# Scarcity in the Modern World

# Scarcity in the Modern World

## History, Politics, Society and Sustainability, 1800–2075

Edited by Fredrik Albritton Jonsson,
John Brewer, Neil Fromer and Frank Trentmann

BLOOMSBURY ACADEMIC
LONDON • NEW YORK • OXFORD • NEW DELHI • SYDNEY

BLOOMSBURY ACADEMIC
Bloomsbury Publishing Plc
50 Bedford Square, London, WC1B 3DP, UK
1385 Broadway, New York, NY 10018, USA

BLOOMSBURY, BLOOMSBURY ACADEMIC and the
Diana logo are trademarks of Bloomsbury Publishing Plc

First published in Great Britain 2019

A catalogue record for this book is available from the British Library.

Library of Congress Cataloging-in-Publication Data
Names: Brewer, John, editor. | Fromer, Neil Alan, editor. | Jonsson, Fredrik
Albritton, 1972- editor. | Trentmann, Frank, editor.
Title: Scarcity in the modern world : history, politics, society and
sustainability, 1800-2075 / Edited by John Brewer, Neil Fromer, Fredrik
Albritton Jonsson & Frank Trentmann.
Description: London ; New York, NY : Bloomsbury Publishing Plc, 2019. |
Includes bibliographical references and index.
Identifiers: LCCN 2018033017 (print) | LCCN 2018035305 (ebook) |
ISBN 9781350040922 (ePUB) | ISBN 9781350040939 (ePDF) |
ISBN 9781350040915 (hardback)
Subjects: LCSH: Scarcity. | Supply and demand–History. |
Economics–Sociolotical aspects.
Classification: LCC HB801 (ebook) | LCC HB801 .S33 2019 (print) | DDC 338.5/213–dc23
LC record available at https://lccn.loc.gov/2018033017

ISBN:     HB:      978-1-3500-4091-5
          ePDF:    978-1-3500-4093-9
          eBook:   978-1-3500-4092-2

Typeset by Integra Software Services Pvt. Ltd.
Printed and bound in Great Britain

To find out more about our authors and books visit www.bloomsbury.com
and sign up for our newsletters.

# Contents

# List of Illustrations

## Figures

## Tables

# Notes on Contributors

**Fredrik Albritton Jonsson** is Associate Professor of British History, Conceptual and Historical Studies of Science at the University of Chicago. His research ranges from the British Empire to environmental history and the Anthropocene. He is the author of *Enlightenment's Frontier: The Scottish Highlands and the Origins of Environmentalism* (Yale University Press, 2013) and co-author of *Green Victorians: The Simple Life in John Ruskin's Lake District* (with Vicky Albritton, University of Chicago Press, 2016). His new project focuses on the history of the stationary state and the rise of cornucopianism in the nineteenth century.

**John Brewer** is Eli and Edythe Broad Professor Emeritus in Humanities and Social Sciences at Caltech and Faculty Associate of the History Department, Harvard University. His many books include *The Pleasures of the Imagination: English Culture in the Eighteenth Century* (HarperCollins, 1997), which won the Wolfson Prize; *The Sinews of Power: War, Money and the English State, 1688–1783* (Knopf 1989); and (with Frank Trentmann) *Consuming Cultures, Global Perspectives: Historical Trajectories, Transnational Exchanges* (Oxford and New York: Berg, 2006). He is currently engaged in a study of Vesuvius in the eighteenth and nineteenth centuries.

**Heather Chappells** is Researcher and Instructor in Geography at the University of British Columbia in Vancouver, Canada. She is an interdisciplinary social scientist bringing perspectives from geography, sociology and science and technology studies to address the sustainable governance of networked resources. Her research focuses on the dynamics of infrastructure systems and their interface with practices of sustainable consumption, primarily in the energy and water sectors. Recent projects and papers have examined the dynamics of disruption and demand, including responses to drought and energy shortages. Her publications include *Infrastructures of Consumption: Environmental Innovation in the Utility Industries* (Earthscan, 2005) and *Sustainable Consumption: The Implications of Changing Infrastructures of Provision* (Edward Elgar, 2004).

**Elizabeth Chatterjee** is Permanent Lecturer in Political Science at Queen Mary University of London. She was formerly a postdoctoral scholar at the University of Chicago and a fellow of All Souls College, Oxford. Her research explores energy policy and political institutions in India, including recent publications in *Contemporary South Asia* (2017) and *World Development* (2018). Her current projects examine the comparative politics of climate change targets and electric statecraft in India in the economic reform era.

**Jörg Friedrichs** is Associate Professor in Politics at the University of Oxford, Department of International Development, and St Cross College. His theoretical interests are concentrated in the fields of international relations and political sociology. He takes a broad transdisciplinary approach to research. He is the author of a new intercultural theory of international relations (*International Theory*, 1/2016). His most recent book is *Hindu-Muslim Relations: What Europe Might Learn from India* (Routledge, 2018). Among his earlier publications, he has a book entitled *The Future Is Not What It Used to Be: Climate Change and Energy Scarcity* (MIT Press, 2013).

**Neil Fromer** is Executive Director of the Resnick Institute, Caltech's endowed programme for energy and sustainability. Neil works across the campus to develop new ideas and research technologies related to a sustainable future and to translate those technologies quickly from the lab to the marketplace. Neil's scientific background is in the interactions of light and matter, and he has over a decade of experience working on solar energy technologies. However, he has also been involved in research on energy storage, clean fuel generation and use, smarter energy and water distribution systems, and energy efficiency. His current focus is on issues related to new technology adoption in major urban infrastructure and the design of centralized systems that allow new technologies to be incorporated rapidly and at multiple scales.

**Walker Hanlon** is Assistant Professor at NYU Stern School of Business and Faculty Research Fellow at the NBER. He studies innovation and economic growth over the long term as well as the impact of pollution on health and population with a particular focus on nineteenth-century Britain. His recent publications include 'Necessity Is the Mother of Invention: Input Supplies and Directed Technical Change', *Econometrica*, January 2015, 83(1), pp. 67–100; 'Coal Smoke and Mortality in an Early Industrial Economy', with Brian Beach, *Economic Journal*, 2017.

**Amber Huff** is a social anthropologist and political ecologist based at the Resource Politics Cluster at the Institute of Development Studies and a member of the STEPS Centre at the University of Sussex. Her primary focus is on the politics of conservation, but broad areas of interest include the politics of nature, conflict, environmental policy, rural livelihoods and human adaptability and the politics of resource struggles in southern Africa. Her research investigates relationships among environmental policy change and well-being at the political and geographic margins, the role of land and investment reforms in exacerbating conservation and mining-related conflicts, and how dominant discourses of scarcity and security are increasingly entangled with both scientific framings of environmental change and sustainable development policy. She is currently leading projects on governance at the 'resource nexus', mining conflicts and natural resource marketization in southern Africa.

**David Lamoureux** completed his PhD in History at the University of Cambridge on a global history of the infrastructural and architectural development of Lagos as a capital city in the twentieth century. His recent publications include 'Comprendre l'Organisation spaciale de Lagos, 1955–2015' in *Hérodote: revue de géographie et de* *géopolitique*, 4.159 (2015), pp. 112–125, as well as 'Remembering the Lagos-that-was to Understand the Lagos-that-is' in Dey Your Lane: *Lagos Variations*, ed. Azu Nwagbogu (Brussels: Centre for Fine Arts/Snoeks, 2016), pp. 174–181. He currently works in Bangui, Central African Republic.

**Lyla Mehta** is Professorial Fellow at the Institute of Development Studies, UK, and Visiting Professor at Noragric, Norwegian University of Life Sciences. She uses the case of water and sanitation to focus on the politics of scarcity, rights and access to resources, resource grabbing, gender, power and policy processes. Her work concerns gender, displacement and resistance and climate change and uncertainty from 'below'. She has extensive research and field experience in India and southern Africa. Lyla has engaged in advisory work with various UN agencies as well as advocacy with NGOs and social movements in Europe and India. Relevant publications include *The Politics and Poetics of Water: Naturalising Scarcity in Western India* and *The Limits to Scarcity: Contesting the Politics of Allocation.*

**Hugh Rockoff** is Distinguished Professor at Rutgers, the State University of New Jersey, and Research Associate of the National Bureau of Economic Research. His research focuses on the history of monetary policy and financial regulation in the United States, and on wartime economic controls. He is the author of books on the U.S. Free Banking Era and the history of price controls in the United States, and of numerous papers in professional journals. His most recent book is *America's Economic Way of War: War and the US Economy from the Spanish-American War to the Persian Gulf War* (Cambridge University Press, 2012). He is also the author, with Gary Walton, of a textbook, *History of the American Economy*. Other publications include 'The Wizard of Oz as a Monetary Allegory', *Journal of Political Economy*, August 1990, 739–760; 'Why Didn't Canada Have a Banking Crisis in 2008 (or in 1930, or 1907, or … )?', with Michael Bordo and Angela Redish, *Economic History Review*, February 2015, 218–243; and 'Not Just the Great Contraction: Friedman and Schwartz's *A Monetary History of the United States, 1867 to 1960*', with Michael Bordo, *American Economic Review, Papers and Proceedings*, May 2013, 61–65.

**Jean-Laurent Rosenthal** is Rea A. and Lela G. Axline Professor of Business Economics and Chair, Division of the Humanities and Social Sciences at the California Institute of Technology. He taught at UCLA's Department of Economics from 1988 to 2006. He was the co-editor of *The Journal of Economic History* (2010–2014). His research focuses on understanding what institutions encourage economic growth and wealth formation. More specifically, his investigations included changes in property rights at the time of the French Revolution, on credit markets in Europe, on law and the organization of enterprises (France, Germany, United States and UK) and on wealth inequality. He is the author or co-author of several books, including *Before and Beyond Divergence: Institutions and Prosperity in China and Europe 1000–1800* (with R. Bin Wong, Harvard University Press, 2011) and *Surviving Large Losses: Financial Crises, the Middle Class, and the Development of Capital Markets* (with Philip T. Hoffman and Gilles Postel-Vinay, Harvard University Press, 2007).

**David Rutledge** is the Tomiyasu Professor of Engineering, Emeritus at Caltech and a former chair of the Division of Engineering and Applied Science there. He is a founder of the Wavestream Corporation, a manufacturer of transmitters for satellite uplinks. He is a winner of the Teaching Award of the Associated Students at Caltech and a fellow of the Institute of Electrical and Electronic Engineers. He is the author of 'Estimating Long-term World Coal Production with Logit and Probit Transforms', in *International Journal of Coal Geology*, Vol. 85, 2011, pp. 23–33.

**Sigrid Schmalzer** is Associate Professor of History at UMass Amherst. Her research focuses on social, cultural and political aspects of the history of science in modern China. Her first book, *The People's Peking Man: Popular Science and Human Identity in Twentieth-Century China*, was published by the University of Chicago Press in 2008 and won the Sharlin Memorial Award from the Social Science History Association. Her latest book, *Red Revolution, Green Revolution: Scientific Farming in Socialist China*, appeared in 2016 (University of Chicago Press).

**Hiroki Shin** is Research Fellow in the Department of History, Classics and Archaeology, Birkbeck College, University of London, and the co-investigator of the AHRC-funded 'Material Cultures of Energy' project. After completing his PhD on the social history of money in modern Britain, at the University of Cambridge, he has worked on projects related to transport and energy history at the University of York and University of Manchester. His research interests relate to the historical interaction between tangible and intangible commodities (money, mobility and energy) and their consumers. His recent publications include 'Have Consumer Movements Enhanced Transport Justice? Passenger Representation on Britain's Railways before 1947', in Colin Divall, Julian Hine and Colin Pooley (eds.), *Transport Policy: Lessons from History* (Ashgate, 2016); 'The Art of Advertising Railways: Organization and Coordination in Britain's Railway Marketing, 1860-1910', in *Business History* (2014); 'Paper Money, the Nation, and the Suspension of Cash Payments in 1797', in *Historical Journal* (2015).

**Emma Stephens** is Professor of Economics at Pitzer College in Claremont, California. She received her PhD in Economics from Cornell University in 2007 and has done research on subsistence farming systems, commodity market participation, spatial market networks and technology adoption in sub-Saharan Africa. Her work on food markets and food security has appeared in a number of journals, including *Journal of Agricultural Economics* (2011), *Food Security* (2012) and *Agricultural Systems* (2017).

**Frank Trentmann** is Professor of History at Birkbeck College, University of London, and also Professor at the Centre for Consumer Society Research, University of Helsinki. His research and publications have focused on civil society, globalization and consumption, including the books *Free Trade Nation* (Oxford 2008) and the *Oxford Handbook of the History of Consumption* (2012, editor). He was the director of the £5 million 'Cultures of Consumption' research programme and principal investigator of the AHRC-funded project 'Material Cultures of Energy'. His latest book is *Empire of*

*Things: How We Became a World of Consumers, from the 15th Century to the 21st* (Allen Lane/Penguin and HarperCollins, 2016).

**Richard Wilk** is Distinguished Professor Emeritus of Anthropology at Indiana University. Trained as an economic and ecological anthropologist, his initial research on farming and family organization in Belize was followed by work on consumer culture, globalization, television and the emergence of national cuisines. At the same time, he has pursued research on energy consumption and consumer culture in the United States. His most recent books are *Rice and Beans* (Bloomsbury 2012, with Livia Barbosa), *Teaching Food and Culture* (Left Coast Press, edited with Candice Lowe) and *Exploring Everyday Life* (Rowman & Littlefield 2015, co-authored with Orvar Lofgren and Billy Ehn).

# Introduction

Fredrik Albritton Jonsson, John Brewer, Neil Fromer
and Frank Trentmann

Climate change has given the issue of scarcity new urgency, with intense debates about a future world crippled by drought and shortages of food, energy and materials. But humans have had to face the challenge of scarcity for a long time. Resources are limited and never enough to fulfil all needs and wants. This dialectic between demand and supply has sharply accelerated since the Industrial Revolution. *Scarcity in the Modern World* anchors current concerns about scarcity in its longer history. It explores the making, meaning and managing of scarcities – past, present and future – from the eighteenth century all the way to today's forecasts of fossil fuels, renewable energy and water use in 2075. By taking a longer and multidisciplinary view, this book offers a new way of tackling the current challenge of meeting the needs of the people on the planet in an increasingly resource-stressed environment. It also recognizes that this challenge is complex and cannot be addressed by a single discipline but requires a concerted effort to think about its political and social as well as technical and economic dimensions.

Discussions of scarcity, of course, are nothing new. But they have predominantly been conducted by science and engineering disciplines and by the humanities and social sciences in isolation from each other. What is novel and path breaking about this book is that it brings together experts from across these disciplines and introduces readers to different ways of thinking about scarcities. The book shows how scarcity has evolved in history and follows the interplay between political, economic, social and natural forces in different times and places, ranging from industrial Britain and the United States to colonial Lagos, Mao's China, post-colonial India and sub-Saharan Africa. Together, the chapters in this book reveal the variety of ways in which regimes, societies and individuals have lived with scarcity. Intrinsically relative, the precise nature and thrust of scarcity is shaped by constellations of power and by decisions about trade-offs and distribution as well as about supply. In addition, the book has a methodological ambition: it follows the dynamics of scarcity at multiple scales of time and space. It discusses the growing influence of future visions and predictions for diagnoses of the present. And it shows how our understanding of scarcity is enriched by looking at local as well as global scales.

It may be tempting to search for a universal analysis and theory for scarcity, but this would be to miss fundamental disagreements about the nature of scarcity. Interpretations of scarcity have diverged in the past and will continue to differ in the future. We cannot simply wish these differences away. Instead, we need to understand these different perspectives and explain their respective power in particular situations in particular times and places. The aim of this book is to help readers wishing to confront current challenges to understand how these alternatives have evolved. Throughout this book, readers will find a number of recurrent themes or tensions, relating to the development of a shortage or resource scarcity, the response to such a situation or the potential limits of future resource use. These include a tension between global and regional views versus local views concerning challenges or solutions to resource issues, as well as the role of institutions and individuals in coping with scarcity.

Perhaps the most prominent theme concerns the extent to which resource scarcity arises from intrinsic natural limits placed on human development by the planet and the laws of physics, as opposed to its manufacture as a result of social hierarchy, political will, or cultural or financial dominance of one group over others. To some extent this tension is driven by methodological differences between the disciplines of researchers investigating the questions. If we take a broader view, however, we are left with a strong sense of the hybrid character of scarcity. The problem of biophysical limits cannot be separated from questions of power, distribution and value. Most cases do not fall into a simple divide between those that are purely natural and those that are socially constructed. Many of the chapters that follow recognize that societies faced certain challenges at a particular moment that had certain natural or physical characteristics, such as low rainfall or a harsh winter that froze coal in the ground. At the same time, these physical factors do not exist in a vacuum. They acquire force by the way in which politics, society and man-made infrastructures deal with such challenges. Indeed, academic and popular understandings of scarcity play a crucial role in determining what authorities and societies think can or cannot be done. There is no single road from shortages to scarcity. This book gives readers the opportunity to view scarcity from a number of vantage points to gain a better sense of the interaction between social and material factors critical in formulating effective responses in the future. In their chapters, experts from different disciplines examine the making of scarcity; the power of projection; strategies of coping, managing and innovating; and the dynamics of distribution.

## Part One: Making Scarcity

This part looks at a wide range of academic disciplines – economics, human development, anthropology and environmental science – in search of a basic definition of scarcity. While our authors disagree in fundamental ways, they also share a great deal of common ground in their approaches. Perhaps most importantly, all of our authors agree that any meaningful analysis of scarcity will have to deal with questions of history, government and institutional frameworks. They also cast doubt on the quest for a purely physical definition of scarcity. While no one would deny that environmental problems have become more systemic and urgent in the post-war period, each chapter, in its own way, insists that excessive concern with natural limits and physical scarcity tends to distract from deeper social and political dimensions of the problem.

The modern debate about scarcity usually takes as its departure point the economic thought of T.R. Malthus. For Malthus, writing on the eve of the nineteenth century, the most pressing problem of political economy was the force of exponential population growth. Malthus argued that divergent growth rates of population and agricultural improvement threatened to undermine social progress. He couched his warning explicitly as a prediction about future famine. Malthus suggested that the population of England could double in the coming twenty-five years but that the nation would face a serious crisis of subsistence in the subsequent generation. Famously, Malthus saw scarcity principally in biophysical terms: the explosive natural force of human reproduction exposed the physical limits to economic growth and social equality. Even though his forecast of English famine did not come to pass, Malthus's political economy has enjoyed a long afterlife in evolutionary theory, ecology, eugenics and post-war environmentalism. Indeed, the lasting appeal of Malthusian thought may ultimately derive from its tendency to conceal the political roots of scarcity.

Yet even the most cursory look at the past reveals how closely connected questions of scarcity are to the exercise of power. Institutions that secure access to food and freshwater have been fundamental to statecraft for millennia. Examples of large-scale systems of provisioning can be found in ancient Rome, the Ottoman Empire, Qing China as well as in France in the age of absolutism. State-sponsored irrigation goes back even further in time. Anxieties about social instability frequently propelled these elaborate arrangements. Famine, drought and other environmental disturbances threatened the legitimacy of political elites. If we define social power as the effective control of bottlenecks, then the security of the food supply surely represents one of the most important sources of authority in all societies.

Scarcity arguably remains as potent a political issue as ever, but accelerating technological change and economic growth have fundamentally transformed how we think about it. Modern agriculture and manufacturing production have created a world of unprecedented material abundance. Yet economic growth has simultaneously exacerbated social divisions around the world and produced new forms of environmental threats. Little wonder, then, if scarcity is increasingly seen as a problem of distributive justice and technological change rather than biophysical limits. The four chapters in this part all reflect this profound shift.

Jean-Laurent Rosenthal looks to economic theory for a foundational definition of scarcity. He argues that it is best understood through the institution of market transactions. All goods that carry a positive price are considered scarce. An increase in price indicates growing scarcity. It follows that shortages arise when goods carry too low a price. Broadly speaking, a shortage describes a condition where a certain group of consumers receive less of a good or service than it desires. Such a shortage may have a variety of underlying environmental, social and political causes. From the perspective of economic theory, the best remedy for a shortage is to let the price change. The increase in price delivers a signal that encourages producers to increase supply or discover a substitute. For Rosenthal, the economic definition of scarcity offers several distinctive advantages. He regards it as a powerful analytical tool that does not enforce a particular prescriptive orientation and is therefore especially well suited to build bridges between disciplines.

Amber Huff and Lyla Mehta approach the problem of scarcity from a comparative perspective of water use in developing countries. They stress the tensions between three competing disciplinary frameworks: (1) the universalist account associated with the discourse of 'Limits to Growth' and 'Planetary Boundaries', (2) the managerial and technical optimism associated with environmental economics and (3) the structural-distributional perspective linked to the discipline of human development. Huff and Mehta take a pessimistic view of these differences, emphasizing that the three perspectives are so distinct as to be incompatible with each other. The Planetary Boundaries framework stresses the physical character of water scarcity and does so on a highly abstract planetary scale, with little concern for social complexity and local variation. By contrast, the managerial framework favours market-oriented solutions and sees scarcity as the product of market failure. It tends to reduce social and ecological problems to a question of price and engineering fixes. Instead, Huff and Mehta champion a perspective that begins with the political context of local water use. They insist that the analysis of scarcity should begin with issues of distribution and power. Technological fixes and market solutions often exacerbate these underlying inequalities rather than overcome them.

Richard Wilk examines scarcity through the lens of anthropological analysis. He rejects universal and objective definitions of welfare and poverty in favour of a hybrid perspective that recognizes them as subjective and physical at the same time. Anthropology reveals how cultural dynamics shape the market forces of supply and demand, for example how consumer fads create new forms of scarcity in a globalized market economy. Wilk draws on his fieldwork in Belize to challenge conventional understandings of abundance and poverty. Among the Q'ueqchi' Mayan speakers, work was seen as crucial to secure moral status, yet members lived relatively self-sufficient lives, free of the many social needs imposed by market economies. Only through more regular exposure to the outside world did the Q'ueqchi' discover the idea of scarcity as a form of injustice.

The chapter by Neil Fromer considers how the threat of anthropogenic climate change and the imperative of energy transition have transformed the question of scarcity in the last few decades. From the disciplinary perspective of environmental science and energy policy, climate change is very much a problem of abundance: the burning of fossil fuel stock has produced an excess of carbon dioxide in the atmosphere. There is also no shortage of renewable energy to replace fossil fuel. What is lacking is the right technology and infrastructure to capture, store and distribute renewable energy in ways that can meet future demand and help satisfy the social needs created by the fossil fuel economy. Fromer also stresses the importance of calibrating energy use to assist developing countries. Data from the Human Development Index suggests that improved access to energy is most critical for improving welfare in developing countries.

# Part Two: The Power of Projection

As we see in the introductory chapters, experiences or perceptions of scarcity are built, depending on your viewpoint, from physical limitations of resources, from failure to control consumption or from political/social hierarchies that inhibit equitable distribution of resources. In Part Two we look at the role of projections in shaping these perspectives. What is the 'reality' of future resource availability? Which aspects of our constraining forces are physical, which are infrastructural and which are social? How accurate are our predictions of the future or our extrapolations of global circumstances from local ones (or our own perceptions)?

Importantly, the perception of resource abundance or scarcity strongly colours our view of possible future growth, and our views of growth will in turn colour our view of resource scarcity. Aside from moments of shock, arising from either natural disasters (such as floods, droughts or fires) or man-made ones (war, refugee migration), our perceptions of resource availability are driven by projections of future development and future consumption. As such, these projections are generally used to provide limits: either limits to available development or limits to future consumption. The chapters in Part Two explore and unpack this concept of projection and limitation, as viewed from multiple contexts.

The first chapter in this part, 'Growth in the Anthropocene', takes a historian's lens of growth and abundance, and applies it to the Anthropocene, the concept that the spread and impact of human life on the planet is so large that we have entered a new geologic age dominated by our own footprint. Albritton Jonsson outlines the techno-economic analyses that are used to justify this argument, projecting the current footprint of human activity into the future to determine a 'risk level' for the planet should we continue on our current path. These narratives drive towards an era of planetary stewardship and possibly a new form of geopolitics in the name of this stewardship, perhaps above individual liberty. Most of those developing the narrative of the Anthropocene use it as a motivating force for curbing growth in some sense; at the very least, a prerequisite to avoiding catastrophe is drastic change to human behaviour around the world. Alternately, some 'ecomodernists' use the concept in an attempt to double down on the human influence on the planet and extrapolate continued growth with technology coming to the rescue. As Albritton Jonsson asks, 'Will the Anthropocene give rise to new social movements and cultural forms or will it simply perpetuate the culture and politics of the late Holocene?'

In 'The Great Resources Myth', Rutledge provides an in-depth analysis of the change in forecasts and actual production of several coal and hydrocarbon producing regions. He notes that despite the variable nature of production and future estimates, it is possible to deduce ultimate production amounts and the time to reach this amount from a careful mathematical analysis of the growth of production. The chapter then applies the analysis to current active production regions to develop an alternative 'global final production' for fossil fuels that is distinct from estimates put forward by the IPCC (Intergovernmental Panel on Climate Change), for instance. It is fruitful to think about Rutledge's analysis, focused solely on predicting total production of a resource from early data on production and availability, in the context of the social and environmental trends that led to changes in coal production in England or in Pennsylvania. Rutledge hypothesizes that the fading production of hydrocarbon energy sources over the next fifty years will provide renewables the appropriate time and space to further decrease costs and drive the next energy transition. In the absence of the broader narrative of the effects of climate change on the global population, it is hard to see such a shift in energy sources emerge on its own.

The last chapter in this part, 'Escapology, or How to Escape Malthusian Traps', attempts to update Malthus in a modern context. Friedrichs argues that Malthus's original thesis, in which an exponentially growing population will outpace increases in resource production and lead to famine, war and death (and the shrinking of the population back within limits), is still sound but the conclusions are incomplete. He continues by examining exit strategies from this trap that were dismissed by Malthus's original analysis. By applying this general model framework (i.e. a constraint on one function describing growth by another independent function), the chapter recasts the great acceleration of the Anthropocene as a neo-Malthusian trap. Friedrichs attempts to project escapes from the classic challenge of overpopulation to problems of ecosystem collapse and environmental degradation. Such approaches, he argues, are largely temporary and ultimately come back to fundamental carrying capacity of the planet: Can the human population develop technological solutions, governance solutions or combined solutions that allow for growth (to improve the quality of life of those on the planet) while controlling the effects of growth or avoiding the constraints defined by the planet?

These chapters on projection demonstrate the important power that comes from our ability to look at data from the present and predict the future, to encompass the ultimate limitations for the planet and for human society. From this comes our ability to recognize an impending global challenge, whether it is climate change, overconsumption of freshwater or ecosystem collapse.

Projections are ultimately about limits, and these chapters examine these limits in a global context. As a result, they inherently tend towards a more natural view of scarcity – assuming optimal and equitable distribution of resources across the globe and across socio-economic classes, when will we reach our fundamental limits? If all shortages are actually situational then these projections are largely irrelevant and serve as a justification for either maintaining or adjusting the status quo. In fact, in all three chapters, we see evidence of projections used for justification of a previously held world view: either that the planet has a fundamental limit for stability or that technological development will create new solutions, with the assumption that market mechanisms or policies will emerge and align in support of those technologies.

The limits of Malthus come from the needs of a growing system (population for Malthus) with an external constraint. For Malthus, food production was considered independent from the complexity of society driving the population growth, a simplifying assumption which was proven incomplete by the previous two centuries of growth.

The Planetary Boundaries that Albritton Jonsson outlines face the same concern. In the long history of the planet (compared to which human existence is practically unnoticeable), we see the true capacity of the planet to adjust to variations and compensate changing environments. The limits set by those espousing this view recognize that humans have flourished in a tiny window of stable time and that staying there is better than leaving. However, the environment of prehistoric humans was nonetheless different than that of modern humans, and the prospect of leaving the stability of the Holocene is one humans will have to face eventually, for man-made causes or not.

Therefore, one must ask the question, to who's benefit is continued growth, or controlled growth, or even controlled contraction? Friedrichs's discussion of depredation of subalterns and outsiders presents an account of power that has been followed by the few who managed to secure and hold on to power. The names and approaches change, but the methods remain somewhat similar. It is in the interest of those with power to maintain the status quo and project resources as scarce or abundant to perpetuate their own position.

These chapters provide notable contributions focused on global analyses of resource scarcity, which not only help project future constraints but also tend to neglect social context. Balancing the need to stay within Planetary Boundaries for sustainable growth with the need to provide stable energy sources to the billions of people on the planet that lack adequate access requires contextualizing these projections. How one views their immediate world and positions it within the global context determines what is believed to be essential. What is worth protecting for those who have the means to insulate themselves from shocks of any impending constraints? For those with no access to clean water, global limits to consumption will not matter. Similarly, Rutledge's analysis may show a possible transitional future for fossil fuels, with global coal nearly at an end and oil and gas providing energy to a growing population while we find alternatives. However, without providing a rationale for future decreases of hydrocarbon production, it is far from the only future possible. Once developed, what will displace it?

Will there be a global solution to our projected futures or only many local ones? To give context to these projections, you have to define the scale of the solution. Is there an us and a them or only an us?

## Part Three: Coping, Managing and Innovating

In this part, two economists, a geographer and an historian examine different responses on different scales and by different entities – states and governments, individual industries and households – to circumstances of 'scarcity'. The environments may be very different – the crisis of resources provoked by the Second World War in the United States, the collapse of cotton imports into Britain during the American Civil War of 1861–65, the Chinese famine of 1959–61 during the Great Leap Forward and the drought in the United Kingdom in 2006 – but all four chapters ask what lessons can be learned from the ways in which scarcity was defined and understood, and what responses it provoked.

Hugh Rockoff's chapter, 'U.S. Mobilization during the Second World War as a Model for Coping with Climate Change', is both an economic history and a thought experiment. It asks how a nation and its government responded to the abrupt and sudden challenge provoked by the demand to reallocate resources under radically changed circumstances, namely the outbreak of the Second World War, but it also uses this particular case to see what lessons can be learned for dealing with other sorts of scarcity, notably those caused by climate change. In his historical case study, Rockoff focuses particularly on the need to build new infrastructure (e.g. the building of pipelines and highways), the development of new industries(notably synthetic rubber and development of the atomic bomb) as well as the reallocation of populations and the raising of extraordinary revenue (via both taxation and borrowing) to pay for the war. He shows how the sense of crisis and the call for patriotic effort and sacrifice to cope with wartime scarcities made possible a series of policies – greater taxation and government deficit spending, rationing and price controls – and a level of government engagement with the free market that was accepted during hostilities but was controversial (and opposed) both before the war and after 1945. His conclusions about the value of his case study to other problems of scarcity are mixed. On the one hand, he argues that an affluent capitalist economy has the capacity and resources to adapt quite quickly to wartime scarcities; on the other, he sees a strong sense of short-term crisis and a consequent willingness to make patriotic sacrifices and changes of behaviour as unlikely in the face of longer-term and less obviously tangible threats to resources posed by the likes of climate change.

Just as Rockoff shows that the interruption of supplies of natural rubber from the Far East stimulated technological developments and a massive expansion in the synthetic rubber industry, so in his chapter, 'Scarcity and Innovation: Lessons from the British Economy during the U.S. Civil War', Walker Hanlon looks at the technological response to the collapse of the supply and escalation in prices of American cotton provided for the British textile industry. Yet, unlike Rockoff's American case, where the state played an active role in responding to shortages, the response in laissez-faire nineteenth-century Britain was market led. What, Hanlon asks, might have been the positive effects of a shortage that adversely affected the 450,000 workers (out of a British population of twenty million) in the cotton industry, the largest manufacturing sector of the economy? Some of the shortfall of American cotton was replaced by inferior cotton from India, but the plant was dirtier than its American counterpart and more difficult to process. Examining patent applications, he shows a remarkable increase in patent applications for devices to improve the preparation of cotton, one not found in other textile industries such as woolens, silk and linen. Scarcity prompted technological innovation. But, as Hanlon shows, this did not lead to long-term structural change in the textile industry. The renewal of American cotton imports after the war saw a reversion to old practices and a decline in the number of patents.

Just as Rockoff and Hanlon focus on the short-term responses to scarcity, Sigrid Schmalzer examines the different understandings of the devastating effects of the Chinese famine that accompanied Mao's Great Leap Forward of 1958–60. She places the terrible suffering of these years within the context of the long-standing analyses of scarcity associated with Thomas Malthus and Karl Marx. She shows how Mao and the regime embraced Marx's critique of Malthus (and Charles Darwin), seeing scarcity not simply as a consequence of the laws of nature but as the outcome of political decisions about resource allocation. But the Maoist regime's critique of the Malthusian law – that population growth will inevitably produce poverty and scarcity – depended upon a voluntarist model of economic growth, in which scarcity would be overcome by the collective determination of the people to achieve economic transformation and break through to a socialist utopia. As Schmalzer explains, the problem of growth was therefore ideological: it was seen as a matter of commitment to short-term sacrifice for ultimate gain, of getting peasants to understand their long-term interests. This vision occluded the conflict between local and national needs, peasants and factory workers, and led Mao to argue against redistribution as a solution to peasant suffering, which he saw as necessary to the path towards modern industrialization. It also led the regime to emphasize (in the manner of Darwin and Malthus) the natural climatological causes of famine. As Schmalzer shows, subsequent analyses of the famine have had a complex and quite ideologically freighted history, in which, somewhat paradoxically, Leftist commentators have been willing to give some credit to climate (in a Malthusian manner) while critics of socialism have advanced explanations more usually associated with the political analysis of the Marxist tradition. This Chinese case points out the importance of issues of scale, both spatial (the conflict between the peasant village economy and that of the nation) and temporal (short-term pain for long-term socialism). And, as Schmalzer concludes, scholars are now beginning to understand the famine in yet another way by framing it within a long-term history of cycles of famine in China that date back centuries rather than decades.

Heather Chappells in her chapter, 'Encounters with Scarcity at a Micro-Scale: Householders' Responses to Drought as a Continuum of Normal Practice', also examines issues of scale and historical framing, but in a way that emphasizes individual memory and personal history rather than the macro forces of climate and economy. Like Lyla Metha in Chapter 3, she wants to move beyond an analysis of aggregate populations and water scarcity, recovering the wide range of responses to and understandings of drought. Key to this, according to Chappells, is both memory – the recollection of previous shortages marked by reservoirs with receding water levels or the introduction of standing pipes – and conceptions of what characterized 'normal' water provision. Such ideas of normality varied according to widely different familial water use and priorities, which did not necessarily accord with more general ideas such as those taken up by water companies. These, in turn, shaped expectations about the drought of 2006 and the ways in which different households responded to it. While attending to such variety, Chappells argues that we should see scarcity, and responses to it, as operating along a continuum that connects the past to the present and another that links notions of normality and disruption. The varied understanding and experience of drought is embedded in different routines and different experiences of the everyday.

All four chapters demonstrate how both definitions of scarcity and the responses they elicit are context-driven. In every case the mechanisms for coping, managing or innovating were driven by specific political, economic and social actors, from the state to the household, with their own agendas. They all carried a certain historical and ideological baggage. And they all raise the question of agency – its possibility and its (sometimes severe) constraints – the question of what can and should be done to cope with a particular scarcity, and what is the proper and appropriate body to do so.

## Part Four: Dynamics of Distribution

That scarcity is not necessarily caused by a failure in supply but often the result of a failure in distribution has been a central insight of Amartya Sen's work. The great Bengal famine of 1943 and mass starvation in Bangladesh in 1974, he showed, happened not because there were too many mouths to feed but because there was a breakdown in people's exchange entitlements, that is, their ability to obtain enough food. In this part, a political scientist, an economist and three historians expand on this insight by examining the different dynamics behind such distributional crises. They follow the troubled story of electrification in colonial and post-colonial India, the battles over water and land in overcrowded colonial Lagos, competition over scarce energy in Japan and socialist East Germany (GDR) after the Second World War, all the way to food shortages in the Sahel region of Africa today.

Scarcity is relative. This means we cannot just think of it as the absence of abundance. Rather, we need to face up to the coexistence of the two: scarcity amid abundance. The chapters in this part track the forces that create or enable such twinned constellations across space and time. In contemporary India this means energy surplus for some groups and in some regions but lack of access to electricity for others. In colonial Lagos, imperial rulers were trying to monopolize scarce water and land for themselves. In the GDR and post-war Japan, there was ample energy at certain times but not at others. In Burkina Faso and Mali in 2012, a combination of regional variations in food production and violence limited distribution of food between markets.

Power is a major theme that runs across these chapters. They illustrate just how many types and techniques of power are involved in the uneven distribution of resources that leave some short, while others have plenty or, at least, enough. There is first of all Big Power: that of empires over colonial subjects. The British Empire, Elizabeth Chatterjee stresses, showed remarkably little interest in electrifying India; in the early twentieth century, the few power stations and networks in operation were mostly the work of local businessmen or Indian princes. In colonial Lagos – the subject of David Lamoureux's chapter – British rulers tried hard to squeeze out the local population from scarce water and equally scarce land. Then there is the power of interest groups and coalitions. Energy shortages in Japan and Germany after the Second World War, Hiroki Shin and Frank Trentmann reveal, articulated conflicts between industrial and private users and reflected the ruling political system's priorities and vulnerabilities. After the popular uprising of 17 June 1953, which almost toppled the socialist government in East Germany, the regime was careful not to interfere directly in household's energy use and, instead, focused on rationing industrial users. In India since the 1960s, electricity has sparked its own kind of scarcity politics, where farmers and middle classes, especially in poorer states, have used subsidies to reserve scarce energy to themselves and their constituents. Markets themselves can be more or less powerful and efficient, as Emma Stephens shows for Burkina Faso and Mali, where more distant areas were less responsive to price changes and market signals than others. We have here an example of the incomplete power of markets to distribute scarce resources effectively, with remote areas failing to respond to local production shortfalls despite local price spikes. Finally, the chapters also illustrate other subtle forms of power, such as influence over the temporal organization of day and night that decides not only 'how much' but 'when' people can access electricity.

Power is hierarchical and itself unevenly distributed but that does not mean it flows in one direction only. As these chapters show, distributional crises are both produced by power but they also produce new political opportunities and alliances, prompting resistance as well as attempts at gaining control over scarce resources. In the case of colonial Lagos, for example, the British land grab and attempts to siphon off scarce water involved an alliance with the local elite but at same time galvanized protests from disenfranchised colonial subjects who came to demand their share in development and local politics. In Japan, energy shortages mobilized housewives. A well-intentioned focus on how to overcome present scarcities should not distract from their potential of politicizing subjects in the past.

Methodologically, these chapters show the merit of attending to scarcity in a concrete setting but do so by locating it comparatively or transnationally in order to question larger narratives about the modern world. The haphazard process of electrification in India both tells us about the endemic reproduction of energy shortages on the subcontinent and challenges a broader Western narrative of modernization and climate change. From a Western perspective, it has been tempting to see industrial capitalism with the help of imperialism expanding outwards from a Western core to the rest of the world. From an Indian perspective, the process looks rather different, as Chatterjee points out in her account of the fractured and uneven advance of electrification. Democracy together with India's federal system created its own political arenas where farmers have often outwitted industrialists. Within a region such as the Sahel, a comparison of responses to price signals in different areas shows that a food shortage should not be treated as a singular phenomenon but as the result of spatial variations. Not all markets failed equally in Mali and Burkina Faso in 2012: some were more efficient than others. Aid and market reforms should consequently be prioritized for the less integrated markets.

For the 'advanced' West, conversely, we should not naively assume that modernity has erased scarcities. Industrial development and mass consumption have created their own distinct pressures. In Western countries, the growing share of household demand for gas, electricity and water, especially since the 1950s, reminds us that the pressure on resources and their contribution to climate change is now widely (if unevenly) dispersed across the population and can no longer be laid just at the feet of big industry. Comparative analysis also reminds us that there is no single natural or rational mechanism with which authorities decide who should get what and when. What is considered a 'normal' and non-negotiable arrangement of quotas and hours in one culture can be considered unthinkable or unacceptable in another. The GDR, for example, tried to get a grip on energy shortages by expanding night shifts in factories, while in Japan the authorities held tight to a customary divide between work-time during the day and private family time for evenings and nights.

Together, the chapters in this part demonstrate the value of examining scarcity through a range of methods and with the help of diverse sources. They follow interest groups in the formation of political coalitions; apply econometric models to measure the differences in food prices between markets over time; study urban planning schemes, maps and colonial correspondence; and they mine national and local archives for information about how authorities tried to set priorities and how different groups of users actually responded during times of shortage. The variety of perspectives, we hope, will inspire readers and researchers to look at the distributional politics of scarcities in their own fresh ways.

## Outlook and policy implications

Faced with ongoing issues around dwindling resources and global-scale shortages, solutions will have to be multidisciplinary – we cannot 'policy' or ration away these problems, nor can more efficient markets solve them, nor can technology on its own. Only in concert can they make an impact.

### The importance of interdisciplinary discourse in solving resource challenges

This book advances a well-rounded view of scarcity, which adds anthropological, geographical, sociological and historical observations to those of economics and engineering. One particular strength of this book, which sets it apart from the existing literature, is that it combines scientific and engineering expertise as well as knowledge from the social science and humanities. The chapters that look at the future of coal and renewable energy, or recent food distribution issues, have very immediate and practical concerns. Equally, current thinking will benefit from the insights of historically informed chapters about the generation and distribution of shortages in colonial and post-colonial settings and the responses and conflicts arising from these.

Throughout this book, we see perspectives on scarcities past and present, short-term shortages brought out by natural and man-made disasters as well as systemic overuse of resources and destruction of the natural environment from development or waste. The interdisciplinary nature of the contributions allows us to address each concept individually from multiple perspectives and tease out implications for our current and future challenges.

Resource scarcity lies at the intersection of engineering, economics, politics and human behaviour. We spell out what can be learnt by admitting history and anthropology to the table where current scarcities are discussed. Two themes of particular relevance concern the status of scarce resources and the political forces that govern their uneven social and regional distribution. Both of these urge caution about technological fixes. The balance of future energy use will require an understanding of energy as a commodity and whether end-users view energy and technology developments as providing added value beyond that of the commodity. The anthropological, historical and geographical perspectives in this book will be pertinent because they show how people perceived the value of the goods they consumed. Such perspectives offer a direct counterpoint to the technological changes required and described. Similarly, attention to the role of politics in both the developed and developing world illustrates the significant role played by political ideas and institutions in shaping the dynamics of scarcity.

The reality of the current human condition on the planet is one of extreme inequality, driven by an abundance of resources to be exploited, a large and growing global population, and practices of consumption that lead to environmental degradation, including the beginnings of feedback loops that threaten to alter the functioning of global ecosystems. This is the true balancing act at the heart of questions about the natural or manufactured nature of scarcity. Systemic inequality in the face of large-scale resource exploitation may not lead humans to run out of needed resources but threatens to disrupt the balance of natural feedbacks on which civilization rests. Humans are also now an urban organism, with more than half of the population living in cities. These circumstances are unique in human history, and it is tempting to use the scale and the uniqueness of the challenge to ignore the lessons from the past, as well as those disciplines of the humanities and social sciences that highlight the stories behind the development of society. Each of the chapters taken alone addresses a way of framing a particular shortage. However, taken together they do something more, weaving together a narrative of both technical and social relevance, demonstrating that no issue of resource scarcity or abundance is the result of a single force (technical or societal), and therefore no issue can be handled entirely by one disciplinary approach. The historical, anthropological, sociological and political science views of scarcity illuminate the power of local and regional governance, the importance of giving voice to the voiceless and the roles of individuals and communities to improve their own world.

The data science, forecasting tools and economic analysis outlined in the chapters show a system that can work in harmony with the social concepts above, local incentives driven by global priorities and vice versa. However, that requires a level of trust and support from quite different groups and interests in the world, especially from those that have traditionally been on the losing end of power struggles and global commerce. Does the farmer in Africa trust that the global network of water and food distribution is there for his benefit as well as those at the top? In an increasingly constrained and interconnected world, who sets the priorities for society?

## Practical implications: The example of the California drought since 2010

This book shows how technological, governance- and market-based solutions are all necessary to resolve persistent scarcity challenges. It also highlights the tension between global and regional perspectives of stressed resources with local perceptions of scarcity driven by structural inequality, mismanagement or neglect. To illustrate how these multiple viewpoints develop and inform policy and actions in practice, let us now turn to a specific case. The historic drought since 2010 focused a global lens squarely on the practices of water use and storage in California. The history of water politics and infrastructure in California, the circumstances of this drought and the new normal for precipitation, and the response to both the onset of drought and the onset of rain serve to highlight the interdisciplinary nature of the challenges we will face in resource management moving forward and illuminate the different strands of thought encompassed in this book.

One theme explored throughout this book covers the natural limits to scarce resources. California receives precipitation largely in the winter months, and most of the state is dry for the summer months. Rain is sporadic – most of the rain falls in a few large storms, and the difference between a wet and dry winter might be only 2–3 storm events. The state sees about three wet years out of every ten, with the other seven coming in drier than average. The precipitation that falls as snow in the Sierra Nevada Mountains is the dominant storage of water from the wetter winter months to the drier summer months, with the snow melt filling the Sacramento and San Joaquin rivers, which run from the mountains through the Central Valley and into the San Francisco Bay. Finally, several areas around the state have significant underground reservoirs with porous soil and rock able to capture and hold water below the surface. The hilly or mountainous terrain around much of the state means that water often doesn't stay long enough to percolate into groundwater basins, and seasonal flooding was common before flood control measures were introduced. While average precipitation is quite high, the variability associated with the natural system is severely limiting from the standpoint of human development, including both farming and urban environments. Nevertheless, from a global resources standpoint, and averaged over time, the state is not 'short' of water – average rainfall (including water equivalent in snowfall) is more than twice the average applied water usage, more than enough to supply water for urban, agricultural and environmental uses.[1] Nonetheless, we see nearly constant water stress in parts of the state, owing to uneven distribution of this water, complex water rights and usage restrictions, and interactions between environmental water uses and human uses. Is the scarcity on view here natural based on the variability and arrival of drought conditions or systemic and man-made based on poor governance and incomplete infrastructure? This has become a political argument in California pitting environmentalists versus developers, urban centres versus agricultural producers.

Several chapters dig into this tension, investigating the building of distribution infrastructure and regulation to support human development, and the environmental consequences of these interventions. For example, we note that California is crossed and re-crossed with aqueducts, and covered with dams and man-made reservoirs. Built over more than a century, these conveyances and storage facilities smooth the lumpiness of the area's natural water delivery mechanism, and together with the time release of water through the snow melt, provide more predictable flows of water for development. The construction of the aqueducts allowed for both the growth in farming in the Central Valley and the delivery of water to the large urban population in the southern part of the state. In addition to flood control districts installing dams, many of the rivers were channelized to manage the incredibly variable flow. Of course, dams, reservoirs and channelized rivers lead to numerous unintended consequences for the environment. The concrete dams and rivers limit groundwater recharge, affect the natural flow of sediment that support coastal areas and, of course, limit the

---

[1]  Average precipitation total across the state is roughly 193 million acre-feet/year, and average applied water use is roughly 76 million acre-feet/year. An acre-foot is the water it takes to cover an acre of land one foot deep, which is ~326,000 gallons or 1.2 million litres, and roughly the water used by two average Southern California families in a year (see information from the California Department of Water Resources (https://www.water.ca.gov/Water-Basics) and from the Public Policy Institute of California (http://www.ppic.org/publication/water-use-in-california/)).

movement of fish and other river life, affecting ecosystem balance both near the coast and upstream.

As highlighted in Part Three, acute crises provide a framework for action by individuals, communities and the private sector. In this example, the human and natural environmental factors provided the context for what became an intense five years' drought. Very low levels of rain and snow for several years decreased the surface water availability for urban and agricultural users as well as for the environment. This brought on a number of responses. First, an amplification of the constant fighting over environmental regulations. Second, as the drought worsened, individuals and water districts again began to look for new infrastructure projects to provide current supply, future storage of water and perhaps more stability – in fact, the development of new reservoirs in response to a severe drought in the 1990s made the first three years of this drought almost unnoticeable to Southern California, perhaps exacerbating the problem. A rash of projects were begun, including the completion of a desalination facility between Los Angeles and San Diego, and the approval of a plan to recycle waste water in LA county. Water districts began investment in research and development of new technologies, from low-flow fixtures to advanced leak detection, to make their systems more efficient. In the Central Valley, farmers anxious to have enough water to maintain fields of trees[2] began digging even more wells and depleting the underground water stores. Finally, policy and regulatory actions were initiated that would have been difficult or impossible to bring forward in a non-emergency situation. Some were temporary, such as the mandatory restrictions in urban water use. Some temporary actions were focused on funding longer term changes – funding for landscape changes and infrastructure development. Some actions were aimed at systemic changes, such as the final passage of the Sustainable Groundwater Management Act in 2015. Most of these solutions, whether bottom up or top down, are fundamentally about using less water (efficiency and technology) or finding new sources of water (with significant environmental and/or economic costs). Although groups also began collecting data and advocating for more comprehensive water-trading markets throughout the state, little headway was made to create a better governance strategy for distribution across the state – solutions were being implemented largely by local groups.

Amid the fights for access to enough water, we are seeing a change to the patterns of precipitation around which the built infrastructure was designed. The current system of water distribution was devised and constructed before the impact of anthropogenic climate change began to reshape regional weather patterns. Higher heat will increase demand for water, and changing weather patterns are projected to bring larger storms and less snowpack storage, and more variability even if total rainfall remains about the same. Relying on outdated infrastructure will certainly lead to more stress, more fighting and more uncertainty.

Here, in the industrialized West, we see an example of the limits imposed by nature, our ability to change those limits (intentionally or not), technical and infrastructure

---

[2] The shift from annual to perennial crops in the Central Valley over the past 2–3 decades is coupled to the way water has been used and delivered around the state, and it is beyond the scope of this discussion.

developments to manage a chronic challenge and mitigate the effects of an acute one, and a political and economic fight over unequal distribution with haves and have-nots. We see here the same lack of action without crisis that concerns those around the world that see a lack of action on sustainable resource development as a major concern for the future. This case study shows the need for inclusion of all the voices at the table with a view towards a sustainable solution for managing resource scarcity – those that view water scarcity as a natural limit and those that view it as structural and man-made; for local and global viewpoints; for environmentalists, farmers and urban water users.

### Lessons for the future: The importance of a model of global leadership with local voices

In 2015, the United Nations released the Sustainable Development Goals (UNSDGs), a set of seventeen guiding principles that try to address the needs of all members of all societies in a more equitable and sustainable fashion.[3] The goals include ending poverty and hunger, providing access to health care and education, clean water and sanitation, clean energy and healthy ecosystems, among many others.

Like other modern efforts, the UNSDGs are data-driven and often techno-optimistic in nature. Indeed, some of the challenges are clearly in need of new technology to help move the needle – perhaps most notably producing enough food where it is needed to feed 10 billion humans. What is unique about the UNSDGs is the recognition that a sustainable future requires gender equity, strong institutions and an educated population, as well as fair and equitable distribution of resources.

Modern (Eurocentric) societal approaches to resource distribution have been almost entirely economic – we insist that energy resources be developed and priced based on a market with internal and external costs. Environmentalists have long railed against the exclusion of environmental costs from the market. Environmental justice advocates have done the same for the lack of attention paid to the unequal distribution of those costs. Perhaps it is time to recognize that human values require a different framing of energy, water, food and many other resource distribution challenges. Whether one agrees with the concept of the Anthropocene as described in this book, the size of the global population and the impact humans now have on planet-scale systems are formidable.

While still framing the problem in somewhat standard economic parlance (including a goal dedicated to economic growth), the UNSDGs allow us to begin a different global discussion, driven by local needs and challenges and recognizing that all people deserve access to the resources that define a healthy and productive life. It remains to be seen whether the UNSDGs will truly integrate the voices of the people at the bottom of the distributional pyramid, or provide teeth to enforce potentially difficult transitions, or encourage markets for new technologies and infrastructure to be developed that align with these goals rather than the existing market forces. Can

---

[3]   http://www.un.org/sustainabledevelopment/sustainable-development-goals/.

a programme, designed to bring people out of poverty in a sustainable way while changing the approach of developed societies to resource use without disrupting their quality of life, really walk that tightrope? To do so requires us to recognize both sides of resource scarcity – the possibility of fundamental limits to human exploitation of the planet's resource in juxtaposition with the realization that most instances of scarcity are at least partially manufactured or exacerbated by existing power structures. And it means greater attention to the temporal and spatial scales involved in scarcities that all too frequently transcend the political and territorial logic of governments and their publics. The knowledge that can be gained from the chapters of this book gives an insight into how we might do better moving forward.

# Part One

# Making Scarcity

# 2

# Scarcity: Language and Politics

Jean-Laurent Rosenthal

Scholarly projects that bring together experts from many different disciplines face problems of language and definition. When these deal with complex and important problems, conversations across the disciplines often become difficult. This is particularly true when these collaborations occur like the trading rings of Malinowski – infrequently and with a constantly set of changing characters.[1] Once everyone has finished elaborating one's disciplinary identity the project is largely over. Certainly, there is not enough time to evolve a common language. This chapter began as an impromptu comment offered at the start of a conference that pleaded for some definitional clarity. Now as then, I advocate for a definition that starts with the economists' definition and then widens the problem.

This chapter makes two claims. The first claim is that scarcity is at the heart of economics, and it is useful for all scholars to consider how economists think about scarcity. The second claim is that although the economists' definition is part of an analytic construct that explains how the world of resources works, it is not prescriptive. It's merely a tool of analysis which must be attended to in order to make prescriptive decisions, which belong to the broader realm of ethics and politics.

Scarcity is at the heart of economics. Going back to the birth of the discipline in the eighteenth century, economists recognize that scarcity is an essential feature of the distribution of both factors of production and goods and services that individuals consume. An efficient economy deals with scarcity well, while an inefficient one does not. Since Adam Smith, economists have debated how to deploy markets and organizations to best take advantage of the resources available to society. They have recognized the primacy of government in affecting the balance between markets and organizations. Most of the contributions to this book take on a problem of scarcity and either explicitly or implicitly propose an alteration in the institutional equilibrium to produce a 'better' social outcome. That puts them all in the vein of analyses pioneered by Smith, Coase and other scholars of economic institutions.[2]

---

[1] B. Bronislaw Malinowski, *Argonauts of the Western Pacific: An Account of Native Enterprise and Adventure in the Archipelagoes of Melanesian New Guinea* (London: G. Routledge & Sons, 1922).

[2] Adam Smith, *An Inquiry into the Nature and Causes of the Wealth of Nations* (London, 1776). Ronald Coase, 'The problem of social cost', *The Journal of Law and Economics*, 3 (1960): 1–44.

Requiring that analyses of scarcity start with the economists' definition risks the critique of disciplinary imperialism. Nevertheless, starting there does have some tangible pay-offs. Consider the situation with fossil fuels. In 2014, oil prices were near $100 a barrel, a situation that at the time people imagined implied the near arrival of the historical production peak due to resource exhaustion. Since then, however, oil prices have fallen by half. This is partly due to an abundance of natural gas and the fact that many experts argue that the energy transition to renewable will occur long before we run out of fossil fuels. Oil was scarce in 2014, and it still is now but the problem of fossil fuels is in fact their abundance. One reason such stark changes in the scarcity of oil can arise is that it has many substitutes. When they become more abundant, oil becomes less scarce even if total proven reserves do not change. Contrast this with water in the Central Valley of California, in the aggregate it is abundant (billions of gallons are used each year), but changes in the types of crops grown have made farmers far less resilient to drought than they had been in the past. Thirty years ago, the dominant crops in the Central Valley were annuals and planted acreage could follow short-term water supply variation. The construction of the California aqueduct brought massive increases in water supply and farmers shifted more and more acreage to fruit and nut trees. These permanent crops require water in both wet and dry years. In dry years, water is in fact more scarce today in the Central Valley than it had been thirty years ago *despite* the fact that aggregate supply is larger than it was in the 1960s. Conversely, Africanized bees are rare in California but they are not scarce. Scarcity thus has little to do with abundance or rarity; it's a social phenomenon that invites inquiry.

## The scarcity of economics

The problem of scarcity is central to economics for one simple reason. A good or service is scarce if it has a positive price. Something that is abundant does not have a positive price. To fix ideas, oranges are scarce and I have to pay about two dollars per pound for them at my local farmer's market (the two dollars is the positive price). Conversely, garbage is abundant and I have to pay a company to take it away (it has a negative price because company gets my garbage each week and my 20 dollars a month). That scarce goods have positive prices is both pithy and lies at the heart of economics, and it has at least four important implications. First, because most everything is scarce, coping with scarcity is like living with air or working under gravity. Given that this conference is not about trivialities it is about something other than simple scarcity. Second, if a good has a positive price, something must be given up to consume it. The trade-off across goods in consumption is a classic problem for economists. Third, it also follows that as a good gets scarcer its price goes up. That implies the reward to producing more of it (and of consuming less of it) goes up. So does the reward for producing substitutes. Just how quickly these responses occur is another classic issue. Fourth, if we consider not consumption but production, if a factor is scarce (expensive) that implies that the alternative factor is abundant and cheap, then substitute factors are also scarce. Finally, there is a corollary: scarcity or positive price means that there is an abundance of demand. So far we have gone no further than economics 001, but that does not mean these ideas are not relevant.

Even if we admit that scarcity is ubiquitous, we must still face the complicated problem of allocation (who ends up with the scarce good/factor). In many cases, the allocation of scarce goods occurs in a market and price is determined by the interaction of supply and demand. Although supply and demand curves are intellectual constructs of the nineteenth century, humans have been behaving as though they participate in market exchange for as long as the data allow us to look. As a child growing up in Provence, I went to the wholesale produce market where large amounts of fruits and vegetables were auctioned. If quantities were small and the weather in major cities was warm, the price for fruits tended to be higher. In particular, a good can become scarce when demand increases. That is after all the whole purpose of marketing and advertising. One can debate whether advertising efforts are manipulating our preferences or providing valuable information about the products we seek to consume, it remains that social information has long been a central element of how demand evolves. The price of a good falls (rises) when demand for it falls (or rises) faster than supply adjusts. Similarly, the price of a good rises when supply falls faster than demand adjusts. One element of demand for fruits is temperature in major markets, an element of supply involves weather in producing areas. Of course, variation in demand and supply comes from a variety of sources including environmental, technological or social and obviously from interaction between these sources.

Varying levels of scarcity are generally not an issue for the market mechanism – price adjusts lead to a new market equilibrium (consider the variations from $30 to $144 per barrel in the price of oil over the last fifteen years). Once the adjustment has occurred, the individuals with the highest willingness to pay end up with the good in question. When evaluating the allocation one (scholar, politician, citizen) may well find fault with who receives the good and who does not. There are two reasons for this. First, there is classic market failure when the market does not reach privately efficient outcomes due to transaction costs.[3] Second, there are cases where the market allocation leads to larger social costs because willingness to pay depends more on ability to pay than on the private benefit of the good. In both cases, one can identify a group of consumers that does not end up with the good but would derive very high benefits. Market failure may lead to government intervention in the allocation. Such intervention often aims to make the good available at below market price to some fraction of consumers. In many cases, such intervention leads to shortages.

## Shortage and overstock

Again, a reminder of the economic definition of a shortage seems in order. Shortage is a situation where buyers remain in the market after the supply has been exhausted.

---

[3] George Akerlof, 'The market for "lemons": Quality uncertainty and the market mechanism', *The Quarterly Journal of Economics*, 84, no. 3 (1970): 488–500.

The reader will have clearly divined that a shortage can only occur with a scarce good and that just like scarcity's opposite is abundance, a shortage's reverse in an overstock. Shortages arise when the price is too low, overstocks when it is too high. Economists have a simple solution to either situation: let the price change. It is often assumed that because the market mechanism allocates the resource in question to the individuals with the highest willingness to pay, there can be no shortages or overstock. This logic works for strawberries, electricity, medical care and even nuclear power plants.

A broader definition covers most of what the chapters in this book describe as either scarcity or shortage: there is a group that receives less of the good or service than would be desirable. A shortage is thus quite distinct from scarcity and is independent of whether or not there exists a market mechanism to allocate the good or service under consideration.

Obviously, the market price is not the only allocation mechanism. Even the most capitalist firms may choose not to let it play out. Certainly, the stock-outs of popular Christmas toys in the United States occur in a market but firms do not usually raise prices when they discover they have the 'it' gift of the season. Instead, they allow a first-come-first-serve mechanism to replace the price mechanism (the same was true until recently about tickets to concerts and the like). Second, many goods and services are not allocated through markets but through some administrative procedure (e.g. passports). Third, whether goods or services are allocated by private or public entities, recipients may or may not face a unit price and that unit price may or may not reflect supply conditions to the entity supplying it. To be more specific, for most of its history, Sacramento made water available to its residents in return for a hook-up fee but it did not metre consumption. Similarly, local water boards could not raise prices to reduce consumption by urban residents during the latest drought in California because a law designed to limit corruption did not allow local water boards to make a profit. Instead, local water boards instituted rationing with mandatory consumption cuts. Rationing is evidence of a shortage.

Understanding shortage in the short run (while supply is fixed) requires specifying two alternatives: first, what the allocation might look like if the market mechanism were allowed free range and, second, what the social desirable allocation of current supply might be. For instance, what to do when the number of flu shot vaccines is cut in half? One could imagine a market mechanism where every person who wants to be vaccinated for the flu must purchase a dose by biding at a weekly online auction. This mechanism will avoid any economic shortage, because at the price of the auction no one wants to buy who does not want to buy. On the other hand, allocating vaccine this way might well raise eyebrows, since the elderly and the poor with low ability to pay and poor access to the internet might get very few doses even though they may need them the most. An advocate for the poor or the elderly may well speak of a shortage of vaccine, because those populations have access to far fewer doses than before the decline in supply. Yet even though we might measure in the elderly's access to vaccine, the use of the term 'shortage' is not a positive statement because there is no shortage. It is a normative statement that the market allocation is socially inefficient. For normative reasons, a social planner might well come up with a score that takes in age, pre-existing conditions, occupation and so forth and then allocate the vaccine using that score at cost. This will produce shortage because healthy middle-age male university professors' tendency to hypochondria will likely make them want to get vaccinated, but the scheme will deny them access to the vaccine.

Understanding shortage in the long run requires dealing with two types of adaptation: increases in supply and the search for substitutes. To return to one of my California examples, two adaptations to the recent drought and attendant water shortage have included reinjecting either rainwater or treated wastewater into the aquifer, have accelerated in the past decade. Both adaptations represent increases in supply that can be tapped when surface water deliveries fall short. Should such programmes diffuse maximally, then urban water users are much less likely to face rationing programmes. One might think this is a better mechanism than raising water prices in periods of drought because it reduces the burden on the poor. These are also adaptations that do not run afoul of the 'no profits' rule. Yet increasing water supply through reinjection requires considerable capital outlays and because water district must balance their books everyone will face an increased cost of water, and the poor may well prefer a tiered pricing system where high-volume consumers pay a high price and those revenues go into long-term supply expansion.

The development of substitutes for water is harder to imagine but consider a more strict definition of the problem where the service is surface water. The main source of water for Southern California comes from surface water from dams in Northern California and from the Colorado River, but groundwater has always been an important source of water. An increase in supply for Southern California could simply involve purchasing surface water rights in the Central Valley. But an alternative (substitute) to surface water shortfalls in drought years would be better ground-water management.

Separately from understanding shortage as social scientists, there is also another very important issue: namely, the use of scarcity and shortage in a normative sense (as we saw in the vaccine example). While using a market to allocate a scarce good is a guarantee of efficiency, it makes no guarantee of fairness. The tension between efficiency and fairness produces a political rather than economic debate. Consider the short run first. In the case of a sudden positive shock to supply, we may find it unfair that the least efficient producers face sudden losses. Similarly, in the case of a sudden negative shock to supply, we may find it unfair that the poor have to absorb most of the reduction in consumption. In both cases, there is likely to be demand for political intervention to reign in the market response. In one case, there will be overstocks (as in the mountains of butter accumulated as a result of European Union subsidies in the 1970 and 1980s). In the other, there will be shortages and rationing. In the long run, dealing with a large positive supply imbalance one can let the market push out the least efficient producers who may have been in the business longest or the political process may intervene and such interventions can be extremely persistent (the English Corn Laws or Japan's closed market for rice). The same is true for large persistent demand imbalances that can lead to the takeover of an industry by the state or some local government (e.g. the progressive nationalization of railroads around the world). Using the language of scarcity and shortage should illuminate the political debate not obscure it.

## From economics to politics and history

Starting with the economists' definitions for scarcity and shortage has two consequences. First, it disentangles the positive issues from the normative ones. Indeed, using these definitions we can quantify differences in outcomes based on different allocation mechanisms. The second consequence is that it makes starkly clear that if we are to understand how societies deal with scarcity or shortage, we need to bring in politics and history at the very least and more likely all the other disciplines of the social sciences. Indeed, even the greatest intellectual contortionist will be unable to rationalize on the basis of economic efficiency, the allocation of water in California, English Corn Laws, Japan's closed market for rice and the myriad approaches to vaccination across the world.

3

# Untangling Scarcity

Amber Huff and Lyla Mehta

## Introduction

Even though scarcity has a very long philosophical history, its dominant contemporary notion is a relatively recent innovation. Over the years, scarcity has had a profoundly influential 'social life' and has become intertwined with ideas of growth, progress, abundance and sustainability. Natural resource scarcity is often discussed as a failure to manage finite resources in the face of global population growth, and this 'tragedy of the commons' conceptualization[1] has come to be seen as a natural, universal and self-evident characteristic of the human condition.

Since the 1970s, resource scarcity has been cast and recast in relation to different problems by academics, civil society and policy players. Debates over 'limits to growth',[2] sustainability and the future survival of humankind,[3] environmental valuation and accounting,[4] and violent conflict and security[5] have all been situated in terms of the normative notion of scarcity. More recently, growing concerns over climate change, volatility in global markets and debates on sustainable development, 'Planetary Boundaries' and the Anthropocene[6] have sparked a renewed interest in scarcity.

Since the 2008 World Economic Forum, key global players, including intergovernmental organizations, international NGOs, financial actors and members of the corporate sector, have highlighted growing water, food, climate and energy security and scarcity threats and the need to resolve them through the so-called nexus

---

[1]  G. Hardin (1968), 'The Tragedy of the Commons', *Science*, 162 (3859): 1243–1248.

[2]  D. H. Meadows, D. L. Meadows, J. Randers, and W. W. Behrens (1972), *The Limits to Growth: A Report for the Club of Rome's Project on the Predicament of Mankind*, New York: Universe Books.

[3]  G. H. Brundtland (1987), *Our Common Future*, Oxford: World Commission on Environment and Development.

[4]  D. W. Pearce, A. Markandya, and E. Barbier (1989), *Blueprint for a Green Economy*, Vol. 1, London: Earthscan.

[5]  T. F. Homer-Dixon (Summer 1994), 'Environmental Scarcities and Violent Conflict: Evidence from Cases', *International Security*, 19 (1): 5–40.

[6]  J. Rockström et al. (2009), 'Planetary Boundaries: Exploring the Safe Operating Space for Humanity', *Ecology and Society*, 14 (2): Article 32.

approach.[7] Discourses of land, water, energy and mineral scarcity have been used as a justification for large-scale resource acquisitions by governments and investors. These so-called land and water 'grabs' have led to dramatic changes in local lives, livelihoods and access to resources.[8]

Yet, even though natural resource scarcity is widely recognized as a problem, it is not clear how it is to be dealt with and how it should shape our priorities and inform our decisions, either in the here and now or in the future. Part of this uncertainty stems from the fact that despite its ubiquity, scarcity is a contested concept. It is often used imprecisely and means different things to different people. Its assumptions and implications vary across a number of different disciplines and fields of practice that deal with problems at the intersection of humans and nature. Given the resurgence in scarcity debates in recent years, here we evaluate diverse conceptions of scarcity in a historical context while also critically engaging with scarcity's taken-for-granted nature.

We begin this chapter by highlighting problems with conventional asocial and apolitical notions of scarcity that are heavily associated with neoclassical economics and Malthusian thinking, particularly concerned with natural resources. We then unpack dominant conceptualizations of scarcity, and discuss how applications and understandings of scarcity vary across contemporary disciplines and literatures. We present a heuristic of three dominant themes that emerge from a wide review of literature that relates to resource use and scarcity. These include (1) the 'systems, boundaries and thresholds' position, (2) the 'technological and managerial fix' position and (3) the 'structural-distributional' position. We then discuss what implications might these different framings of scarcity carry for our ability to imagine and plan for possible futures. This is an important exercise, as each of these three positions implies different trade-offs between considerations of economic growth, environmental sustainability and equity, and each has different implications for action and development, which we illustrate with respect to water. We conclude by proposing why the structural and distributional position is best placed to consider both the political economy of resource control and accumulation alongside issues concerning environmental justice, ethics and sustainability.

## Disaggregating conventional notions of scarcity

Dominant notions of natural resource scarcity bring together two primary sets of ideas from classical political economy and neoclassical economics. In terms of the former,

---

[7]  J. Allouche, C. Middleton, and D. Gyawali (2014), *Nexus Nirvana or Nexus Nullity? A Dynamic Approach to Security and Sustainability in the Water-Energy-Food Nexus*. STEPS Centre, STEPS Working Paper 63; H. Hoff (2011), *Understanding the Nexus*. Background Paper for the Bonn 2011 Conference: The Water, Energy and Food Security Nexus, Stockholm Environment Institute; World Economic Forum (2014), *The Future Availability of Natural Resources: A New Paradigm for Global Resource Availability*, Geneva: World Economic Forum.

[8]  J. Franco, L. Mehta, and G. J. Veldwisch (2013), 'The Global Politics of Water Grabbing', *Third World Quarterly*, 34 (9): 1651–1675.

from Malthus comes the idea of a natural mismatch between the human tendency for population growth and the earth's capacity to support an increasing population at a high level of well-being.[9] In terms of the latter, the idea of scarcity as the mismatch between unlimited human desires and limited means to fulfil them originated with the 'marginalist revolution' of the 1870s that laid the foundations of neoclassical economics.[10] The assumption follows that scarcity is a natural phenomenon or a set of natural limits existing prior to human society and politics, and that atomistic self-interested decision-makers will push these limits in pursuit of satisfying unlimited desires.

But wants and desires do not have to be endless and unlimited[11] and are also socially mediated and constructed.[12] While growing populations and associated demands for water, food and technology can certainly result in shortages and environmental damage, one must crucially ask if the fixation with overpopulation distracts from focusing attention on more crucial aspects of resource access and allocation. To what extent is this thing we think of as natural scarcity in fact associated with dominant modes of production, patterns of consumption, distribution of power in society (e.g. along gender, caste and ethnicity and other axes of social difference) and political decisions regarding terms of trade, state planning, centralizing technologies, tenure arrangements, conservation and so on?

Mehta has argued that 'scarcity' has emerged as a totalizing discourse in both the North and the South with science and technology often expected to provide solutions.[13] Considering this, it is important to ask how 'wide-angle' approaches to natural resource scarcity obscure complexities, politics, experiences, uncertainties around natural resource availability, and why notions of scarcity as promoted by multilateral and bilateral donors, government bureaucracies and think tanks usually triumph over diverse local experiences, understandings and solutions to problems of natural resource availability. Do aggregate projections and technical assessments of resource availability capture their multifaceted nature and embeddedness in culture, history and politics? If scarcity isn't one concrete thing, what are the competing and overlapping assumptions, narratives and ideas that make up the totalizing discourse of scarcity? Our heuristic of three dominant themes emerges from a wide review of literature that relates to resource use and scarcity. It highlights how different disciplines attribute different causes and solutions to scarcity. We turn to present these now.

### Theme 1: Systems, boundaries and thresholds

The 'systems, boundaries and thresholds' position frames scarcity in terms of absolute biogeophysical limits to earth system functioning. The fundamental premise of this

---

[9] T. R. Malthus (1798), *An Essay on the Principle of Population*, London.
[10] B. Fine (2010), 'Economics and Scarcity: With Amartya Sen as Point of Departure', in L. Mehta (ed.), *The Limits to Scarcity: Contesting the Politics of Allocation*, 73–91, Vol. 73–92.
[11] W. Leiss (1988), *Limits to Satisfaction: An Essay on the Problem of Needs and Commodities*, Canada.
[12] S. Rayner (2010), 'Foreword', in L. Mehta (ed.), *The Limits to Scarcity*, x–xvi, Vol. 73–92, London: Earthscan.
[13] L. Mehta (ed.) (2010), *The Limits to Scarcity: Contesting the Politics of Allocation*, London.

position is that the earth is a complex ecological system that involves relationships between biophysical and social elements and processes, which are compromised through human activities. In this vein, human activities have cumulatively brought about profound changes to the earth's biophysical characteristics and ecological processes to the extent that the capacities of the planet to support human life and socio-economic development is threatened, resulting in ecological collapse, global financial instability and growing economic inequalities.[14]

The origins of this position can be directly traced to the 1970s, with the hugely influential publication of the Club of Rome's *Limits to Growth* and the popularization of debates in the early environmental movement on the relative contributions of population, technology and growing affluence to negative environmental impacts and crises. Of the contemporary positions we discuss in this chapter, this one is most associated with the neo-Malthusian preoccupation with relationships between population growth and both societal and ecological collapse. Today, this position is closely aligned with ecological economics and, in broad terms, it is mostly concerned with large-scale systems dynamics across timescales, the environmental consequences of increasing consumption and an absolute conception of environmental scarcity.[15] This position is also reflected to varying degrees in work in several interdisciplinary areas, which use systems-focused approaches to understand human–environment/ society–nature relations and engage with the challenges of sustainable development and global environmental and climate change. Such areas include human ecology, environmental studies, sustainability science and earth system science (ESS).[16]

Exemplars of this position that have recently risen to prominence include the concept of the Anthropocene and the Planetary Boundaries (PB) approach. Originally coined by Paul Crutzen[17] over a decade ago, the concept of the Anthropocene views Earth as an evolving 'planetary' system that has entered a geologic time interval, in which human activities rival global geophysical processes in terms of influencing changing global conditions.[18] PB disaggregates and conceptualizes these proposed changes in terms of nine 'Planetary Boundaries' (some of which remain un-quantified) that represent a 'safe operating space' (SOS) for humanity. The nine system processes or boundaries include climate change, ocean acidification, stratospheric ozone depletion, atmospheric aerosol loading, biogeochemical flows that interfere with nitrogen and

[14] M. R. Chertow (2000), 'The IPAT Equation and Its Variants', *Journal of Industrial Ecology*, 4 (4): 13–29; F. P. Saunders (2014), 'Planetary Boundaries: At the Threshold... Again: Sustainable Development Ideas and Politics', *Environment, Development and Sustainability*, 17 (4): 823–835.

[15] I. Røpke (2005), 'Trends in the Development of Ecological Economics from the Late 1980s to the Early 2000s', *Ecological Economics*, 55 (2): 262–290; 'Theories of Practice – New Inspiration for Ecological Economic Studies on Consumption' (2009), *Ecological Economics*, 68 (10): 2490–2497.

[16] K. Rasmussen and F. Arler (2010), 'Interdisciplinarity at the Human-Environment Interface', *Geografisk Tidsskrift-Danish Journal of Geography*, 110 (1): 37–45.

[17] P. J. Crutzen (2002), 'Geology of Mankind', *Nature*, 415 (6867): 23; 'The "Anthropocene"', in E. Ehlers and T. Krafft (eds.), *Earth System Science in the Anthropocene*, 13–18.

[18] Rockström et al., 'Planetary Boundaries'; W. Steffen, J. Grinevald, P. Crutzen, and J. McNeill (2011), 'The Anthropocene: Conceptual and Historical Perspectives', *Philosophical Transactions of the Royal Society of London A: Mathematical, Physical and Engineering Sciences*, 369 (1938): 842–867; W. Steffen, Å. Persson et al. (2011), 'The Anthropocene: From Global Change to Planetary Stewardship', *AMBIO*, 40 (7): 739–761.

phosphorous cycles, freshwater, land systems change, biodiversity loss and chemical pollution.[19]

However, as Galaz and colleagues argue, '[p]lanetary boundaries' are not fixed nor certain, but represent model-derived best-guess estimates of 'an uncertainty zone around a potential threshold'.[20] In this perspective, we see not only an attempt to demonstrate the cumulative effects of human activities on particular planetary thresholds but a scaled-up concept of scarcity implicitly applied to the resource uses and patterns of consumption that comprise the ecological SOS supporting crucial systems and processes. PB proponents stop short of specific timescale predictions or specifications of how, precisely, large-scale changes and breaches will impact human life. As a result, this approach remains at best speculative and descriptive of processes under way, despite the urgency of the messages that radical immediate change is necessary for the survival of the species. Because of its planetary-level focus, PB has little relevance to understanding how these processes are unfolding in real-world places and ecosystems, or what is at stake in people's lives in an immediate sense. Still, it has a powerful narrative to frame and justify a range of policy approaches concerning global environmental change. However, the tone is rhetorical and prophetic rather than predictive in a way that is particularly useful to inform specific interventions at local and meso-scales.

### Theme 2: The technological and managerial fix

The 'technological and managerial fix' position is more optimistic and argues that investment in technological, market-driven and managerial solutions will allow global society to mitigate, and also adapt to, resource crises, across sectors of society and scales from local to global, without compromising goals of environmental sustainability and inclusive economic growth into the future. This position is reflected in contemporary ideas about sustainability and sustainable development that dominate international political discussions, which are fundamentally about shifting and managing scarcity over space and time, in both an ecological and an economic sense.

For technological optimists, scarcity is conceptualized as the opposite of abundance and as arising from a failure to identify innovative solutions to emerging problems, inefficient technologies or a lack of technical management of resources. The focus on abundance highlights human technological inventiveness in time of need and projects that into the future. Literature taking a 'fix' approach is heavily influenced by development economics and environmental economics and generally demonstrates faith in markets: support for donor- and state-led governance and resource management solutions to problems of environmental degradation to rectify global as well as localized environmental problems. Scarcity and other environmental problems are seen as an expected consequence arising from flawed policies that result in market failures and governance failures.

---

[19] Rockström et al., 'Planetary Boundaries'; W. Steffen et al. (2015), 'Planetary Boundaries: Guiding Human Development on a Changing Planet', *Science*, 347 (6223): 1259855.

[20] V. Galaz et al. (2012), 'Planetary Boundaries' – Exploring the Challenges for Global Environmental Governance', *Current Opinion in Environmental Sustainability*, 4 (1): 80–87.

The technological and managerial fix position on scarcity is particularly interesting in terms of the ways that its proponents construct compelling narratives justifying technical or market intervention. Much of this genre uses the language of ecological limits (particularly in the framing of narratives of crisis), natural capital, the global commons and global goods, ecosystem services, all of which originated in or possess particular salience in ecological economics,[21] especially in order to discuss problems and crises. Key contemporary examples of the influence of this position include the UN-led 'Green Economy' approach (and 'green' growth and 'green' development more broadly) and World Economic Forum's food-water-energy 'nexus'.

While it is widely understood that 'environmental damage is not equity-neutral',[22] these approaches remain debated, particularly by social scientists, due to a number of unresolved questions around equity outcomes, and the environmental, economic and social claims of their proponents are widely contested. On a basic level, policymaking for green development often occurs without guidance on the means of assessing unanticipated conflicts, trade-offs and synergies that arise as programmes and projects are implemented, and evidence-based studies that objectively document triple win outcomes are rare.[23] In fact, green growth schemes may be particularly risky in terms of potential negative consequences for poor people, which might outweigh any direct or indirect benefits resulting from aggregate economic growth. Schalatek, Wichterich and Unmüßig and colleagues see the green economy as a market-based approach that justifies the commodification and enclosure of resources and commons, undermining livelihoods, justifying land and green grabs[24] and dispossessing local people – especially women food producers.[25]

In 'fix' thinking, broadly, technological choices that are exercised are often considered to exist outside politics. But in reality, these are deeply political – and contestations around technological, institutional or market solutions are sites of politics and cannot be seen as neutral arbiters to resolve decisions on how best to deal with and manage resource scarcity.

[21] R. B. Richardson (2013), *Building a Green Economy: Perspectives from Ecological Economics*, East Lansing: Michigan State University Press.

[22] S. Dercon (2014), 'Is Green Growth Good for the Poor?', *The World Bank Research Observer*, 29 (2): 163–185.

[23] J. Baker, E. J. Milner-Gulland, and N. Leader-Williams (2012), 'Park Gazettement and Integrated Conservation and Development as Factors in Community Conflict at Bwindi Impenetrable Forest, Uganda', *Conservation Biology*, 26 (1): 160–170; N. Suckall, L. C. Stringer, and E. L. Tompkins, 'Presenting Triple-Wins? Assessing Projects That Deliver Adaptation, Mitigation and Development Co-benefits in Rural Sub-Saharan Africa', *AMBIO*, 44 (1): 34–41; E. L. Tompkins et al. (2013), *An Investigation of the Evidence of Benefits from Climate Compatible Development*, Sustainability Research Institute Paper No. 44.

[24] S. M. Borras et al. (2011), 'Towards a Better Understanding of Global Land Grabbing: An Editorial Introduction'; J. Fairhead, M. Leach, and I. Scoones (2012), 'Green Grabbing: A New Appropriation of Nature?', *Journal of Peasant Studies*, 39 (2): 237–261.

[25] L. Schalatek and K. Burns (2013), *Operationalizing a Gender-Sensitive Approach in the Green Climate Fund*, Washington, DC: Boell Foundation; B. Unmüßig (2012), *The Green Economy–The New Magic Bullet?* Berlin: Heinrich Böll Foundation; C. Wichterich (2012), *The Future We Want: A Feminist Perspective*.

Furthermore, often technology and market fixes are both the 'problem' and the 'solution' – for example, interventions such as large dams are made out to be the 'solution' for scarcity in water-starved areas but they are also 'problems' around which prominent social movements have emerged. Similarly, privatization models or large-scale foreign investments in water and land are purported to be the 'solution' to efficiently manage scarcity – but their impacts on human well-being and people's basic rights and dignity can often be problematic, especially in the world's poorest countries. These issues are taken up directly in the structural inequality/distributional position to which we now turn.

### Theme 3: The structural-distributional position

Contrary to the previous two positions, which both naturalize scarcity in different ways, this position argues that environmental degradation and resource scarcity are not, in fact, 'natural' but result from inequitable institutional arrangements that result in gross inequalities in access to resources.[26] This position advances a sociopolitical perspective on scarcity drawing on a variety of disciplinary approaches including political ecology, political economy, discourse analysis and human development approaches. This position resists universalized notions of scarcity as well, emphasizing that the precise ways that people in different social groups perceive and experience scarcity will vary across different environmental settings, at different scales (from the household to community, nation and the global world) and on the basis of relations of power and production.[27] It also focuses on how access to and control over resources are contested in these different settings and at these different scales, resulting in competing claims and conflicts shaped by uneven power relations.[28]

Ross distinguishes between socially generated scarcity (insufficient necessities for some people and not others) and absolute scarcity (insufficient resources, no matter how equitably distributed). For him, neoliberalism has encouraged a pro-scarcity climate distinguished, economically, by deep concessions and cutbacks, and, politically, by the rollback of 'excessive' rights. He argues that the two kinds of scarcity have been conflated either intentionally in order to reinforce austerity measures against the poor or inadvertently due to ignorance about how natural resources are produced and distributed.[29] The human development approach to scarcity breaks down macro and aggregate understandings of scarcity. It would argue that scarcity regarding access to basic resources is unacceptable in the twenty-first century. This is particularly

---

[26] P. Dasgupta (1997), *Environmental and Resource Economics in the World of the Poor*, Resources for the Future Lecture, Washington, DC: Resources for the Future; UNDP (2006a), *Human and Income Poverty: Developing Countries*, New York: United Nations Development Programme; K. Watkins (2006), *Human Development Report 2006-Beyond Scarcity: Power, Poverty and the Global Water Crisis*, UNDP Human Development Reports.

[27] L. Yappa (1996), 'Improved Seeds and Constructed Scarcity', in R. Peet and M. Watts (eds.), *Liberation Ecologies: Environment, Development, and Social Movements*, 69–85, New York.

[28] R. Peet and M. Watts (1996), *Liberation Ecologies: Environment, Development, Social Movements*, New York: Routledge.

[29] A. Ross (1996), 'The Lonely Hour of Scarcity', *Capitalism, Nature, Socialism*, 7 (3): 3–26.

so because scarcity is not 'natural' but generated through sociopolitical processes, through exclusion, biases and discrimination.[30] For example, in India, so-called lower caste women are still denied access to certain wells. In apartheid South Africa, the inequalities based on discriminatory policies were huge. Consequently, around 80 per cent of the poor in rural areas had no access to water or sanitation in 1994 at the birth of the new South Africa.[31] A human development approach draws on Amartya Sen's entitlements analysis (see below). Thus, it is important to look at questions of power and of social values, distribution and justice in how problems of scarcity emerge and how they, and responses to them, are experienced.

A human rights approach to resource scarcity would seek to integrate the norms, standards and principles of the international human rights system into the plans and policies related to natural resources management at the international, national and sub-national levels. Key principles would include accountability, transparency, empowerment, participation, non-discrimination (equality and equity) and attention to vulnerable groups (see HLPE 2015).[32] Human rights approaches can assist in building social consensus and in mobilizing commitments to facilitate a fairer use of resources and to empower poor people. Policies and programmes that are designed from a human rights point of view are more likely to be equitable, sustainable and have the potential to eliminate extreme poverty. Clearly, there are many links between the violation of human rights and the economic, social, cultural and political deprivations that characterize poverty. Despite the challenges in their implementation,[33] the realization of all human rights can guide efforts to reduce, and ultimately eradicate, poverty.[34]

Finally, due to growing international investments in resources, there is a need to protect the rights of vulnerable and marginalized groups. While there have been several initiatives to protect the interests of foreign investors in international trade agreements, there is no concomitant protection for communities affected by these investments; their rights are assumed to be protected by their national governments, which is not always sufficient. Even national states have found it hard to protect public policies in the courts set up to arbitrate for investors. Defining the extraterritorial obligations of the investors as well as the government in the host country is essential to ensure that vulnerable people's basic rights are protected. It is also important to consider the human rights obligations of states towards persons outside their territories, including state obligations to protect people from the extraterritorial activities of private-sector actors based in their country. The land acquisitions on the part of foreign investors around the world are a good case in point. In some cases, there are severe violations to

---

[30] UNDP (2006), *Human Development Report 2006-Beyond Scarcity: Power, Poverty and the Global Water Crisis*; L. Mehta (2005), *The Politics and Poetics of Water: The Naturalisation of Scarcity in Western India*, New Delhi.

[31] S. Movik (2012), *Fluid Rights: South Africa's Water Allocation Reform*, Cape Town: Human Sciences Research Council Press.

[32] HLPE (2015), *Water for Food Security and Nutrition*, Rome: FAO.

[33] L. Mehta (2006), 'Do Human Rights Make a Difference to Poor People? The Case of Water in South Africa', in P. Newell and J. Wheeler (eds.), *Rights, Resources and Accountability*, London.

[34] C. M. Sepulveda, C. Nyst, and H. Hautala (2012), *The Human Rights Approach to Social Protection*, Ministry of Foreign Affairs of Finland.

rights to food, livelihoods, water and so on.[35] We now tease out these different themes and approaches to scarcity through the case of water.

## Water: Perspectives on scarcity and resource challenges

The availability of water fluctuates in space and time and it is relevant when assessing water allocation and actual water distribution. The fluidity of water also implies downstream effects on people and uses and the need to look at wider impacts across a range of scales (i.e. within a watershed or basin). Thus, due to the fluid nature of water, far-reaching impacts such as scarcity and pollution can extend across entire river basins. In 2015, 663 million people around the globe lacked access to safe drinking water and 2.4 billion people lacked access to improved sanitation with about 946 million people defecating in the open.[36] This situation undermines good health, nutrition and human dignity. Access to water can be particularly challenging for smallholders, vulnerable and marginalized populations and women. Women and girls are often responsible for water collection and may spend between thirty minutes and six hours per day collecting water, undermining their health, educational and life chances. Poor water quality affects human health and ecosystems' functioning. Climate change will add irregularity and uncertainty to the availability of water in many regions.[37] Water, however, is a contested resource and has multiple meanings for different social groups and actors. It is simultaneously a natural molecule or $H_2O$, essential for the ecological cycle, a spiritual resource for millions who worship at holy river banks and oceans, a commodity which can be mined, bottled, sold and traded and a life-giving element without which human survival is not possible. These multiple meanings of water are rarely captured in global water assessments or dominant water scarcity and 'water wars' debates.

### Systems, boundaries and thresholds and water scarcities

How much water is available for human use in a given period of time? The earth's land surface receives about 110,000 km³ of rainfall annually.[38] More than half of this water is evapotranspired (transmitted from soils and through plants to the air); and about 40,000 km³ becomes available in dams, lakes, rivers, streams and aquifers for human and environmental uses.[39] Aquifers receive approximately 13,000 km³ of this annual run-off.[40]

---

[35] Franco et al., 'The Global Politics of Water Grabbing'.
[36] UNICEF and WHO (2015), *Progress on Sanitation and Drinking Water*, 2015 Update and MDG Assessment.
[37] HLPE (2015), *Water for Food Security and Nutrition*.
[38] A cubic kilometre is the amount of water in 400,000 Olympic-sized pools, or the average annual consumption of ~18 million UK residents.
[39] UN Wwap (2012), *The United Nations World Water Development 42 Report 4: Managing Water under Uncertainty and Risk*, Paris.
[40] P. Döll (2009), 'Vulnerability to the Impact of Climate Change on Renewable Groundwater Resources: A Global-scale Assessment', *Environmental Research Letters*, 4 (3): 035006.

Water is a critical limiting factor for food production, but is also central to energy production, and it is widely agreed that freshwater scarcity presents one of the most pressing crosscutting challenges in the future.[41] According to the European Commission, pressures on water availability will continue to grow – not only through the need to feed and hydrate a growing global population but also from changes in patterns of consumption across the board.[42] The increasing water demand for global resource production is a result of both the overall increase in the amount of resources needed to meet global needs and increases due to the mounting intensification in production systems.

Amid this projected increasing demand and mounting need for trade-offs among competing uses of water resources (discussed below), climatic change means that rainfall and water availability are likely to become more uncertain.[43] From a Planetary Boundaries perspective, the ocean and the atmosphere are the two great 'fluids' of the planet, and the distribution of energy by latitude, over the land and sea surfaces and within the ocean, plays a major role in their flow and circulation. In earth's current climate context, a range of global surface temperatures and atmospheric pressures allow the three phases of water to be present simultaneously, with ice and water vapour playing critical roles in the physical feedbacks of the global climate system.[44]

However, the Planetary Boundaries and systems approach is not able to capture sufficiently the distributional limitations to water use and views scarcity in absolutist terms. In particular, with respect to global freshwater availability it is now well established that there is adequate global supply but of course in different regions, there is already water stress. As the HLPE (High Level Panel of Experts on Food Security and Nutrition) argues, while annual renewable freshwater resources are adequate at global levels to meet human water needs,[45] these resources are very unevenly distributed across the globe. Per capita annual renewable water resources are particularly low in the Middle Eastern, North African and South Asian regions. There are also significant variations in water availability within regions and countries. Uneven water resource distribution can translate into uneven capacity to grow food and affect food availability and access and also affect different social groups differently. Such nuances are not captured in the analyses at a planetary or global scale.

## The technological and managerial fix position and water scarcity

The technological and managerial fix position shares a concern with the systems, boundaries and thresholds position regarding the degradation of water resources due to agricultural intensification and competing pressures on water resources in a rapidly

[41]  Chatham House (2012), *Resources Futures*, London: Chatham House; SABMiller and WWF (2014), *The Water-Food-Energy Nexus: Insights into Resilient Development.*
[42]  European Commission (2012), *The European Report on Development 2011/2012: Confronting Scarcity: Managing Water, Energy and Land for Inclusive and Sustainable Growth.*
[43]  W. Steffen et al. (2015), 'Planetary Boundaries: Guiding Human Development on a Changing Planet', *Science*, 347 (6223): 1259855.
[44]  Ibid.
[45]  HLPE, *Water for Food Security and Nutrition.*

changing world characterized by global population growth, rapid urbanization and changing preferences for consumer goods. Here, however, the emphasis tends to shift from the physical consequences of these factors to the market dimensions (including internalization of externalities to correct 'market failures'), trade-offs, for example, between the provision of water and infrastructure to agricultural and extractives sectors and the role of water availability and price in decisions on where to invest and where to produce.[46] According to SABMiller and WWF, the demand for increasingly scarce resources to fuel development is shaping trends in resource control and commodity markets across the world.[47] International businesses 'experience the effects in terms of higher and more volatile input and raw material costs', while consumers see their patterns of spending altered by the ever-increasing cost of basic necessities.[48] At the same time, while agriculture is dependent on renewable resources, and thus may have a long-term outlook, a judicious management of land and water resources (as well as transport corridors and associated infrastructure) is viewed as necessary to avoid declining productivity, reduced access to the necessary renewable resources and potentially isolated assets.[49]

From a nexus perspective, the use and management of water requires an integrated approach that takes into account both land and energy issues.[50] Since the 1990s, water-sector reforms have been influenced by the concept of Integrated Water Resources Management (IWRM), which calls for 'co-ordinated development and management of water, land and related resources, in order to maximize welfare in an equitable manner without compromising the sustainability of vital ecosystems'.[51] IWRM is thus broadly in line with a water-energy-land (WEL) nexus perspective.[52] However, as a vast literature has revealed, IWRM has tended to be idealized, abstract and difficult to implement, especially in sub-Saharan Africa where complex formal and informal rights, as well as customary land and water arrangements, prevail.[53] IWRM implementation, in fact, may have resulted in an unwarranted policy focus on managing water instead of improving poor people's access to water. Furthermore, the newly created institutional arrangements have often been prone to elite capture and failed to address historically rooted inequalities.

Other dominant solutions to scarcity involve technical and market-driven approaches. As discussed, since the Dublin Declaration of 1992, water is increasingly seen as having economic value in all its competing uses. Accordingly, efficient resource management is equated with water having a price and the price signal is thus evoked

[46] Chatham House (2012), *Resources Futures*; WWF (2015), *African Ecological Futures*.
[47] SABMiller and WWF (2014), *The Water-Food-Energy Nexus: Insights into Resilient Development*.
[48] Ibid.
[49] WWF, *African Ecological Futures*.
[50] European Commission (2012), *The European Report on Development 2011/2012: Confronting Scarcity: Managing Water, Energy and Land for Inclusive and Sustainable Growth*.
[51] GWP (2000), 'Integrated Water Resources Management', in *TAC Background Papers No. 4*, Stockholm: Global Water Partnership Technical Advisory Committee.
[52] European Commission (2012), *The European Report on Development 2011/2012*.
[53] L. Mehta, S. Movik, A. Bolding, B. Derman, and E. Manzungu (2016), 'Introduction to the Special Issue: Flows and Practices – The Politics of Integrated Water Resources Management (IWRM) in Southern Africa', *Water Alternatives*, 9 (3): 389–411.

as a way to solve water scarcity problems.[54] Thus, in the past two decades, water has moved away from being viewed as a common good (however impure) and a public service to a commodity being managed according to economic principles.[55] In part, this has to do with the growing influence of powerful players, such as the World Bank and transnational corporations that have paved the way for controversial water privatizations around the world. In the name of 'efficiency' and 'scarcity', solutions have included water reallocation through water markets, water permits and different privatization models. Private-sector involvement in water provision was also imposed on many debt-ridden countries in the course of the economic restructuring of the 1990s. There are arguments claiming that poor people are willing to pay for water[56] and, relatively speaking, poor people pay far more than the rich for water (see below). Still, experiences with privatization of water have not always been poor-friendly.[57] One reason has to do with the nature of water markets. The high level of monopoly and low competition do not naturally lead to high responsiveness to user needs, and there is often no incentive to service non-profit-making sectors (such as rural areas and the urban poor) or to invest in unprofitable sectors (such as wastewater and sanitation). Often prices have been raised beyond agreed levels within a few years of privatization, and people who could not pay have been cut off (for South African examples, see McDonald and Ruiters, 2005; Dawson, 2010).[58]

### The structural-distributional position and water access and scarcity

Water scarcity is a complex phenomenon and can be analysed differently from social, political, meteorological, hydrological and agricultural perspectives.[59] Scarcity of water is typically examined through two lenses. The first is 'physical water scarcity', which compares the amount of renewable water annually available per capita in a particular area with predetermined thresholds to identify water-stressed and water-scarce areas, respectively.[60] The second lens is 'economic water scarcity'.[61] This refers to the fact that physical availability of water does not necessarily mean that water is available for use or is accessed. In some areas, while there may be abundant water available, the lack of infrastructure means that the water is not available where it is needed or

[54]  Ibid.
[55]  M. Finger and J. Allouche (2002), *The Transformation of the Global Water Sector: The Role of the World Bank and 'Public Service TNCs'*. Ibid.
[56]  M. A. Altaf, H. Jamal, and D. Whittington (1992), *Willingness to Pay for Water in Rural Punjab, Pakistan*, in *Water and Sanitation Report 4*, Washington, DC: The World Bank.
[57]  M. C. Dawson (2010), 'The Cost of Belonging: Exploring Class and Citizenship in Soweto's "Water War"', *Citizenship Studies*, 14 (4): 381–394.
[58]  Ibid; D. McDonald and G. Ruiters (eds.) (2005), *The Age of Commodity: Water Privatization in Southern Africa*, London: Earthscan.
[59]  M. Falkenmark and M. Lannerstad (2005), 'Consumptive Water Use to Feed Humanity – Curing a Blind Spot', *Hydrology and Earth System Sciences Discussions*, European Geosciences Union, 2005, 9 (1/2): 15–28.
[60]  M. Falkenmark and C. Widstrand (1992), 'Population and Water Resources: A Delicate Balance', *Population Bulletin*, 47 (3): 1–36.
[61]  D. Molden (2007), *Water for Food, Water for Life: A Comprehensive Assessment of Water Management in Agriculture*, London.

of an appropriate quality for use. For example, according to UNEP, an estimated 51 million people in the Democratic Republic of the Congo, around three quarters of the population, had no access to safe drinking water in 2011, even though the country is considered water rich, with more than half of Africa's water reserves.[62] In such countries and regions, the challenge is economic water scarcity or lack of investments, appropriate infrastructure or management, rather than physical water scarcity, to provide for the needs of the population, including water for food security and nutrition. Both these portrayals of scarcity, however, tend to direct attention to natural and economic forces rather than look at human-induced land and water use practices and at sociopolitical considerations and how scarcity can be socially mediated or constructed.[63]

However, these lenses of physical and economic water scarcity do not necessarily consider the way in which the distribution of and control over water is social differentiated by gender, caste, race, occupation and other categories. In his entitlements approach, Amartya Sen has argued that the per capita food availability decline (FAD) is a misleading way to assess hunger and famine, since hunger is more about people not having access to food due to wider social and political arrangements as opposed to there not being enough food to eat.[64] Similarly, aggregate views of water scarcity can be problematic because they can hide real inequalities in water access determined by property rights, social and political institutions, and cultural and gender norms. People's lack of access to water may have little to do with physical scarcity per se but may instead be due to exclusions arising from social positioning, gender or because of the way water is managed, priced and regulated.[65] For example, deeply rooted traditional or historical inequalities can limit women and other vulnerable groups' access to land and thereby to water for agricultural uses, which hampers livelihood strategies and negatively impacts food security.

Gender and other markers of identities continue to mould water allocation and access among users. Cultural norms in much of the developing world dictate that women and girls are responsible for water collection, and they may spend several hours per day collecting water. Unequal power relations within the household, and women's minimal control over household finances or spending, can force women into a daily trudge (taking precious time) for fetching cheaper or free untreated water, which may result in health problems or increased poverty and destitution. This time could instead be used to focus on livelihood and agricultural activities, attending school and to improve maternal and infant health.[66] This situation is worsened by the fact that women are often excluded from decision-making processes regarding water management projects or natural resource allocation.

[62] UNEP (2011), *Towards a Green Economy: Pathways to Sustainable Development and Poverty Eradication.*
[63] L. Mehta (2005), *The Politics and Poetics of Water: The Naturalisation of Scarcity in Western India,* New Delhi; UNDP (2006), *Human Development Report 2006-Beyond Scarcity: Power, Poverty and the Global Water Crisis.*
[64] A. Sen (1981), *Poverty and Famines: An Essay on Entitlement and Deprivation;* A. Sen (1983b), 'Poor, Relatively Speaking', *Oxford Economic Papers,* New Series, 35 (2): 153–169.
[65] L. Mehta (2014), 'Water and Human Development', *World Development,* 59: 59–69; UNDP, *Human Development Report 2006-Beyond Scarcity.*
[66] Mehta, 'Water and Human Development'; WHO/UNICEF Joint Monitoring Programme 2012.

Mehta distinguishes between 'lived/experienced' scarcity (something that local people experience cyclically due the biophysical shortage of food, water, fodder etc.) and 'constructed' scarcity (something that is manufactured through sociopolitical processes to suit the interests of powerful players).[67] Her focus was water scarcity in western India and the role of the dam-building lobby and rich irrigators and agro-industrialists in promoting large dams over more decentralized approaches to deal with water scarcity in the drylands. A similar approach to water is provided by the 2006 Human Development Report entitled 'Beyond Scarcity: Power, Poverty and the Global Water Crisis'[68] which has explicitly focused on the role of power relations and unequal access in determining water scarcity. It also argues that the global water crisis is overwhelmingly a crisis for the poor. The distribution of water in many countries mirrors the distribution of wealth, and vast inequalities exist in both. The United Nations Development Programme (UNDP) estimates that almost two in three people who lack access to clean water, and over 660 million people without adequate sanitation, live on less than two dollars per day. Furthermore, not only do the poorest people get access to less water, and to clean and safe water, but they also pay some of the world's highest water prices.[69] Overall, the public sector retains, at least in principle, the reach and the mandate to clarify rights, set prices, resolve trade-offs and ensure safe water and sanitation access for the poor and excluded, whether as a service provider or supporter, or through contracts with private firms, but in many water scarce regions, the largest local water footprints are due to industrial and extractive activities.[70]

In recent years, reforms based on the IWRM have brought water rights to the forefront of the policy agenda. In some cases, governments have declared water resources to be property of the state, which allows governments to allocate water rights within an integrated resource management framework. In other areas, reforms have involved formal water permitting based on government discretion within a formal water economy. With some notable exceptions, both approaches have failed to incorporate substantive pro-poor redistributive provisions, an equity failure that has been exacerbated by poor implementation practices that reflect drastically uneven power relationships, backing urban, industrial and high-growth industry claimants against agricultural and rural claimants.[71] In Tanzania, for example, even though the government owns all land and water, water extraction is fee-based and requires a permit potentially excluding the poor from water use rights. Although customary rights are recognized (but require conversion to permits), the tension of recognizing them alongside formal rights has meant poor treatment of customary users of land

---

[67] L. Mehta (2005), *The Politics and Poetics of Water: The Naturalisation of Scarcity in Western India*, New Delhi.

[68] UNDP, *Human Development Report 2006-Beyond Scarcity.*

[69] Ibid.

[70] Chatham House, *Resources Futures*; European Commission (2012), *The European Report on Development 2011/2012.*

[71] HLPE, *Water for Food Security and Nutrition*; UNDP, *Human Development Report 2006-Beyond Scarcity.*

and water[72] despite the fact that smallholders produce most of the food in the country. In an even more severe situation, such uneven power relationships and the absence of appropriately implemented water rights frameworks can open up the possibility of 'water grabs'.[73] According to Franco and colleagues, 'water grabbing is a process in which powerful actors are able to take control of, or reallocate to their own benefit, water resources used by local communities or which feed aquatic ecosystems on which their livelihoods are based'.[74]

Conflict situations can exacerbate unequal or lack of access to water, can threaten provision of water and can divert attention from food production to other priorities. In such situations, the poor become the victims not only of the conflict itself but also of hunger and waterborne diseases. Water insecurities also persist in occupied areas such as Palestine when restricted water withdrawals enforce unequal access and use. For example, Israelis consume over three times as much water per capita per day (300 litres compared to 73 litres), but strict military orders restrict water withdrawals and access for Palestinians living in occupied areas.[75]

## Discussion and conclusions

In this chapter, we have demonstrated that scarcity and resource management debates involve multiple contested framings and narratives that essentially tell a story about a problem, including its causes, appropriate interventions and likely outcomes. We presented three positions: the systems, boundaries and thresholds position, the technological and managerial fix position and the structural-distributional position. Despite substantial differences, there are important areas of agreement between all three positions. First, work reflecting all three positions acknowledges the importance of complex relationships, and even what can be thought of broadly as 'feedbacks' between resource systems and society (including economic systems), particularly in the context of the intensification of resource use and economic growth. Second, all three positions are in broad agreement that limitations exist in regard to sustainable use of natural resources. This is an area of consensus even if notions of sustainability, the nature of the limits (e.g. absolute vs relative vs social), their causes (e.g. growth processes vs external costs vs structural barriers to access) and appropriate solutions are contested. Third, work from all three positions reflects the idea that different sustainability needs and relational dynamics are at play in regard to different types of natural resources. Fourth and likewise, even with technological progress, increasing complexity in the operating environment constrains the exploitation of existing and future resources. Despite these shared underpinnings, we believe it is not really

[72] B. Vorley, L. Cotula, and M.-K. Chan (2012), *Tipping the Balance: Policies to Shape Agricultural Investments and Markets in Favour of Small-scale Farmers*.

[73] UNDP, *Human Development Report 2006-Beyond Scarcity*.

[74] Franco et al., 'The Global Politics of Water Grabbing'.

[75] S. Gasteyer, J. Isaac, J. Hillal, and K. Hodali (2012), 'Water Grabbing in Colonial Perspective: Land and Water in Israel/Palestine', *Water Alternatives*, 5 (2): 450–468.

possible to reconcile the three dominant positions on natural resource scarcity. The systems, boundaries and thresholds position, the technological and managerial fix position and the structural-distributional position represent three distinct approaches (with different philosophical assumptions and disciplinary roots) as to what scarcity fundamentally means, its causes, its consequences and its implications for sustainability and development. They are thus not simply different analytical lenses through which to view and interpret objective facts about natural resources and scarcity.

From a systems, boundaries and thresholds position, scarcity is absolute and biophysical. Scarcity occurs when people alter any of three characteristics of the natural world: (1) the amount of finite non-renewable resources that exist, (2) the quality or integrity of renewable resources and ecosystems and (3) the functions of planetary resource and biogeochemical systems. This framing has been an effective motivator of popular environmental movements and broadscale policy discussions of issues like global climate change adaptation and mitigation. With its overarching emphasis on biogeochemical processes, global environmental integrity and the survival of the human species, 'planetary thinking' of the systems, boundaries and thresholds orientation is broad in scale to say the least. We agree with the idea that planetary thinking is important to understanding the scale and magnitude of the cumulative environmental damage that resource intensification has created, but we contend that planetary thinking is not extremely tractable and often neglects consideration of the trees for the forest, so to speak, when it comes to actually understanding the dynamics at play in sustainability issues. By focusing on the selected boundaries, this thinking has abstracted the perceived challenges from the way in which a person actually interacts with resources (e.g. an individual eats food but doesn't interact with nitrogen and phosphorus cycles directly). Furthermore, 'planetary' processes play out and are experienced in the social and environmental milieu of particular places. The causes, costs, gains, consequences and hazards associated with environmental change, degradation and scarcity are contextual and highly uneven across the world. This is the idea behind the Principle of Common But Differentiated Responsibilities (PCBDR), which recognizes historical differences in the contributions of developed and developing countries to global environmental problems, and differences on the basis of respective capacities and responsibilities to tackle these problems. But it is important to remember that the historical inequalities and dependencies alluded to by the PCBDR are often mirrored on a sub-national level, playing out in terms of cross-regional dependencies, urban–rural differences and class-based and gendered relations.

From a *technological and managerial fix perspective*, which has close associations with neoclassical economics, scarcity is not a problem of absolute biophysical limits as described above. Rather, scarcity is a set of more abstract economic problems that arise due to market failures. Natural capital is viewed as essentially substitutable both in production and as a direct provider of utility. In this framing, scarcity creates business and growth opportunities and catalyses sustainability transitions through market-driven processes of innovation and increased efficiency in production, allowing for adjustments in inputs and substitutions in production processes. In the absence of widespread market failures, decoupling growth from resource use and substituting processes are seen as ameliorative responses to specific and temporary resource shortages and as contributing to continued growth. However, underpriced resources can lead to over-exploitation and misappropriation, resulting in degradation of ecosystems. Further, persistent market failures are associated with concerns over resource prices and volatility in markets, as such failures increase the risk of supply disruptions, and supply is unable to respond accordingly to rapid changes in demand. As this happens, small changes in demand can result in significant swings in prices. From this perspective, recommendations are scaled and, on one hand, tend to focus on the growth imperative more than limiting tangible ecological or extractive impacts. On the other hand, solutions emphasize the need to manage valuable ecosystems and realize economic values inherent, yet un-captured, in natural landscapes. Solutions range from local development and management projects involving, for example, carbon forestry and reforestation aimed at linking local producers to markets for products to facilitating private investment in technological, market-based and managerial solutions that promise to allow global society to mitigate and adapt to resource crises, across sectors of society and scales from local to global, while enhancing opportunities for growth. From a technological and managerial fix position, unpriced or underpriced resources result in 'market failures' that become evident as economic agents fail to integrate full costs into calculations and decisions about resource use, resulting in 'external effects', or 'externalities'.

By contrast, we argue for the need of the *structural-distributional position*, which places politics at the centre of understandings of scarcity, and breaks down macro and aggregate understandings of scarcity to argue that scarcities result from contextual factors that produce a lack of access to the basic necessities of life and restricted opportunities by which people can make the choices that lead to a healthy and fulfilling life. Scarcity is explicitly politicized; it is not viewed as a natural phenomenon that can be isolated from planning models, allocation politics, policy choices, market dynamics and local power, social and gendered dynamics in particular resource environments. Environmental degradation and discrepancies in resource access often go hand in hand and result from inequitable decision-making and institutional and governance arrangements. While technical and managerial solutions to resource scarcities are not inherently inimical to considerations of social and environmental equity, such considerations are often secondary to goals of profitability, pricing and economic growth that may be more important to more powerful stakeholders.

While some may argue that perceptions of scarcity can drive positive change and investment in, say, sustainable and low-carbon infrastructure and technology, or can be the catalyst to launching a discussion about how existing resources are distributed, often scarcity can be used to justify certain interventions over others. In the name of scarcity, coupled with fears of teeming numbers, controversial interventions such as large dams, nuclear energy, biotechnology and militarization are often put forward as solutions by politically powerful actors while excluding discussions and deliberations of more suitable and more equitable alternatives.[76] The result is that

---

[76] N. Hildyard (2010), '"Scarcity" as Political Strategy: Reflections on Three Hanging Children', in L. Mehta (ed.), *The Limits to Scarcity*, 149–164, London: Earthscan; Mehta, *The Limits to Scarcity*; N. Xenos (2010), 'Everybody's Got the Fever: Scarcity and US National Energy Policy', in L. Mehta (ed.), *The Limits to Scarcity: Contesting the Politics of Allocation*, 31–49, London: Earthscan.

efficiency arguments usually prevail over equity arguments. The 'scare' of scarcity remains a means of diverting attention away from the causes of poverty and inequality that may implicate the politically powerful. As a result, scarcity is also a powerful tool to colonize the future and to shape it in certain ways.[77] Thus, the political strategy of scarcity is obscured with scientific language as it continues to be remodelled as a concept to justify the means and interventions of the powerful. At the same time, neo-Malthusian crisis arguments are given new life and an additional explanatory power when the future is colonized through scarcity arguments. From a critical, yet forward-looking perspective, we must ask how this contemporary politics of scarcity can in fact limit our thinking about sustainability and our collective capabilities to envision and realize alternatives to the future scenarios and options that others present us.

This is not to deny that scarcities (in a number of senses) exist for many and that environmental problems (not least due to the wanton over-exploitation of resources and climate change) are among our greatest challenges. However, this position resists seeing scarcity as a constant variable that can be blamed for our woes. Instead, we need to be aware of the politics of allocation and the ways in which scarcity is politicized and, in fact, constructed in popular and policy debates, especially in ways that suit the interests of powerful players.[78] Often, the problem lies in how we see scarcity as a *natural* phenomenon, which distracts from due consideration of the ways in which it is socially generated and experienced. Scarcity is rarely the natural order of things but usually the result of exclusion and unequal social and power relations that legitimize skewed access to and control of resources. As such, scarcity should be thought of relationally, as a situation that results from particular types of social, political and market relationships in which access and control is monopolized by more powerful social actors. Furthermore, a number of researchers have identified ways in which conventional visions of scarcity that focus on forecasts, aggregate numbers and physical quantities are privileged over local knowledges and experiences of scarcities that identify problems (and solutions) in different ways.[79]

While technological innovation and resource management regimes have great potential for addressing scarcity and sustainability issues, it is assumed that technological progress and market forces will resolve crises. Still often technology and market fixes are both the 'problem' – the driver of climate change, environmental degradation and localized resource depletion – and the proposed 'solution' to the problems that they have themselves created. For example, interventions such as large dams are made out to be the 'solution' for scarcity in water-starved areas but they are also 'problems' around which prominent social movements have emerged. Hydroelectric power is the 'solution' to growing energy demand in emerging economies, but hydroelectric projects are associated with downstream 'problems' that threaten fisheries and livelihoods. This observation highlights the fact that pathways to sustainability should not be viewed as

---

[77] Hildyard, '"Scarcity" as Political Strategy'.
[78] Mehta, *The Politics and Poetics of Water*; Mehta, *The Limits to Scarcity*.
[79] Hildyard, '"Scarcity" as Political Strategy; Mehta, *The Politics and Poetics of Water*; I. Scoones (2010), 'Seeing Scarcity: Understanding Soil Fertility in Africa', L. Mehta (ed.), *The Limits to Scarcity*, 165–178, London: Earthscan.

independent from the drivers of the problems that they are meant to address. There are no silver bullets.

From this viewpoint, solutions to scarcities should be oriented towards dismantling the institutions and structures that focus disproportionate social and environmental risks and vulnerabilities on some and not on others, as well as dismantling the structural barriers that cause suffering and deprive people of capabilities and well-being. These structures and barriers are contextual and will vary by country, region and demographics, so 'bottom-up' approaches that place vulnerable people and the landscapes that they depend on at the centre of policy consideration are required. This goes beyond assuming from 'above' how people relate to their local environments and what people need to live fulfilling lives, to putting the perspectives and voices of real people into programming for sustainability.

This is important because the understandings that dominate policy debates at the international and national levels are frequently at odds with the perceptions, knowledge and experiences of local resource users and workers in the fields and factories of the world. While we concur that pressing sustainability problems can be addressed, sometimes through technical intervention, we insist that they must be understood contextually and holistically, taking into account expert perspectives as well as the knowledge of a range of other, often less considered but more directly or intimately experienced, stakeholders.

Our position on scarcity holds that processes of resource intensification have resulted in severe environmental damage globally, but there have been clear 'winners' and 'losers' in terms of the distribution of the benefits and costs of this intensification. This position appreciates problems across scales (from the household to the planet) and privileges the ways in which dynamics at play in global sustainability issues are manifest in different places or resource environments. Proposed solutions need to be viewed in both social and ecological contexts, including the context of uneven global distribution of development, privilege, wealth and environmental risk, and downstream and externalized impacts of proposed courses of action as well and ways to enhance the rights and well-being of poor and marginalized people. Different actors in different social positions can bring unique understandings to the problems based on their experiences and expertise. This position which largely privileges the structural and distributional aspects of scarcity is an important step towards enhancing ethics, equity and environmental justice in addressing sustainability issues.

# Acknowledgements

We thank Frank Trentmann and Neil Fromer for their helpful comments and Lina Forgeaux for her immense help with formatting the references. This chapter draws on work commissioned by the World Wide Fund for Nature (WWF). See IDS, *Natural Resource Scarcity: Framings, Forecasts and Implications for the Future*, 2016.

# 4

# Rethinking the Relationships between Scarcity, Poverty and Hunger: An Anthropological Perspective

### Richard Wilk

*My mother gazed silently out of the window until I asked her what she was thinking. 'I am thinking', she said, 'that there must be a lot of rich people in this country'. Astonished, I exclaimed, 'How can you gaze upon that, and declare that there are rich people here?' 'Ah', she countered, 'if there are this many poor people here, there have to be a lot of rich people.*

Sidney Mintz describing his mother's reaction
while driving through El Fanguito, a slum in San Juan, Puerto Rico.[1]

Anthropology has a surprisingly limited amount to say about shortage and poverty. By classifying their object of study as traditional and tribal society, past generations of anthropologists tended to define these issues out of existence. Economic anthropologists depended on the influential work of economist Carl Polanyi to reassure themselves that 'traditional' societies did not follow rules of economics, which were applicable only to modernity, capitalism and money.[2] Even when anthropologists studied people who toiled in mines, on plantations and in factories, they could dismiss daily misery and hunger as products of colonialism and conquest, assuming that poverty did not exist before European arrival. Consequently, in this chapter, I will not try to summarize what anthropologists have had to say on the topic but will instead use anthropological tools and concepts to try to understand how poverty and shortage can simultaneously be objective 'facts of life' and culturally and historically relative constructions with shifting and complex meanings.

The advantage of the anthropological denial of poverty as an objective category is that it leads us to question any simple attempt to equate wealth with quality of life and the lack of wealth with misery. As in the recent literature in 'happiness studies', opening

---

[1] Mintz, Sidney, quoted in Donald Lewis Donham (1990), *History, Power, Ideology: Central Issues in Marxism and Anthropology*, 51, Berkeley.
[2] Karl Polanyi (1944), *The Great Transformation*, New York.

this question requires a kind of ethical and political dance around the problem of what might be called 'happy peasants'.[3] Even the very earliest urban dwellers in Mesopotamia expressed a romanticized view of the simple life of the rural farmer, complaining of the complexity and moral hazard of the prosperous life. Throughout philosophy and religion, we are presented with a contradictory set of moral precepts about poverty, on one hand a form of misery requiring charity and empathy, and on the other hand a source of moral purity, contact with nature, authentic social values and common virtues. The overlay of moral and ethical discourse should prompt us to ask whether there is anything objective at all in either of these precepts.

## Scarcity and poverty as hybrids

Bruno Latour uses the term 'hybrid' for a concept that combines aspects of both the natural and the social. Despite the efforts of modernists to separate the two, to make an absolute philosophical distinction between the physical and the cultural, reality has a way of moving back and forth in their gap between. This is reflected in a division between the natural and social sciences as well as in the distinction between qualitative and quantitative methodologies, emic and etic, measureable and incalculable, universal and particular.[4] Before I read Latour, I argued that 'quality of life' was a hybrid concept that had both objective and subjective aspects which could not be separated from each other. Subjective perceptions are just as real as medical conditions and lifespan, so there is no way to make objective health a proxy for the perception of health, or vice versa.[5]

Similar issues arise in the search for an objective definition or calculation of poverty. Definitions of poverty can be very precise without being accurate. They constantly change and are usually out of date by the time they are instituted; at one time in the United States, a gallon of beer a day was considered the bare minimum needed by a working man.[6] While it is useful to define poverty according to some absolute (e.g. living on US$1 or less a day) or didactic and moralizing purposes, most serious scholars agree that these comparisons are very imperfect measures of well-being.[7] Even something as basic as the physical qualities of an environment that make it comfortable have proven resistant to universals, again because of the hybrid nature of the concept of comfort even the basic physical needs for water and nutrition are extremely difficult to calculate given the enormous plasticity of the human and the subjectivity of what we mean by good health.

---

[3]  Bruno Frey and Alois Stutzer (2002), *Happiness and Economics: How the Economy and Institutions Affect Human Well-Being*, Princeton, NJ.
[4]  Bruno Latour (2012), *We Have Never Been Modern*, Boston.
[5]  Richard Wilk (1999), 'Quality of Life and the Anthropological Perspective', *Feminist Economics*, 5 (2): 91–93.
[6]  Daniel Horowitz (1985), *The Morality of Spending*, Baltimore, MD.
[7]  David Gordon (2006), *The Concept and Measurement of Poverty*, in Christina Pantazis, David Gordon, and Ruth Levitas, *Poverty and Social Exclusion in Britain: The Millennium Survey*, Bristol.

The recent outpouring of research and popular writing on well-being and happiness, and the older concept of a 'standard of living' make similar universalistic claims when they could better be understood as hybrids, along with many other attempts to reduce subjective states to objective measureable conditions. Something crucial is always lost along the way. So far attempts to use brain imaging to find out what people are 'really' feeling has only added complexity to what is really an unsolvable problem. Or perhaps rather than being a *problem*, hybridity is a fundamental feature of human culture and experience that we can never escape.

## Resources and shortage, prices and extinction

If poverty and lack are partially subjective qualities, can we at least find some sort of objective measure of shortage? Shortage presents itself as a kind of quantitative measure of the balance between supply and demand; too much demand and not enough supply is a condition of relative shortage accompanied and measured by a rise in prices. Even non-human primates and other animals balance supply and demand in making choices.[8] But even in their case, 'demand' is a product of the tastes and desires of individual primates, who differ from one another in ways that are fluid and at least partially social (depending on their rank, sex and age) and cultural (a product of training and learning). Further, 'supply' is also a product of complex interactions within markets, which are themselves socially mediated (or 'embedded', to use Grannoveter's term[9]).

Environmental economists typically divide the world's resources into two kinds of 'natural capital': those that are constantly renewed by life and natural processes ('flow resources') and those that exist in a fixed quantity, spread or concentrated in or on the earth.[10] Physical scientists have tended to focus on the limited supplies of non-renewables like fossil fuels and valuable minerals, most recently those which are heavily used in manufacturing electronics, like germanium, coltan and rare earths. We often hear about a helium shortage or the drastic decline in the number of rubies found in Burma because the deposit is 'mined out'.[11] Environmentalists put much of their hope for sustainable economies on an expected future when supplies of fossil fuels decline and renewable fuels become cheaper.

The shortages of non-renewable resources, however, are absolute only in theory. Instead, the term 'shortage' really means 'rising in price'. It is perfectly normal for the cost of any non-renewable resource to rise over time, as the most accessible and therefore

[8]   Cécile Fruteau, Bernhard Voelkl, Eric Van Damme, and Ronald Noë (2009), 'Supply and Demand Determine the Market Value of Food Providers in Wild Vervet Monkeys', *Proceedings of the National Academy of Sciences*, 106 (29): 12007–12012.

[9]   Mark Granovetter (1985), 'Economic Action and Social Structure: The Problem of Embeddedness', *American Journal of Sociology*, 91 (3): 481–510.

[10]  James J. Sullivan and H. Fernando Arias (1972), 'Concepts and Principles for Environmental Economics', *Environmental Affairs*, 2 (3).

[11]  This is not a terribly original point; economists and environmental sciences have been thinking about issues of depletion, markets and prices for centuries.

the cheapest materials are depleted, though new technologies can suddenly make new supplies accessible. As a consequence of the rise in prices, it becomes economically feasible to mine or quarry or pump deposits that are less concentrated, more distant or require more expensive technology and power. As a consequence, there is never an *absolute* shortage of gold, only a shortage of gold that can be mined at less than the market price. Higher prices prompt the exploitation of deposits which were once considered uneconomic. The actual supply of gold is infinite for all practical purposes, since a vast amount is dissolved in the ocean (20 million tonnes, at 13 billionths of a gram per litre) and melted into the earth's core. Once all of the 'sweet' light crude oil is pumped out of the ground, the price goes up and it becomes feasible to drill in deep water or to exploit tar sands and other less accessible sources. Nitrogen is present in endless profusion in our atmosphere, but fixing that gaseous nitrogen into liquid ammonia or solid ammonium nitrate, our most important crop fertilizers, requires a great deal of energy. As the cost of natural gas rises (or falls with the development of new technologies like fracking), the cost of nitrogen fertilizer follows.[12]

Oil supplies were low in the early 2000s amid fears that we were at 'peak oil' – now the United States is the world's largest producer of fossil fuels once again and oil prices are down. The real danger from the exploitation of non-renewable resources is not shortage, it is price. As a resource becomes more expensive to extract or new technologies are required, any producer will look for ways to shed some of the costs onto other people or agents, what economists call rent-seeking. There are also the externalities, costs of extracting and using resources which are not paid by anyone or which are dumped onto a public that does not directly benefit. The 'dead zone' in the Gulf of Mexico is the consequence of allowing excess fertilizer to drain off into watercourses. So far nobody is held responsible for cleaning nitrogen out of run-off water or trapping it more deeply in the soil. The 12–13 million metric tonnes of nitrogen fertilizers used every year in the United States remains cheap to farmers because they don't have to pay the cost of the indirect damage it causes, which are shed on taxpayers or fishermen, who are already subsidizing cheap fuel and paying artificially high prices for crops protected from foreign competition.[13,14] Rising levels of methane, $CO_2$ and other greenhouse gases in the earth's atmosphere are just more of those unaccounted externalities, which keep shortages at bay only by shifting around costs and benefits.

A shortage of a renewable flow resource, on the other hand, can lead to its extinction or create such a degree of scarcity that the item is said to be 'economically extinct'. Before mineral oil, the global oil economy depended on the rendered fat of billions of animals, from whales, sharks and walrus to penguins and herring, permanently eliminating some stocks while others have taken hundreds of years to even partially recover. Much of the field of natural resource management and theories of common

---

[12] Vaclav Smil (2004), *Enriching the Earth: Fritz Haber, Carl Bosch, and the Transformation of World Food Production*, Cambridge.

[13] The figures on nitrogen fertilizer come from government statistics (http://www.ers.usda.gov/data-products/fertilizer-use-and-price.aspx

[14] The story of crop subsidies is covered in detail by Colin Sage (2011), *Environment and Food*, New York and Winson Anthony (2013), *The Industrial Diet: The Degradation of Food and the Struggle for Healthy Eating*, New York.

property has developed in response, but in many cases growing scarcity is the indicator of a problem that may be too advanced to solve.

As a non-renewable resource becomes scarcer, and demand continues despite the rise in price, extractive industries have a strong incentive to keep exploiting stocks in decline. As the price of a pelt, a trophy or a medicinal plant rises due to increased scarcity, it may become a luxury, what marketers call a 'positional good'. This seems to happen most often when people have trouble distinguishing the quality of a product themselves, and price becomes a measure of quality. Caviar from the Caspian Sea or elvers from the Atlantic Coast of the United States are good examples; their rarity and high price makes them more, rather than less attractive (the so-called Veblen effect, or Veblen good, often conflated with 'snob' and 'bandwagon' effects[15]). Small, sessile and concentrated resources can be particularly vulnerable (abalone for example), but they are also relatively easy to convert into property or contained in territory that can be owned and protected.[16] Migratory animals such as salmon can also be very vulnerable to over-exploitation, for obvious reasons. Even extremely abundant species like the passenger pigeon can be over-exploited to the point of extinction; some bounce back from extremely low populations (American alligators), while others never seem to recover (Atlantic codfish). The physical reality of Veblen effects is revealed by astonishing experiments showing that medications that are labelled as more expensive and given more elaborate packaging have more physical efficacy (measured objectively) than the same medicine with a cheaper price tag.[17]

One kind of shortage occurs during the interval between rising prices and new production. In food markets there is almost always a lag because it can take a year to grow a new crop, two or three to increase beef production and up to eight with tree crops. Technology makes a difference in lowering the price or increasing the supply of non-renewables. Higher efficiency, substituting machines for humans and increased scale all provide opportunities for increasing production and making new sources of supply feasible. Because of the lag between price rise and the invention and adoption of new technology, this creates a rhythm of alternating shortage and glut, which may be muted or exaggerated by a futures market, which brings the money of speculators into play. Shortage is therefore a normal and expected part of the operation of markets; loss and gain are closely connected to one another in global capitalism, even though the connections are often difficult to trace.

By increasing efficiency and lowering prices, improvements in technology can also destroy stocks of renewable resources. Fisheries are a good example – time and time again, the prospect of increased efficiency has lured investors and fishers into investing in bigger boats, larger engines, longer nets, radar and sonar, to the point where boats are so effective and efficient that they can drive a species into commercial extinction before catch limits or other regulations can be brought into play.[18] Technologies of

[15] Harvey Lebenstein (1950), 'Bandwagon, Snob, and Veblen Effects in the Theory of Consumers Demand', *The Quarterly Journal of Economics*, 64 (2): 183–207.
[16] James Acheson (1988), *The Lobster Gangs of Maine*, Durham.
[17] Luana Colloca (2017), 'Effects Can Make You Feel Pain', *Science*, 358 (6359): 44.
[18] Charles Clover (2008), *End of the Line: How Overfishing is Changing the World and What We Eat*, Berkeley.

enforcement rarely keep up with new forms of production, allowing space for illegal exploitation of resources which can quickly lead into a downward spiral.

My point here is simply that scarcity affects the value of different kinds of goods or resources in very different ways. This variation is not a direct product of nature but involves an interaction between nature and humans mediated by technology, markets and culture (as well as the complex and often unpredictable dynamics of ecosystems and their tolerance of externalities). The yield of a particular crop may be large and sustainable, but the costs of the resources and technologies necessary to produce and market that food may rise quickly, creating a shortage that has little to do with nature. In a globalized market economy, conflict and political strife are much more likely to create shortages than any kind of natural catastrophe or advance in some sort of productive technology. But we need to also take account of the cultural changes in taste and preference that can suddenly increase demand for a product, the fad super foods quinoa or açai for example, creating a form of scarcity that may subside into bust as quickly as it arises. Once again scarcity is a relationship and an active and complex process, rather than a stable state or a natural limit set by physical need or ecological laws. These are exactly the same problems that crop up in any attempt to define poverty.

## Creating shortage

Many shortages have nothing to do with the quantity of goods or materials available. Geographers would redefine shortage as a problem of *location*, that food is not getting to the people who need it most. Scarcity is also an obvious product of *allocation*; in the United States we grow enough corn to feed everyone in the world, but instead we feed almost half of it to animals and use half of the rest to make ethanol for vehicles. Similarly, if Americans ate much less meat, there would be enough grain available to make everyone in the world obese.[19]

Governments are also agents of shortage. Some countries have created an ideology of scarcity, even in the midst of abundance, as a way of promoting savings or bolstering nationalism in times of war.[20] Governments always prohibit the unlicensed sale of many drugs, cigarettes, alcohol (and salt in the past), and raise their prices in order to collect excise taxes and improve public health. Prices are a familiar form of rationing that can be seen as a benign way of turning private vice into public virtue. More serious regional shortage can quickly lead to hoarding, which raises prices, but when demand goes down, hoarders hold onto their stocks waiting for even higher prices instead of letting them onto the market. Unless government intervenes, large-scale starvation can result, and rationing and public distributions are also subject to free riding and corruption.

[19] Heinz-Willhelm Strubenhoff, 'Can 10 billion People Live and Eat Well on the Planet? Yes', *Brookings* blog on future development, 28 April 2015 (https://www.brookings.edu/blog/future-development/2015/04/28/can-10-billion-people-live-and-eat-well-on-the-planet-yes/).

[20] Laura Nelson (2012), *Measured Excess: Status, Gender, and Consumer Nationalism in South Korea*, Columbia and Helen Veit (2013), *Modern Food, Moral Food Self-Control, Science, and the Rise of Modern American Eating in the Early Twentieth Century*, Durham.

Just as shortages can lead to panic and alienation, they are also tools of social integration, as exposed in systems where the goal of an exchange of goods is not the goods themselves, but the social connections created through the acts of exchange (Mauss and Durkheim among others). Napoleon Chagnon described a case among the Yanomamo where two villages that had been self-sufficient sought to create an alliance. The relationship began with a series of reciprocal feasts with large amounts of meat and drink. As exchange broadened, one group 'forgot' how to make baskets and the other unlearned pottery-making, so they had to trade with the each other, which eventually led to marriages and close alliances cemented by kinship ties.[21] Kaufman describes exactly the same kind of 'learned inability' among many of the French couples whose daily lives he studied.[22]

Shortage is the very foundation of consumer capitalism, which depends on the cultivation of desires, constantly seeking to turn envy or dreams into concrete wants and from there into needs.[23] This could be reframed as a process of inventing and disseminating new forms of shortage, a viewpoint that resonates in a curious way with Bataille's description of consumer society as a system that endlessly promotes waste.[24]

Artificial shortages are well known in ethnographic accounts of what was once called 'primitive money'. The painstakingly woven red feather belts of the Santa Cruz Islands, like the stone money of Yap and the shell necklaces and armshells traded in the Kula ring were made from rare materials, but their real value came from their individual histories, something that could not be forged or created through craft.[25] Only elders and famous people could imbue objects with power and value, as Elvis did with the scarfs he threw to hysterical fans. These goods also circulated in limited spheres of exchange, so that in Bohannon's famous example of 'spheres of exchange' among the Tiv, brass bars could only be exchanged for slaves, white cloth and cattle.[26] Particular kinds of goods were sequestered from the cash economy, a practice interpreted by some anthropologists as a kind of moral economy and by others as a deliberate strategy by elders to control the flow of important goods.

## Defining poverty

One of the tenets shared by classical liberalism, Marxism and mainstream religious philosophy is that the poor should not be blamed for their condition. At best they are innocent and misfortunate, and at worst they are victims whose suffering should be blamed on others or on a cruel and unfair system. It is anathema among anthropologists

[21] Napolean Chagnon (1992), *Yanomamo: The Last Days of Eden*, San Diego.
[22] Jean-Claude Kaufmann (1998), *Dirty Linen: Couples and Their Laundry*, London.
[23] Illich gives a succinct definition of this process, which has been discussed thoroughly in more recent literature on consumption and consumer behaviour; see Ivan Illich (1977), *Toward a History of Needs*, New York.
[24] Georges Bataille (1991), *The Accursed Share*, trans. Robert Hurley, New York.
[25] See chapters in Cynthia Werner and Duran Bell (eds.) (2004), *Values and Valuables: From the Sacred to the Symbolic*, 21–48, Walnut Creek.
[26] Paul Bohannan (1959), 'The Impact of Money on an African Subsistence Economy', *The Journal of Economic History*, 19 (4): 491–503.

to 'blame the victim', and instead the usual practice is to use ethnography to create empathy for the poor and their suffering.[27] On the contrary, many of the people that anthropologists study have a very firm idea that poverty reflects moral failings and may be divine (or mundane) punishment for various kinds of bad behaviour. Rather than seeing material wealth as a form of hazard, in many cultures wealth is a reward for virtue; as in the Prosperity Theology of many global Protestant sects, wealth is the recognition of right living according to God's rule.[28]

The philosopher John Ladd, for example, quotes early twentieth-century Navajo elders to the effect that 'the good man is a prosperous man, and the bad man is a poor man', quoting an informant who said, 'He's no good. He is going to be hard up, wear poor clothes, poor shoes, he is going to be raggy.' The Navajo child is taught to work hard so he can have 'good Hogan (house), lots of horses, lots of jewelry'[29] To further illustrate this point, I return to my fieldwork (1979–80) with Q'eqchi' (Mayan) speakers in the southern Belizean rainforest.

At the time many of the Q'eqchi' villages were self-sufficient in food and only partially embedded in a monetary economy. They grew rice and reared hogs for the market, but within the village little cash circulated; instead people traded labour through a system of rotating work groups that made subsistence farming relatively reliable and food circulated in what could be called a moral economy.[30] Many features of the subsistence economy acted to reduce the risk of serious food shortage, though there were still lean seasons and hunger caused by disasters like hurricanes. From an outsider's perspective the communities I worked in seemed very egalitarian, with few wealth differences between households. Yet when I did household inventories, I found that some possessed radios, shotguns, bicycles and new clothes, and had many hogs and chickens, while others existed almost entirely outside the cash economy, eating little beyond corn tortillas, chilli and their own chickens and eggs. Scarcity was a product of changing seasons and the vagaries of weather, rather than the market for rice or the national economy.

One of my constant tasks was learning a new and complex language without any help from books, a skill I needed in order to approach my research question about whether or not greater participation in the cash economy was leading to greater economic differentiation or even the emergence of social stratification.[31] Unable to find

[27] Nancy Scheper-Hughes (1992), provides one of the most popular and well-known examples of this kind of ethnography; *Death without Weeping: The Violence of Everyday Life in Brazil*, Berkeley.

[28] Ilana Van Wyk (2016), *The Universal Church of the Kingdom of God in South Africa: A Church of Strangers*, Cambridge.

[29] John Ladd (1957), *The Structure of a Moral Code: A Philosophical Analysis of Ethical Discourse Applied to the Ethics of the Navajo Indians*, 209, Cambridge.

[30] See Richard Wilk (1995), 'Learning to Be Local in Belize: Global Systems of Common Difference', in Daniel Miller (ed.), *Worlds Apart: Modernity through the Prism of the Local*, 110–131, London, and Richard Wilk (ed.) (1989), *The Household Economy: Reconsidering the Domestic Mode of Production*, Boulder, CO; see also James Scott (1976), *The Moral Economy of the Peasant: Rebellion and Subsistence in Southeast Asia*, New Haven, CT.

[31] This was a difficult task, because of the powerful hegemony of the idea that 'we are all equal here, like a family'. Most houses were identical, built by the same rotating labour groups, and everyone dressed alike. I did find some differences inside the houses; some families had radios, more clothing, a shotgun for hunting, more dishes and cookpots.

a word in my dictionary for 'poor' or 'poverty', I tried to find it by quizzing my language teacher Juan Cal. He did not seem to understand the word I was trying to translate. So I asked him something like, What would you call a man who does not have enough food for his family, and does not have any money to buy a new axe or some rice in the shop? The word I got in response was already in my Spanish-Q'eqchi' dictionary as *perezoso* which is best translated as 'lazy'. He said the only reason someone would have no money or food is if they were not willing to work, because you could always grow corn or other kinds of food, grow rice to sell or work for someone else.

Based on my own liberal assumptions, I was taken aback and continued to push, asking what you would call someone who was sick or crippled and unable to work. Juan said the only reason that would happen is if you were unlucky or misfortunate, probably because of witchcraft, caused in turn because you had done something bad to a person. In a culture where hard work is highly valued, in some ways the measure of a person's participation in a moral community, poverty was itself an indicator of some sort of moral failing and consequent retribution. It was part of a moral balance at the meeting of the corporeal and the supernatural. Juan just did not see poverty as a phenomenon that defined groups of people in an unjust world. Similarly, people have a moral relationship with the deities of the forest and hills, so any scarcity resulting from a bad harvest is also an indication of a failure to perform proper rituals of propitiation. This is quite extraordinary coming from a member of a culture that has suffered 500 years of conquest, exploitation, serfdom and flight.

Later in my fieldwork I spent time in a village on the highway, where many men worked as day-labourers on large foreign-owned farms. Here people regularly said they were poor because every day they saw members of other ethnic groups including East Indians, Creoles and Garifuna, driving cars and trucks, living in houses built from cut lumber or concrete, working in clean offices instead of out under the hot sun. The Q'eqchi' village schools were the worst in the country, they had no doctors or village clinics, no running water or electricity, their wages were low and when they went into town they were cheated by merchants and openly insulted and badly treated in public. Their children died from easily cured diseases like measles. Poverty was defined categorically, as a consequence of being an Indian, and it reflected fundamental injustice that began with the arrival of Cortez. With a growing consciousness of this inequality, poverty has emerged as a political issue and is fundamental in motivating a protracted legal struggle to get the government to recognize their land rights.[32] Scarcity is now understood as injustice.

I did my first fieldwork at a critical moment when the concept of poverty was incomplete, and some Q'eqchi' people still lived in a world of abundance. They might have a shortage of rain, a lean time caused by insects or storms, an accident or sickness that sapped their vitality, but these were problems out of human control, in the hands of god and the 13 'hill-valley spirits' called Tzuultaq'a, who truly owned the wealth of nature. In the Q'eqchi' world of that time, shortage was not part of nature; it was

---

[32] Mai Campbell and James Anaya (2008), 'The Case of the Maya Villages of Belize: Reversing the Trend of Government Neglect to Secure Indigenous Land Rights', *Human Rights Law Review*, 8 (2): 377–399; I have been involved as an expert witness in these legal cases since 1995.

a product of racism and oppression at the hands of the government and other ethnic groups. By contrast, village life was envisioned as cooperative and secure, with an egalitarian ethos and an assertion that 'we may not have money, but we are rich in food and family'. Q'eqchi' people often said to me that they lived a much better and happier life than what they saw among 'rich' outsiders – that as farmers they were truly wealthy in the things that mattered.

The notion of the earth as a cornucopia, the only real source of wealth, reminds some anthropologists of the physiocratic economic philosophers of the Enlightenment.[33] But it also reflects the efforts of many peoples around the world who do not want to trust their future to a cash economy that has never been a reliable source of income and has often been the partner of intrusive and threatening authority. But when the earth itself betrays you, when the game disappears and foreigners loot the forest for rosewood, as it is cut up by roads and property lines, confidence in the voluntary refuge of self-sufficiency falls apart, along with the common property resources that made a village economy viable and secure. The land itself becomes another kind of wealth, easily lost and impossible to regain.

As an outsider and observer of Q'eqchi' communities, they appeared to me to be oppressed people. But they did not understand or feel poverty until they encountered wealth. So when did they become poor? When did they leave a world of abundance and begin to experience the endless shortages that drive a market society, the constant 'ratchet' of rising expectations so characteristic of consumer culture?[34] It is one thing to say someone else is poor, but it is another thing entirely for that person to think of themselves as impoverished. Yet today you can still travel to many rural areas in the world where people feel that they live superior lives to those outsiders who think they are wealthy, and this is more than consolation, making the best of a bad situation. Money and income appear hegemonic in Manhattan, but not in some small parts of southern Belize.

This subjective element has obvious effects on behaviour. For example, in most Q'eqchi' villages where I worked in the 1970s, you could not buy corn with money. You could ask to borrow some, but there was a clear rule that corn, game, fish and wild fruit were gifts from god, and not to be bought or sold among Q'eqchi' people. The poor are often known for their sharing and generosity to one another, a stereotype that is based on a way of survival on the margins of a cash economy. In southern Belize in 1980, a couple could build a house and make a living with nothing more than a machete, a bucket, a few piglets and a comal (a metal griddle for making tortillas). Today, Q'eqchi' people living in towns find that they need cash for everything, and the fact that they

---

[33] Stephen Gudeman and Alberto Rivera (1990), *Conversations in Columbia: The Domestic Economy in Life and Text*, Cambridge.

[34] Elizabeth Shove has discussed the ratcheting of standards of living, though Vance Packard and other earlier critics of consumer society noted how easy it was to rise in income and status and how difficult it is to drop. There are echoes of this idea in the sociological concept of aspirations and reference groups, the idea that at every rung of the status ladder, people aspire to those a step above. Elizabeth Shove (2003), 'Converging Conventions of Comfort, Cleanliness and Convenience', *Journal of Consumer Policy* 26: 395–418; Salomon Rettig, Frank N. Jacobson, and Benjamin Pasamanick (1959), 'Subjective Status and the Nature of the Reference Group', *The Journal of Social Psychology*, 50 (2): 233–240.

have so little is now enough for them to feel poor. But the question remains, Where along this continuum, if at all, does a shortage of cash become a state of mind?

Because poverty is (partially) a malleable and relative concept, it is often experienced through comparison with a reference group. Creole Belizeans made this point very clear to me when I was interviewing people who had migrated abroad and then returned to Crooked Tree village in 1990. When I asked if they had been better off when they were working illegally in the United States, many gave me a version of 'better to be poor in the USA than well off down here'. They explained that the poor in the United States have access to clean water, toilets and electricity, things absent in much of rural Belize. Nevertheless, perceptions of poverty quickly adjust to circumstance; more than one person told me that it was 'harsh' to see just how rich Americans were and to know that as an immigrant they would never have that level of income and luxury.

For this group, the ratchet of rising expectations did not lead to high aspirations and a climb up the ladder out of poverty. At least living in Belize you see everyone in the village in the 'same pot'. And as many people said, the pace of life in the United States is too fast; people never have time to take it easy with family and friends, a variation of the idea that 'we may not have money, but we have family and community'. This seems superficially comparable to the choices that fall under the label 'voluntary simplicity' or 'simple living' in the United States and other rich countries; though there is a sense of choice for those returning to rural life in Belize, it is a stark binary. By contrast, the middle-class 'downshifters' in the United States have a wide range of options open to them and often a safety net that keeps them from falling too far.

Belizeans have been reminded of their relative wealth by the flood of economic and political refugees from Honduras, Guatemala, El Salvador and other nearby countries in the 1980s and 1990s. Most of the menial and agricultural jobs in the country are now filled by 'aliens' who are happy with wages that most native Belizeans find far too low. This leads to resentment, but it also reminds everyone that while Belize may be poor compared with the United States, it is rich compared with Honduras. Poverty, like scarcity, is always a relative and comparative concept, embedded in a wider system of values.

## Voluntary poverty

In the 1990s I did some brief fieldwork with a 'simple living' group in the United States; I also briefly served as a consultant for a national 'voluntary simplicity' organization in 2003–4 and attended one of their conferences, as well as other regional meetings. At one of those national meetings, the executive board invited a group of educators at a traditionally black college to attend. There was a huge gap of understanding between the two groups.[35] The black educators saw their job as uplifting people out of poverty, while the entirely white contingent from the Simplicity Forum was preaching

---

[35] A report on that meeting is available online at http://rootsystemsinstitute.net/simplicity/files/ws_report_2004.pdf.

'downshifting'. This meant working less, living with lower income and owning 'less stuff', being more self-sufficient and sometimes renouncing successful careers for a rural existence at a slower pace.

The distance between aspiring black educators and meditating affluent white people exposes the real difference between wealth and poverty in the United States today – that wealth allows choices, including the choice to be 'poor'.[36] Luxury, paradoxically, can be expressed through disdain for material comfort ('roughing it' and 'adventure travel') and an exaggerated form of thrift, traits that demonstrate just this element of volition. Once a family or individual has *escaped* from scarcity and poverty, they learn to value cultural and social capital in a way that is often expressed by a disdain for money and material goods, spiritual values instead of hedonism, a cycle which probably goes back to early civilizations.

Belize has always been a destination of choice for the 'Mosquito Coasters', who are searching for a simpler life far from whatever city or suburb they came from. They often act out their fantasy about simplicity by spending huge amounts of money on things like windmills, minihydro generators, organic gardens and solar panels, or even whole sustainable communities and green Ecolodges. Becoming poor in this particular way has become a very expensive business. The fantasy farms, beach cottages and holistic mud baths sometimes employ the children and even the grandchildren of Q'eqchi' people I interviewed in the 1980s. While some still live in rural farming communities, most now live in highway-side villages where they compete with one another for low-paying jobs in resorts, restaurants, shrimp and banana farms or orange groves. These communities are plagued by alcohol addiction and drug use, interpersonal and sexual violence, widespread theft and the more organized violence of youth gangs. Perhaps at a certain point the rich cease being a reference group, and just seem like aliens from another planet.

## Scarcity, abundance and taste

Taste, like poverty, is a concept that lies in the uncomfortable hybrid ground between structure and agency, the individual and the social, free will and determinism. Taste has a completely ambiguous status, depending on which scientists are engaged with it. Cognitive science locates taste in the brain, physiologists in the retro nasal cavity and the taste buds, and food scientists in the food itself. While taste and scarcity may seem distant and unrelated concepts, they are actually closely linked through the false objectivity of economics which treats 'demand' as an exogenous variable. While taste can refer to all kinds of preferences, its prototypical meaning comes from food, a conceptual arena where the relationship between taste and scarcity, shortage, poverty and hunger is especially clear.

---

[36] Ironically, a number of different groups in the United States are now busy trying to portray poverty as a *disease*, the product of natural conditions which can be cured in much the same way as alcoholism or measles. Taking this particular construction apart would require another lengthy paper.

In a paper on the politics of taste in a Liberian refugee camp in Ghana, Trapp discusses the relationship between necessity and taste in reference to a small snail called 'kiss meat'.[37] In Liberia the snails were considered a great delicacy, but in the privation of refugee life they became a sign of poverty, of the necessity of gathering wild food when there was no money to buy meat from the store. As many scholars have noted, being forced to eat something, anything, can easily transform its valence from positive to negative and its flavour from delicious to disgusting.[38] This observation thoroughly deranges the objectivity of economics and palsies the invisible hand of the marketplace by opening the relationship between supply and demand to the social, cultural and psychological.[39]

My recent research on the environmental effects of taste for fish emphasizes this point.[40] Fish considered a gourmet delicacy in one place are often rejected as 'trash fish' in others. Some species of fish are sold a long distance from their origin, going through many steps of preparation and transformation before they are deemed edible. And in Euro-America, certain fishing methods and species are closely associated with class position and the cultivation of cultural capital through mastery of arcane and sometimes mystical lore.[41] 'Game' fish are protected, exalted and mystified in ways that transcend their role as food, so that eating one becomes a form of sin against nature. In the process they lose their edibility and become curiously akin to 'trash' fish. In fact many of the rejected trash fish are actually indigenous, while the game fish are often introduced and could be seen as invasive species.[42]

One curious trend that is emerging in my research is a principle of abundance and taste. Commercial fishing is clearly a business, with the goal of maximizing catches of desirable fish. But what makes fish desirable? It turns out that in most markets, the most abundant fish are considered the least desirable and tasty, a curious translation of market principles into bodily experience. The same principle applies in most recreational fisheries as well, where the most common and abundant fish, the ones most easily caught, are usually dismissed as 'trash fish' that are thrown back or destroyed. The status and edibility of a trash fish is not just low, it is negative. Trash fish are often considered rank, disgusting and dangerous, the killers of the eggs and young

---

[37] Micah Trapp (2016), 'You-Will-Kill-Me-Beans: Taste and the Politics of Necessity in Humanitarian Aid', *Cultural Anthropology*, 31 (3): 412–437. See also Elizabeth Dunn (2011), 'The Food of Sorrow: Humanitarian Aid to Displaced People', in Coleman Leo (ed.), *Food: Ethnographic Encounters*, 139–149, New York.

[38] Falk makes a convincing argument that rather than being opposites, the enticing and the disgusting are in close proximity: Pasi Falk (1994), *The Consuming Body*, London.

[39] It is ironic that economists are now celebrating one another with Nobel prizes for discovering this, given that anthropologists and others have been proving exactly the same point for over a century.

[40] Richard Wilk (2014), 'The Politics of Taste and Assimilation', in Bendix Regina and Maichaela Fenske (eds.), *Political Meals*, 315–323, Münster.

[41] William Washabaugh (2000), *Deep Trout: Angling in Popular Culture*, New York. Randy Kadish (2013), *The Way of the River: My Journey of Fishing, Forgiveness and Spiritual Recovery*, Saw Mill River Press.

[42] The introduction of game fish like black bass and rainbow trout into innumerable lakes and streams around the world has caused untold environmental disruption and the extinction of many indigenous species.

of other better fish, often reputed to eat offal and excrement, to live on the 'bottom' and accumulate poison in their flesh. They are not simply undesirable, they are evil, and government agencies sometimes engage in extermination campaigns or offer fisherfolk a bounty.

Consider the common saltwater blue mussel. They were a pest in Long Island Sound, where I lived as a teenager, encrusting docks and boats, and making it difficult to walk on beaches. I was encouraged to smash them with rocks whenever possible; their only use was as bait for better fish (though I was always encouraged to buy bait rather than catch my own). As mussels started to appear on cosmopolitan European-inspired menus in the area, people began to eat them as 'moules marinière', but they did not eat the ones on their docks and beaches, the ones that were free and easily gathered. The mussel that appeared in supermarkets and fish stores were imported from Canada, where the water was thought to be more pure and the shellfish safer. I have seen the same thing in many places; for example in Sweden, most people do not collect local clams or cockles, though they are almost comically abundant. North American suburbanites spend untold millions trying to protect themselves and their gardens from white tailed deer, and thousands are injured every year in automobile collisions. While many would be willing to pay exorbitant prices for venison in a restaurant, how many would be willing to hack the perfectly edible hams and fillets from a roadkill (as I have done several times)?

Surely, some of this aversion comes from fear of pollution or a disdain for the labour of foraging (which is now gaining cultural capital through the influence of the New Nordic cuisine). But another part of it stems, I think, from an internalization of the rules of the marketplace. If something is abundant it is undesirable. If it is scarce, it must be valuable. Marketers work on this principle all the time by placing new products with celebrities and creating 'limited edition' goods that are only available in special stores. Creating artificial scarcity can build up demand; Fiji water got its start in the United States by giving cases of free water to celebrities, but holding it off the market for several months. Once demand had built up, the water was very slowly dribbled out to the market, and it still retains some of the sympathetic magic of celebrity. Of course, it is chemically identical to the water that comes almost free from the tap.[43] My point here is that taste intervenes in the connection between value and scarcity in a way completely alien to conventional economics. Even a substance like gold, whose value seems concrete and historically unassailable, is subject to changes in taste. Despite claims that it is 'the most useful metal', almost 80 per cent of production still goes into jewellery, in other words ornamentation subject to fashion.[44] The one single unassailable truth about taste is that it will always change over time.

[43]  Richard Wilk (2006), 'Bottled Water, the Pure Commodity in the Age of Branding', *Journal of Consumer Culture*, 6 (3): 303–325.
[44]  https://www.gold.org/about-gold/gold-demand/sectors-of-demand.

# Conclusion

To reiterate some of my major points, rarity is not in itself the cause of shortage. Instead, shortage is a relationship between people and nature mediated by markets, and, paradoxically, the most important and dangerous shortages are those of renewable resources rather than fixed stocks like fossil fuels or metal ores. Social regulation of property, access, rights and values is ultimately more important in creating or reducing scarcity than any aspect of the physical environment. Finally, there is a close relationship between abundance and value that does not come from market position or economic calculation. Instead, living in a consumer culture leads to a kind of inverse fetishism, where abundant resources can become dangerous and liminal. Because of this complex relationship, scarcity and abundance can never be stabilized in the long run – they are inherently dynamic, and any form of stability comes at the cost of great effort.

It would be easy to conclude that anthropologists' contribution to understanding scarcity is an application of cultural relativism that undermines any form of universal definition of the phenomena. On the contrary, the lack of a universal and objective definition moves the concept of scarcity into a realistic engagement with everyday struggles over value and sufficiency, the substance of politics and religion. It does no good to pretend that scarcity is a completely natural phenomenon or that it is an artificial creation with no connection to a material world. Hybridity is uncomfortable and ethically ambiguous, but recognizing the hybrid nature of poverty leads us towards more nuanced analysis and hopefully more effective action that does more than cast the poor as passive or blameworthy victims.

This analysis implies that no measurement of scarcity can be entirely objective or free of moral and political values. Any appeal to 'basic needs' should be treated with scepticism, even those which specify nutritional or medical minima. Furthermore, because scarcity is so often determined by markets and pricing, any measurement based on price must include an estimate of elasticity of supply – in other words, how will supply respond if prices go up or down? And since scarcity is always a relative concept, we must always include a referent – scarce compared to what?

# 5

# Renewable Energy:
# A Story of Abundance and Scarcity

Neil Fromer

## Introduction: Scarcity and abundance of energy

Contemporary discussions of renewable energy present a disconnect. On the one hand, we often think about energy challenges in terms of scarcity and depletion, highlighting challenges for energy access in the developing world or the inability of renewables to reliably replace fossil fuels in the developed world. Yet we also know that renewable energy opportunities abound, making conventional energy systems more robust, creating jobs and providing energy in remote, off-grid locations.[1] With the recent adoption of both the Paris climate agreement and the United Nations Sustainable Development Goals (UNSDGs),[2] businesses, governments, NGOs and academic communities are engaged in a robust debate about the future energy demand and the best way to meet that demand in a sustainable manner. While it is certain that continued burning of fossil fuels to power human civilization will have significant consequences for ecosystems all over the globe, it is unclear what the consequences might be for a rapid shift from the existing infrastructure to one powered by renewable energy sources. Opponents of strategies that move quickly to high penetrations of renewables cite economics, reliability and expanding energy access as key challenges that renewables will struggle to overcome. To some extent this is a circular problem, as the issues faced by renewables stem in large part from attempts to incorporate them into an existing infrastructure built for fossil fuels.

In this chapter, we will attempt to separate the legitimate technical challenges for a renewable energy future from those that are the result of a tilted playing field created

---

[1]  See, for example, Varun Sivaram (May 2017), 'The Global Warming Wild Card', *Scientific American*, 316: 48–53 or U.S. Dept. of Energy (2017), *Staff Report on Electricity Markets and Reliability*, August 2017. https://energy.gov/downloads/download-staff-report-secretary-electricity-markets-and-reliability.

[2]  http://www.un.org/sustainabledevelopment/sustainable-development-goals/. On 25 September 2015, countries adopted a set of goals to *end poverty, protect the planet* and *ensure prosperity for all* as part of a new sustainable development agenda. Each goal has specific targets to be achieved over the next fifteen years.

by more than a century of fossil energy dominance. Understanding this difference can help set policy and drive customers to think holistically about the adoption of renewable energy.

Then we illustrate that, even under aggressive projections for increased energy access and consumption over the next thirty years, there is no looming threat of a lack of energy resources to power the planet; rather, there is an abundance of energy available and in fact significantly more potential for renewable energy than for traditional non-renewable sources. What is lacking is a system for energy capture, conversion and distribution that is satisfactory to meet our projected future demands in a sustainable way. Thinking about future energy scarcity in this context, then, requires a nuanced understanding of interrelated challenges:

- Technological limitations to capturing, converting, storing and distributing the energy in sunlight and wind in a cost-effective manner
- Physical infrastructure limitations related to the use of outdated systems designed for old technologies that make it more challenging to connect renewable technologies to the homes and businesses that use this energy
- Social infrastructure limitations, such as government regulations or societal/cultural expectations, that affect the ways in which users are willing or able to interact with the energy system
- Limitations created by our requirements for sustainable human development and environmental health.

Some of these limitations are natural or economic limits (materials, energy density, variability of supply), and some are 'manufactured' based on the physical and social infrastructure we have already built, creating a playing field tilted against the incorporation of clean energy solutions. Sometimes these limitations interact, exacerbating or improving the situation. All of these limitations must be addressed in the coming years to have a realistic chance of meeting our societal goals for mitigating climate change while increasing energy access. The solutions we develop to address them will also interact, potentially complicating their effectiveness. However, with careful implementation, these interactions can be virtuous and aid in a global energy transition.

## Energy availability and human development

### Historical and current energy use

Energy abundance has long been a driver for productivity and economic development. Prior to the Industrial Revolution and the advent of a modern energy infrastructure, very few opportunities existed to improve human economic progress – those with resources could purchase the physical labour of animals or humans (as employees or as slaves). The development of fossil energy and electrification cannot be understated in terms of the effect on productivity and quality of life.[3] Fossil fuels are incredibly dense, meaning even a small amount will provide a significant benefit. For example, the usable energy from just 20 g of oil converted to mechanical work at a reasonable efficiency is roughly equivalent to an hour of manual effort from a healthy adult.[4] For those people living in the developed world today, this provides unprecedented access to economic mobility, with the related improvements seen in health, life expectancy and overall quality of life. In 2015, the United States consumed the energy equivalent to nearly 2,300 million tonnes of oil, more than 7.1 tonnes of oil per person. At 20 g of oil per hour of manual labour, our energy consumption is similar to every person in the United States having forty people doing hard labour 24/7 to support their lifestyle.[5]

Of course, not every country in the world uses energy at the rate that the United States does. Nor does increased energy use universally translate into increased quality of life. As the Industrial Revolution arrived and the income per person in the developed world grew explosively, a subset of humanity in the developing world actually has fared worse and falls today arguably below the standard of living from pre-industrial times.[6]

In fact, if we look at energy use per capita and compare it to indicators of wealth or quality of life, we can see this discrepancy clearly. For developing countries, increasing energy use is strongly correlated with improvements in quality of life, while for countries above an annual usage of ~3,500 kilograms of oil equivalent/person/year, this correlation becomes weaker or disappears altogether, depending on the particular measure used. Many such measures exist, and for demonstration we will look at the Human Development Index (HDI) as calculated by the UN for each country. The HDI is an index that incorporates economic prosperity (via the GDP), life expectancy and education data to create a score for overall development.[7] Figure 5.1 plots HDI as a function of energy consumption for a number of countries in 2013 and clearly shows both a strong increase in HDI as a function of increasing energy at low values, and a huge range of energy consumption for those countries with high HDI. This result implies something important about the relationship between quality of life and energy consumption. It is important to increase energy access for people with very low consumption, but it is also possible to decrease energy consumption (sometimes drastically) for those at the high end.

If we look only at economic output and compare the relationship between GDP and energy consumption for a developed country to that relationship in a developing country, the importance of increased energy access for the future of the developing world can be clearly seen. Figure 5.2 compares the GDP and energy consumption

---

[3] Greg Clark (2007), *A Farewell to Alms*, 1–23, Princeton.
[4] A well-trained athletic individual can sustain a power output of ~225 Watts over several hours, or an average energy expenditure of 0.225 kWh. At a conversion of ~11.63 kWh/kg of oil equivalent, this is the equivalent of 19.3 g of oil.
[5] British Petroleum, *BP Statistical Review of World Energy 2016*: http://www.bp.com/en/global/corporate/energy-economics/statistical-review-of-world-energy.html
[6] Clark, *A Farewell to Alms*, pp. 1–23.
[7] Data from the United Nations: http://hdr.undp.org/en/content/human-development-index-hdi. Note that numerous other metrics for development or quality of life have been created – it is not our intention to advocate for any one measure but point out the general trends connecting these measures to energy consumption, as done here.

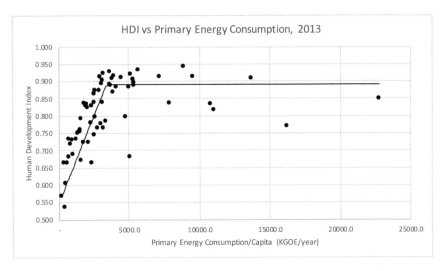

**Figure 5.1** HDI vs energy consumption per capita for 2013. *Note*: Below ~3,500 kg of oil equivalent per year, increases in HDI are directly correlated to increases in energy consumption. Above that value, HDI remains largely high as energy consumption continues to increase. The line is presented as a guide to the eye. *Source*: HDI data from the UN, energy consumption data from the BP Statistical Review of World Energy.

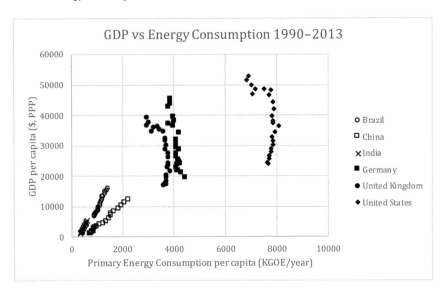

**Figure 5.2** GDP vs primary energy consumption from 1990 to 2013 for six countries. *Note*: The data show a positive correlation between energy consumption per capita and GDP per capita for developing countries, and GDP growth that is largely decoupled from energy consumption in the developed countries. *Source*: GDP data from the World Bank.[8]

[8]  Data from the World Bank Data Portal. Available from: http://data.worldbank.org/ (accessed February 2017).

for China, India and Brazil between the years 1990 and 2013. Over that time, GDP in those countries increased significantly (2.4x in Brazil, 4.6x in India and 12.5x in China) and energy consumption increased significantly as well (1.5x, 1.7x and 2.9x, respectively). It also shows the data for the United States, the UK and Germany, and the story is quite different. Although all three developed countries also saw an increase in GDP of roughly 2x, the energy consumption in all three *fell* during that same period, with 2013 consumption per capita 10–20 per cent below 1990 levels. In addition, while GDP/person in the United States is only 16.5 per cent higher than Germany in 2013 (16 per cent), energy consumption is 78 per cent higher during the same period.

## Projections for future energy use

This sets the stage for us to project future energy demand. In keeping with the recent sustainable development goals set by the UN, we need to project energy demand assuming an increase in energy availability for those developing countries. The 2017 revision of the UN world population prospects estimates between 9 and 10 billion people will live on the planet in 2050.[9] There is a significant body of existing research dedicated to predicting future energy use trends by country and population.[10] Rather than attempt to reproduce those projections, we will create a simple range of potential energy use scenarios in 2050 that assume (with some significant optimism) a noticeable enhancement of human lives around the planet. This is embodied in the UN sustainable development goals released in 2015, including ending poverty and hunger worldwide and ensuring affordable access to energy, clean water and sanitation.[11] Addressing energy access around the globe will clearly not be easy nor do we propose mechanisms for accomplishing the UN goals – however, if we assume we are going to achieve universal energy access, what might that look like? To do this will require a substantial increase in energy use in the developing world. The range of scenarios discussed below reflect how much of focus the developed world places on energy efficiency in the coming decades and which pathways the developed world follow to increase energy use.

A simple estimate of global energy demand would be to scale per capita energy demand so that every person on the planet had an energy footprint equal to that of the average person in the United States today – admittedly a very high estimate – which would mean that 2050 global energy demand would be between 59,000 and 69,000 million tonnes of oil equivalent (MTOE), approximately 4.5–5.25x the global consumption in 2015. We can call this the 'high-use' scenario for future energy.

We saw above that there is an approximate threshold level of energy consumption per capita that separates those developing areas of the world from the developed areas – below ~3,500 KGOE/person/year, increased energy consumption led strongly to

---

[9] United Nations, Department of Economic and Social Affairs, Population Division (2017), World Population Prospects: The 2017 Revision. April 2017. Accessed from: https://esa.un.org/unpd/wpp/.

[10] See, for example, the U.S. Energy Information Agency, *International Energy Outlook 2017*, September 2017. https://www.eia.gov/outlooks/ieo/.

[11] See, for example, the United Nations Sustainable Development Goals knowledge platform. https://sustainabledevelopment.un.org/sdgs.

increased GDP and quality of life, with diminishing returns for consumption above that point. If we aim for an average global energy consumption of 3,500 KGOE/person/year, we have consumption between 30,000 and 35,000 MTOE globally in 2050, or 2.3–2.65x the 2015 global consumption. We can call this the 'low-use' scenario. As stated, this 'low-use' case is still a very optimistic one, as it implies a large increase in energy access around the globe.

Note that while this represents a significant net increase in global per capita energy use, the 'low-use' scenario actually requires a huge decrease in energy consumption across the developed world. Is it possible to drastically reduce our energy footprint? Most experts on carbon emissions reductions have said that achieving deep decarbonization (reductions of 80 per cent or more in $CO_2$ emissions) will require a large increase in energy efficiency.[12] The best way to affect such a change is still a matter of much debate, although the data above suggest that it is feasible at the macro-scale to cut U.S. energy consumption by nearly a factor of 2 with limited effect on GDP, or more broadly with a limited effect on quality of life. Meanwhile, the roll-out of new energy technologies and increased energy availability in the developing world will need to accelerate as drastically to have hope of meeting our goals as a society.

## Options for future energy supply

Is it possible to power the planet in 2050 and beyond under any of these scenarios? Will 2–5x our current energy consumption be feasible? To meet the demands projected above, overall energy production will need to grow by 2.4–4.85 per cent/year from 2015 to 2050, with overall growth in primary energy over the last decade coming in just under 2 per cent/year.[13]

Predictions for the total energy available from coal, oil and natural gas on the planet vary widely, and the methodology and reasons for this variation will be discussed later in this book. Most projections for future fossil fuel availability are based on either proven or total reserves, which is an economic calculation based on the cost of extraction of the resources, rather than the total amount of material in the earth's crust. However, the World Energy Council predicts total resources well above 10,000,000 MTOE for the total of available oil, coal and natural gas (regardless of the recoverability).[14] If we imagine that the energy consumption increases at a constant annual rate between 2015 and 2050 to the amount predicted in the scenarios above, this is between 165 and 350 years of fossil fuels. However, meeting all or most of our demand with fossil energy will create another abundance – $CO_2$. Atmospheric $CO_2$ is now over 400 ppm for the first time in recorded history and will stay above that level for the foreseeable future. Addressing the threat of a changing climate due to abundant $CO_2$ in the atmosphere will be a costly endeavour and we are already seeing some of

---

[12] See, for example, Macdonald et al. (2016), 'Future Cost-competitive Electricity Systems and Their Impact on $CO_2$ Emissions', *Nature Climate Change*, 6: 526.

[13] British Petroleum, *BP Statistical Review of World Energy 2016*.

[14] World Energy Resources Report (2016), *World Energy Council*. Available from: www.worldenergy.org.

the effects, which will intensify by mid-century and in the years beyond. The stated goal of the Paris Climate accord was to keep global average temperature rise below 2 degrees, and if possible below 1.5 degrees. Based on the long-lived nature of carbon dioxide in the earth's atmosphere, this can be translated to a total amount of emissions that can be released before crossing the 2 degrees threshold. A careful analysis of the carbon budget arrives at the consensus that a total of 800 billion tonnes of carbon dioxide can be emitted from 2017 onwards – any more and we will exceed 2 degrees of temperature rise.[15] Although different fossil fuels have different carbon intensities, this is significantly less than the $CO_2$ that would be emitted by consuming only the proven reserves of coal, oil and natural gas.

However ample the potential to burn fossil fuels is, there is also ample renewable energy resource available in the form of incoming solar radiation. It is estimated that the average solar energy resource for the continent of Africa (energy from the sun hitting the surface averaged over the year) is roughly 150,000 terawatt-hours/day (TWh/day). Globally, a low estimate for the average solar resource is approximately 470,000 TWh/day. Converting this to tonnes of oil equivalent gives approximately 40,000 MTOE/day in solar energy that reaches land on the populated continents of the planet – well more than 2x our annual consumption in 2015.[16] While the changing climate in the future might alter expected solar or wind resources, it is not expected to reduce these averages significantly.

It is clear from these estimates that there is no looming threat of lack of energy resources to power the planet; rather, there is an abundance of energy available and in fact significantly more renewable energy resource than non-renewable resources. This tells us that any scarcity in energy, renewable or fossil-based, is created not by a lack of the critical resources but by the lack of a comprehensive system for conversion and distribution that is satisfactory to meet projected future demands in the right place at the right time.

In 2015, renewable sources provided 2.8 per cent of the global energy demand. To meet global demand in 2050, following our estimates above, renewable energy production would need to grow by 12.5–15 per cent per year between 2015 and 2050. While large, this growth rate is quite feasible given that over the past ten years, global utility-scale solar energy production has grown at an annual rate of 50 per cent/year and wind power at 23 per cent/year.[17]

If there is not an issue with energy resource scarcity, what is the concern? Why can't we simply continue to scale solar and wind energy until we meet the target production? There are a number of issues that will arise as the scale of renewable energy production increases around the globe. Some of these issues can be traced back to other types of scarce resources, and many are related to the distribution of energy, materials and people around the planet.

[15] Global Carbon Budget (2016), from *the Global Carbon Project*. http://www.globalcarbonproject. org/.
[16] Data on average Solar Insolation from SOLARGIS global insolation maps. https://solargis.info/.
[17] British Petroleum, *BP Statistical Review of World Energy 2016*.

## Potential limitations to abundant clean energy

Above, we saw that the raw energy resources exist to power the planet entirely by renewable energy, even including large increases in global energy demand to meet the goals of sustainable development and energy access. However, while solar energy reaching the planet might be abundant, that is only the beginning of the challenge. Fossil fuels may not be renewable, but they are abundant and they are dense, as we saw above. Energy from the sun is renewable, and abundant, but is not particularly dense – at midday, sunlight delivers roughly 1,000 W/m^2 of power. Currently, commercially available modules exist to convert sunlight to electricity at efficiencies as high as 22 per cent, with average panels achieving ~16 per cent conversion efficiency. This means a square metre of available roof or ground area might contribute as much as 200 W of power at midday. Depending on latitude and local weather conditions, however, this square metre of area might generate 650 kWh of electricity in a year in a favourable location such as the southwest United States, the Sahara or the Atacama Desert (the electricity that could be generated in an average modern power plant by of ~150 KGOE) or as little as 250 kWh in places like Germany, Scandinavia or the pacific northwest (roughly 56 KGOE).[18]

The relative sparseness of solar energy has important implications – it takes a lot of area to provide the power needed, and it takes a lot of material to convert that energy into a useful form. In addition to the sparseness is the often-discussed fact that solar energy is intermittent: we have power when the sun is shining, but none when it isn't – weather, night-time and seasons creating both predictable and unpredictable variations on a timescale from minutes to years. Finally, while it is clear that we have abundant solar energy and existing technology to turn that energy into electricity, electricity accounts for only a fraction of our total energy use. To truly replace fossil fuels, we need to be able to convert solar energy not only to electricity (electrical energy) but also to fuels (chemical energy) and heat (thermal energy).

These three concerns, availability by location, by time and by type, drive the concerns about future deployment of solar energy to meet our goals. Conversion and storage require specific technologies and materials, storage and distribution require infrastructure and the details of each might serve to constrain growth. We will break these potential constraints into three types: technological limitations to capturing, converting, storing and distributing the energy to meet all of our projected future use (is it technically possible to turn the available resource into energy for the whole planet to use?); infrastructure limitations that make it more challenging to connect renewable technologies to the homes and businesses that use this energy (even if it is technically possible is it feasible to build such a system?); and economic, social or environmental limitations that might make it harder to challenge status quo energy systems (can this ever be cost-effective, and what does that really mean?). These concepts are not mutually

---

[18]  1 kg of oil equivalent converts to 11.63 kWh of electrical energy content, but in a conventional fossil fuel power plant, you might convert ~40 per cent of that energy into usable electricity, so for this purpose we use 4.4 kWh/KGOE.

exclusive, and solving some of the infrastructural problems may open up a wider range of potential technologies or create a different set of technological constraints.

There are many in-depth studies of the feasibility of a high renewable energy system.[19] The goal of this chapter is not to dive into the details of these analyses, but rather to highlight the ways in which these constraints contribute to scarcity rather than abundance of renewable energy solutions.

## Technological limitations

Here we look at the purely technological challenges associated with increasing renewable energy use to 100 per cent. In other words, for what aspects of a purely renewable energy future are there technological gaps that can't be met with any available or near-term technology. Recall that installed energy assets, like power plants or electricity transmission lines, typically live for at least 30–50 years, so to target 2050 means that new technologies need to start rolling out in the next few years. Many of the currently available solutions are not yet cost-effective based on the system we have in place, and research on new materials and technologies will be necessary to meet our goals, but we will address those issues later and focus here on gaps without any clear technical solution.

Perhaps the most commonly discussed issue with solar and wind energy is that they are variable and intermittent sources of electricity. As discussed above, renewable electricity comes with predictable and unpredictable variations from seconds or minutes in duration up to seasonal or even annual timescales. Our analysis of available solar resource is based on annual averages that do not take into account these variations at all, when in fact the difference between summer sunlight and winter sunlight may be the most important issue for using solar energy. We need short-term storage (minutes to hours) to deal with variability in weather or other emergency situations; we need storage from hours to days to deal with day–night cycles and longer term weather patterns; and we need storage up to several months to deal with seasonal variations in the available resources. As a result, recent discussions of penetration of solar and wind power have logically begun to focus as much or more on electrical storage than on conversion technology.

Although most focus is currently on batteries, both as a way to store electrical energy electrochemically in either a distributed or centralized fashion, many other technologies exist for storing electricity, including thermally (by heating or cooling materials) or mechanically (in a rotating flywheel, as compressed gas or by moving water or materials uphill). The current focus on batteries is driven by demand for portable battery systems for portable electronics and electric vehicles, and as a result, the focus remains on lithium-based batteries that can provide the high energy and

---

[19] See, for example, Mark Jacobson et al. (2015), 'Low-Cost Solution to the Grid Reliability Problem with 100 per cent Penetration of Intermittent Wind, Water, and Solar for All Purposes', *Proc Natl Acad Sci*, 112: 15060–15065, or Christopher Clack et al. (2017), 'Evaluation of a Proposal for Reliable Low-Cost Grid Power with 100 per cent Wind, Water, and Solar', *Proc Natl Acad Sci*, 114: 6722–6727.

power densities (energy and power per unit mass) needed for making lightweight systems. This flavour of battery systems may also be the most effective way to solve short-term storage needs on the electricity grid.

However, lithium battery technologies are not the best for high total energy applications, especially long-term stationary storage applications where weight may be less important than total system cost. A host of other materials are being investigated for these purposes, but come with fundamental challenges in terms of the available materials,[20] the capacity and duration of the solution, the efficiency and cost to deploy it.[21] For long term, seasonal energy storage, there has yet to be any electrical storage to match the storage provided by pumping water uphill into reservoirs when energy is available and then recovering that energy in a hydroelectric power station when it is needed. However, the construction costs and environmental impacts of building new dams make it challenging to imagine deployment of new hydroelectric storage at a scale required to accomplish our seasonal or year over year energy storage needs.[22]

Similarly, discussions about renewable energy tend to focus on electricity, since we have available, deployable solutions to convert solar and wind energy into electricity. However, electricity accounts for only a fraction of total energy use – in 2015, approximately 4,300 TWh of electricity were generated, again assuming average fossil power plant efficiencies, this is the equivalent of 977 MTOE, or roughly 40 per cent of primary energy demand. Large amounts of primary energy are used in the construction and industrial manufacturing sectors and of course in transportation. Traditionally, these demands have been met with various types of fuels, as they are dense and transportable. Even if we succeed in generating abundant electricity in a renewable fashion, and in electrifying most/all of our light duty transportation fleet and domestic fuel consumption, we will need to develop technology for making some fuels in a renewable fashion. Success here would also provide another form of long-term storage for renewable electricity, which could be converted to fuel and stored for months or even years if needed.

Fossil fuels are derived originally from the sun (plants die and create biomass that with pressure and time are converted to fuel). However, plants are not terribly efficient at converting sunlight into fuel – a careful accounting for the energy inputs yields an overall sunlight to fuel efficiency of 1–2 per cent for the best plants (such as switchgrass).[23] Although we continue to make strides on the science and technology, we have yet to develop systems to convert biomass into fuels that are scalable, long-lived and efficient enough to be cost-effective, except in certain specific applications like the capture of biogas from landfill or sewage waste processing. Conventional biofuels (corn ethanol) compete with food crops and have only a small benefit over

[20] Albertus Wadia and Srinivasan (2011), 'Resource Constraints on the Battery Energy Storage Potential for Grid and Transportation Applications', *J. Power Sources*, 196: 1593–1598.

[21] Steven Chu, Yi Cui and Nian Liu (2017), 'The Path towards Sustainable Energy'. *Nature Materials*, 16: 16–22.

[22] Clack et al., 'Evaluation of a Proposal for Reliable Low-cost Grid Power with 100 per cent Wind, Water, and Solar'.

[23] Nathan Lewis and Daniel Nocera (2006), 'Powering the Planet: Chemical Challenges in Solar Energy Utilization', *Proc Natl Acad Sci*, 103: 15729.

fossil fuels in their carbon footprint. 'Next-generation' biofuels, using waste biomass, are better, since they don't compete with food production, but it remains a difficult scientific challenge to convert those materials to usable fuels and chemicals.

We can use inorganic materials to convert sunlight to fuel – for instance, using electricity (from solar panel) to split water into hydrogen (a fuel) and oxygen. The best systems can do this at high efficiency, but rely on rare, expensive materials that make the process more expensive than generating hydrogen from methane. Recent research has demonstrated systems that can convert sunlight to hydrogen at 10 per cent efficiency using only relatively common elements.[24]

However, the grand challenge of artificial photosynthesis, creating carbon-based fuels in this way, remains outside of our reach for the time being. New scientific understanding of the chemistry of carbon dioxide is needed, and this remains a scientific research project. However, it is essential to develop these techniques, as not only fuels but also industrial chemical inputs must be replaced with renewable sources. A barrel of crude oil generates gasoline, jet fuel and other fuels, but also generates hydrogen and ethylene and other light hydrocarbons that are used as inputs in chemical plants. Replacing gasoline use with renewable alternatives means we will need to develop replacements for these other petroleum products, or we will continue to need to dig oil from the ground.

In addition to timing and type of energy, the sparseness of solar and wind energy leads to a physical constraint – how much energy can be generated locally and how much must be sent in via transmission or distribution networks? As mentioned above, in some areas, the resource is low enough (or variable enough) that large amounts of land and materials might need to be devoted to the effort. Although we will discuss the ability of infrastructure to alleviate this challenge later, it is important to know that in some cases the sheer amount of material required might be a constraint. There have been several review papers that address the general availability of metals and semiconductor materials that have important properties for the conversion of solar or wind energy into electrical, mechanical or chemical energy, and scarcity of these materials might limit growth of new technology solutions.[25]

## Infrastructural limitations

In the United States and other developed countries, the discussion of renewable energy deployment is often one of comparative economic advantage between renewable and fossil energy. This is a skewed discussion from the start, because the existing infrastructure was built for the outdated technology, and this creates bottlenecks for alternative deployment. Our networks for delivering and using energy resources (which

---

[24] Erik Verlage et al. (2015), 'A Monolithically Integrated, Intrinsically Safe, 10% Efficient, Solar-Driven Water-Splitting System Based on Active, Stable Earth-Abundant Electrocatalysts in Conjunction with Tandem III-V Light Absorbers Protected by Amorphous TiO2 Films', *Energy & Environmental Science*, 8: 3166.

[25] See, for example, Cyrus Wadia et al. (2009), 'Materials Availability Expands the Opportunity for Large-Scale Photovoltaics Deployment', *Environmental Science & Technology*, 43: 2072–2077.

includes both the physical infrastructure and the social/regulatory infrastructure that was developed to manage it) were built based on outdated rules and an outdated understanding of technology. Two hallmarks of this outdated paradigm are:

1. They are designed to generate abundance, rather than mitigate scarcity. Focus on making sure that there is a surplus of cheap and reliable energy to be used when needed, with no concern for finite amounts or for consequences of overuse. Emphasize oversupply to give some measure of reliability.
2. Measuring the system while in operation is hard to do. We do as little measurement as possible, and use those limited measurements to infer as much as possible about the health of the system as a whole.

These two points lead to large centralized development, which is easier to measure and control. They also lead to a focus on maximizing capacity to deliver resources as a good proxy for reliability. This also simplifies the measurement process.

The system works very well when capacity far outstrips demand most of the time, when power flows in one direction from centralized generator to distributed user and when supply can be scheduled to match demand. Solar electricity, in particular, forces a change to these assumptions. Our energy demand predictions above show that we need to become much more efficient with our energy inputs, so excess capacity will not be available for reliability. Although solar and wind power are being deployed in large power plants connected to users by high-voltage transmission lines, they are also increasingly being deployed in smaller amounts closer to (or as a part of) the end-user's networks. This means power will flow in more complex patterns, affecting the performance of the hardware as well as the markets that facilitate the delivery of electricity. And the intermittent nature of solar and wind power means that scheduling supply to match demand is more difficult and sometimes impossible.[26]

The relationship between power and energy resources is important to understand as the focus for the electricity sector tends to be power, obscuring some of the challenges and opportunities available. In particular, the capacity to deliver power is generally cited as the constraint, based on the existing infrastructure. Power is energy delivered for a specific duration at a particular time, as compared to the total annual energy production or consumption throughout the year. These quantities are connected through the capacity factor: the energy delivered over a year as a fraction of the total energy available from a generator (if it was producing its rated power 24 hours a day, 365 days a year). The capacity factor for the entire U.S. generation fleet in 2015 was ~39 per cent – there is generation capacity for more than 2x the energy delivered based on the nameplate capacity of the generators. Solar generators, however, can only generate power for the fraction of the day during which the sun is shining. In deserts and other high-resource areas, this gives a capacity factor approaching 35 per cent, but in most urban areas it is less than 25 per cent. Note that storage does not change this calculus

[26] Matthew R. Shaner et al. (2018), 'Geophysical Constraints on the Reliability of Solar and Wind Power', *Energy Environmental Science*, 11: 914–925, or Friedrich Wagner (2016), 'Surplus from and Storage of Electricity Generated by Intermittent Sources', *European Physical Journal Plus*, 131: 445.

– while coupling solar energy generation with energy storage allows power delivery to shift in time to help match supply and demand, a solar panel's capacity factor is determined by location (weather, shading and overall sunlight).

Conversely, we can define the load factor as the ratio of the average power delivered over a year to the peak power demand. This gives us a measure of how 'smooth' our demand is. In California, the load factor is decreasing (getting lumpier over time) and is close to 50 per cent. During this time, average energy consumption has remained fairly constant, but peak demand has increased. Projections from the California Independent System Operator (CAISO) for future electricity demand in the state see this trend continuing and being exacerbated by solar deployment. This highlights a problem for increasing solar penetration in developed countries, known as value sag. The more solar energy you have on the grid, the less it is worth, since it all comes at the same time of the day.[27] Areas with high penetrations of renewable energy, such as California and Germany, are already seeing the need to 'curtail' renewable energy on cool, sunny days – there is more power available than is needed at that time of day.

Vehicle electrification and electrification of other fuel uses will perhaps exacerbate these problems, as we will create a larger demand for electricity at times when renewable sources may not be available. However, increased electrification of these systems will also increase flexibility in our demand, and increased capability to measure and control demand and supply together might offer the ability to attack supply versus demand from both ends at once, i.e. attempt to make the renewable sources as dispatchable as possible to meet critical demand, but also make demand as flexible as possible to match available supply. Creating a new infrastructure paradigm that values local use of local resources first, and measures and optimizes in real time based on the available resources, can be much more efficient from the standpoint of energy generation and use. However, it might require end-users to redefine the efficiency of their systems – to create a more holistic measure of the efficiency of generation and use of energy, rather than looking at capacity factors and uptime for power plants and industrial facilities separately. For residential and commercial energy uses, this is in fact much easier to accomplish, as we tend to be very inefficient in our use of assets like cars and appliances.

In our estimates of future energy use, the high-use scenarios involve little focus on conventional energy efficiency, while the low-use cases will require a massive decrease in energy use by the United States and many other developed countries. Even the high-use case will require some investment in energy efficiency to hold the energy use in the developed world fixed as we move into the future.

As stated above, we have seen the developed economies become more efficient in their energy use in recent years, with overall decreases in the energy used per capita while GDP rose, or at the very least with energy use growing at a much slower rate than economic growth.

---

[27] Varun Sivaram and Shayle Kann (2016), 'Solar Power Needs a More Ambitious Cost Target', *Nature energy*, 1: 16036.

The global energy data presented above shows that it is possible to sustain high GDP at energy use much closer to the threshold value of 3,500 KGOE/person/year. Countries such as Germany and the UK are already much more efficient by this measure than the United States is.

The most conservative arguments against the feasibility of this level of decarbonization point to our existing economy and extrapolate the cost (in terms of economic competitiveness) associated with becoming more efficient. Perhaps instead we need to apply a comparative analysis and identify, by region and by economic sector, what is driving energy use at the current levels and what allows other regions/sectors to be more efficient. Such approaches have been used to analyse carbon emissions reduction policies, and applying this technique to energy consumption of cities/regions could identify best practices and opportunities for investment with significant energy efficiency gains.[28]

It is clear from long-term energy efficiency trends in places like California, and more recent trends in energy efficiency improvements worldwide, that there is room to grow here. The true gains will come when we are able to look at the system as a whole and invest in technologies that increase energy efficiency even if they reduce efficiency in other aspects of our industry. However, the system as built does not provide adequate incentives for efficiency, and the lack of measurement or baseline makes it hard to incorporate system efficiency in a holistic manner. Nonetheless, when possible to measure it, we appear to be able to do more than is generally realized.[29]

It is important to note that not all measures designed to increase energy efficiency will have their intended effect. Sometimes referred to as Jevons paradox, it has been observed in numerous areas that increases to efficiency in any process often lead to increased, rather than decreased, consumption. However, if efficiency increases are driven by scarcity or cost, rather than technology improvements, consumption can be driven down, at least in the short term. Thus, careful design of programmes to increase overall energy efficiency is required to avoid the paradox and actually decrease consumption.

Recall that traditionally energy infrastructure relied on excess capacity to deliver energy as a proxy for reliability or system resilience. Here is a dangerous trap – as long as we are providing excess capacity, human activity will expand to consume it. Any concept for adaptable infrastructure for a renewable energy future will need to address this paradox and develop the ability to provide reliable service without implicitly encouraging wasteful use. This could be the hardest challenge in the design of a future energy infrastructure and is as much or more of a social engineering challenge as a technological one.

---

[28] Yuli Shan et al. (2018), 'Assessment of $CO_2$ Reduction Potentials in Chinese Cities', *Science Advances*: EAAQ0390.

[29] See, for example, John Laitner, *Calculating the Nation's Annual Energy Efficiency Investments*, American Council for an Energy-Efficient Economy, February 2013. http://aceee.org/research-report/e133.

## Economic, environmental and developmental limitations

In the end, the development of new technology and new infrastructure needs to be an economic one – either the capital cost of development and deployment will rival than of conventional energy systems, or political will or social responsibility will rise to the challenge and demand a change via policy, or by recognizing the unpriced externalities related to fossil energy use and incorporating those costs into systems making them more expensive, or we will not sustain the renewable energy transition.

Again, the infrastructure is tilted against renewables – in this case, the market infrastructure. Energy economics are built based on a combination of large upfront capital outlays and a market to incorporate current and future marginal costs based on fuel prices. Renewables do not have this structure, once the initial capital is spent, fuel costs are not an issue, and operations and maintenance costs are often smaller than at a large fossil energy plant. Thus, the deployment of large amounts of renewable energy can lead to negative price shocks and other issues that threaten the existing markets for energy or electricity. This leads grid operators, utilities and power plant operators to undermine the value of renewable energy. Designing a new infrastructure that incorporates a new way to evaluate the costs and benefits of solar energy is required.

By forcing clean energy alternatives to fit into the system designed for fossil fuels, but not incorporating the environmental costs of those incumbent technologies, we are creating a false choice – economics versus environment. When we talk of the environmental impacts of fossil energy systems, including damage to human health and natural ecosystems, and the threat to our infrastructure posed by climate change, we can identify costs that should be included in an overall analysis of costs and benefits for renewable energy. However, large variations exist in methodology for calculating the cost associated with these impacts.[30]

As discussed at the start of the chapter, there is an abundance of fossil fuel in the earth's crust. Unless we leave it there, we will suffer the effects of climate change. Unless a system is put in place that allows renewable energy sources to compete, within an infrastructure that also supports the expansion of clean energy into developing parts of the world, it will be impossible to avoid perhaps catastrophic global warming. Ultimately, there are a number of different balances we must strike as we attempt to clean the energy supply and expand energy access in the under-resourced areas of the planet. In the developed world, strengthening (rather than weakening) the environmental controls is imperative, and determining appropriate costs for new development that incentivizes clean energy deployment in the near term is essential. Once India has set a path for growth based on fossil fuels, it may be too late to change the trajectory.[31]

Above, we laid out some of the challenges and opportunities to be addressed. It is still an open question how to design systems (either from the ground up or by retrofitting our existing infrastructure) to accomplish a stable, sustainable energy

---

[30] See, for example, William Nordhaus (2017), 'Revisiting the Social Cost of Carbon', *Proc Natl Acad Sci*, 114: 1518, and references therein.

[31] Sivaram, 'The Global Warming Wild Card'.

system for the planet. We end with a short outline or vision of what such a renewable energy infrastructure might look like to guide the next generation of science and engineering research, as well as the policymakers who will need to design/update markets and regulations.

## A vision for a renewable energy future

Any detailed attempt to design a future energy system based entirely on renewable resources must tackle all of the above challenges, and there are a number of modelling efforts under way to do this.[32] Here we simply lay out a general vision or approach to making the system more resilient to large penetrations of renewables, with the realization that the trajectory we take to get there might vary based on local resources, technological developments and infrastructure investment.

Perhaps a robust approach would start with an overall system that can be layered with local resources applied locally whenever possible, but that cascades out to incorporate longer distance and larger scale to provide backup, resilience and smoothing of the variations in time and space discussed above. This takes advantage of the relative ease of measurement and communication over short and long distances in real time. Local control allows a better balance between development and environmental considerations and ownership of issues created, while a regional, national and/or global framework provides reliability and long-term sustainability. In developed areas, identify the smallest set of infrastructure changes that allow an approximation of such an approach, while in developing areas, such an architecture can be put in place at the outset. Invest in technology development to improve efficiency, develop long-term energy storage and renewable fuel development for maximum flexibility. Approach the design with these three basic principles in mind:

1. Turn renewables into 'baseload' power sources that can be dispatched as needed.
2. Use our communications infrastructure to aggressively manage the demand for energy, shifting uses to make the best use of renewable energy when available. If we can truly make demand flexible, there is a lot of room for overall system efficiency improvements to best use renewable energy.
3. (Re)build infrastructure to utilize renewable resources more effectively, including large-scale projects that connect geographically distinct regions of the country/ planet together (smoothing variability) to small-scale upgrades of hardware and controls for the electricity distribution system to allow two-way power flow and pooling of distributed resources.

---

[32] See, for example, Macdonald et al., 'Future Cost-competitive Electricity Systems and Their Impact on $CO_2$ Emissions', Mark Jacobson et al., 'Low-Cost Solution to the Grid Reliability Problem with 100 per cent Penetration of Intermittent Wind, Water, and Solar for All Purposes' or Clack et al., 'Evaluation of a Proposal for Reliable Low-Cost Grid Power with 100 per cent Wind, Water, and Solar', and references therein.

In areas with significant infrastructure in place, the third point is often complex, expensive and time-consuming, as the projects require significant regulatory approvals as well as land and materials. In developing economies, however, smarter infrastructure deployment can be done for roughly the same cost as a more conventional system, allowing a more flexible system from the outset.

## Scarcity and abundance in energy revisited

This chapter has attempted to motivate the reader to think about the necessity of increased energy consumption around the globe and the challenge to the health of the planet that might come from such an expansion. We've made the case that there is no global shortage of energy, and that in fact the supply of fossil fuels available to meet current and future energy demand, coupled with the global system for exploitation of these resources, creates an entrenched set of interests that look to expand their services to the developing world while tightening their grip on the global supply chain. So how do we conceive of scarcity within the global energy system? We have reached a point in time (in fact, we may already be well past it) where continued exploitation and use of fossil fuels will have massive, negative global-scale consequences, even as they will continue to provide significant benefits to local communities and individuals around the planet. Renewable energy systems exist that can provide the local benefits of energy generation and quality-of-life improvements connected without the negative consequences of climate change. The success of deploying renewable energy globally will rest on changing the paradigm for energy delivery, from built infrastructure, to new energy trading market designs, to alternate regulatory/governance structures. And like those other examples, such a solution will require the collective action of local communities with a global perspective.

Part Two

# The Power of Projection

6

# Growth in the Anthropocene

Fredrik Albritton Jonsson

The dream of earthly abundance has a long history. We can track a rich variety of words in the English language for improvement, growth and development from early modern alchemy to neoclassical economics. During the Stuart Age, magicians and projectors imagined cornucopia through transmutation, instauration and political arithmetic. In the Enlightenment, the lexicon of improvement shifted to utility, comparative advantage and compound interest. Victorians in turn conceived of wealth as the product of steam, coal and iron. In the twentieth century, the language of plenty expanded to include concepts of substitution, gross national product, take-off, information society and present value. Curiously, this cornucopian vocabulary emerged more or less in tandem with a language of scarcity and limits, including concepts such as soil exhaustion, the stationary state, geometric increase, surplus population, the coal question, the limits to growth and environmental sustainability. That parallel movement is hardly a coincidence. Competing predictions of abundance and scarcity have fed on each other over the course of the modern period. The prospect of accelerating change has provoked countervailing visions of physical limits. These mutually constituted imaginaries closely reflect a context of technological innovation and globalization as well as demographic strain and ecological degradation.[1]

In recent years, the debate about the future of growth has produced a new approach rooted in geology and earth system science. The concept of the Anthropocene was coined in 2000 by the chemist Paul Crutzen and biologist Eugene Stoermer to draw attention to a major rupture in the history of the planet. In geological terms, the science of the Anthropocene suggests that we have entered into a new epoch, leaving behind the relatively stable environment of the Holocene. The start of the Anthropocene signals a shift in the fundamental condition of the earth system, including multiple interconnected threats to the safe function of the system and the future of economic development. The conceptual framework of Planetary Boundaries expands on this understanding of planetary risk by charting quantitative limits for sustainable growth. By defining the economy as a subset of the earth system, this approach overturns conventional notions of scarcity and abundance. In the case of climate change,

---

[1] Fredrik Albritton Jonsson (2014), 'The Origins of Cornucopianism: A Preliminary Genealogy', *Critical Historical Studies*, 1 (1): 1–18.

accelerating carbon emissions are overwhelming the natural system, creating a new kind of scarcity of sinks. In the case of land use and biodiversity, economic development threatens both genetic diversity and functional traits within ecosystems. Here too we face a new kind of scarcity. Biodiversity comprises a non-renewable stock from which we draw food, medicine and industrial raw materials. Economic growth must be kept within certain boundaries to safeguard the sources, sinks and flows of the earth system.[2]

From the beginning, Crutzen and Stoermer deployed the concept of the Anthropocene in many registers, weaving together elements of environmental science, history and ethics. The unprecedented rupture of the Anthropocene signals a break both in the history of humanity and the life of the planet. Never before have humans been able to alter the global climate of the Earth. Fossil burning and other features of the modern economy are interfering with the earth system processes that keep the planet stable for humans. The promise of the Industrial Revolution – that humans can master the natural world – is now in doubt. Yet paradoxically, the Anthropocene imagines failure as a form of superhuman agency. The impact of economic growth on ecosystems around the world is so great that it now resembles a geological force. There is no way of disavowing this super-agency. Global threats must be met with 'planetary stewardship'.

It should come as no surprise that some observers have reacted to the provocative pronouncements about the Anthropocene with strong scepticism or outright hostility. These critics worry that the analysis of planetary change focuses too much attention to future effects and not enough on historical causes. They also warn that the notion of geological agency obscures and detracts from the analysis of specific social forces and actors. Is the analytical lens of earth system science really appropriate for thinking about politics on a human scale?[3]

This chapter examines the science of the Anthropocene by exploring three closely related concepts: the Great Acceleration, Planetary Boundaries and the 'environmental envelope' of the Holocene. Taken together, they challenge and recast conventional ideas of scarcity and abundance by placing economic development in a planetary and geological framework. The chapter concludes by considering the ways in which Anthropocene science is producing rival ideological interpretations, including competing concepts of transcendental ingenuity and envelopes of stability. Such a process of appropriation suggests that the Anthropocene framework might become a new battlefield for the long-standing conflict between cornucopian and Malthusian interpretations of the environment.

***

[2]  P. J. Crutzen and E. F. Stoermer (2000), 'The Anthropocene', *IGBP Newsletter*, 41 (May): 17–18; Johan Rockström et al. (2009), 'Planetary Boundaries: Exploring the Safe Operating Space for Humanity', *Ecology and Society*, 14 (2).

[3]  Dipesh Chakrabarty (2009), 'The Climate of History', *Critical Inquiry* (Winter); Julia Adeney Thomas (2014), 'History and Biology in the Anthropocene: Problems of Scale, Problems of Value', *American Historical Review*, 119; Andreas Malm and Alf Hornborg (2014), 'The Geology of Mankind: A Critique of the Anthropocene Narrative', *The Anthropocene Review*, 1: 62; cf. Richard B. Norgaard (2013), 'The Econocene and the Delta', *San Francisco Estuary and Watershed Science*, 11: 3.

**Figure 6.1** 'The Great Acceleration'. *Source*: International Geosphere-Biosphere Programme. Downloaded 16 March 2017. http://www.igbp.net/news/pressreleases/ pressreleases/planetarydashboardshowsgreataccelerationinhumanactivity since1950.5.950 c2fa1495db7081eb42.html.

At the heart of the Anthropocene discourse is a common image of exponential growth on a planetary scale in the form of a cluster of J-curves spiking upwards together over the last two hundred and fifty years. Among the twenty-four indicators shown in Figure 6.1, we find a mixture of social developments and environmental trends: carbon dioxide, tropical deforestation, shrimp aquaculture, methane, paper production, dam building and urban population growth. In each curve, the second half of the twentieth century marks a moment of steep increase: the Great Acceleration. By juxtaposing social development with threats to the earth system, the graphs illustrate how human activities have been reshaping the planetary environment in the course of just three generations. The speed and magnitude of these anthropogenic changes have come to exceed the capacity of the earth system to absorb the environmental damage generated by economic growth. Such a conception of the Anthropocene also recognizes the central importance of climate change as a driver of global change yet insists that climate change is but one among several growing threats to the stable functioning of the biosphere.

Some of the leading scholars of the Anthropocene have adopted the Planetary Boundaries concept. This precautionary model predicts that unsustainable economic development will trigger irreversible and non-linear changes to the earth system. There are nine areas of risk: land system change, biodiversity loss, climate change, oceanic acidification, the supply of freshwater, aerosol loading, ozone depletion, nitrogen/phosphorus and 'novel entities'. Land use is changing rapidly, thanks to urbanization, agriculture and population pressure. The rate of biodiversity loss (changes in biosphere integrity) is increasing in many ecosystems. Acidification is affecting marine biodiversity as well as the capacity of oceans to absorb carbon dioxide. The supply of freshwater in many regions is deteriorating. Aerosol loading and ozone depletion threaten the stability of the earth system's atmosphere. Industrial agriculture has disturbed the global nitrogen and phosphorous cycles. Finally, the introduction of novel entities such as microplastics, organic pollutants and radioactive particles may pose a risk not just at the local or regional level but also worldwide.[4]

'Planetary Boundaries' represent approximate quantitative values for thresholds of environmental risks beyond which we can expect non-linear and irreversible change on a continental or planetary level. Most famously, climate scientists have warned that atmospheric $CO_2$ concentrations above 350 parts per million (ppm) signify unacceptable danger to the welfare of the planet and humanity. The big rise in emissions that brought us past this threshold happened in the past three generations. While the origin of fossil fuel burning goes back to the Industrial Revolution (which set us on a path beyond the Holocene's natural atmospheric $CO_2$ variability of 260 to 285 ppm), the truly dramatic rise in atmospheric carbon dioxide, from 310 to 400 ppm, has occurred between 1950 and 2015.

A third widely circulated image from the International Geosphere-Biosphere Programme focuses not on the Anthropocene itself but its climatological and evolutionary prelude.[5] The graph shown in Figure 6.3 marks temperature changes over the past 100,000 years, as measured by changes in $\delta^{18}O$ (the difference in the ratio between oxygen isotopes $^{18}O$ and $^{16}O$). It bridges the conventional divide between history and prehistory, seeing them as part of a single story. Early human migration in the Pleistocene took place in the context of sharp temperature oscillations between glacial periods ('ice ages') and interglacial periods. Agriculture emerged once temperature stabilized in the long plateau of the Holocene. Will Steffen defines the Holocene as the 'environmental envelope', which made possible the growth of complex societies. It is the 'only global environment that we are sure is a "safe operating space" for the complex, extensive civilization that Homo Sapiens has constructed'. A stable environment is seen here as the prerequisite for development. The Holocene gave 'humanity ... the freedom to pursue long-term social and economic development'. According to Steffen, the 'overarching long-term goal for humanity' requires that the earth system remain in a 'Holocene-like' state. In concrete terms, Jan Zalasiewicz and Mark Williams point to the crucial role of sea levels in fostering complex societies. The relative stability of sea levels over the last five thousand years has permitted the

---

[4]   Johan Rockström, Will Steffen et al. (2009), 'A Safe Operating Space for Humanity', *Nature*, 461, 24 September; Will Steffen, Jacques Grinevald, Paul Crutzen and John McNeill (2011), 'The Anthropocene: Conceptual and Historical Perspectives', *Philosophical Transactions of the Royal Society A* 369 842–867; cf. Will Steffen, Åsa Persson, Paul Crutzen et al. (2011), 'The Anthropocene: From Global Change to Global Stewardship', *Ambio*, 1–23; Will Steffen and Johan Rockström (2015), 'Planetary Boundaries: Guiding Human Development on a Changing Planet', *Nature*, January 2015.
[5]   'Anthropocene' International Geosphere and Biosphere Programme. http://www.igbp.net/globalchange/anthropocene.4.1b8ae20512db692f2a680009238.html.

build-up of fertile sediments on coastal plains and in river deltas across the planet. Such 'additions to the terrestrial landscape' have been 'most amenable for human life' by spurring intensive agriculture, population growth, urbanization and coastal trade.[6]

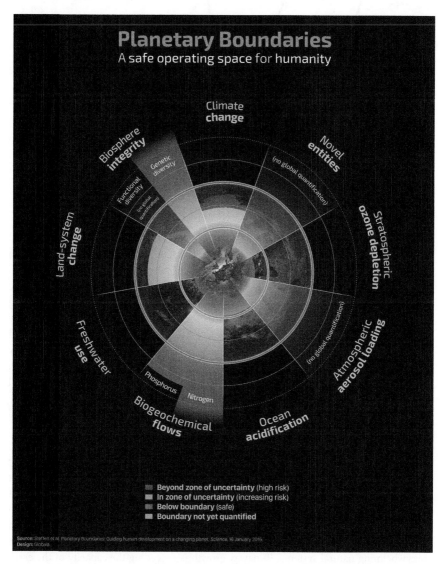

**Figure 6.2** Planetary Boundaries: A safe operating space for humanity. *Source*: https://www.stockholmresilience.org/research/planetary-boundaries.html. F. Pharand-Deschênes/ Globaïa

[6] Steffen et al., The Anthropocene: From Global Change to Global Stewardship, p. 9; Jan Zalasiewicz and Mark Williams 2012, *Goldilocks Planet: The 4 Billion Year Story of Earth's Climate*, 211–213, Oxford University Press.

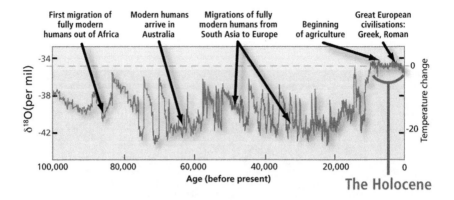

**Figure 6.3** Graph from the International Geosphere-Biosphere Programme website on the 'Anthropocene'. *Source*: Downloaded 16 March 2017. http://www.igbp.net/globalchange/anthropocene.4.1b8ae20512db692f2a680009238.html.

It follows from the argument about climatological stability that the 'environmental envelope' of the Holocene made possible not only sedentary agrarian society but also (in conjunction with fossil fuels) the Industrial Revolution and the Great Acceleration. During the Holocene, economic development did not yet interfere with the basic functions of the earth system (the economy was growing within a 'safe operating space'). Although anthropogenic changes in the earth system became increasingly common during the early decades of the Great Acceleration, it still enjoyed a level of environmental stability comparable to the late Holocene. In part, this relatively easy entry into the Anthropocene can be attributed to the temporal lag between carbon dioxide emissions and their material effects. Such generational lags have been a central feature of Anthropocene experience so far.

The Planetary Boundaries framework shifts the old debate about scarcity and abundance into a new register by placing waste and pollution in the context of earth system processes. The 350 ppm boundary for carbon dioxide concentration in effect asks us to imagine how abundance creates environmental risk. The Great Acceleration generates waste products and pollution of such magnitude and at such a high rate of change that they cannot be absorbed by natural systems on a timescale meaningful to humans. What we used to think was infinite and inexhaustible – the ocean and the atmosphere – turn out to be all too finite. This notion of planetary sinks can be understood as a new form of scarcity, conceived not as a shortage of resources but as a problem of man-made waste overwhelming natural systems. Runaway growth is exceeding the capacity of the earth system to absorb harmful pollutants. To counter this threat, some observers call for an ethos and policy of precautionary abstention. Affluent consumers need to leave what remains of our fossil fuels – coal, oil and natural gas – unused in the ground.[7]

---

[7]   Natural sinks might be engineered to absorb increased levels of waste and pollution, for example through bio-energy with carbon capture and storage (BECCS). The Paris Agreement includes an

The idea of the carbon sink must be understood in the context of the carbon cycle. Over the span of geological time, the amount of carbon in the atmosphere has fluctuated greatly. Through natural processes such as volcanic eruptions and chemical weathering, carbon has moved from the atmosphere and back into the lithosphere. Since life on earth requires carbon as a fundamental building stone of all organic structures, plant species form a major carbon sink by means of photosynthesis. Ancient plant life in turn has become coal, gas and oil deposits in the lithosphere through processes of compression and sedimentation. When humans burn fossil fuels, they release ancient carbon back into the atmosphere in the form of carbon dioxide. Another significant sink for carbon can be found in the earth's oceans. So far, the oceans have played an important role in diverting anthropogenic carbon dioxide from the atmosphere. Yet climate change also threatens this process. Carbon dioxide dissolves in seawater through a chemical reaction with a molecule called carbonate ion ($CO3-2$). But with rising levels of carbon dioxide in the atmosphere, there is not enough carbonate ion in the seawater to absorb the excess. At the same time, oceanic acidification diminishes marine life and therefore curtails its capacity to take up excess carbon dioxide.[8]

Climate change and new forms of land use are also threatening the diversity of life on the planet. Biodiversity is a foundational kind of resource, arguably more significant than any kind of mineral stock in maintaining the human economy and the biosphere itself. Will Steffen insists that biodiversity is as crucial as a stable climate for human development. Charles Langmuir and Wally Broecker single out biodiversity as the 'ultimate nonrenewable resource'. While it is true that life on the planet has survived multiple mass extinctions, the recovery of biodiversity occurred on a geological rather than a historical timescale. From a human perspective, a mass extinction event would create a novel form of biological and ecological scarcity through the rapid reduction of the number of species and viable ecosystems. Since biodiversity is so crucial to the human economy, biological scarcity would probably produce severe economic scarcity of different kinds as well. In the updated account of the Planetary Boundaries framework, Will Steffen and Johan Rockström call attention to two different aspects of biodiversity. The first trait is genetic diversity, which gives the biosphere the capacity to adapt to 'abiotic change'. The second dimension of biodiversity captures the range, distribution and abundance of 'functional traits' in ecosystems. What matters here is not just the absolute survival or extinction of a population but its relative distribution across ecosystems. Ecologists warn that many populations face 'biological annihilation' as their range is dramatically curtailed and their numbers drop precipitously. While the fate of the charismatic megafauna intermittently enters the public spotlight, most people will not spare more than a passing thought for

---

ambitious programme of carbon sequestration, the construction of artificial sinks over coming decades. But it is currently unclear whether these technologies can deliver results on a scale that matches the emerging threats. Another problem here is that negative emissions technologies might themselves produce carbon emissions.

[8] David Archer (2009), *The Long Thaw: How Humans Are Changing the Next 100,000 Years of Earth's Climate*, Princeton University Press, pp. 104–113; Charles H. Langmuir and Wally Brockner (2012), *How to Build a Habitable Planet: The Story of Earth from the Big Bang to Humankind*, 606, Princeton University Press.

more foundational life forms like insect pollinators or phytoplankton. The Planetary Boundaries framework incorporates proxy measures for the depletion of biological and ecological diversity, including the global extinction rate and the biodiversity intactness index (BII).[9]

***

The protection of biodiversity and other Planetary Boundaries requires an integrated approach. The study of how the planet became habitable has emerged as a unified field of investigation under the name of earth system science. We can trace this aspiration back to the conjectural histories of the planet presented by the Enlightenment naturalist Comte de Buffon and the Romantic explorer Alexander von Humboldt. But as a formal field, earth system science came into its own during the Cold War with the advent of satellite monitoring and computers capable of processing large quantities of data. Not by coincidence, NASA led the way in pioneering an integrated approach. Earth system science logically extends to the field of astrobiology, which inquires into the habitability of other planets and the evolution of life across the universe.[10]

In the Anthropocene literature, the growth of climate science in the post-war era is characterized as a pivotal moment in the unfolding of a new planetary consciousness.

Libby Robin and her colleagues Paul Warde and Sverker Sörlin argue that the modern concept of the 'environment' emerged at the beginning of the Great Acceleration. The experience of global environmental change brought on a new understanding of the vulnerability of the biosphere to human influence. Increasingly, the future of the planetary environment became an object of quantitative expertise and prediction.[11]

The discourse on the Anthropocene introduces a new politics of nature. The practical point of declaring the coming of a new epoch is to urge citizens to maintain the biosphere in a condition as close to the Holocene as possible. The Planetary Boundaries framework expands on this precautionary norm by setting forth a quantitative and multidimensional model of environmental risk. Will Steffen and Johan Rockström recommend a regime of 'planetary stewardship' to safeguard biodiversity and other vital earth system processes. Humans have to 'take responsibility' for the impact of the global economy on the earth system. Stewardship also carries a moral obligation of 'social equity'. Developing countries need assistance in leapfrogging to renewable

---

[9]   Will Steffen et al. (2011), 'The Anthropocene: From Global Change to Planetary Stewardship', *Ambio*, 40: 747; Langmuir and Brockner, *How to Build a Habitable Planet*, pp. 593–594; Johan Rockström and Will Steffen (2015), 'Planetary Boundaries: Guiding Human Development on a Changing Planet', *Nature*, 347 (6223), 13 February; Gerardo Ceballas, Paul Erlich and Rodolfo Dirzo (2017), 'Biological Annihilation via the Ongoing Sixth Mass Extinction Signaled by Vertebrate Population Losses and Declines', *Proceedings of the National Academy of Science*, 114 (30).

[10]  Clive Hamilton and Jacques Grinevald (2015), 'Was the Anthropocene Anticipated', *The Anthropocene Review*, 2 (1): 59–72; Paul Edwards, *A Vast Machine: Computer Models, Climate Data, and the Politics of Global Warming*, Cambridge, MA: MIT Press, 2010.

[11]  Will Steffen, Paul J. Crutzen and John McNeill, 'The Anthropocene: Are Humans Now Overwhelming the Great Forces of Nature', *Ambio: A Journal of the Human Environment*, 36 (8): 617 Table I; Libby Robin, Sverker Sörlin, and Paul Warde, *The Future of Nature: Documents of Global Change*, Yale University Press, 2013.

energy sources, while rich countries must voluntarily cut their fossil fuel emissions. But beyond such abstract ethical language, there is no serious attempt to elucidate what kind of government is best fit to turn these ideals and forecasts into policy.[12]

Some critics fear that the Anthropocene might become a Trojan horse for authoritarian forms of government. In a nod to Michel Foucault's concept of biopolitics, Christophe Bonneuil and Jean-Baptiste Fressoz warn that the 'geo-power' of the Anthropocene leaves little room for democratic practice. There is indeed a striking absence of conventional liberal concepts in this discourse – one looks in vain for any discussion of justice and law, virtue and rights. However, on a more charitable reading, such omissions could also be understood as pragmatic concessions in the face of intractable international divisions. The exquisite vagueness of the term 'stewardship' leaves maximum space for unorthodox political alliances.[13]

On the face of it, the norms of the Anthropocene might appear quite conservative. After all, the task of 'stewardship' (itself a term derived from ancient religion) is to keep the global economy within 'Planetary Boundaries' and return the biosphere to a 'Holocene-like state'. Such a precautionary model rejects the standard narrative of the Industrial Revolution, viewing it not as the great liberation from the shackles of nature, but a Pandora's jar that carries devastating unintended consequences. The time lags involved in the history of carbon emissions also carry a certain conservative implication. It took more than a century to discover and confirm the carbon footprint of industrial capitalism. What other dangers might be unleashed by our present technologies in the future?[14]

Clive Hamilton rightly observes that Anthropocene politics involves a world-making project. The discovery that humans pose a basic threat to the vital functions of the earth system represents a fundamental watershed in human politics and culture. There is no turning back from this moral responsibility. But to be effective, the new 'super-agency' requires knowledge and action on a planetary scale. To purge fossil fuels from the economy and reorient it towards renewable energy will require sweeping social change informed by scientific expertise. Moreover, this project must necessarily be indefinite in temporal terms. The Planetary Boundaries are presumably permanent and will therefore need to be policed indefinitely.[15]

In his 2002 manifesto 'The Geology of Mankind', Paul Crutzen calls for 'scientists and engineers to guide society towards environmentally sustainable management'. The aim is to change 'human behavior at all scales'. The blueprint for global sustainability published in 2016 by Paul Hawken is fully in keeping with Crutzen's manifesto. It envisions a hundred ways to reduce the carbon footprint of the world economy, from small changes in everyday behaviour to the introduction of epic new technologies. Among Hawken's 'coming attractions' are marine permaculture, solid-state wave

---

[12] Steffen et al., 'The Anthropocene': The Problem of Inequality is Implicit in Paul Crutzen's Early Work on 'Geology of Mankind', *Nature*, 415, 3 January 2002.

[13] Christophe Bonneuil and Jean-Baptiste Fressoz (2013), *L'Événement Anthropocène*, Seuil.

[14] For the image of Pandora's jar and the Industrial Revolution, see E. A. Wrigley (2010), *Energy and the Industrial English Revolution*, Cambridge: Cambridge University Press.

[15] Clive Hamilton (2017), *Defiant Earth: The Fate of Humans in the Anthropocene*, 64, 121, Malden, MA: Polity Press.

energy, hydrogen-boron fusion, direct air capture and enhanced weathering of minerals. The latter two technologies would increase carbon capture through the making of artificial sinks.[16]

As it happens, Anthropocene science has already produced a self-consciously cornucopian ideology of its own. The 'ecomodernist' group associated with the Breakthrough Institute – including its leaders Ted Nordhaus and Michael Shellenberger – has proposed that the Anthropocene should be seen in a positive light, not as a tragic deviation from Holocene stability but rather as an opportunity for technological creativity and cultural flourishing: in short, an age of abundance rather than scarcity. This anti-declensionist view of the future is accompanied by an exuberant account of human adaptation in the Pleistocene. The geographer Erle Ellis insists that the entire period of the Holocene should be renamed the Anthropocene in recognition of how deeply humans have transformed the biosphere in the past. More recently, Ellis and paleoecologist Mark Maslin have pushed the starting point even further back into the Pleistocene. Proposing a starting date for the Anthropocene around 50,000 years ago, they note that 'human social and cultural capacities to alter its environmental processes' have 'accumulated' and 'scaled up' in 'complex and historically contingent ways' ever since. In a similar spirit, the Hall of Human Origin at the Smithsonian Museum of Natural History, an exhibit funded by the David H. Koch foundation, presents human evolution as a series of adaptations to prehistoric climate change. Material constraints here serve as foils for biological and technological innovation. The instability of climate in the Pleistocene epoch figures not as an impediment to complex society but as the crucible for what we might call a transcendental form of ingenuity.[17]

The structural analogy between the Pleistocene past and the Anthropocene future rests on a series of controversial assumptions. By starting the Anthropocene in the Pleistocene, Erle Ellis and Mark Maslin reject the special significance of the climatological stability of the Holocene. They also conflate two dramatically different landscapes of human development. Why should evolutionary adaptation in a virtually unpopulated world serve as a credible model for life in the Anthropocene? Other ecomodernists tend to downplay the political, technological and ethical difficulties surrounding a transition to renewables. Because they assume that high growth rates will be possible in the foreseeable future, they show little interest in problems of environmental justice. The power of human ingenuity will overcome those apparent limits.

In sharp contrast, the most vocal advocates of Planetary Boundaries invoke the stability of the Holocene as a foundation of human flourishing. The connection

---

[16] Crutzen, 'Geology of Mankind', 23; Paul Hawken (ed.) (2016), *Drawdown: The Most Comprehensive Plan Ever Proposed to Reverse Global Warming*, New York: Penguin.

[17] Ted Nordhaus, Michael Shellenberger and Jenna Mukuno (2015), 'Ecomodernism and the Anthropocene', *Breakthrough Journal*, Summer; Erle Ellis et al. (2016), 'Involve Social Scientists in Defining the Anthropocene', *Nature*, 7 December, corrected 13 January 2017; Ruth Defriez (2014), *The Big Ratchet: How Humanity Thrives in the Face of Natural Crisis*, Basic Books; for critical commentary, see Ian Angus, 'Another Attack on Anthropocene Science'. http://climateandcapitalism. com/2017/01/24/another-attack-on-anthropocene-science/; William J. Burroughs (2005), *Climate Change in Prehistory: The End of the Reign of Chaos*, Cambridge University Press.

between sea levels and civilization suggested by Mark Williams and Jan Zalasiewicz provides a powerful case in point. Stable coastlines have been critical for the development of complex societies, in terms of agricultural productivity, population growth, urbanization and commerce. If ocean levels rise dramatically, much of coastal civilization will be in jeopardy. Hundreds of millions of people will be displaced. Major agricultural regions will be inundated, creating scarcity of arable land and food. Some of the greatest cultural treasures on the planet Earth will also be destroyed.[18]

Such a tragic understanding of Holocene stability is strongly connected to a normative subtext. The Planetary Boundaries model implies that the Holocene provided a uniquely benign environment. In ethical terms, the model assumes a strong fit between the natural and the social world: the development of civilization is tied to the accident of a brief climatological epoch in the history of the planet. But this aggregate picture of the Holocene as the 'environmental envelope' of 'civilization' contains a developmental bias. The advocates of Holocene stability are committed to preserving the type of society that emerged at the end of the Holocene, that is, regimes dedicated to scientific rationality and bureaucratic management (we should remind ourselves again that these texts shy away from explicit discussions of the merits of liberal democracy and particular forms of political economy). Ironically, the rise of these scientific and managerial forms of rationality in the late Holocene was closely tied to the windfall of fossil fuel energy and the rise of cornucopian expectations about economic growth. Will Steffen and Johan Rockström suggest in their 2009 essay, 'A Safe Operating Space for Humanity', that human civilization must be reoriented towards the biophysical context of development according to the principles of 'ecological economics'. Yet at the same time, they also emphasize the possibility of growth *within* the Planetary Boundaries: 'The evidence so far suggests that, as long as the thresholds are not crossed, humanity has the freedom to pursue long-term social and economic development.' However, in a more recent article on planetary stewardship, Steffen and his co-authors seem to take a more pessimistic perspective, citing John McNeill's classic environmental history *Something New under the Sun*.

> A core value of post-World War II contemporary society is ever-increasing material wealth generated by a growth-oriented economy based on neoliberal economic principles and assumptions, a value that has driven the Great Acceleration but that climate change and other global changes are calling into question.

So far, the Planetary Boundaries approach has mostly avoided hard questions about the distribution of the ecological footprint and environmental justice. It sets aggregate boundaries, but does not comment on the social distribution of emissions. How can

---

[18] Zalasiewicz and Williams, *Goldilocks Planet*, pp. 211–213. Another way to assess the significance of the 'environmental envelope' of the Holocene would be to examine the impact of rapid climate change on food production, including drought and heat tolerance in different crops. This investigation should also extend to topics such as insect pollination and freshwater availability.

an equal level of development become available to all people on the planet without disrupting the basic cycles of the earth system?[19]

We are left with a series of vexing challenges. The push to keep the earth system in a 'Holocene-like state' requires large-scale social and technological change. But the imperative of technological transformation might also pave the way for ideologies that prioritize technical fixes over more fundamental social change. This problem is compounded by closely related issues of ethical comportment and social psychology. Late Holocene ideologies tend to associate social status and psychological well-being with constant consumption, material abundance and indefinite economic growth ('affluenza'). What are the political prospects for an alternative outlook that favours simple living and slow growth or even stationary economies? In politics, technological innovation is commonly associated with boldness, progress and hope. But does an optimistic view of the Anthropocene ignore and conceal the true nature of the new epoch? Conversely, can a tragic sense of the Anthropocene sustain deeper social change and a reorientation of the economy towards justice and care? Much will depend on the nature of the responses to the unfolding crisis. Will the Anthropocene give rise to new social movements and cultural forms or will it simply perpetuate the culture and politics of the late Holocene?[20]

---

[19] W. Steffen and J. Rockström (2009), 'A Safe Operating Space for Humanity', *Nature*, 461: 474–75; Steffen et al., The Anthropocene: From Global Change to Global Stewardship, p. 13; John McNeill, *Something New under the Sun: An Environmental History of the Twentieth Century World*, W.W. Norton, 2000; Amitav Ghosh (2016), *The Great Derangement: Climate Change and the Unthinkable*, University of Chicago Press.

[20] On the perils of optimistic thinking in the Anthropocene, see Clive Hamilton (2014), 'The Delusion of the "Good Anthropocene": Reply to Andrew Revkin', 17 June. http://clivehamilton.com/the-delusion-of-the-good-anthropocene-reply-to-andrew-revkin/.

# 7

# The Great Resources Myth

David Rutledge

## Introduction

World energy production has increased dramatically since the Second World War. Figure 7.1 shows the historical production, split into coal, hydrocarbons and alternatives. Hydrocarbons here include oil, natural gas and natural gas liquids. Alternatives are everything else. Initially this meant fuelwood. Hydroelectric generating plants came on line in the 1880s and nuclear power began in the 1950s. More recently, wind turbines, solar photovoltaics and biofuels have become significant. As shown in Figure 7.1, there is a noticeable drop in hydrocarbon production in the years after 1979. In 1979, the Shah of Iran was deposed, and the following year Saddam Hussein led Iraq in an attack on Iran. Oil production in both countries collapsed, and the price of oil more than doubled. Since then world hydrocarbon production has risen at a slower pace. This does not necessarily mean that the total production of hydrocarbons in the long run will drop, but it does indicate that production will be drawn out. Decision-makers often make the assumption in speaking that climate policy can make coal and hydrocarbon production drop. So far, there is little evidence to support this. The most important international agreement to limit coal and hydrocarbon carbon dioxide emissions has been the Kyoto Agreement, which was signed in 1997 and in force through 2012. There is no hint of a drop in coal and hydrocarbon production during that period in Figure 7.1 or even a deceleration.

The goal of this chapter is to estimate how much coal and hydrocarbons will be burned in the long run and the time frame. The time is important for considering the transition to alternatives. Our approach is based on curve fits to the production histories. We will compare the results with reserves and with the business-as-usual scenario used by climate scientists in their climate models. This scenario is called RCP8.5, where RCP stands for Representative Concentration Pathway.

Figure 7.2 shows the data in Figure 7.1, re-plotted on a per-person consumption basis. There is a common pattern as a new source is introduced. First consumption rises. Then there is a shock, like a war or an accident, and the consumption levels out. For example, from 1926 until the Iranian Revolution, hydrocarbon production per person increased by ten times. But since 1979, production has stayed around 1toe per person. Coal production per person rose steadily in the years before the First

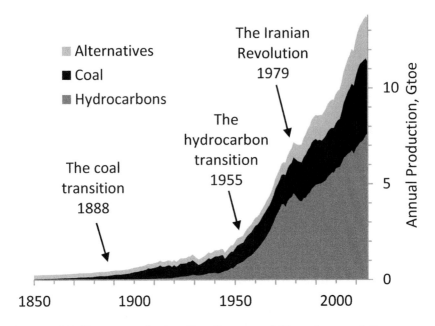

**Figure 7.1** World energy production. *Note*: Gtoe means billions of tonnes of oil equivalent. The toe is taken to be 42 GJ. *Source*: Data from the BP *Statistical Review*,[1] the Food and Agricultural Organization of the United Nations,[2] Arnulf Grubler[3] and Brian Mitchell.[4]

World War, but was relatively flat afterwards at 0.4 toe per person until 2000, when lower-income countries, especially China, began a build-out of their electrical grids. In the 1950s, the conventional wisdom was that nuclear power would replace coal and hydrocarbons when the oil fields and coal mines played out. In 1956, M. King Hubbert suggested that nuclear power could pass oil in the United States by 2000.[5] In Isaac Asimov's 1951 science fiction tale *Foundation*, nuclear power dominates at all levels from planetary supplies to personal reactors. Initially, nuclear electricity generation did grow at a rapid rate, 30 per cent per year annualized from 1965 to 1975.[6] But after the Chernobyl explosion in 1986, this stopped. Following the Fukushima core meltdowns in 2011, nuclear power may have entered a declining phase.

[1] BP (2017), *Statistical Review of World Energy*. Available from: http://www.bp.com/en/global/corporate/energy-economics/statistical-review-of-world-energy.html (accessed 14 August 2017).
[2] Food and Agricultural Organization of the United Nations (FAO), FAOSTAT online data base. Available from: http://faostat.fao.org/ (accessed 14 August 2017).
[3] Arnulf Grubler (2003), *Technology and Global Change*, Cambridge: Cambridge University Press.
[4] Brian Mitchell (2007), *International Historical Statistics*, 5th edition, Basingstoke: Palgrave Macmillan.
[5] King Hubbert 1956, *Nuclear Energy and the Fossil Fuels*, Publication 95, Houston, TX, Shell Development Company. Available from: http://www.hubbertpeak.com/hubbert/1956/1956.pdf (accessed 14 August 2017).
[6] BP, *Statistical Review of World Energy*.

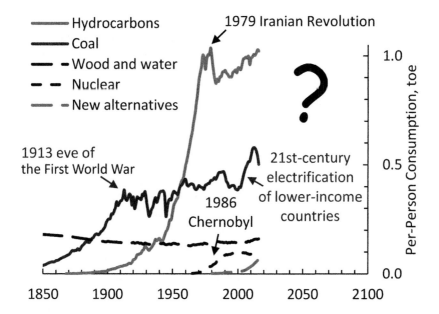

**Figure 7.2** World per-person energy consumption. *Source*: Population from the United Nations Population Division.[7] *Note*: New alternatives are all alternatives except for nuclear and hydroelectric power.

Many governments encourage the development of new alternatives to fossil fuels, particularly wind and solar power for electricity and biofuels for transportation. Wind and sunshine are variable and only partly predictable. We do not know how an electricity grid dominated by wind turbines and solar panels would actually work. The solar contribution in 2016 was still small, only 1.3 per cent of the world's electricity,[8] although the share of production reached 10 per cent in sunny California.[9] Nevertheless, the fundamental solar resource is enormous, and the solar capacity growth rate is spectacular, 50 per cent on an annualized basis from 2006 to 2016.[10]

## British coal

British coal is a good test case because the production cycle is essentially complete. The UK was the dominant coal producer in the nineteenth century and there was an intense debate at that time about its long-term coal supplies. Economist Stanley Jevons

[7]   United Nations Population Division. Available online from: http://www.un.org/en/development/desa/population/publications/index.shtml (accessed 14 August 2017).
[8]   BP, *Statistical Review of World Energy*.
[9]   California Energy Commission. Available from: http://www.energy.ca.gov/almanac/electricity_data/electricity_generation.html (accessed 14 August 2017).
[10]  BP, *Statistical Review of World Energy*.

started the discussion with his 1865 book, *The Coal Question*.[11] At that time the UK accounted for a remarkable 73 per cent of the world's cumulative production. Before Jevons, people had typically calculated a static lifetime based on the current production. In modern language this is the reserves-to-production ratio, or $R/P$ ratio. The British $R/P$ ratio, according to Edward Hull, the pre-eminent coal geologist of the day, was a reassuring 1,100 years.[12] However, Jevons deduced that production had been rising at 3.5 per cent per year. Further, he argued that production would continue to rise in this exponential fashion, and that the increase would become unsustainable sometime in the twentieth century. A Royal Commission was appointed to study the issue. Their report, published in 1871, was a stinging rebuke of Jevons and a classic example of a bureaucracy doubling down.[13] Hull had assumed a minimum seam thickness of 2 feet down to a depth of 4,000 feet, but the Commission decided on a 1-foot minimum down to 4,000 feet. Such seams were not mined then; they are not mined now. This raised the estimate of mineable coal from Hull's 81 Gt (billion metric tons) to 149 Gt. In addition, they rejected Jevons's assumption of exponential growth in favour of a gentle rise. The Commission estimated that coal would run out in 2231. With minor revisions, the Commission's estimate formed the basis for the British reserves for a hundred years.

Figure 7.3 shows what actually happened. As Jevons predicted, British coal production continued to rise, albeit at a slower rate. By 1913, production had reached 292 Mt. The annualized growth rate between 1865, when Jevons published his book, and 1913 was 2.2 per cent per year, compared with the 3.5 per cent/year growth that Jevons observed. In the following year, 1914, war erupted in Europe, and 40 per cent of the miners of military age volunteered for military service.[14] The 1913 output was never exceeded. Production has been falling ever since, the decline halted by neither the 1946 nationalization by Clement Atlee's Labour government nor the 1994 privatization by John Major's Conservative government. In 1972 there were 803 active longwalls.[15] The last British longwall, Kellingley Colliery, shut down in 2015. British coal is done except for a handful of tiny drift mines and some small short-term surface mines.

Jevons was sketchy in his perception of the course of the production decline, but he was correct in his prediction that the time frame for significant future production was closer to a hundred years than a thousand years. On the other hand, the Royal Commission failed spectacularly in its resource estimate. The cumulative production through 2016 is 27.5 Gt, only 18 per cent of the Commission's 149 Gt. The collapse

---

[11] Stanley Jevons (1866), *The Coal Question; An Inquiry concerning the Progress of the Nation, and the Probable Exhaustion of our Coalmines*, 2nd edition, revised, London: Macmillan and Co.

[12] Edward Hull (1861), *The Coal-Fields of Great Britain*, 2nd Edition, London: Edward Stanton.

[13] Royal Commission (1871), *Report of the Commissioners Appointed to Inquire into the Several Matters relating to Coal in the United Kingdom*, Vol. 1, London: the Royal Stationery Office, Her Majesty's Stationery Office.

[14] Barry Supple (1987), *The History of the British Coal Industry. 1913–1946 The Political Economy of Decline*, Oxford: Oxford University Press.

[15] William Ashworth (1986), *The History of the British Coal Industry, Vol. 5, 1946–1982, the Nationalized Industry*, 80, New York: Oxford University Press.

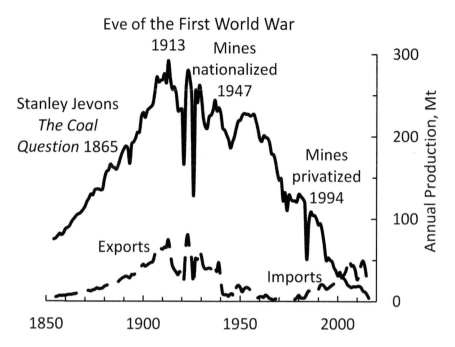

**Figure 7.3** The history of British coal production.[16,17] *Note:* At the peak in 1913, the UK was the world's largest coal exporter, exporting 33 per cent of its production. By 2015, imports had reached 85 per cent of consumption.

in production was associated with great social stress, with strikes by Arthur Scargill's National Union of Mineworkers against the Conservative governments of Edward Heath in 1972 and 1974 and Margaret Thatcher in 1984. The thrashing Thatcher gave the miners left a legacy of bitterness that lingers today.

## Characterizing resources

We distinguish between reserves, resources and occurrences (Figure 7.4). Reserves are coal and hydrocarbons that are *proved* by a measurement within a specified distance and *economic*, meaning that someone could make money by producing them. Modern reserves are quoted on a recoverable basis, where an allowance is made for the coal and hydrocarbons that will be left behind when production has ended. For resources, we require that the coal and hydrocarbons be economically interesting, with a significant chance that they will be produced in the future. Otherwise they are occurrences.

[16] BP, *Statistical Review of World Energy*.
[17] Mitchell, *International Historical Statistics*.

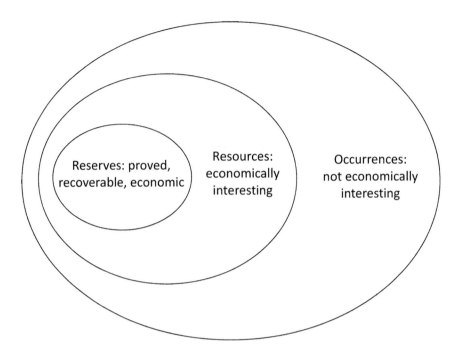

**Figure 7.4** Criteria for reserves, resources and occurrences.

The first detailed survey of world coal reserves was published in 1913 for the 12th International Geological Congress in Toronto. The reserves were updated for the World Power Conference in 1924 and then again in 1929. Beginning in 1936, this was put on a more regular basis with a series of *Statistical Yearbooks*. These surveys used the same criteria for seam thickness and depth as the Royal Commission, and like the Commission, it was intended that the reserves be appropriate as an estimate of future production. The work has continued to the present under the World Energy Council (WEC). Recently, it was published every three years as the *Survey of World Energy Resources*.[18] The last survey was published in 2013, 100 years after the Toronto meeting. The WEC surveys are the most important historical reference for world coal reserves, and other listings are primarily derived from them.

For hydrocarbon reserves, we will use the BP *Statistical Review* series that started in 1981.[19] The situation with oil and gas reserves is quite different from coal. Coal is a rock. It is often visible at outcrops, and this makes it easy to identify most of the major coal fields. By contrast, oil and gas are located in geological traps. These are hard to find and new fields are still being discovered. Unlike coal reserves, hydrocarbon reserves have generally not been taken to be appropriate as estimates of future production.

---

[18] World Energy Council (WEC), various editions of *Survey of Energy Resources* and the earlier *Statistical Yearbooks* of the World Power Council, The more recent surveys are available online at: https://www.worldenergy.org/publications/ (accessed 14 August 2017).

[19] BP, *Statistical Review of World Energy*.

## Production curve fits

For our projections, we will work with the cumulative production, $q$, where we add up annual production numbers as we go along. Cumulative production curves are typically s-shaped, although sometimes new technology or a new market will cause a second cycle. We define the ultimate production, $U$, as the total production in the long run, past and future. Until the last well is plugged or the last mine is sealed, $U$ must be estimated rather than calculated directly. We write the time when the cumulative production has reached 0.9 $U$ as $t_{90}$. This time is an appropriate way to answer the question, "How long will oil last?" By $t_{90}$ production is often collapsing, and this is associated with economic stress. For British coal, $t_{90}$ was 1973, at a time of miners' strikes. Our projections for $U$ and $t_{90}$ are based on a logistic model for the cumulative production. The approach is to linearize the cumulative production with the logit transform. The details are given in a 2011 paper in the *International Journal of Coal Geology* by the author.[20] We imagine ourselves in the position of a Victorian engineer making a new projection for $U$ each year. These calculations would certainly have been possible at that time. The logistic function was invented by P.F. Verhulst in 1838 to make projections for national populations.[21] However, no one thought of applying the logistic function to coal production then. The historical evolution of the projections for $U$ are shown in Figure 7.5. They are unstable in the early years, but they settle down after 1871. The transition is indicated in the figure by a shift from a dashed curve to a solid line. The projections form a damped oscillation with the actual cumulative production approaching from below. The projections have a ±19 per cent range, and it is clear that this range will capture the actual value of $U$.

After they have stabilized, the projections are satisfactory, but what can we say about the evolution of reserves? In Figure 7.6, we compare the projections with the reserves history. The plot shows original reserves, which are the sum of reserves and cumulative production. Before 1968, the reserves are minor updates of the Commission's numbers. However, in 1968, the reserves collapsed from 169 Gt to 16 Gt. This crash of reserves is a common feature in mature coal regions. It signals a transition in the basis of the reserves accounting from all the qualified coal in the country to just the coal that is within the grasp of the existing mines. The shift acknowledges the lack of opportunities for new mines.

For the UK, reserve estimates were available very early in the production cycle. However, they were much higher than the eventual production and they stayed high. On the other hand, the projections for $U$ from curve fits to the cumulative production stabilized before the peak in production and the range of the projections captures the actual production.

[20] David Rutledge (2011), 'Estimating Long-term World Coal Production with Logit and Probit Transforms', *International Journal of Coal Geology*, 85: 23–33. Available from: http://www.sciencedirect.com/science/article/pii/S0166516210002144?via%3Dihub (accessed 14 August 2017).
[21] Pierre Verhulst (1838), 'Notice sur la loi que la population suit dans son accroissement', *Mathematique et Physique*, 113–121.

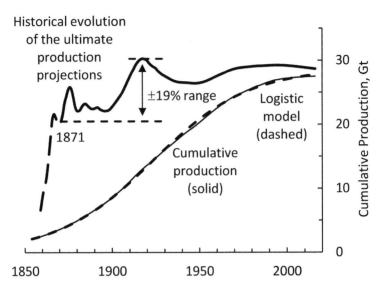

**Figure 7.5** Historical evolution of the projections for the ultimate production, *U*, of British coal. *Note*: The logistic model is also shown for comparison with the cumulative production.

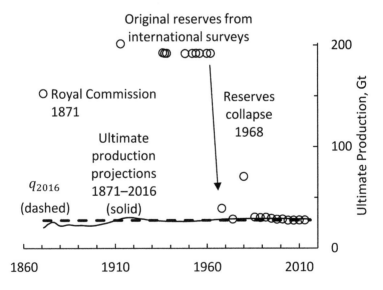

**Figure 7.6** Evolution of the projections for the long-term production, *U*, of British coal compared with reserves reported in international surveys.[22] *Note*: The cumulative production for the appropriate year is added to the reserves to make them comparable to the projections. These are labelled as original reserves. Hull's estimate and that of the Royal Commission are also shown.

[22]  World Energy Council, *Survey of Energy Resources*.

**Table 7.1** Projections vs reserves in mature coal regions

| Region | Cumulative production, $q$, Gt (2016) | Cumulative production fraction of original reserves, $q/R_o$ (reserves year) | Ultimate production projection range, $\Delta U$, Gt (starting year) | % of peak production at $t_{90}$ ($t_{90}$) |
|---|---|---|---|---|
| United Kingdom | 27.5 | 18% (1871) | 20.5–30.3 ±19% (1871) | 45% (1973) |
| German hard coal | 12.1 | 5% (1913) | 8.8–12.7 ±18% (1946) | 53% (1985) |
| France and Belgium | 7.2 | 23% (1913) | 4.3–8.5 ±33% (1900) | 58% (1970) |
| Pennsylvania anthracite | 5.0 | 42% (1921) | 3.1–5.1 ±24% (1900) | 41% (1952) |
| Japan and South Korea | 3.6 | 21% (1936) | 2.6–4.0 ±20% (1946) | 63% (1986) |
| Median percentages | na | 21% | ±20% | 53% |

The German classification of hard coal (*Steinkohle* in German) includes both bituminous coal and anthracite. German hard coal statistics are from the Statistik der Kohlenwirtschaft.[23] Other production data from the BP *Statistical Review*[24] and Brian Mitchell.[25] Reserves from the surveys of the World Energy Council.[26]

It turns out that the British pattern is typical. Table 7.1 shows the data from the UK and four other mature coal regions. For each of these regions the current annual production is less than 1/1000 of the cumulative production. The middle column shows that the small fraction of the early reserves that the UK has produced is comparable to others. The median fraction is 21 per cent. The highest is 42 per cent, from the Pennsylvania anthracite fields. In addition, the projections for the long-term production have captured the actual value for each region. For the entire group, the median projection range was ±20 per cent. The table also shows how large the production was at $t_{90}$ compared to the peak production. The median is 53 per cent of the peak, with a range of 41 to 61 per cent. This means that at $t_{90}$, production is likely to be about half of the peak value. It is interesting that for France $t_{90}$ was 1970. Not coincidentally, in 1974, France started an aggressive nuclear power programme. The lowest share of the original reserves produced is German hard coal, with only 5 per cent. What makes this interesting is that German hard coal production has been subsidized for many decades at several times the world market price. One might have expected the fraction produced to be higher than 42 per cent yield for the Pennsylvania anthracite mines, which have not had government subsidies. Shutting down a German mine is a political decision, not an economic one. The schedules are negotiated years in advance. The last two mines, Prosper-Haniel and Ibbenburen, are set to shut down in 2018, and that will be the end of more than 200 years of coal mining in the Ruhr. This behaviour is different from hydrocarbons, where it is common for the early reserves to

---

[23] German hard coal production statistics are from the Statistik der Kohlenwirtschaft e.V. Available from: http://www.kohlenstatistik.de/ (accessed 14 August 2017). The data for the early years were obtained by email correspondence with the agency.
[24] BP, *Statistical Review of World Energy*.
[25] Mitchell, *International Historical Statistics*.
[26] World Energy Council, *Survey of Energy Resources*.

be less than the production that follows. Technology plays a different role for coal and hydrocarbons. For oil and gas, horizontal drilling and fracking have recently increased production in oil and gas reservoirs and made production possible in source rocks that could not be economically produced previously. For coal, improved longwall mining technology has reduced recovery because it is less flexible than the manual working it replaced. On the other hand, labour productivity and safety improved dramatically with longwall mining.

## Active coal regions

We can extend this analysis to the active coal mining areas of the world. Table 7.2 shows the results for ten active regions that, together with the previous mature regions, cover the earth. For two regions, the curve fitting process failed to converge mathematically. These are Latin America and Asia. Asia as defined here excludes China, Japan, South Korea and Asiatic Russia, because these are included in other regions. For these two cases, we use the original reserves as an estimate of future production. Note that historically, original reserves have been higher than the subsequent production. This introduces a high bias to our world projection for $U$. By far the highest ultimate is for China, 32 per cent of the world ultimate. For comparison, China accounted for 46 per cent of the coal produced in the world in 2016. China also differs from the others in that $U$, 254 Gt, is considerably greater than original reserves, 174 Gt. The problem here is that China has only rarely responded to the WEC surveys. The Chinese reserves date from 1992. It is a fair observation that the Chinese have shown less interest in surveying and reporting reserves than Europeans and Americans. There is a more recent reserves estimate from the Chinese National Bureau of Statistics in 2003. In this case, the reserves, 189 Gt, plus 2003 cumulative production, 37 Gt, is 226 Gt, which is closer to the projection of 254 Gt.

The table gives a world total calculated by adding up the regional results, including the mature coal regions. How long will the world's coal last? $t_{90}$ is 2066. The projection for $U$ is 784 Gt, including a cumulative production of 368 Gt. $U$ amounts to 64 per cent of the reserves plus cumulative production, which is 1,220 Gt. Figure 7.7 shows how the projections and world reserves have evolved over time. Several factors have reduced the reserves with time. Early reserves were based on a limited number of measurements, often on outcrops, and it was often assumed that the coal seams were shallow and continuous over great distances. Later more detailed surveys have revealed areas where the seams had been eroded away. Other seams were in geological basins, or synclines, where the seams were too deep to work. Many countries used the seam criteria established by the Royal Commission at first. Over time countries adopted more conservative seam criteria and recovery factors. The U.S. reserves serves as a good example of this evolution. In 1913, the reserves were 4 Tt. In 2013, the reserves were 237 Gt. American coal reserves fell by 94 per cent in 100 years. On the other hand, the projections have been reasonably stable, with the projections varying in a ±9 per cent range since 1998.

**Table 7.2** Projections vs reserves for the active coal regions of the world

| Region | Cumulative production, $q$, Gt (2016) | Ultimate production projection, $U$, Gt | Original reserves, $R_o$, Gt | Ultimate production projection range, $\Delta U$, Gt | $t_{90}$ projection |
|---|---|---|---|---|---|
| Australia | 14 | 45 | 88 | 27–48±28% | 2072 |
| China | 79 | 254 | 174 | 145–254 ±27% | 2063 |
| Africa | 10 | 16 | 41 | 13–16±9% | 2065 |
| Europe | 78 | 115 | 178 | 82–119 ±18% | 2067 |
| Russia | 30 | 48 | 221 | na | 2064 |
| Western US | 20 | 38 | 162 | 38–51 ± 15% | 2047 |
| Eastern US | 51 | 72 | 144 | 72–78 ± 4% | 2064 |
| Canada | 4 | 5 | 10 | 5–6 ± 14% | 2036 |
| Asia | 25 | na | 117 | 81–117 ±18% | 2075 |
| Latin America | 3 | na | 18 | 12–24 ±33% | 2084 |
| World (including mature regions) | 368 | 784 | 1,220 | 659–784 ±9% | 2066 |

Cumulative production is calculated through 2016. The projection ranges are calculated since 1996. For Asia and Latin America, the ranges reflect the changes in the reserves during this period. The Russian projection is based on production in Soviet times, and there is no modern range. Production data from the BP *Statistical Review*[27] and Brian Mitchell.[28] Reserves from the surveys of the World Energy Council.[29]

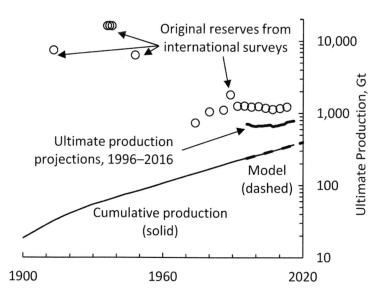

**Figure 7.7** Evolution of the projections for the ultimate production, $U$, of world coal compared with the original reserves. *Note*: The model curve is the sum of the fifteen individual regional logistic models. Note the logarithmic scale.

[27] BP, *Statistical Review of World Energy*.
[28] Mitchell, *International Historical Statistics*.
[29] World Energy Council, *Survey of Energy Resources*.

## Hydrocarbons

Next we turn to hydrocarbons. We start with the hydrocarbon data in Figure 7.1 and apply the same procedure to make projections that we did for coal. In this case it is interesting to show the linearized plot (Figure 7.8). The effect of the slowdown after the Iranian Revolution is a change in slope of the plot, which is associated with a delay in $t_{90}$ from 2041 to 2080.

Figure 7.9 shows how the projections and reserves have evolved for hydrocarbons over time. In contrast to coal, for hydrocarbons $U$ is higher than the original reserves. Hydrocarbon reserves have increased steadily. In recent years, world oil reserves increases have been dominated by the Canadian tar sands and Venezuelan Orinoco heavy oil. Their share of world reserves increased from 4 per cent in 1998 to 23 per cent in 2016.[30] In the 1970s, the major OPEC (Organization of the Petroleum Exporting Countries) producers nationalized their oil fields. In the following years, they increased their oil reserves dramatically. At that time there were discussions about basing production quotas partly on reserves, and this may have encouraged countries to raise their reserves. There has been a great deal of discussion of whether the OPEC reserves increases were justified, but there were no definitive answers.

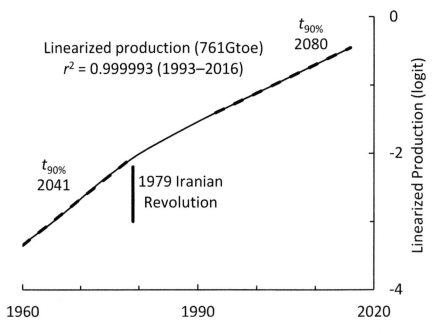

**Figure 7.8** World hydrocarbon production linearized by the logit transform with the optimized value of $U$, 761 Gtoe. *Note*: The projection for $U$ is found as the value that gives the highest value of $r^2$ (square of the correlation coefficient) from 1993 to 2016. The dashed lines are trend lines that give projections for $t_{90}$.

---

[30] BP, *Statistical Review of World Energy*.

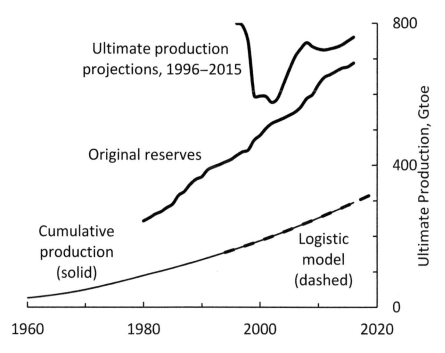

**Figure 7.9** Evolution of the projections for the ultimate production of hydrocarbons, compared with the BP reserves.[31]

**Table 7.3** Combining the results on an energy basis, with coal converted to toe at 2t/toe.

| | Cumulative production, Gtoe | Ultimate production projection, Gtoe | $t_{10}$ | $t_{90}$ | Original reserves, Gtoe |
|---|---|---|---|---|---|
| Hydrocarbons | 295 | 761 | 1977 | 2080 | 688 |
| Coal | 184 | 392 | 1947 | 2066 | 610 |
| Combined | 479 | 1,153 | 1970 | 2076 | 1,298 |

*Note*: Cumulative production is through 2016. The time $t_{10}$ is the year that the cumulative production reached $0.1U$.

Table 7.3 shows the projections for hydrocarbons and coal and the total, while Table 7.4 gives the same information in terms of carbon dioxide emissions. Note that the projection for ultimate production for coal in energy terms is only 52 per cent that of hydrocarbons. This reflects the fact that hydrocarbon production passed coal in energy terms in 1955, and there is no sign that this will change in the future. Coal has a higher carbon coefficient than oil and gas, but the $CO_2$ emissions are still somewhat higher for oil and gas. The exhaustion time $t_{90}$ for hydrocarbons and coal together is almost the same in terms of energy and carbon, 2076 vs 2075.

[31] Ibid.

**Table 7.4** Combining the results on a carbon-dioxide emissions basis using the carbon coefficients in the 2015 BP *Statistical Review*[32]

|  | Cumulative production, GtC | Ultimate production projection, GtC | $t_{10}$ | $t_{90}$ | Original reserves, GtC |
|---|---|---|---|---|---|
| Hydrocarbons | 216 | 583 | 1977 | 2080 | 527 |
| Coal | 199 | 423 | 1947 | 2066 | 659 |
| Combined | 415 | 1,006 | 1968 | 2075 | 1,186 |

*Note*: Cumulative production is through 2016.

## Alternatives

A $t_{90}$ for fossil fuels of 2076 should be associated with an increasing share for the alternatives. Figure 7.10 shows the alternatives share over time. In 1850, it was 83 per cent. Energy in 1850 meant fuelwood, mostly. For a hundred years after 1850, the share for alternatives decreased steadily, first because of coal in the 1800s and then later because of oil and gas. The alternatives finally bottomed out at 10 per cent

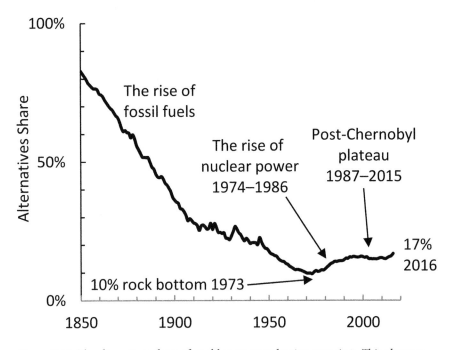

**Figure 7.10** The alternatives share of world energy production over time. This plot uses the same data as in Figure 7.1. This is shares of all energy, not just electricity.

[32] Ibid.

in 1973, the year of the Yom-Kippur War and Arab boycotts. Afterwards alternatives grew because of the build-out of nuclear power plants, reaching 14 per cent by 1986, the year of the Chernobyl disaster. From 1987 until 2015, alternatives were on a plateau at 15±1 per cent. Alternative electricity capacity has been added, particularly in wind and solar generation. Wind and solar together reached 5 per cent world of electricity generation in 2016. However, this has been offset by a declining electricity share for nuclear power from 16 per cent in 1986, the year of Chernobyl, to 11 per cent in 2016. And the electricity grid is the good news for alternatives. In comparison, the biofuels share of energy consumption in 2016 was only 0.6 per cent[33] and electric vehicles were only 0.5 per cent of 2016 American vehicle sales. The most popular vehicle, the Ford F pickup, outsold the most popular electric vehicle, the Tesla Model S by 28:1.[34] All of this means that it is difficult to say how the shares of the alternatives will evolve.

However, we can deduce something about the costs. Governments often argue that switching to alternatives will save consumers' money. For example, in the fact sheet for President Barack Obama's proposed Clean Power Plan, it was stated that consumers would see energy bills reduced by $85 per year in 2030.[35] Europe is much farther along in wind and solar electricity generation than the United States is. How are European residential electricity prices faring? Figure 7.11 shows residential electricity prices versus wind and solar capacity in OECD Europe countries. Generally speaking, the countries with higher per-person wind and solar capacity also have higher residential electricity prices. The highest prices are more than twice the lowest ones. European households typically spend the equivalent of $1000 per year on electricity. The problem with high residential electricity prices is that some people in cold places will have trouble paying for heating and some people in hot places will forgo air conditioning.

We can use the data to deduce a wind and solar surcharge, $s$, per kilowatt hour. One way to proceed is to imagine a mythical OECD Europe country that has no wind and solar generation, a European Kentucky. The dashed line in the figure is a regression line. The relationship is tight enough ($r^2 = 0.79$) that we can take the $y$-intercept of the regression line as an estimate of the price of residential electricity in this mythical country. This gives 16¢/kWh for the no-wind, no-solar price. We can compare this with the average population-weighted price of residential electricity for these countries. For this we need the residential electricity consumption, which is given in the IEA's 2016

[33] Ibid.
[34] American electric vehicle sales. Available from: http://insideevs.com/monthly-plug-in-sales-scorecard/ (accessed 14 August 2017). Other vehicle sales are from the WSJ Market Data Center. Available from: http://online.wsj.com/mdc/public/page/2_3022-autosales.html (accessed 14 August 2017).
[35] Barack Obama (2015), fact sheet. Available from: https://www.whitehouse.gov/the-press-office/2015/08/03/fact-sheet-president-obama-announce-historic-carbon-pollution-standards (accessed 14 August 2017).

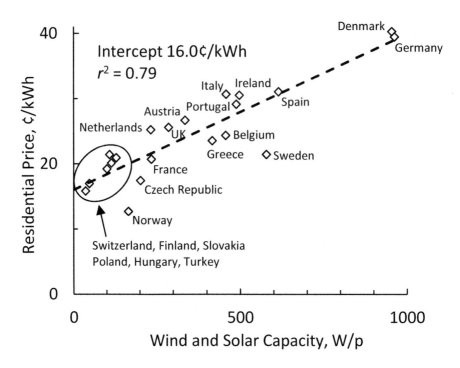

**Figure 7.11** Residential electricity prices calculated at market exchange rates, plotted against the per-person wind and solar capacity.[36] These are the OECD Europe countries that are tracked in the BP *Statistical Review. Source*: The residential electricity prices are taken from the IEA's 2016 *Electricity Information*,[37] the wind and solar capacity from the BP 2016 *Statistical Review*[38] and populations from the United Nations Population Division.[39] *Note*: All values are for 2014, except for residential electricity prices for Spain, which were not available. Spanish prices are from 2011, adjusted with a 2014 deflator.

*Electricity Information*.[40] This works out to 26¢/kWh. We associate the difference, 10¢/kWh, with wind and solar power and divide by the wind and solar generation share in these countries, 10 per cent in 2014.[41] This gives

$$s = 10¢/\,kWh\,/10\% = \$1/\,kWh$$

for the wind and solar surcharge. No European government tells their citizens that wind and solar energy are costing consumers an extra dollar per kilowatt hour. However, that is what the data indicate. On the contrary, governments typically calculate the cost of

[36] David Rutledge (2015), 'Will the President's Clean Power Plan Save Consumers Money'. Available from: https://judithcurry.com/2015/08/10/will-the-presidents-clear-power-plan-save-consumers-money/ (accessed 14 August 2017).
[37] International Energy Agency (IEA) (2016), *Electricity Information*, Paris, France.
[38] BP, *Statistical Review of World Energy*.
[39] United Nations Population Division.
[40] International Energy Agency, *Electricity Information*.
[41] BP, *Statistical Review of World Energy*.

generating electricity from a solar panel or a wind turbine that is isolated from the grid. Customers, on the other hand, need access to an electrical grid 24 hours a day. Electricity must be supplied when the wind does not blow and the sun does not shine. Shadow generators and transmission lines must be added to balance the wind and solar generators.

## Discussion

The critical observation in this chapter is that for the five mature coal regions, the median ultimate production is only a fifth of the early reserves. It is easy now to see what went wrong. The criteria that the Royal Commission adopted in 1871, a minimum seam thickness of 1 foot and a maximum depth of 4,000 feet, were too optimistic. Today most underground production comes from longwall mines. In longwall mining, there is a line of self-advancing roof supports that shield a shearing machine that progresses back and forth across the coal face. Longwall mining is safer and more efficient than hand hewing, but it requires a seam thickness of a metre and a level block of several square kilometres to be economic. Another factor that contributes to exaggerated reserves is government influence. Coal reserves are the responsibility of government bureaucracies and governments take pride in having large reserves. While an oil company is penalized severely in the stock market for overstating reserves, there is no penalty for a government that does the same thing. It was similar when OPEC countries nationalized their oil fields in the 1970s. Previously their reserves came from international oil companies. After the national oil companies took over, OPEC oil reserves doubled over the next twenty years.[42] A final factor is that fossil fuel production, particularly underground coal mining, must be acceptable to the society on the surface. Producing a two-metre seam causes substantial subsidence. In earlier times when many of the people in the town above had fathers and brothers working underground, the disturbance was acceptable. The miners' pay put food on the table. However, now the mining operations are substantially automated, and many of the people above are government workers who do not feel they are dependent on the mine. When the social support breaks down, it becomes difficult to get a permit to open a new mine. When there are no new mines in a country, the end is just a matter of time. The existing mines work out the resources within the twenty-kilometre radius of the access shaft where the faces can be ventilated, and then they shut down, one by one. The shafts are filled in to stabilize the sites, and the network of roadways collapses. There is no going back.

The conventional wisdom is that there are long time constants in the atmospheric carbon cycle and in the climate system. This means that the critical input for climate models is the ultimate production of fossil fuels, projected here as 1006 GtC. Our projection is completely different from the IPCC's business-as-usual scenario, RCP8.5, where total fossil-fuel carbon-dioxide emissions are 5.6 TtC.[43] Coal dominates the

---

[42] Ibid.
[43] IIASA, RCP data base. Available from: http://www.iiasa.ac.at/web-apps/tnt/RcpDb (accessed 14 August 2017).

emissions in the scenario and a large multiple of the coal reserves would be burned.[44] This is contrary to the historical experience that only a small fraction of early coal reserves are consumed. This means that the models greatly overestimate the climate impact of burning fossil fuels.

## Concluding thoughts

Fossil fuels differ from the other scarce commodities discussed in this book. The supply of fossil fuels is finite, and it was recognized early that at some point we will move away from fossil fuels. The historical production data for fossil fuels are comprehensive, and this makes it possible to validate mathematical models that describe their eventual exhaustion. Moreover, there has been intense worldwide interest and support for developing alternatives that have lower environmental impacts than fossil fuels.

Logistic projections differ from the typical reports that energy economists produce like the BP *Energy Outlook 2035*.[45] The energy outlooks use much shorter time frames, typically twenty years rather than the sixty years implied by $t_{90}$. The twenty-year time frame is too short for considering the transition to alternatives or the impacts of climate change. In addition, the energy outlooks are essentially demand models with little consideration given to resource scarcity. Logistic projections can work with a longer time frame, and they allow a resource to become scarce.

In electronic engineering the rise time of a voltage pulse is conventionally calculated as the difference between the time that the voltage reaches 90 per cent and 10 per cent of the final value. We can calculate a projected fossil-fuel era lifetime in this fashion as the difference between $t_{90}$ and $t_{10}$. In Table 7.3, this gives 106 years. From the perspective of human history, the fossil fuel era will be brief. We just happen to be in it. That said, a $t_{90}$ of 2076 for fossil fuels indicates that scarcity is not imminent, even though it is true that at times gasoline may be more expensive than commuters might like. An aggressive renewables programme should not be justified on the basis of concern about the scarcity of world fossil fuels.

In the years since 2000, electricity has arrived for hundreds of millions of people. A working electrical grid brings an enormous improvement in the quality of life. Communities can power pumps and filters to provide clean water, eliminating many diseases. Food can be refrigerated all the way from the wholesaler to the home to prevent spoiling. A hospital can run an operating room. Families can fend off the heat and cold. The agent of their deliverance has been coal, because it is the cheapest of the fossil fuels. Nevertheless, it was the policy of the Obama administration to discourage

[44] Keywan Riahi, Shilpa Rao, Volker Krey, Cheolhung Cho and Vadim Chirkov, Guenther Fischer, Georg Kindermann, Nebojsa Nakicenovic, Peter Rafaj (2012), 'RCP 8.5, A Scenario of Comparatively High Greenhouse Gas Emissions', *Climatic Change*, 109: 33–57.

[45] BP (2016), *Energy Outlook 2035*. Available from: http://www.bp.com/en/global/corporate/energy-economics/energy-outlook.html (accessed 14 August 2017).

construction of coal power plants in low-income countries in favour of alternative sources of energy.[46]

It should be appreciated that the transition to alternatives will be expensive and slow. Germany is often considered exemplary in its alternatives programme, but its experience is also a warning. In 2004, wind and solar power contributed 1.8 per cent of German primary energy consumption. Ten years later, in 2014, the wind and solar share had risen to 6.8 per cent.[47] For this modest increase, German residential electricity prices rose from 0.17€/kWh to 0.30€/kWh.[48]

For a global perspective, we return to Figure 7.1. In the figure, the alternatives share for world energy in 1996 was 16 per cent. Twenty years later, after more than three trillion dollars[49] have been spent on renewables, the share was 17 per cent. It should be appreciated that the main cost is not the wind turbines and the solar panels, but the rest of the system. A major factor that contributes to the cost is that every watt of wind and solar power must be induced by a government programme. If the price of electricity were the only criterion, the worldwide capacity of wind and solar would be zero. At some point in the future, we must shift to alternatives, but for now we are in the position of St Augustine, who wrote "Grant me chastity and continence, but not yet."

[46] John Kerry (2014), 'Remarks on Climate Change', 16 February, in Jakarta. Transcript available from: https://2009-2017.state.gov/secretary/remarks/2014/02/221704.htm (accessed 14 August 2017). Video available from: https://food-health-vika.com/video/P-yDzHApXiw/Secretary-Kerry-Delivers-Remarks-on-Climate-Change-in-Indonesia/ (accessed 14 August 2017).

[47] BP, *Statistical Review of World Energy*.

[48] International Energy Agency, *Electricity Information*.

[49] International Energy Association (IEA) (2017), *World Energy Investment*, Paris, France. This publication gives world investments in renewables for the electricity grid from 2000 to 2016 in Figure 1.2. Available from: https://webstore.iea.org/world-energy-investment (accessed 5 June 2018).

# 8

# Escapology, or How to Escape Malthusian Traps

Jörg Friedrichs

## Introduction

Thomas Malthus is the thinker of scarcity par excellence. He has received a bad press, but undeservedly so. As we will see, many problems of the contemporary era have a structure that is similar to the classical Malthusian problem of overpopulation. Hence, a Malthusian framework remains promising. The fundamental logic is simple enough: one function grows so fast that it exceeds the limits posed by another function, with overshoot leading to dire consequences.

For Malthus, the first function was population growth. In his view, population was growing faster than the second function – food production. The result was a particular form of scarcity, namely food scarcity, leading to disastrous consequences. Today, parallel cases abound. Environmental impact and greenhouse gas emissions (first function) exceed the earth's regenerative capacity and the capacity of the climate system to absorb greenhouse gases (second function). The likely consequences are environmental havoc and runaway climate change. They may turn out dreadful enough to deserve the epithet 'Malthusian'.

Malthus gave us helpful clues on how to think about the logical structure of such problems, but less so on how to escape them. This is a shortcoming, but it is no excuse for abandoning his framework. The Malthusian framework remains unsurpassed as a way of thinking about scarcity. Hence, abandoning it would seem unwise. Unpleasant as it may be to contemplate Malthusian traps, we should rather think harder about ways to escape them ('escapology').

In this chapter, I discuss a variety of Malthusian and neo-Malthusian traps, as well as ways of escaping them. Based on a model of the classical overpopulation trap, I discuss a variety of escape routes starting with the solutions and non-solutions suggested by Malthus (moral restraint, vice and misery), followed by strategies of shifting the problem to subalterns and outsiders, and culminating in cornucopian solutions like exponential industrial growth and technical progress.

Subsequently, I move to the neo-Malthusian challenges of the contemporary era, from climate change to energy scarcity.[1] After a brief outline of the traps threatening the foundations of contemporary industrial civilization, I survey conceivable ways of dealing with them. In doing so, I revisit the escape routes discussed previously and ponder which of them, if any, may be available, eventually in a modified form, to deal with looming scenarios of neo-Malthusian crisis.

## The Malthusian trap

Malthus's *Essay on the Principle of Population* (1798) has an oft-quoted statement that neatly summarizes his theory: 'Population, when unchecked, increases in a geometrical ratio. Subsistence increases only in an arithmetical ratio.'[2] The basic idea is that population grows exponentially, but the growth of a society's means of subsistence is only linear. Linear growth in food supply cannot make up for the skyrocketing needs of an exponentially growing population. Conversely, exponential growth of population outpaces the linear increase of subsistence. As population grows faster than subsistence, food intake per capita shrinks inexorably. At some point, population growth runs against the hard limit posed by minimum food intake per capita – with tragic results.

Malthus was aware that population can temporarily exceed its long-term limits. For example, there can be good harvests for twenty or thirty years. In that case, population levels may exceed the long-term subsistence base. Malthus cautioned, however, that this can happen only for so long. The longer such overshoot lasts, the greater the overpopulation. With growing overpopulation, the famine bound to occur after a bad harvest will then be even more devastating. If the famine is not sufficient to decimate population to a viable level, then other calamities such as war and pandemics may do so. A combination of famine, war, pandemics and deviant behaviour ('vice and misery') will decimate population to a level consistent with the means of subsistence until the cycle starts anew.[3]

During his lifetime, Malthus re-proposed his theory several times: first in the two-volume version of the *Essay* of 1803 and then in further iterations, with the last edition appearing in 1826.[4] These modifications, however, left the model intact in all its axiomatic elegance (Figure 8.1).

---

[1]  For further details, see Jörg Friedrichs (2013), *The Future Is Not What It Used to Be: Climate Change and Energy Scarcity*, Cambridge, MA: MIT Press.

[2]  Thomas Malthus (1798), *An Essay on the Principle of Population, as It Affects the Future Improvement of Society*, 14, London: J. Johnson.

[3]  For further discussion, see Jörg Friedrichs (2014), 'Who's Afraid of Thomas Malthus?', in Michael J. Manfredo et al. (eds.), *Understanding Society and Natural Resources: Forging New Strands of Integration across the Social Sciences*, 67–92 at 68–70, New York: Springer.

[4]  Thomas Malthus (1826), *An Essay on the Principle of Population; or, A View of Its Past and Present Effects on Human Happiness*, London: John Murray; cf. Donald Winch (1987), *Malthus*, Oxford: Oxford University Press.

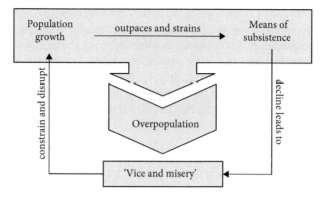

**Figure 8.1** The Malthusian trap.[5]

## Escape routes from the Malthusian trap

Logically speaking, the solution to the Malthusian problem is closing the gap between exponential growth in population and linear growth in subsistence. This can happen either through 'vice and misery' or through a managed solution. One way of achieving a managed solution is to constrain population growth. Another way is exponential growth in the means of subsistence. Malthus called for the former and discarded the latter, but modernity has shown that it is possible, at least temporarily, to increase agricultural yields at a pace exceeding population growth. Most of history has neither followed classical Malthusian nor modern cornucopian patterns. Instead, the most common way of dealing with the problem of overpopulation has been to shift the problem to subalterns and outsiders. Let us discuss these escape routes in turn.

### Moral restraint, vice and misery

Malthus himself contemplated one solution and two non-solutions to the overpopulation trap. His preferred solution was 'moral restraint', or the voluntary renouncement of procreation in a religiously correct and morally virtuous manner. He contrasted this with 'vice', or objectionable forms of non-reproductive sex. Failing population control, Malthus argued, the consequences were dire, leading to 'misery', or social calamities such as famine and war decimating the population.

By moral restraint, Malthus sought to control reproductive behaviour in ways acceptable to him as an Anglican. Married couples should engage in sexual moderation to curtail the number of their offspring, and non-married people should renounce sexual intercourse altogether. Malthus had a visceral dislike for 'vice', which included any form of controlling reproduction by means other than moral restraint. To him, social institutions such as prostitution and infanticide were immoral and hence unacceptable.

---

[5] Reproduced from Friedrichs, 'Who's Afraid of Thomas Malthus?', p. 70.

But was it realistic to expect people to control their reproductive instinct? Malthus had doubts about that. Tragically, 'misery' remained the most likely way for the system to return to equilibrium. For religious and humanitarian reasons, however, Malthus could not embrace misery because it relied on tragedy to run its course. He detested destructive forms of population decimation such as warfare, genocide, famine, pandemics and other calamities. By labelling the alternatives pejoratively as 'vice and misery', Malthus made clear that for him moral restraint was the only acceptable option.

### Depredation of subalterns

In restricting conceivable escape routes to moral restraint, vice and misery, Malthus overlooked the fact that humans have a habit of shifting problems that they cannot solve to their fellow humans. In the course of history, humans have developed two additional ways of escaping the Malthusian trap by shifting the burden to others: the depredation of subalterns and the depredation of outsiders.

Let us begin with the depredation of subalterns. A popular objection to Malthusian theory is that equality might somehow solve the problem of overpopulation and poverty. Critics claim that there is enough for all to go round if only food were distributed more evenly. Historically, the opposite seems to be the case. Inequality has been a solution to the Malthusian problem!

The history of institutionalized inequality started in a seemingly innocuous way, with affluent and hence 'complex' hunter-gatherer communities relying on the collection, storage and redistribution of surplus food. The strategy was for the community to store food as an insurance against famine.[6] Most typically, the people specializing in storage and the provision of other public goods would be 'big men' or priests, acting on behalf of commoners. In hunter-gatherer and other so-called primitive societies, those controlling food stocks were compelled to meet the expectations of their fellow tribespeople lest the latter would walk away or revolt against their leadership.[7] Originally, this conditional form of inequality amounted to a social bargain that benefited both sides. From a Malthusian perspective, it created a suitable buffer to protect the community as a whole if not from vice then at least from misery.

Inequality became institutionalized, or structural, when, with the Neolithic or agricultural revolution, property of land became private and privilege became hereditary, with more and more people extracting rents from other people rather than resources from nature.[8] Primitive accumulation enabled the upper echelons of 'civilized' societies – warriors and priests, bureaucrats and merchants – to amass capital, lock in privilege and thereby escape from the Malthusian trap.

---

[6]   Alain Testart (1982), 'The Significance of Food Storage among Hunter-Gatherers: Residence Patterns, Population Densities, and Social Inequalities', *Current Anthropology*, 23 (5): 523–537.

[7]   Marshall Sahlins (1963), 'Poor Man, Rich Man, Big-Man, Chief: Political Types in Melanesia and Polynesia', *Comparative Studies in Society and History*, 5 (3): 285–303.

[8]   Douglass C. North and Robert Paul Thomas (1977), 'The First Economic Revolution', *Economic History Review*, 30 (2): 229–241; Mary K. Shenk et al. (2010), 'Intergenerational Wealth Transmission among Agriculturalists: Foundations of Agrarian Inequality', *Current Anthropology*, 51 (3): 65–83.

To some degree, the elites kept using the resources extracted from the community to produce public goods. They bolstered their legitimacy and served their societies by investing in irrigation systems and distributing food rations during famine. Increasingly, however, they would have kept a handsome portion of the surplus for themselves. In extremis, this allowed them to ensure their own survival over and above that of the commoners. Chances of survival were stacked in favour of the elites by the fact that many of them had specialized in coercion.[9] Short of an invasion or mutiny, the elites had thus ensured themselves against the Malthusian trap.[10]

Agent-based modelling confirms that the emergence of inequality went hand in hand with Malthusian population dynamics.[11] Originally this worked best in those areas where agriculture relied on grain, which was easy to appropriate.[12] Since the beginnings of agriculture, the mechanisms have become more intricate, owing to higher levels of social differentiation and stratification. What is more, the exemptions from the Malthusian trap have come to extend far beyond the initial classes of warriors and priests, bureaucrats and merchants. Nevertheless, even in the contemporary era, famines arise in situations where food remains available in sufficient quantity to some but not others – far from refuting Malthusian theory, this is a result of problem shifting as outlined in this section.[13]

The bottom line is that structural inequality serves, at least in part, as a social buffer, or insurance policy, against the Malthusian trap. Elites seek privilege for many other reasons including sheer advantage, but inequality lies hidden in plain sight as a way to deal with the Malthusian problem.

## Depredation of outsiders

Having discussed the depredation of subalterns, let us move to the depredation of outsiders. The paradigmatic case is pastoral nomadism. Let me exemplify this by the evolution of nomadism on the Eurasian steppe, a model that may also apply to nomadic pastoralists in other world regions.[14]

---

[9] This is not to say that war and violence started with agricultural civilization. See Lawrence H. Keeley (1996), *War before Civilization: The Myth of the Peaceful Savage*, New York: Oxford University Press; Steven A. LeBlanc (2003), *Constant Battles: The Myth of the Peaceful, Noble Savage*, New York: St. Martin's Press.

[10] Serge Svizzero and Clement Tisdell (2014), 'Inequality and Wealth Creation in Ancient History: Malthus' Theory Reconsidered', *Economics & Sociology*, 7 (3): 222–239.

[11] Simon T. Powers and Laurent Lehmann (2014), 'An Evolutionary Model Explaining the Neolithic Transition from Egalitarianism to Leadership and Despotism', *Proceedings of the Royal Society B*, 281 (20141349).

[12] Joram Mayshar et al. (2015), 'Cereals, Appropriability and Hierarchy'. Barcelona GSE Working Paper No. 842.

[13] Amartya Sen (1981), *Poverty and Famines: An Essay on Entitlement and Deprivation*, Oxford: Clarendon.

[14] David W. Anthony (2007), *The Horse, the Wheel, and Language: How Bronze-Age Riders from the Eurasian Steppes Shaped the Modern World*, Princeton, NJ: Princeton University Press; Christopher I. Beckwith (2009), *Empires of the Silk Road: A History of Central Eurasia from the Bronze Age to the Present*, Princeton, NJ: Princeton University Press; Iver B. Neumann and Einar Wigen (2018), *The Steppe Tradition in International Relations: Russians, Turks and Eurasian State Building, 4000 BCE–2017 CE*, Cambridge: Cambridge University Press.

The origin of pastoral nomadism remains debated.[15] Regardless of the details, it must have occurred after the agricultural revolution when, due to decisive technological advances in farming, herding became an increasingly differentiated and spatially segregated activity.[16] Nomadic pastoralism may have emerged in Mesopotamia when settled agriculture became too intensive to allow for the presence of large herds on fertile lands, with segments of the population moving away from farming centres and specializing in animal husbandry.[17] Herdsmen migrated to marginal areas that were unsuitable for farming and became pastoral nomads. In the wilderness, pastoral populations were constrained by the number of their livestock, which in turn was constrained by how many animals their land base could support.[18] Their lifestyle allowed for a level of social complexity and organization that was impressive in and of itself, but could hardly rival the sedentary societies developing around the same time.[19] Importantly, however, pastoral nomadism awarded distinct military advantages. Horses were available in large numbers, and the entire tribe was mobile so that in a military campaign, it was not necessary to leave behind a garrison to protect cattle and kin.[20]

This is where the depredation of outsiders comes into play. As the ancient Greek historian Herodotus noted about the Scythians: 'Since they have no towns or strongholds, but carry their homes around with them on wagons, since they are all expert on using their bows from horseback, and since they depend on cattle for food rather than on cultivated land, how could they fail to be invincible and elusive?'[21] Owing to military prowess and supplemented by trade, including the taxation of caravans traversing the Silk Road, the depredation of outsiders enabled levels of social complexity and material wealth that the steppe would otherwise not have supported.

One of the consequences of this predatory strategy was a revised social bargain among nomads. Whereas previously nomadic leaders offered a stock of spare animals in exchange for the loyalty of their followers, now they offered access to wealth from neighbours to those willing to submit to their leadership so that, united, the nomads would become a formidable force. Well-organized nomadic hordes were able to raid their sedentary neighbours and extract tribute from them, as happened when the Scythians started looting Mesopotamia in the seventh century BC.

A few centuries later and further to the East, Central Asian tribes began a succession of at least fifteen nomadic empires and supra-tribal federations raiding China, starting

---

[15] Anatoly M. Khazanov (1994), *Nomads and the Outside World*, 2nd edition, Madison: University of Wisconsin Press, Chapter 2.

[16] Andrew Sherratt (1981), 'Plough and Pastoralism: Aspects of the Secondary Products Revolution', in Ian Hodder, Isaac Glynn and Norman Hammond (eds.), *Pattern of the Past: Studies in Honour of David Clarke*, 261–305, Cambridge: Cambridge University Press.

[17] Susan H. Lees and Daniel G. Bates (1974), 'The Origins of Specialized Nomadic Pastoralism: A Systemic Model', *American Antiquity*, 39 (2): 187–193.

[18] Neil Roberts (2014), *The Holocene: An Environmental History*, 3rd edition, 241–242, Chichester: Wiley-Blackwell.

[19] William Honeychurch (2014), 'Alternative Complexities: The Archaeology of Pastoral Nomadic States', *Journal of Archaeological Research*, 22 (4): 277–326.

[20] Neumann and Wigen, *The Steppe Tradition in International Relations*, Chapter 2.

[21] Herodotus (1998), *The Histories. Translated by Robin Waterfield*, Oxford: Oxford University Press, IV:46.

with the Xiongnu around 200 BC and ending with the final defeat and extermination of the Zunghars around 1750.[22] It is possible to see the interaction between China and its nomadic steppe neighbours as a case of competitive cultural coevolution, with the nomads preying on their sedentary neighbours.[23]

On the one hand, nomadic populations were constrained by their land base. On the other hand, they supplemented their subsistence base with agricultural products and luxuries acquired from neighbours through raiding, trading and the extortion of tribute. Together, raiding, trading and tribute worked as an effective insurance against the Malthusian trap of overpopulation.

## Depredation of subaltern outsiders

While it is possible to contemplate the depredation of subalterns and outsiders separately, they tend to occur in combination. Some societies predominantly rely on one form of depredation only, but the historical norm is the depredation of people who are *both* subalterns *and* outsiders.

Steppe nomads, for example, moved from the depredation of subalterns to the depredation of outsiders and then further to the depredation of subaltern outsiders. Initially, pastoral nomadism relied less on the depredation of outsiders than on inequality among nomads.[24] As in the case of advanced foragers and agricultural societies, this started as an insurance against Malthusian misery. While foragers and agricultural societies relied on storage, nomads relied on clan leaders holding a stock of surplus cattle that they would borrow from their followers during and after a famine. Inequality had advantages for both sides, although the elites must have benefited more. Commoners benefited from the fact that leaders would vouch for their survival in times of hardship, providing emergency aid and restocking their herds.[25] Leaders and their clans benefited even more: their lifestyle was lavish, and they were the last to starve. Structural inequality was ensconced in the social bargain between nomad leaders and their followers, and contributed to solving the Malthusian problem.[26]

As societies grew larger, sedentary civilizations became more hierarchical, whereas nomadic societies remained rather egalitarian. The reason was that herders could walk away and move to another part of the steppe when they felt their leaders were asking too much. Hence, even tribal leaders were mostly compelled to pursue a pastoral way of life rather than becoming rentiers, as was common in agricultural societies. This was disappointing for ambitious upstarts. What could an aspiring tribal leader do to obtain

[22] J. Daniel Rogers (2012), 'Inner Asian States and Empires: Theories and Synthesis', *Journal of Archaeological Research*, 20 (3): 205–256.

[23] Thomas J. Barfield (1989), *The Perilous Frontier: Nomadic Empires and China*, Cambridge, MA: Blackwell. See also Nicola Di Cosmo (2002), *Ancient China and Its Enemies: The Rise of Nomadic Power in East Asian History*, Cambridge: Cambridge University Press.

[24] Small hordes of herders exhibit similar material inequalities as small-scale agricultural societies. See Monique Borgerhoff Mulder et al. (2009), 'Intergenerational Wealth Transmission and the Dynamics of Inequality in Small-Scale Societies', *Science*, 326: 682–688.

[25] Anthony, *The Horse, the Wheel, and Language*, pp. 154–155.

[26] Foragers, farmers, herders – structural inequality originates in the provision of storage as a public good.

more resources and a more exalted status? He could raid outsiders, and preferably sedentary outsiders who had accumulated wealth and were easy to locate. Thanks to the depredation of outsiders, sedentary or otherwise, tribal leaders and their entourage were able to elevate themselves to a status that nomadic egalitarianism would otherwise not have supported.[27]

Territorial conquest took the arrangement to the next level. Given their military strength, nomads were in a position to spin off excess populations who would leave the steppe and become conquerors. The nomadic conquerors would then not only extract resources from the vanquished but also become their political overlords. In other words, they would move to the depredation of subaltern outsiders. China under Kublai Khan and Persia under Tamerlane are cases in point.[28]

This stands for a more general pattern prevailing in cases of conquest. If it is true that the Aryans managed to establish themselves as upper castes after their invasion of India many thousand years ago, then this must have protected their descendants from starvation and other Malthusian calamities while also increasing the plight of the lower castes. The same seems to apply for great migrations, whenever an invading population subdues an indigenous population. Similarly, classical empires from China to Rome and colonial empires from the Portuguese to the British have relied on military superiority to impose themselves on, and extract resources from, the populations brought under their control.

It bears emphasis that both the depredation of subalterns and of outsiders, as well as any combinations of the two, are particularistic solutions. They do not solve the Malthusian problem as such but shift it from certain individuals or groups to others. For example, the ability of elites in agricultural societies to extract resources from commoners insured them against the risk of starvation during a famine. Commoners, by contrast, could not count on the same level of food security. Similarly, the ability of nomads to loot resources from sedentary populations improved their own food security while aggravating the food insecurity of the sedentary populations, especially during a period of drought and famine. Hybrid solutions, such as empire-building and colonialism, similarly shift the burden from the well-to-do to those less fortunate, rather than addressing the problem as such.

## Cornucopian solutions

Malthus thought the only way to close the gap between the exponential growth of population and the linear growth of subsistence was to curb population. Industrial modernity has shown that it is also possible, at least temporarily, to close the gap by exponential growth in subsistence. The last two centuries have seen extended periods of exponential economic growth outpacing population growth and enabling a handsome increase in per capita wealth, defying Malthusian expectations.

---

[27] Neumann and Wigen, *The Steppe Tradition in International Relations*, Chapter 2.
[28] Ibid., Chapter 3.

It is important to note, however, that this has come on the back of resource exploitation and technical progress. Thanks to cheap energy and abundant raw materials, including fossil fuels and other mineral resources, humans escaped the Malthusian trap. Enhanced resource exploitation went hand in hand with technical progress since the Industrial Revolution.

Together, resource exploitation and technical progress have enabled an unprecedented increase of human carrying capacity. World population has grown from about 1 billion in 1800 to 7.34 billion in 2016. Although population growth has been faster than ever since the agricultural revolution, industrial society has temporarily abrogated the Malthusian trap of overpopulation.[29] The 'green revolution' of the 1970s has defused the 'population bomb'[30] for another two generations. Serial doublings of the economy, including enhanced agricultural yields, have produced the cornucopian notion that abundance is the norm and scarcity an unacceptable aberration and deviation from it.[31]

The mobility of people, goods and capital has further contributed to this happy state. In previous centuries, migration to 'underpopulated' landmasses such as America and the import of raw materials and foodstuffs from colonies mitigated the Malthusian problem for Europeans, typically at the expense of indigenous populations (depredation of subaltern outsiders). While migration remains attractive, there are hardly any underpopulated landmasses left and migrants now mostly move in reverse direction, from the Global South to the richer industrial North. International trade and capital flows also enhance global carrying capacity, although today globalization may be levelling off.

Due to the so-called demographic transition, world population is slowly moving away from patterns of exponential growth. Nevertheless, it is still on track to grow by more than half, from around 7.3 billion in 2013 to about 9.7 billion in 2050 and 11.2 billion in 2100.[32] Although fertility is now at or below replacement level in most parts of the world, the populations of most countries will continue to grow for a very long time due to so-called demographic momentum.[33] Even so, the world population is showing signs of moving towards a plateau over the coming century.

At first sight, this amounts to an impressive battery of cornucopian escape routes from the Malthusian trap: resource extraction and technical progress; globalization; and the demographic transition. Alas, most of these putative escape routes are temporary rather than permanent. Resources are limited, and technical innovation may stall.[34] Infinite growth on a finite planet is impossible. Globalization may level off or even

---

[29] Antony Trewavas (2002), 'Malthus Foiled Again and Again', *Nature*, 418: 668–670.

[30] Paul R. Ehrlich (1968), *The Population Bomb*, New York: Ballantine Books.

[31] H. Charles, J. Godfray et al. (2010), 'Food Security: The Challenge of Feeding 9 Billion People', *Science*, 327: 812–818.

[32] UN (2015), *World Population Prospects: The 2015 Revision*, New York: United Nations.

[33] Wolfgang Lutz and K.C. Samir (2010), 'Dimensions of Global Population Projections: What Do We Know about Future Population Trends and Structures?', *Philosophical Transactions of the Royal Society B*, 365: 2779–2791.

[34] Deborah Strumsky, José Lobo and Joseph A. Tainter (2010), 'Complexity and the Productivity of Innovation', *Systems Research and Behavioral Science*, 27 (5): 496–509.

disintegrate. The demographic transition may not withstand an epochal reversal of economic growth and a decline of modern accomplishments such as the education of women. If we imagine the demise of industrial society and related blessings, then most countries of today's world are hopelessly overpopulated. Malthus may turn out to be right after all.

The industrial era has created a 'fool's paradise' of sorts that temporarily abrogates the worst aspects of Malthusian tragedy. Once industrial civilization enters a terminal decline, the Malthusian problem of overpopulation may yet come to haunt humanity. To make a bad situation worse, the challenge is not just overpopulation but also a host of additional neo-Malthusian traps.

## Neo-Malthusian traps

Neo-Malthusian traps are problems that have the same logical structure as the classical Malthusian trap. One function ($f_1$) outpaces and strains another function ($f_2$). The system has some inertia built into it, enabling temporary overshoot. Given the inexorable decline of the second function, however, overshoot leads to significant systemic disruptions, ultimately constraining the first function and thus bringing the system back to equilibrium – but only after a devastating crisis (Figure 8.2).[35]

For example, greenhouse gas emissions may overwhelm the homeostatic regulation of the climate system. Fuel depletion may lead to a decline in production capacities, leading to a situation where declining supply cannot meet rising demand. In the meantime, overshoot may occur in the form of irreversible global warming and unsustainable levels of fuel consumption. This may then lead to catastrophic climate change and energy scarcity. Ultimately, some new equilibrium is unavoidable. However,

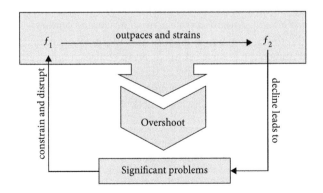

**Figure 8.2** The logical structure of Malthusian traps.[36]

---

[35] This section is a condensed version of Friedrichs, 'Who's Afraid of Thomas Malthus?', pp. 70–85.

[36] Reproduced from ibid., 71.

getting there may entail the demise of industrial society. The following neo-Malthusian theories follow this kind of logical template.

- *Environmental neo-Malthusianism.* According to ecological footprint analysis, overshoot results from society's environmental impact outpacing and straining ecosystem services, leading to environmental degradation and thus undermining the earth's regenerative capacity.[37] Unless society finds a way to reduce its impact to whatever ecosystem services are able to replenish, this is bound to lead to Malthusian calamities that are difficult to fathom and will force humanity's environmental impact back to sustainable levels.[38]
- *Climate-based neo-Malthusianism.* When greenhouse gas emissions outpace the ability of the climate system to absorb them, climate change may cause serious trouble to human civilization, which appears ill-prepared for more than 2°C of global warming. Especially when accompanied by positive reinforcements after possible tipping points,[39] human misery may ultimately force a reduction of climate stresses but the climatic perturbation may last for centuries and the social and political consequences are bound to be catastrophic.[40]
- *Energy-based neo-Malthusianism.* Given the heavy dependence of industrial society on energy, fossil fuel depletion may lead to a decline, or even reversal, of economic growth. Insofar as industrial civilization needs economic growth to be sustainable, some authors argue that fossil fuel depletion may trigger the demise of prevailing social and economic models, forcing a new equilibrium at lower levels of energy throughput. It may be possible to reach such an equilibrium in the long term, but only after a long emergency.[41]

The neo-Malthusian theories listed thus far are deceptively simple. They provide powerful narratives, but they are inadequate as tools for prediction and guidance. The environment, climate system and energy sector are more complex than suggested by such theories. Fortunately, it is possible to develop more sophisticated and fine-grained models. The following complex neo-Malthusian theories are of particular interest.[42]

- *Limits to Growth.* The seminal work by Donella Meadows and colleagues remains the most influential neo-Malthusian modelling exercise.[43] Both in the original

---

[37] Mathis Wackernagel and William E. Rees (1996), *Our Ecological Footprint: Reducing Human Impact on Earth*, Gabriola Island, BC: New Society.

[38] WWF (2016), *Living Planet Report 2016: Risk and Resilience in a New Era*, Gland: WWF.

[39] Timothy M. Lenton et al., 'Tipping Elements in the Earth's Climate System', *Proceedings of the National Academy of Sciences of the USA*, 105 (6) (2008): 1786–1793.

[40] Naomi Oreskes and Erik M. Conway (2014), *The Collapse of Western Civilization: A View from the Future*, New York: Columbia University Press.

[41] James Howard Kunstler (2005), *The Long Emergency: Surviving the Converging Catastrophes of the Twenty-First Century*, New York: Atlantic Monthly; John Michael Greer (2009), *The Ecotechnic Future: Envisioning a Post-Peak World*, Gabriola Island, BC: New Society Publishers.

[42] For further details, see Friedrichs, 'Who's Afraid of Thomas Malthus?', pp. 77–85.

[43] Donella H. Meadows et al. (1972), *The Limits to Growth: A Report for the Club of Rome's Project on the Predicament of Mankind*, New York: Universe Books.

study and its updates, the authors have simulated complex interaction effects not only for food and population but also for geological resources and pollution, as well as industrial output.[44]

- *Eco-scarcity Theory*. Thomas Homer-Dixon and colleagues have popularized the neo-Malthusian theory of eco-scarcity whereby land degradation and other environmental strains combine with population pressure to cause economic busts and migratory movements, unleashing political crises and violent conflict further down the line.[45] Zhang and colleagues have presented a model whereby climate change leads to reduced food supply per capita, triggering a complex cascade of interlocking calamities.[46] Zhang et al. tested their model on historical data from the premodern and early modern era. Others have developed similar theoretical models for the study of present and future climate change.[47]

- *Civilizational neo-Malthusianism*. According to Tainter's theory of diminishing returns on complexity, societies constantly face problems.[48] As societies devote resources to address these problems, their complexity increases. Tragically, there are diminishing returns on increasing complexity. Systemic collapse becomes almost inevitable if and when societies have depleted their reserve problem-solving capacity.[49]

## Escape routes from neo-Malthusian traps

Given the structural similarity between classical and neo-Malthusian traps, any possible escape routes are also likely to be structurally similar. Let us therefore revisit the escape routes from the classical Malthusian problem of overpopulation, discussed above. In doing so, let us examine to what extent it is possible to adapt these escape routes and make them work for the solution of the neo-Malthusian problems beleaguering humanity in the twenty-first century.

### Moral restraint, vice and misery

As we have seen, Thomas Malthus himself considered three responses to the challenge of overpopulation: moral restraint, vice and misery. Although the nature of the

---

[44] Most recently, Donella H. Meadows, Jørgen Randers and Dennis L. Meadows (2004), *Limits to Growth: The 30-Year Update*, White River Junction, VT: Chelsea Green.

[45] Thomas F. Homer-Dixon (1999), *Environment, Scarcity, and Violence*, Princeton, NJ: Princeton University Press.

[46] David D. Zhang et al. (2007), 'Global Climate Change, War, and Population Decline in Recent Human History', *Proceedings of the National Academy of Sciences of the USA*, 104 (49): 19214–19219; David D. Zhang et al. (2011), 'The Causality Analysis of Climate Change and Large-scale Human Crisis', *Proceedings of the National Academy of Sciences of the USA*, 148 (42): 17296–17301.

[47] Halvard Buhaug, Nils Petter Gleditsch and Ole Magnus Theisen (2010), 'Implications of Climate Change for Armed Conflict', in Robin Mearns and Andrew Norton (eds.), *Social Dimensions of Climate Change: Equity and Vulnerability in a Warming World*, 75–101, Washington, DC: World Bank.

[48] Joseph A. Tainter (1988), *The Collapse of Complex Societies*, Cambridge: Cambridge University Press.

[49] Temis G. Taylor and Joseph A. Tainter (2016), 'The Nexus of Population, Energy, Innovation, and Complexity', *American Journal of Economics and Sociology*, 75 (4): 1005–1043.

problems has changed considerably, the same classical responses are still discernible in political and academic discourse.

To begin with, the notion of moral restraint remains discernible. For example, environmentalists demand a lower ecological footprint, and environmental economists recommend a conscious strategy of de-growth.[50] These calls lack the theological overtones found in the work of Thomas Malthus, but what else are they if not exhortations for moral restraint? In the classical Malthusian domain of population studies, the idea of moral restraint is still identifiable. Accepted wisdom has it that the demographic transition results from an industrious work ethic where people devote more time to production and less to reproduction. There is evidence to show that educated women have fewer babies. This suggests that development and emancipation lead to moral restraint.[51]

The struggle against 'vice' is also still with us, although it comes in a different guise. Fifty years ago, Paul Ehrlich and others were calling for compulsory birth control as a way to defuse the 'population bomb'.[52] Since then, such intrusive methods have lost legitimacy in the public imagination. Even China is abandoning its one-child policy. Tampering with the reproductive rights of women meets increasing disapproval. Similarly, calling for poor developing countries to forego industrialization in the interest of climate stability sounds vicious from a moral point of view. While different from those made by Malthus, the arguments are still moralistic. One may relate this to a broad shift of contemporary sensitivities towards liberal norms.[53] (Note how this feeds into a cornucopian mindset. Industrious work ethic and related moral restraint does not only reduce birth rates but also boosts investment and growth, closing the Malthusian gap between population and subsistence from both sides.)

Like Malthus, pessimists emphasize that for all its desirability moral restraint seems unlikely. To them, hoping for voluntary de-growth and a deliberate reduction of the ecological footprint is seriously naïve given human nature and industrial lock-in. This leads some observers back to unpleasant scenarios of Malthusian misery. Such authors claim that a sustainability transition is unavoidable, but is likely to come with serious disruptions that risk bringing out the worst in humans.[54] These authors are not cynics. They agree that war, famine, pandemics and other forms of human misery are terrible scourges. Yet, in the absence of moral restraint, they may happen by default.

## Depredation of subalterns and outsiders

Like misery, the depredation of subalterns and outsiders seems outrageous to contemporary sensitivities. Depredation may persist under various guises, such as

---

[50] Peter A. Victor (2008), *Managing without Growth: Slower by Design, Not Disaster*, Cheltenham: Edward Elgar; Tim Jackson (2009), *Prosperity without Growth: Economics for a Finite Planet*, London: Earthscan; William Ophuls (2011), *Plato's Revenge: Politics in the Age of Ecology*, Cambridge, MA: MIT Press.

[51] Ole Jacob Sending and Iver B. Neumann (2006), 'Governance to Governmentality: Analyzing NGOs, States, and Power', *International Studies Quarterly*, 50 (3): 651–672.

[52] Ehrlich, *The Population Bomb*.

[53] Ian Morris (2015), *Foragers, Farmers, and Fossil Fuels: How Human Values Evolve*, Princeton, NJ: Princeton University Press.

[54] Kunstler, *The Long Emergency*; Greer, *The Ecotechnic Future*; Friedrichs, *The Future Is Not What It Used to Be*.

the exploitation of wage labour or unequal terms of trade between industrial and developing countries, but they appear as undesirable downsides of capitalism. Unlike in past historical epochs when the depredation of subalterns and outsiders was a source of pride to those who felt 'superior', they have become an embarrassment.[55] Nevertheless, in practical terms they remain available as escape routes from neo-Malthusian traps for those who are unscrupulous enough to shift the problem to less fortunate people and groups.

In its original form, the depredation of subalterns rested on a sedentary (agrarian) territorial order. In times of globalization, this has changed beyond recognition. Elites have become footloose, and the subalterns depredated can be located on the other side of the globe. This may change once again if neo-Malthusian challenges come to roost. Under such circumstances, elites may want to reterritorialize politics. It may become necessary for them to reassert their rule over discrete communities so that privileged status remains a boon in times of neo-Malthusian vice and misery.

For example, how will the rich be able to defend their luxury resorts in the face of a declining state monopoly of force and with migrants overrunning their compounds? There are two routes open to them. Some super-rich may be willing to move to a defensible position such as a Caribbean island and/or specialize in coercion by acquiring a private army, a strategy that would have to go far beyond the acquisition of bodyguards from a private security company. Others, which will include most members of the elite except for the super-rich, may not be willing or able to go down that route. They will need protection from a state-like entity enforcing law and order within a territory and determining the boundaries of the political community, that is, who counts as a legitimate citizen or resident and who does not. The support of the well-to-do for mass migration may thus be reversed. After supporting and benefiting from globalization for generations, they may come to support not only reterritorialization but also a return to the state as a guarantor of structural inequality.

For other groups, the depredation of outsiders may offer a more promising escape route from neo-Malthusian traps. Neo-nomadism is an interesting case in point. At first glance, nomadism sounds like an unlikely candidate for the solution of contemporary problems. While there are still hundreds of millions of people in Africa, the Middle East, Inner Asia, South Asia and the Far North living a nomadic or semi-nomadic lifestyle, traditional nomadism appears to be a matter of the past.[56] Partly due to climate change, classical nomadism in places like Mongolia and Oman is in decline.[57] Interestingly, however, nomads can be highly adaptive to changing circumstances.[58] Somalia has seen a pastoralist revival after the disintegration of the state in the late 1980s and early

---

[55]  Morris, *Foragers, Farmers, and Fossil Fuels*.
[56]  Anatoly M. Khazanov (2013), 'Contemporary Pastoralism: Old Problems, New Challenges', in Troy Sternberg and Dawn Chatty (eds.), *Modern Pastoralism and Conservation: Old Problems, New Challenges*, 5–23, Cambridge: White Horse Press, at 5.
[57]  Neil Pederson et al. (2014), 'Pluvials, Droughts, the Mongol Empire, and Modern Mongolia', *Proceedings of the National Academy of Sciences of the USA*, 111 (12): 4375–4379; Dawn Chatty and Troy Sternberg (2015), 'Climate Effects on Nomadic Pastoralist Societies', *Forced Migration Review*, 49: 25–27.
[58]  Dawn Chatty (2013), *From Camel to Truck: The Bedouin in the Modern World*, 2nd edition, Cambridge: White Horse Press.

1990s. Only a few years later, Mongolia saw a temporary pastoralist revival when the communist command economy collapsed and unemployment was rampant.[59] Even in the early twenty-first century, nomadism remains a challenge to sovereign territorial statehood and the Westphalian international order.[60]

While it is difficult to imagine billions of people becoming herders, alternate forms of nomadism are already emerging and may further develop as an escape route from neo-Malthusian traps. Migrant groups are the most likely candidates for adopting neo-nomadism in this way. Neo-nomadism requires a willingness to move over long distances in search of resources and to move on once again when resources become scarce. Group cohesion needs to be high because only a strong allegiance to a community of fellow nomads can enable the willingness to see outsiders as a source of resource extraction rather than as fellow humans. This implies a flexible understanding of rights and property, especially those of outsiders, which in turn enables neo-nomads to rely on the depredation of their sedentary host societies. Neo-nomads will depredate sedentary outsiders by default, take over when possible and retreat when necessary.

## Cornucopian solutions?

Cornucopian solutions, such as those outlined earlier, are temporary fixes and rest on the viability of industrial society. Alas, they appear destined to falter in times of neo-Malthusian turmoil. In any case, infinite growth on a finite planet is impossible. Some people argue that dematerialization can enable permanent exponential growth. However, a simple back-of-the-envelope calculation shows that this is not true. Let us demand that the world economy should grow for a century by 3 per cent per annum, without any increase of resource consumption and pollutant emissions. By how much would it be necessary to abate the resource and emission intensity of the world economy (resources consumed and pollutants emitted per unit of GDP)? The answer is: a staggering 94.8 per cent. To have a century of 3 per cent growth *and* reduce resource consumption and pollutant emissions, the abatement would have to be even more drastic.[61]

## Back to the future?

Returning to archaic lifestyles of foraging, pastoralism or subsistence agriculture is hardly an option for billions of people. Nevertheless, authors close to the Transition Town movement recommend horticulture as a way to achieve food security for local communities.[62] In an era when industrial-scale agriculture has become problematic for various social and environmental reasons, they argue, gardening and other

---

[59] Khazanov, 'Contemporary Pastoralism', p. 16.
[60] Nick McDonell (2016), *The Civilisation of Perpetual Movement: Nomadism in the Modern World*, London: Hurst.
[61] For a more extensive discussion of why infinite growth on a finite planet is impossible, see Friedrichs, *The Future Is Not What It Used to Be*, Chapter 1.
[62] Rob Hopkins (2008), *The Transition Handbook: From Oil Dependency to Local Resilience*, Totnes: Green Books.

subsistence lifestyles promise an intriguing 'community solution' to those disaffected with industrial society (maybe because they have been spoilt by its blessings).[63]

The back-to-nature romanticism of such prescriptions is naïve, to say the least. Communitarianism jeopardizes liberal values. A world fragmented into local communities would hardly be amenable to maintaining a cosmopolitan outlook.[64] There is strong evidence to suggest that agrarian societies, including horticultural ones, come with considerable inequality, including gender inequality.[65] A crisis of industrial civilization might push some people into archaic lifestyles, but there is no reason to romanticize the 'simple life'.[66]

## Conclusion

Humankind resembles an escapologist resorting to ever more desperate stunts in order to evade ever more inexorable scarcities imposed by limits to growth. To bring this home, I have presented a variety of Malthusian traps and escape routes. On a final note, let me clarify that not all escapes are created equal. Not every escape is a solution; not every solution addresses the problem; and even those solutions that *do* address the problem may work on some conditions but not others. Applying this framework, let us classify the escape routes presented in this chapter along three dimensions: whether they are solutions or non-solutions; whether they address the problem or shift it elsewhere; and whether they operate in a way that is perennial or conditional (Figure 8.3).

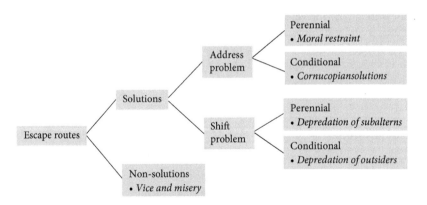

**Figure 8.3** Escape routes from Malthusian traps.

[63] Pat Murphy (2008), *Plan C: Community Survival Strategies for Peak Oil and Climate Change*, Gabriola Island, BC: New Society Publishers; see also Olivier De Schutter (2014), 'The Specter of Productivism and Food Democracy', *Wisconsin Law Review*, 2014 (2): 199–233.

[64] Stephen Quilley (2013), 'Degrowth Is Not a Liberal Agenda: Relocalization and the Limits to Low Energy Cosmopolitanism', *Environmental Values*, 22 (2): 261–286.

[65] Morris, *Foragers, Farmers, and Fossil Fuels*.

[66] Aggressive planetary stewardship or geoengineering might be further options, but I do not discuss them because they would mark genuinely unchartered territory and may have devastating unintended consequences.

Clearly, 'vice and misery' is at best a non-solution. It cannot count as a solution because misery is unacceptable on humanitarian and vice on moral terms. Truth be told, vice and misery are undesirable consequences of a problem unsolved rather than solutions, responses or strategies.

The depredation of subalterns and the depredation of outsiders are solutions, but they shift the problem to others rather than solving it. In doing so, the depredation of outsiders is a conditional rather than a perennial solution because it cannot work in the absence of outsiders to prey upon.[67] While similarly questionable on ethical grounds, the depredation of subalterns may count as a perennial way of shifting the problem because 'the poor you always have with you' (John 12:8).

Cornucopian solutions and moral restraint address the problem head-on. The crux about cornucopian solutions is that they are conditional on the availability of resources that are exploitable in exponentially rising quantities, as well as sinks that are able to absorb the environmental fallout. Only moral restraint solves the problem perennially, once and for all. It will always work *if* (!) and when people are ready to sacrifice parochial short-term interest to collective long-term survival.

From an idealistic viewpoint, we would obviously want a genuine solution that does address the problem in a perennial way. Tragically, such a solution does not seem to be available short of moral restraint, which in theory can solve Malthusian problems forever and for all humankind but remains elusive because we are in overshoot (climate change, resource depletion) and there is an entire moral economy of inaction keeping us humans parochial and short-sighted.[68]

## Acknowledgements

The author is grateful to Einar Wigen and Iver Neumann, as well as the editors and other contributors to this book, for critical comments and helpful suggestions.

---

[67] There is real historical evidence for this. Nomadic 'shadow empires' north of China used to decline during times of imperial crisis in the Middle Kingdom. See Barfield, *The Perilous Frontier*. By the same token, neo-nomads will not be able to prosper without prosperous host societies.
[68] Friedrichs, *The Future Is Not What It Used to Be*, Chapter 6.

Part Three

# Coping, Managing, Innovating at Different Scales

# 9

# U.S. Mobilization during the Second World War as a Model for Coping with Climate Change

Hugh Rockoff

## War as an analogue for environmental catastrophe

The problem of how best to respond to the scarcities that are likely to be created by global warming and environmental degradation directs social scientists in search of historical analogies. There are many examples of droughts, floods, deforestations, and so on, from which much can be learned. But wars can also help us understand how economies respond to extreme challenges. Wars will be especially useful if climate change or pollution reach 'tipping points' when conditions worsen dramatically in short periods of time. In this chapter, I explore the American experience in the Second World War as a model for understanding how best to cope with major scarcities.[1]

Often terms such as 'scarcity' or 'shortage' are used simply to refer to a commodity that is available in amounts smaller than what was available in the past – amounts below 'normal' – or smaller than what is considered adequate given ethical concerns. By these definitions, the United States did not suffer from many shortages during the Second World War. With a few exceptions – most importantly rubber – commodities

---

[1] There is a large literature that describes the mobilization. Donald Nelson was the head of the War Production Board and his memoir, *Arsenal of Democracy: The Story of American War Production*, Harcourt Brace, New York, 1946, although often criticized for its efforts to rationalize his decisions, remains the most important of the memoirs written by participants. Elliot Janeway (1951), *The Struggle for Survival. A Chronicle of Economic Mobilization in World War II*, New Haven, CT: Yale University Press, was the first attempt to explain the economics of the mobilization and draw out the implications for economic policy that received widespread attention. Paul A.C. Koistinen (2004), *Arsenal of World War II: The Political Economy of American Warfare, 1940-1945*, University of Kansas Press, is now the classic description of the political economy of the mobilization. A. Maury Klein (2013), *Call to Arms: Mobilizing America for World War II*, New York: Bloomsbury Press, and Charles K. Hyde (2013), *Arsenal of Democracy: The American Automobile Industry in World War II*, Detroit: Wayne State University Press, are recent histories that do a good job of describing the scale and scope of the mobilization.

were available in amounts that exceeded pre-war production or imports.[2] Again in ordinary conversation and in the discourse of many social sciences there were scarcities in the sense that prices were very high because of increases in demand and/ or decreases in supply. In this sense, there were many scarcities during the Second World War. These were often addressed with great infrastructure projects. There were also many shortages in the economist's sense that demand exceeded supply at the market prices. Prices were often fixed by the federal government to try to prevent inflation and so allocation of available supplies had to be accomplished by some form of non-price method: favouritism, queuing or formal rationing. Undertaking infrastructure projects to increase supplies of materials that threaten to rise in price and the adoption of non-price rationing may be infrequent in peacetime, but they may be needed in the future to deal with atmospheric warming, the exhaustion of fossil fuels and related problems. The war years, in other words, although brief and aberrant in some ways, have much to teach us about how to deal with environmental challenges.

In some respects, the European and Japanese experiences in the Second World War are better analogues for an economy weakened by environmental stresses than the American experience. Bombs dropped by enemy aircraft are, perhaps, a better analogue for severe weather events produced by global warming than the distant challenges faced by the United States during the Second World War. But the American experience is also relevant. The United States faced many supply challenges and did so as a functioning democratic state in which non-war concerns although subordinate continued to influence policy. In other words, the process of decision-making in the United States was much closer to the peacetime norm than it was in Europe or Japan during the Second World War.

In the following section, I describe the state of the economy on the eve of U.S. entry into the war. Next, I consider the attempts to augment supplies of crucial materials with massive infrastructure projects. Then, I look at population movements. Considerable numbers of workers had to be moved to produce munitions and to increase supplies of materials and transport. Global warming and other environmental challenges may require large population movements, for example from low-lying coastal areas or from drought-ridden farming areas. Again, the war has much to teach us about how this can be accomplished.

Despite successful efforts to increase supply, the growth of demand often outpaced supply, and the government faced by the prospect of a wage–price spiral turned to price controls and rationing. Subsequently, I explore this issue in detail. Most of the responses to wartime scarcities required money, in some cases great heaps of money. Then, I describe the monetary and fiscal policies that raised the needed funds. Progressives hoped that the mobilization would be seen as a hugely successful experiment with big government and that as a result the post-war period would experience a strong left turn in American politics. However, this was not to be. I further explore some of the

---

[2]  Supplies of silk (and luffa brushes) were also cut by Japanese military expansion. Silk was used for parachutes, but was replaced by nylon.

reasons why the war experience was not interpreted as Liberals had hoped. In the final section, I summarize the main themes.

## The U.S. economy in December 1941

It is often assumed that mobilization of the U.S. economy in the Second World War was facilitated by a high level of unemployment of both workers and capital that was still present at the onset of the mobilization. There is some truth in this claim, but it is easily exaggerated. The U.S. economy was expanding rapidly in 1940 and 1941. By December 1941, the rate of unemployment had fallen to a level more typical of post-war recessions than of the very high levels that prevailed during the 1930s. Pearl Harbor then and the mobilization that followed pushed unemployment rates to very low levels and hours work to very high levels.[3] All this is illustrated in Figure 9.1,

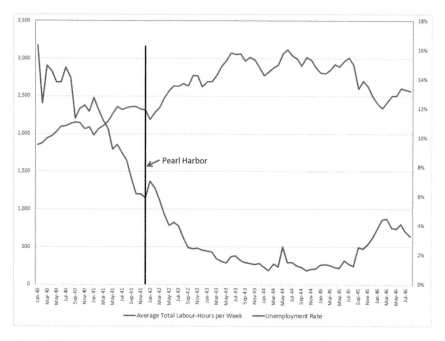

**Figure 9.1** Unemployment and average hours worked per week, 1940–1946. *Note*: Unemployment, the falling line, is measured as a per cent of the labour force on the right axis. Total hours worked per week, the rising line, is measured in millions of hours on the left axis. *Source*: James Frederic Dewhurst, and Twentieth Century Fund, *America's Needs and Resources, A Twentieth Century Fund Survey Which Includes Estimates for 1950 and 1960*, The Twentieth Century Fund, New York (1947) pp. 690–692, columns 1, 3 and 14.

[3]   J. R. Vernon (1994), 'World War II Fiscal Policies and the End of the Great Depression', *The Journal of Economic History*, 54 (4): 850–868.

which shows plots of unemployment measured as a percentage of the labour force and average hours worked per week from January 1940 to August 1946.

Nor was an economy approaching full employment necessarily a negative when it came to mobilization. In peacetime it may be easier to convert a factory which is closed to the production of a new product than one which is going full blast. Financial incentives may be sufficient to convince owners of the closed factory to open it and for managers and workers to go back to work. The same financial incentives may not convince the owners of a factory going full blast to produce a new product. The new product may look more profitable, but why take a risk if things are going well? It may be thoughts about peacetime conversions that lead observers to think that unemployment facilitates conversions. But if we are converting to full-scale mobilization for war, it may be easier to convert the factory going full blast than one that is lying idle. Workers and managers are already in place, all that needs doing is tearing out old production lines and putting in new ones. A combination of financial incentives, patriotism and government orders limiting production of civilian goods may be sufficient to produce rapid conversion. The closed factory can also be brought on line, but there may be delays in assembling workers and managers. The auto industry made this argument when, before Pearl Harbor, they were being pressured to begin some production of weapons. Partial conversion, they claimed, was inefficient. Let us have a good production run, and then when we have to, we will convert 100 per cent to war production. The argument was self-serving, but not without logic.

## New infrastructure

An impressive array of new infrastructure was built in the United States during the Second World War. Production of raw materials, of course, had to be multiplied substantially to meet the needs of the armed forces, and this required expanding existing facilities and constructing new ones. The peak for ingot steel was in March 1944 when 93.8 million long tonnes were produced, an annual rate about 1.8 times the amount produced in 1939. Aluminium production increased by a factor of 6.9 and magnesium production by a factor of 72.[4]

Robert Gordon in a justly famous paper estimated that about $29 billion, including both private and public money, was spent on manufacturing structures and equipment during the war.[5] This would be about $442 billion in today's money using the CPI as the inflator, about $781 billion using the unskilled wage and about $3.04 trillion using nominal GDP.[6]

---

[4]  James Frederic Dewhurst, and Twentieth Century Fund, *America's Needs and Resources, a Twentieth Century Fund Survey Which Includes Estimates for 1950 and 1960* (New York 1947).
[5]  Robert J. Gordon (1969), '$45 Billion of U.S. Private Investment Has Been Mislaid', *The American Economic Review*, 59 (3): 221–238.
[6]  I used the inflators available at www.measuringworth.com (accessed 21 April 2016) and assumed that the expenditures were all made in 1942.

Many of the projects completed during the war would be the subject of intense public attention and consuming political controversy if undertaken today. A list of these projects includes the Big Inch and Little Big Inch pipelines, the Alaska Highway, the synthetic rubber industry, an expanded fleet of ocean transport and the Manhattan Project which built the atomic bomb.

The rapid completion of these projects – which was accomplished without substantially endangering living standards at the time – suggests that large infrastructure projects designed to cope with climate change or environmental degradation could be completed quickly provided adequate funding was available and the usual array of legal obstacles could be overcome. In each of these cases – the Manhattan Project is a partial exception – the project made use of known technologies. Projects designed to cope with the effects of climate change that, by contrast, require the development of new technologies cannot rely on the wartime analogues as evidence that they could be accomplished relatively easily.[7] There are papers and monographs that are devoted to most of these projects. Here I will provide brief summaries that together convey a sense of the scope, speed and diversity of the projects undertaken.

(1) The synthetic rubber industry is perhaps the clearest example of the creation of a new industry to resolve a wartime scarcity. In this case the term 'scarcity' can be given a conventional definition of a severe reduction in the amount of a commodity available. Before the Second World War most of America's rubber came from plantations in the Far East. Those supplies were cut off by the outbreak of the war with Japan. There had been attempts before the war to acquire a stockpile of rubber, but those efforts were half-hearted. Adequate funding to lay in a stock of raw materials that were then in abundant supply, but would not be if the United States became involved in a war that most Americans did not want to join, was not forthcoming from either the automobile tyre industry (the main user of rubber) or the government. Figure 9.2 shows the amount of rubber consumed by type during the war: natural rubber, reclaimed and synthetic. The figure shows the dramatic fall in the consumption of natural rubber. By 1945, consumption of natural rubber was only about 14 per cent of what it had been in 1941. Consumption during the war would have been under more pressure if stocks had not been built up shortly before Pearl Harbor.

As can also be seen in Figure 9.2, the contribution of reclaimed rubber to total production remained roughly constant during the war. The exception is 1943 when consumption was about 16 per cent higher than it had been in 1941. After Pearl Harbor automobile tyres were rationed to limit hoarding and gasoline was rationed to limit driving and conserve the existing stock of tyres. Part of the increase in consumption of reclaim was due to the efforts of the general public who responded enthusiastically to a highly publicized salvage campaign. The reclaim industry, however, had been well established before the war and continued to supply most of the reclaimed rubber from traditional sources. The efforts of patriotic Americans to find rubber by rummaging for old tyres, rubber mats, and so on, made a modest contribution, despite the inspiring

---

[7]  Field (2008) showed that despite many claims to the contrary, total factor productivity did not ratchet upwards over the war period.

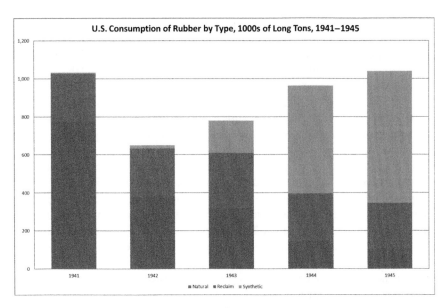

**Figure 9.2** U.S. Consumption of rubber by type, 1000s of long tonnes, 1941–1945. *Source:* Hugh Rockoff, 'Keep on Scrapping: The Salvage Drives of World War II'. NBER Working Paper w13418 (2007) Table 3, p. 53.

news stories about the nationwide search for used rubber. Much of the salvaged rubber could not be turned into tyres, which was the most pressing need. Although helpful, the contribution of the salvage campaign was mostly to morale. The fears of children in particular could be assuaged by making them feel that they were helping to win the war.

Another salvage campaign, incidentally, which was less important in economic terms than it was in political and social terms, was the fat salvage campaign. Americans were encouraged to save cooking fat and turn it in to the local butcher. Fat was needed, Americans were told, to make explosives. The truth, however, was rather different. The amount of fat needed for munitions was only a small fraction of U.S. production. Explosive makers could be sure that they would get their share. The fat salvage campaign was funded by the soap makers. They were concerned that if soap was rationed, some consumers would get used to using less, and that as a result the post-war market for soap would be spoiled.

The real answer to the rubber shortage was synthetic rubber.[8] Automobile tyres of high quality had been made successfully as early as 1934 from neoprene, a synthetic developed in the United States. But the molecule finally chosen to be the workhorse of the synthetic rubber programme was Buna-S, which had been developed by I. G. Farben

[8]  Attilio Bisio, and Vernon D. Herbert, *Synthetic Rubber: A Project That Had to Succeed.* Greenwood Press, Westport Connecticut (1985), provide an excellent overview of the programme. Howard (1947), Frank A. Howard, a Standard Oil chemist and executive, provides an informed participant's view and a defence of Standard Oil's role, in *Buna Rubber: The Birth of an Industry,* Van Nostrand Reinhold Inc., New York (1947).

and Standard Oil. I. G. Farben had invented the molecule; Standard Oil's contribution was scaling up the laboratory processes for mass production. Attempts had been made to convince the tyre companies to invest in synthetic rubber before the war, but these efforts had been frustrated by the low price of natural rubber. To contemporaries the synthetic rubber programme seemed to be slow in getting off the ground. One problem was to decide on the type of synthetic rubber that would form the basis of the programme. A committee appointed by President Roosevelt and headed by Bernard Baruch, the head of the War Industries Board in the First World War, solved that problem by picking Buna S. A further delay was caused by Standard Oil's attempt to receive long-run recognition of its patent rights. But once these issues were settled, facilities were created and came on line rapidly. The Baruch Committee reported in September 1942. By May 1943, Standard Oil had its Butadiene plant (a key feedstock for synthetic rubber) up and running. By 1944, as shown in Figure 9.2, the shortfall in consumption of natural rubber had been offset by production and consumption of synthetic rubber.[9] The synthetic rubber programme, however, was only one of many infrastructure projects.

(2) The Big Inch and Little Big Inch pipelines were completed in 1942 and 1944. Before the war oil had been carried from the Texas oil fields to the New Jersey refineries by rail and barge. German submarine attacks destroyed many of the oil tankers, and the railroads and barges were needed for other purposes during the war. A pipeline was the obvious answer. Pipes had been used for many years to transport oil. But sustainable pressures were low and the oil moved slowly. In the 1930s techniques were developed to create large diameter pipes that could transport oil under high pressure. The government provided the funding for the pipelines through subsidiaries of the Reconstruction Finance Corporation. Legal obstacles that might be raised by local interests during peacetime were limited by wartime patriotism and those that did emerge were easily brushed aside. After the war the pipelines were converted to natural gas and sold to private firms.

(3) Aluminium was needed in large amounts for aircraft, and so the United States undertook a major expansion programme. New plants were financed by the government through the Reconstruction Finance Corporation. Before the war the Aluminum Company of America had a monopoly and had been charged with violating the antitrust laws. After the war several West Coast plants were sold to Henry Kaiser, creating Kaiser Aluminum and competition for the Aluminum Company. Production of aluminium as shown in Figure 9.3 more than quadrupled between January 1941 and the peak in 1943.

One sometimes finds references in general histories of the war to the fact that the government needed to ration steel, copper and aluminium. The story is complex. There was considerable concern during the early phase of the war that the armed forces were letting too many contracts. Confused producers, it was feared, would be working on too many half-finished projects and the economy as a whole might deteriorate because too many resources were devoted to the production of munitions and not enough to the production of goods for the civilian sector. A number of plans were tried to deal with

---

[9]   Howard, *Buna Rubber,* pp. 249–251.

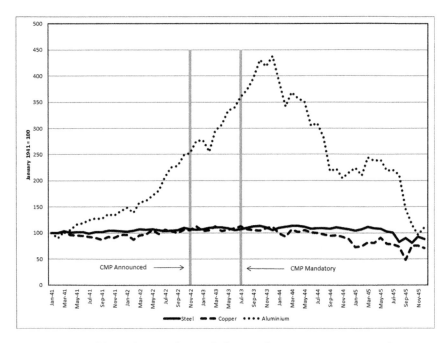

**Figure 9.3** Monthly production of controlled materials, January 1941 to November 1945. *Note*: Production in January 1941 set to 100. *Sources*: Steel: NBER Historical Data Series m01135b. Copper: NBER series m01247b, available at http://www.nber.org/databases/macrohistory/. Aluminium: U.S. Department of the Interior Bureau of Mines, *Mineral Industry Surveys, Primary Aluminum*, January 1947.

this problem. One, borrowed from the First World War, was the priority system. The idea was that each contract would be given a rating by the War Production Board – A, B, C and so on – and producers would be required to finish higher rated contracts first. It sounded good, but in practice it foundered on 'priorities inflation'. Major producers were given the authority to pass on their high priorities to subcontractors and they tended to use the highest justifiable priority. The productive system was flooded with high priorities. The War Production Board responded by introducing higher priorities, but these new and higher priorities soon flooded the system as well. The priorities system clearly was not working.

The response was the Controlled Materials Plan (CMP). Under this system the War Production Board would give the agencies letting contracts for munitions allotments of steel, copper and aluminium (the three 'controlled materials'). Contracts could only be let if there were enough of these basic materials available for its completion. The CMP has been heralded as a great success. One enthusiastic historian of the war effort, Elliot Janeway (1951) claimed that the CMP 'flooded the fighting fronts with firepower'.[10] His claim has been repeated often by historians of the war effort. For one thing, the name

[10] Janeway, *The Struggle for Survival*.

may have appealed to historians anxious to find successful examples of government planning. But consider Figure 9.3 which plots monthly production of steel, copper and aluminium, and shows the dates on which the CMP was announced and when the CMP became mandatory. Although there were modest increases in steel and copper production, they were dwarfed by the increase in aluminium production which was needed in vast amounts for aircraft. But as shown in Figure 9.3 by the time the CMP went into effect, the problem created by a shortage of aluminium had been solved. Production of airframes was soon cut because the supply of planes coming on line was more than adequate. The limiting factor was pilots rather than planes. And with the cut in airframe production came the cut in aluminium production. There is also some evidence, moreover, that the Army Air Force ignored the CMP for a time even after it became mandatory, telling the War Production Board one thing and the aircraft manufacturers something else. The end of this policy of 'double book keeping', as it has been referred to, was more or less coincident with the peak in aluminium production.

(4) The most stunning example of what could be accomplished by the government in a short period of time when financial and legal constraints were removed was the atomic bomb. American progress towards a bomb can be dated from the delivery to President Roosevelt in October 1939 of the famous Einstein–Szilárd letter warning that Germany might build an atomic bomb and urging that the United States build one. Although the general idea of how an atomic bomb would work was understood by physicists, the methods by which one could be constructed were not. The solution was to set several teams to work exploring alternative means of collecting fissionable material and alternative ways of constructing a bomb from those materials. The same approach, setting teams to work on alternative technologies some of which would likely fail, could be employed in meeting environmental challenges. General Leslie Groves, who had supervised construction of the Pentagon, assumed command of the Manhattan Project in September 1942 and acquisition of land at Oak Ridge Tennessee, one of the key sites for the production of the raw material for the bomb began at that time. J. Robert Oppenheimer became the supervisor of the scientific work in July 1943. There were local objections to the acquisition of land at Oak Ridge and the displacement of local residents. There was even a brief congressional investigation. But the urgency of war meant that local resistance would not be allowed to interfere. Work on the site at Los Alamos in New Mexico, where the scientists worked and where the bomb would be assembled, began in December 1942. Only about two and one-half years elapsed from the breaking of ground at Los Alamos and the explosion of the first bomb in July 1945, surely evidence of what can be accomplished when an external threat creates a national consensus.

The best estimate of the cost of the Manhattan Project, at least in an accounting sense, is about $2 billion in wartime dollars.[11] In some ways, this appears to be a relatively small sum, a lot of 'bang for the buck', as one commentator noted. If we inflate with the consumer price index we get a sum of about $25 billion today. But this is not, to my mind, the best way of inflating the cost of the Manhattan Project because many of the expenditures were made for highly trained personnel and specialized equipment

---

[11] Kevin O'Neil (1998), 'Building the Bomb', in Stephen I. Schwartz (ed.), *Atomic Audit: The Costs and Consequences of US Nuclear Weapons*, 33–104, Washington, DC: Brookings Institution Press.

and materials, whose cost has probably risen more rapidly than the consumer price index. Inflating by GDP per capita gives a figure of $61 billion. Or, to take a third approach, expenditures of $2 billion amounted to only about 0.8 per cent of GDP in 1945, or about $139 billion as of 2013.[12] The same project, however, is likely to cost still more today. A large-scale project today that inflicted costs on local interests would face much more effective legal and political resistance with correspondingly higher costs. It was also possible in the Second World War to get many of America's leading scientists and engineers to put their academic careers on hold while they worked on the Manhattan Project. Today, assembling a team of similar eminence would be far harder and far more costly, even if it was for the worthy goal of addressing climate change. Some engineers and executives working on the project, moreover, may have been dollar-a-year men (their salaries were paid by the corporations that employed them in peacetime) and so the costs of their services may not be adequately accounted in the conventional figure. All in all, the largest figure cited above, $139 billion, in other words may well be an underestimate of what it would cost today to do something similar. Nevertheless, the history of the Manhattan Project suggests that much can be accomplished in a short period of time, even when the technology cannot simply be taken off the shelf, when the project is sufficiently urgent.

These examples do not by any means exhaust the list of projects undertaken to meet the unique demands of the war economy. Cargo ships including the famous Liberty ships, machines for decoding the German enigma machines, a highway to Alaska, factories for producing magnesium and many others could be named. The range is extraordinary.

## Redistribution of the population

Global warming is likely to cause the redistribution of the population, for example, from low-lying coastal areas to safer ground or from agricultural regions that are no longer productive because of persistent drought to regions where global warming has increased agricultural productivity. The war experience suggests that given the right incentives this can be accomplished quickly and, given the challenges, relatively smoothly. Figure 9.4 shows interstate migration of the civilian labour force between April 1, 1940, and November 1, 1943. The region that was changed the most was the Pacific Coast, which gained 1.8 million people from other regions. There were, moreover, substantial population movements among the states within these regions and movements within states. The city that was most affected by the war was Los Angeles. One estimate is that 780,000 people moved into the Los Angeles area between April 1940 and April 1944.[13] The redistribution of the labour force was accomplished mainly through financial incentives: there were high-paying jobs to be had in war production centres. William Bendix starred as Chester Riley, a riveter at a California aircraft factory, on a hit radio

---

[12]  The inflation factors were taken from the website www.measuringworth.com (accessed 5 November 2014).

[13]  Arthur C. Verge (1994), 'The Impact of the Second World War on Los Angeles', *Pacific Historical Review*, 63 (3): 289–314.

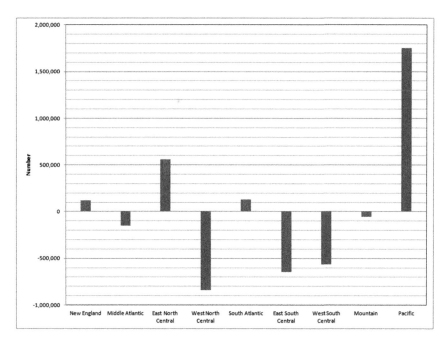

**Figure 9.4** Interregional migration of the civilian population in the United States, April 1940–November 1943. *Note*: New England: Maine, New Hampshire, Vermont, Massachusetts, Rhode Island. Middle Atlantic: New York, New Jersey, Pennsylvania. East North Central: Ohio, Indiana, Illinois, Michigan, Wisconsin. West North Central: Minnesota, Iowa, Missouri, North Dakota, South Dakota, Nebraska, Kansas. South Atlantic: Delaware, Maryland, Dist. of Columbia, Virginia, North Carolina, South Carolina, Georgia, Florida. East South Central: Kentucky, Tennessee, Alabama, Mississippi. West South Central: Arkansas, Louisiana, Oklahoma, Texas. Mountain: Montana, Idaho, Wyoming, Colorado, New Mexico, Arizona, Utah, Nevada. Pacific: Washington, Oregon, California. *Source*: James Frederic Dewhurst, *America's Needs and Resources*, pp. 44–45.

and TV series in the 1940s. The show's title 'The Life of Riley', meaning an ordinary guy living the good life, became an often-used catchphrase in the 1940s.

The federal government attempted to smooth the redistribution by creating agencies and programmes to ease the difficulties produced by mass population movements. A perusal of a list of government wartime agencies reveals the efforts: the Defense Housing Coordinator, the Office of Defense Health and Welfare Services, the Office of Community War Services and the Committee for Congested Production Areas. Undoubtedly, programmes were created in many other agencies to deal with the problems created by mass population movements. One of the motives for price and rent controls, for example, was to prevent profiteering aimed at workers moving into congested production centres. The war experience suggests that financial incentives can produce a rapid redistribution of the population, but also suggests some ways that the federal government can ameliorate the problems created by mass population movements. Some studies are available of how and how well these agencies coped with population movements and more would be valuable.[14]

Of course, Americans have been moving west since the first years of European settlement. Many Americans probably viewed the war as a favourable occasion to make a move that they had long contemplated – a favourable occasion, in other words, to act on Horace Greeley's famous admonition 'Go West Young Man, and Grow Up With the Country.' Some perspective on the long-run trends can be obtained from Figures 9.5 and 9.6. Figure 9.5 shows by census years the percentage of non-white Americans residing in states or territories that were different from the state or territory in which they were born. The largest increase occurred in the war decade 1940–1950. But that increase was also, as can be seen in Figure 9.5, part of a longer-term trend. The exception in this figure is the slight decrease between 1930 and 1940, reflecting the lack of incentives to move. White migration is shown in Figure 9.6. Here again there is a large increase in the war decade, but it appears to have been part of a trend that continued into the 1960s and 1970s.

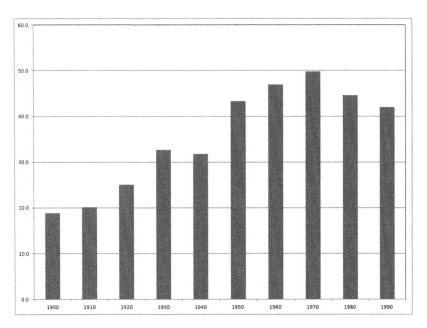

**Figure 9.5** Percentage of non-white Americans residing in a state different from the state in which they were born, by census year, 1900–1990. *Source*: Susan B. Carter, Scott Sigmund Gartner, Michael R. Haines, Alan L. Olmstead, Richard Sutch and Gavin Wright, *Historical Statistics of the United States: Earliest Times to the Present*, Cambridge University Press, New York (2006), Table Ac13-32.

---

[14] William J. Collins, for example, studies the Fair Employment Practice Committee set up in 1941 to provide better access for African Americans to wartime jobs in 'Race, Roosevelt, and Wartime Production: Fair Employment in World War II Labor Markets', *American Economic Review*, 91 (1) (2001): 272–286. Claudia Goldin and Robert Margo study the effects of the National War Labor Board in 'The Great Compression: The Wage Structure in the United States at Mid-Century', *The Quarterly Journal of Economics*, 107 (1) (1992): 1–34.

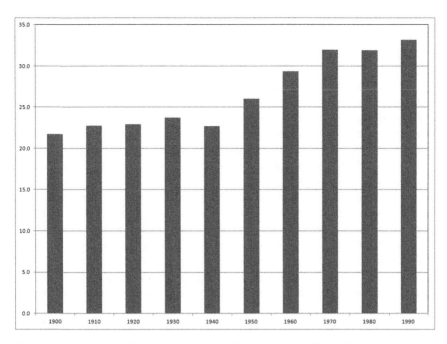

**Figure 9.6** Percentage of white Americans residing in a state different from the state in which they were born, by census year, 1900–1990. *Source*: Susan B. Carter et al., *Historical Statistics*, Table Ac13-32).

## Rationing and price control

It is fair, I believe, to use the phrase 'without seriously damaging contemporary living standards' to convey a sense of how Americans fared during the war. It is deliberately vague because the standard of living during the war is a contested issue. Some statistics even show that Americans were better off during the war than they were in the relatively prosperous years that followed. But Robert Higgs (1992) is surely right that the statistics are misleading because there were fundamental differences between the war economy and the peacetime economies that followed.[15] Production of many consumer durables, for example, was cut off during the war. Prices of products that were available, moreover, are hard to measure because of quality deterioration, black markets and so on. One example that illustrates these difficulties is a problem that was perhaps the major problem facing price controllers during the war, but one which is hardly remembered today: forced uptrading. Manufacturers faced with booming demand and price controls would discontinue production of low-quality-low-priced lines because these were typically the low-profit-margin items produced in bulk. But discontinuing these lines was a burden on low-income consumers who were forced to

---

[15]   Robert Higgs (1992), 'Wartime Prosperity? A Reassessment of the U.S. Economy in the 1940s', *The Journal of Economic History*, 52 (1): 41–60.

'trade up' to higher priced lines. The people compiling the price indexes were aware of this problem, but it was not easy to deal with. There have been many attempts to correct the standard price indexes for these problems.[16] The number of attempts and the range of estimates obtained suggest the difficulty of the problem.

On the other side of the ledger, there were jobs to be had, something that had not been true for a decade. But they were often dangerous jobs, and getting them often meant moving to a congested war production zone with primitive services. New consumer durables were not available, but one could save and plan on buying those goods after the war. The expectation that prices would fall after the war, as the economy fell back into depression, may have made wartime savings seem more valuable at the time than they turned out to be.

But the basics were there. American civilians were well fed during the Second World War. Consumption of sugar and coffee was reduced somewhat below pre-war levels because ocean transport had to be diverted to the war effort. Civilian consumption of meat, on the other hand, which did not require ocean transport, was higher during the war than it had been before.[17] The main reason for rationing food was that demand (pushed up by stimulative monetary and fiscal policies) substantially exceeded supply at the prices set by the Office of Price Administration. Price control, it was felt, was necessary to prevent a dangerous 'wage–price spiral'.

One can think of the wartime equilibrium as a bargain agreed to by three parties. Unions – which had recently become an important factor in labour markets – agreed to a 'no strike' pledge. For the most part this pledge was kept, although the miners did go out on occasion in the coal fields. Employers agreed to a 'no lockout' pledge. And the government agreed to enforce the bargain by fixing prices and wages. Fixing prices without formal ration coupons would have produced forms of non-price rationing that would have been inherently unfair. Queuing would have been common, and then available supplies would have gone to the person who was lucky enough to be in the right line at the right time. Price controls without formal rationing, moreover, would have made it easy to divert supplies to the black market. Rationing increased the fairness of the distribution system and diminished the incentive of people to violate price controls. Everyone would get something. Even so, some pressure to evade the system would remain. Some consumers would get ration tickets for smaller amounts than they wanted to buy at the Office of Price Administration price, and some consumers would get more. One suggestion frequently made by economists is that the authorities permit the organization of a grey market in which consumers could sell excess ration tickets. This makes a lot of sense, but was not tried, as far as I am aware, in

[16]  The best known is Milton Friedman and Anna J. Schwartz (1982), *Monetary Trends in the United States and* the United Kingdom: Their Relations to *Income,* Prices, *and* Interest Rates, 107, University of Chicago Press. Others include Robert J. Barro (1978), 'Unanticipated Money, Output, and the Price Level in the United States', *Journal of Political Economy*, 86: 502; Hugh Rockoff (1978), 'Indirect Price Increases and Real Wages during World War II', *Explorations in Economic History*, 407–420; and Geofrey Mills and Hugh Rockoff (1987), 'Compliance with Price Controls in the United States and the United Kingdom During World War II', *The Journal of Economic History*, 47: 197–213.
[17]  Hugh Rockoff (1984), *Drastic Measures: A History of Wage and Price Controls in the United States*, Cambridge.

the Second World War. Perhaps it was felt that allowing the sale of excess ration tickets would undermine the morale underpinning rationing: sacrifices must be endured for the good of the country.

Although price control and rationing were fairly successful during the period of national unity produced by the war, problems began to develop as the war progressed. One was evasion through quality deterioration and black markets. Some examples of quality deterioration were straightforward: the candy bar shrank and the recipe was altered to use less desirable ingredients. Landlords deferred maintenance on rent-controlled properties. A subtler form of evasion was 'forced uptrading', as we have seen, where manufacturers discontinued low-priced, low-quality, low-profit-margin lines, forcing consumers to 'trade-up' to high-price-high-profit margin lines.

Open black markets were less common, but still a problem. Some supplies of meat, for example, moved in clandestine channels from producers through black market slaughter houses to wholesalers and restaurants where it was sold at prices far above the official prices set by the Office of Price Administration. Black market meat was also sold in meat easies (after the speak easies of prohibition) where one could buy meat without a ration ticket. The black market in meat deepened as the war progressed and undermined support for controls.

After the war ended, the problems of price control and rationing became much harder to address. Labour unions, as we noted, had promised no strikes, but that was taken to mean for the duration of the war. Once the war ended, the United States was hit by a wave of strikes. Workers felt, with some justice, that wage controls had been more effective during the war than price controls because of the evasions discussed above. They felt entitled to wage increases to make up for these losses. Strikes created painful dilemmas for the Office of Price Administration and the War Labor Board, the agencies responsible for regulating prices and wages. By granting price and wage increases in the industry experiencing the strike, the government could help end a strike and restore production. The agencies, moreover, were under great pressure to do so. Especially when it came to consumer durables, the public was anxious to see strikes end and goods that the public had been denied during the war made available again. But by making exceptions to its general rule of no increases in prices and no substantial increases in wages, the government undermined the entire structure of controls and the premise of equality of sacrifice on which it rested. Although many people inside and outside the government hoped that controls would continue, controls quickly disintegrated and were abandoned.

## Financing the war

The rapid transformation of the American economy was made possible by money, lots of it. Elsewhere I have referred to the wartime economy as the 'gold rush of 1942'.[18]

---

[18] Hugh Rockoff (2012), *America's Economic Way of War: War and the U.S. Economy from the Spanish-American War to the Persian Gulf War*, Cambridge University Press.

In 1849 Americans discovered gold in the rivers of California and the rush was on. People quit their jobs in the East and raced to California to pan for gold. The key to the gold rush was the commitment of the federal government to mint gold coins containing a fixed amount of gold: to buy any amount of gold offered and to pay $1.00 for every 25.8 grains of pure gold. Something similar was true in 1942: the federal government was willing to pay high prices for bullets, planes, tanks and factories to produce synthetic rubber and aluminium. Again the rush was on. Indeed, in some respects the deal offered to munition producers in the Second World War was better than the deal offered to the gold miners. The gold miners might rack up costs that exceeded the value of the gold they produced and end up losing money. But in the Second World War, munition producers were offered cost-plus contracts. Higgs (1993) describes the switch to cost-plus contracts and the long-run consequences for military procurement.[19] This is not an interpretation invented many years after the war. During the war many observers recognized what was happening and referred to it as a 'second gold rush'.

It might have been different. Progressives, including many prominent New Dealers, believed that the way to maximize production and minimize the damage to civilian living standards was through detailed planning by federal agencies, such as the War Production Board and the War Labor Board. The idea that received most attention was the 'Reuther Plan', put forward by Walter Reuther, a rising star in the United Auto Workers union, in late 1940. Reuther's plan would have had the entire auto industry converted to the production of military aircraft. The auto companies would pool their efforts: one would produce engines, another would make other parts and a third would assemble the planes. The military would have the lead in deciding who produced what, but industrial councils that included workers would play a prominent role in organizing production. If adopted it would have been a big step towards a much larger role for labour in the corporate decision-making process, one that labour leaders hoped would continue after the war. But the Reuther Plan was proposed before Pearl Harbor. It was discussed for a time, but nothing on this scale could be done until Pearl Harbor and after Pearl Harbor it was largely forgotten.[20]

There are always many entrepreneurs willing to produce and sell to a rich customer. But the skills needed to excel in winning government contracts were not identical with the skills needed to win contracts from private firms. In the Second World War, the entrepreneur who excelled above all others in winning the races for government contracts was the legendary Henry Kaiser who built ships and factories to supply steel, magnesium and aluminium for the war effort. Kaiser had forged strong ties with the Roosevelt administration before the war, but the war provided the range of challenges, and the funds, to turn him into a household name.[21]

---

[19] Robert Higgs (1993), 'Private Profit, Public Risk: Institutional Antecedents of the Modern Military Procurement System in the Rearmament Program of 1940–1941', in Geofrey Mills and Hugh Rockoff (eds.), *The Sinews of War: Essays on the Economic History of World War II*, 166–198.

[20] Alan Brinkley (1995), *The End of Reform: New Deal Liberalism in Recession and War*, 206–209, New York: Random House.

[21] Stephen B. Adams (1997), *Mr. Kaiser Goes to Washington: The Rise of a Government Entrepreneur*, University of North Carolina Press.

To an unprecedented degree the war was financed by raising taxes. Higher personal income taxes, higher corporate taxes and an excess profits tax financed almost 50 per cent of the war expenditures. But the government also relied heavily on borrowing. To some extent financing the war by issuing debt made economic sense. After all, this was rightly regarded as a temporary emergency. Debt could be repaid after the war was over. In modern parlance, taxes could be smoothed over time through wartime borrowing rather than being allowed to spike during the war as would have happened if they had been raised to the extent necessary to finance all of the war. This logic, however, does not work so well when it comes to meeting scarcities arising from environmental damage because this sort of damage is likely to be of long duration or permanent. I also believe that the reliance on borrowing was motivated in part by a desire to hide the cost of the war and to minimize the inevitable unpopularity of a government that imposed higher taxes. There were also concerns by conservatives in Congress that extremely high tax rates – some administration proposals of this sort were rebuffed – might persist after the war.

The contrast with depression era finances was stark. Criticism of the Roosevelt administration's deficit spending during the 1930s was intense and persistent. Roosevelt, although more amenable to deficits, was not indifferent. He believed that a deficit might be necessary in an emergency, but that deficits should be kept as small as possible, and that every effort should be made to return a balanced budget as quickly as possible, a belief on which he acted on several occasions by cutting spending or raising taxes. Once the war began, concern about the deficit evaporated, and the United States ran deficits that would have been inconceivable a few years earlier. This is shown in Table 9.1. In 1939 a highly controversial deficit was 2.8 per cent of GDP; by 1949 the deficit was 22.5 per cent of GDP. The change in federal and state and local spending is shown in Figure 9.7. It shows clearly that although New Deal spending seemed revolutionary to contemporaries, it was dwarfed by spending during the Second World War. Keynes, of course, recognized that war was the one occasion on which American politics would allow 'Keynesian policies' of deficit finance to be used. This was the point that he made in his famous 'open letter' to Roosevelt in 1933. There Keynes pointed to the prosperity produced by deficit spending in the First World War and urged Roosevelt to adopt the same policy to meet the Great Depression.

Although considerable reliance was placed on taxation and borrowing during the war, the government also turned to the printing press. The reason seemed to be a fear of high interest rates on government debt. High rates would have increased the long-run costs of government debt, would have been seen as a sign that the U.S. economy was weakening under the strains of war and would have imposed costs on civilian borrowers as high rates spread through financial markets. Federal Reserve purchases of federal debt (today we call it quantitative easing and think of it as something new) directly added to bank reserves. Increased expansion of lending by the banks then produced further purchases of government debt by banks and their customers. The net result was that nominal rates were held down during the war, the stock of money rose rapidly and the price level more than doubled. The use of borrowing and especially money creation tended to hide the full cost of the war from the average American. Inflation would be blamed on war profiteers rather than on the government's financial policies.

**Table 9.1**  The federal budget deficit in the Great Depression and the Second World War

| Year | Unemployment (per cent of the labour force) | Nominal GNP (billions of dollars) | Federal budget deficit (billions of dollars) | Federal budget deficit (per cent of GNP) |
|---|---|---|---|---|
| 1929 | 3.2 | 103.9 | 0.7 | 0.67 |
| 1933 | 20.6 | 56.0 | −2.6 | −4.64 |
| 1939 | 11.3 | 91.3 | −2.8 | −3.07 |
| 1944 | 1.2 | 211.4 | −47.6 | −22.52 |

*Source*: Hugh Rockoff, *America's Economic Way of War*, p. 173.

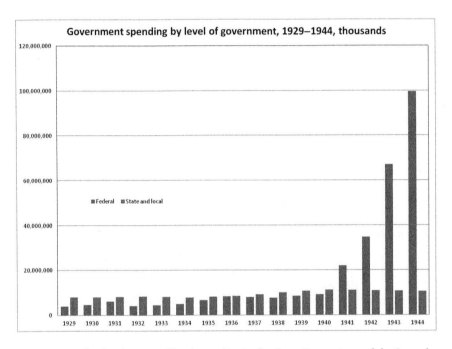

**Figure 9.7**  Federal and state and local spending in the Great Depression and the Second World War. *Source*: Susan B. Carter et al., *Historical Statistics*, Table Ea10-23.

## The rejection of wartime socialism

Progressives might well have hoped that the success of the mobilization would produce a consensus that big government 'worked'. If socialism worked so well during the war, why not in peacetime, or so went the rhetorical question. True, I have argued above that the mobilization probably owed more to the 'gold rush' produced by a flood of no-risk-high-profit contracts than it did to centralized planning. But Progressives might well have hoped that, whatever might be argued against it, the public would see the war as proof of the enormous capacity of the state to do good things and would support Progressive measures after the war.

The reality, however, proved very different. Republicans recovered the House in 1946. Truman defeated Dewey in 1948, but was defeated by Eisenhower in 1952. In general the 1950s are remembered for their conservatism, not for progressive policies rooted in a continuation of wartime socialism. Several interrelated factors help explain the rejection of the wartime model, although it is hard to be definitive. The failure of the wartime model to be maintained after the war can also suggest some possible reasons why the wartime model may have limited contemporary applicability.

(1) The undoing of the potential Progressive interpretation of the war experience, in the sense of detailed control of the economy by the federal government, began well before the war. As Alan Brinkley demonstrates in *The End of Reform* (1995), the public began to lose confidence in New Deal Liberalism in the sense of detailed government control during the 1930s. The National Industrial Recovery Act had not won new friends for detailed government involvement. The recession of 1937–1938, moreover, undermined claims that the New Deal was on the right track economically, and the court-packing episode undermined the claim that the New Deal was on the side of democracy.[22]

(2) The main problem for the wartime model was the unraveling of wartime controls that occurred immediately after the war ended. The transition to the peacetime economy went badly. One problem was a wave of strikes, including strikes by autoworkers, steel workers, miners and railroad workers. During the war, labour unions, with a few exceptions, John L. Lewis's mine workers being the most notable, adhered to the no-strike pledge. But they chafed under a system of wage and price controls they felt was unfair. Wage controls, they believed, were strictly enforced, while producers found numerous ways around strict controls. Above we mentioned forced uptrading. It was particularly irksome to the labour unions. The effect of forced uptrading was not counted properly, they argued, in the price indexes that were then used to determine allowable wage increases. Decontrol of food prices and the end of food rationing were desired by the public, but it also ended badly. Ranchers could see that controls were on the way out, so they had an obvious incentive to keep their animals off the market. The result was meat shortages that angered the public.

(3) Wartime prosperity strengthened the Keynesian argument that the problem of depression had been 'merely' a problem of aggregate demand. This meant – particularly as formulated by Keynes's American followers such as Alvin Hansen, Abba Lerner and Paul Samuelson – that the main thing was to maintain full employment through fiscal policy. Keynes had argued in the *General Theory* that once the problem of aggregate demand had been solved through fiscal policy, the allocation of resources among activities could safely be left to the market. In the *General Theory*, Keynes put it this way:

I see no reason to suppose that the existing system seriously misemploys the factors of production which are in use. There are, of course, errors of foresight; but these would not be avoided by centralising decisions. When 9,000,000 men are

---

[22] Brinkley, *The End of Reform*, pp. 46–47, 86–105, 18–20.

employed out of 10,000,000 willing and able to work, there is no evidence that the labour of these 9,000,000 men is misdirected. The complaint against the present system is not that these 9,000,000 men ought to be employed on different tasks, but that tasks should be available for the remaining 1,000,000 men. It is in determining the volume, not the direction, of actual employment that the existing system has broken down.[23]

Keynes's view rapidly became the view of the overwhelming majority of American economists, and was, for the most part, the lesson that the public at large drew from the war. Detailed planning by government agencies was not needed to counter slowdowns in private spending: increased government spending or tax cuts were.

This view was shared at least to a point even by John Kenneth Galbraith, deputy head of the Office of Price Administration during part of the war, who became the leading economist advocating Progressive policies after the war. In *A Theory of Price Control* (1952), Galbraith argued that if restrictive monetary and fiscal policies had been imposed after the war they would have permitted the gradual release of controls without inflation. Permanent controls, he concluded, did not 'commend themselves to anyone who ever undertook to administer them'.[24]

(4) American manufacturers were quick to take credit, during and after the war, for their production achievements. Progressives might have wanted companies to point out what Progressives regarded as the crucial role played by government finance and direction, but, of course, that is not what the advertisements to be found in magazines and newspapers stressed.

(5) Finally, another part of the story is what historians Arthur Schlesinger Sr. and Jr. (1999) saw as the cycle in American life that alternated between 'public purpose' and 'private interest'. Americans were willing to sacrifice themselves, according to the Schlesingers, for the common good – but only for a while. After they have followed leaders who call for personal sacrifice for the public good, there comes a time when they grow tired of sacrifice and want to pursue their own interests: Liberalism gives way to conservatism.[25] Wars, inevitably, bring a call for sacrifices for the greater good. We can, on this argument, expect wars to be followed by conservative eras of private interest. The era of the Civil War and Reconstruction came to an end in about 1869 and was followed by a conservative period, the Gilded Age. The Progressive era included the First World War and was followed by a conservative turn in national politics: remember President Warren Harding's 'what we need now is normalcy, not nostrums'. It is no surprise, then, indeed it could have been predicted, that the same phenomenon would follow the Second World War.

The lesson that many Americans took from the depression, war and post-war periods taken together was that the success of government planning in wartime was sui generis. It depended on a willingness to cooperate that was possible only

---

[23] John Maynard Keynes (1936), *The General Theory of Employment, Interest, and Money*, 312, London: Macmillan.
[24] John Kenneth Galbraith (1952), *A Theory of Price Control*, 57, Cambridge University Press.
[25] Arthur M. Jr. Schlesinger 1999, *The Cycles of American History*, Boston: Houghton Mifflin.

with the patriotism generated by a major war. Perhaps people recognized the simple psychological fact, or better assumed fact, that people are endowed with a willingness to sacrifice, even to the point of giving their lives, for the common good when the enemy is a human enemy who is attacking one's land. It is not at all clear that the same willingness to sacrifice can be invoked to fight an enemy who cannot be personified.

## What does the war teach us about coping with scarcity?

The American mobilization during the Second World War provides some reasons for guarded optimism about the ability of the United States and other rich nations to cope with the challenges posed by scarcities including those produced by climate change and environmental contamination. In a remarkably short period of time the U.S. economy was drastically reorganized. Production of consumer durables was curtailed and production of munitions was ramped up. Civilian construction was curtailed and large-scale infrastructure projects such as a synthetic rubber industry to replace the natural rubber that was no longer available and the Manhattan Project (the atomic bomb) were completed. Large numbers of workers moved to war production centres, often far from where they were living before the war. Although coping with everyday life during the war could be frustrating, all of this was accomplished without seriously damaging contemporary living standards.

Ultimately, the method behind this transformation was what might be called 'gold rush economics'. The federal government was willing to pay high prices for bullets, guns, planes, aircraft carriers, synthetic rubber plants, long-distance pipelines, air fields and so on; and so people stopped what they were doing and rushed to build them. Workers moved to California to work in aircraft factories, much as they had moved to California in the 1850s to pan for gold.

To be sure, a critically important factor making possible the rapid transformation of the economy was the short-circuiting of the power of special interests to block projects that were in the national interest. After Pearl Harbor the dominant consensus was that an all-out effort was required because the United States faced an immediate and existential threat. Political objections to a rapid transformation of the economy decreased dramatically, although they did not disappear. Concerns about excessive government spending, for example, that had been a political staple during the 1930s all but disappeared after Pearl Harbor. But even during the war, it must be admitted, fear of adverse political reactions to high taxes led to heavy reliance on borrowing. And the fear that high interest rates would generate similar adverse reactions in part accounts for the Federal Reserve's decision to adopt a rigid bond-support programme.

Price controls and rationing enjoyed considerable public support during the war, but proved to be wasting assets. Once the war was won, and patriotic appeals to cooperate lost their force, cracks appeared in the system of controls. A wave of strikes after VJ day was particularly disruptive because they pitted both workers and employers against the government's wage and price controllers. The lesson here is that price controls and rationing, while they might be pressed into service during an environmental emergency, do not appear to be the way to deal with the problem of scarcities over the long term. The infrastructure created during the war, such as the new synthetic rubber industry, however, remained.

The United States, of course, was an unusual case. It was rich. Americans could still live reasonably well even with consumer durables temporarily unavailable and other commodities subject to rationing. The United States had, moreover, an unusually flexible economy. The auto industry, for example, was in the habit of tearing out old production lines and replacing them with new ones to produce new models. American chemical companies were in the habit of building new plants in locations far removed from their home offices. And interregional labour mobility, in particular moving west, was a long-running tradition. The ability of the United States to make rapid adjustments in the Second World War, although a hopeful sign for rich industrial economies, may have less to say about the adjustment process in poorer, less flexible economies, if help is not forthcoming from rich nations.

Other chapters in this book document the wide range of scarcities the world faces, often driven by climate change and environmental contamination. Often these problems seem intractable. The American experience in the Second World War, however, offers some clear evidence that these problems can be addressed rapidly and effectively through a massive infusion of energy and resources without seriously endangering living standards once the political obstacles to a response are overcome.

## Acknowledgements

I thank the participants at the Caltech conference on scarcity for many helpful suggestions and stimulating questions. I also thank my colleague Hilary Sigman for a discussion of the issues involved in trying to make use of the wartime model. Jessica Jiang provided excellent research assistance. I am responsible for the remaining errors.

# 10

# Scarcity and Innovation:
# Lessons from the British Economy during the U.S. Civil War

## W. Walker Hanlon

Throughout history, economic activity has been characterized by periodic shortages in the supply of inputs to production. These shortages come in many forms: adverse weather events that wipe out agricultural production, trade embargoes that squeeze the flow of goods across borders, wars that destroy capital or kill workers and so on. While the form and source of shortages may change over time, there is no evidence of a reduction in the economic importance of these events. In fact, looking ahead, shortages of many crucial inputs, ranging from food and water to oil and land, loom on the horizon.

While we often think of input shortages as negative events, there is also evidence that shortage may play a positive role, by jump-starting innovation. For example, economic historians such as Bob Allen have argued that labour scarcity and high wages in early modern Europe, due in part to the legacy of the Black Death, provided incentives for the development of labour-saving technology and thereby led to the Industrial Revolution.[1] However, tracing the link between input shortages and innovation has often proven elusive, largely because of the difficulty of isolating the impact of scarcity from other factors, as well as the challenge of tracking and quantifying technological progress. Yet understanding the relationship between scarcity and technological progress is crucial: technological change represents perhaps the most promising avenue for adaption in the face of shortage.

In this chapter, I examine the relationship between input shortages and innovation by focusing on one specific historical event: the shortage of cotton caused by the U.S. Civil War on innovation in Britain. At the onset of the U.S. Civil War, Britain's large cotton textile industry was heavily reliant on cotton imports from the U.S. South. Hundreds of thousands of British workers and their families relied on these steady cotton supplies for their livelihood. A combination of factors, including the Union blockade of Southern ports, sharply reduced these supplies during the war (1861–65).

---

[1]   See Robert Allen (2009), *The British Industrial Revolution in Global Perspective*, Cambridge.

The result was a deep depression in the British cotton textile industry lasting through most of the war, followed by a rapid recovery once U.S. cotton supplies resumed. I study how, in an effort to deal with this shortage, British manufacturers developed new technologies that allowed them to utilize lower-quality cotton supplies from India, the second most important cotton-growing nation.

Focusing on such a specific setting comes with both advantages and drawbacks. The main advantage is that it allows us to track the source and timing of the cotton shortage and its influence on both the rate and direction of technological progress. On the other hand, this is just one specific example, so it can provide only one window into understanding the complex relationship between scarcity and innovation. However, this is not to say that these events were unimportant. The British cotton textile industry was the largest and most important sector of the British economy during this period. Hundreds of thousands of people were directly employed by the industry, while many others were indirectly dependent on it. At its height, in the winter of 1862–63, the cotton shortage forced half a million destitute people to seek relief through public welfare or private charities.[2]

This chapter takes an economic history approach to understanding the effects of scarcity. This is distinct from a purely historical approach, both because of the central role played by data and statistical analysis and because the questions asked are grounded in economic theory. It is also distinct from a purely economic approach, because the quantitative analysis depends crucially on a deep understanding of the historical events considered.

Turning to history offers some advantages for understanding the relationship between scarcity and technological progress. In particular, the historical event that I consider offers a sharp change in the availability of a crucial input which, from the point of view of British textile manufacturers, was both unexpected and unrelated to other factors affecting their innovation decisions. At the same time, the economy of nineteenth-century Britain offers a unique environment for understanding the role of market mechanisms in regulating the response to scarcity. Britain during this period was characterized by a very strong laissez-faire ideology, which meant that government intervention in the affairs of private industry was extremely limited. This provides a window into how private innovators responded to the market incentives generated by input scarcity.

My analysis focuses on two questions. First, did the shortage of U.S. cotton shift the direction of innovation? And second, did this shift in innovation patterns persist after the end of the U.S. Civil War?

The first of these questions has to do with directed technical change, that is, the extent to which scarcity of an important input to production affected the direction of innovative activity. This has been a topic debated by economists since at least the work of John Hicks in the 1930s.[3] Much of the work in this area has focused on the impact

---

[2]  See Arthur Arnold (1864), *The History of the Cotton Famine: From the Fall of Sumter to the Passing of The Public Works Act*, London or, more recently, V. Arthi, B. Beach and W. W. Hanlon, *Recessions and Mortality When Migration Matters*, Mimeo, June 2017.

[3]  John Hicks (1932), *The Theory of Wages*, New York.

of labour scarcity. John Habakkuk, for example, argued that labour scarcity in the early United States pushed innovation towards labour-saving technologies.[4]

Recently, theories of directed technical change have been formalized in a series of papers by Daron Acemoglu.[5] The key prediction emerging from Acemoglu's theory is that the impact of input scarcity depends on the substitutability of inputs. For example, if there are two inputs into a production process and it is difficult to substitute between them – an example might be land and labour in early agriculture – then the theory predicts that a reduction in the availability of one of those inputs will shift the direction of innovation towards technologies that economize on the scarce input.[6] On the other hand, if it is fairly easy to substitute one input for another, then the theory predicts that the relative scarcity of one input will push innovation towards technologies that take advantage of other, relatively more abundant, inputs.

While directed technical change theories were designed with the modern U.S. economy in mind, they have a direct application to the response of British cotton textile producers to the cotton shortage caused by the U.S. Civil War. In particular, prior to the Civil War, British cotton textile spinners were using different types of cotton from different locations. The largest supplier of cotton was the Southern United States, which mainly supplied a mid-to-high quality. The main alternative source of supply was India, but Indian cotton tended to be of lower quality and dirtier, which meant that it required more processing and was not usable for all applications. Thus, these different varieties of cotton were similar, but not perfect substitutes. Given this high degree of substitutability, Acemoglu's theory suggests that we should see innovation shift towards taking advantage of the relatively more abundant variety, which during the Civil War meant cotton from India.

In addition to comparing across cotton varieties, we can also consider how producers in other textile industries – wool, linen and silk – responded to the cotton shortage. Unlike cotton, the United States did not play an important role in providing inputs into any of the other major textile industries during this period. Thus, while cotton textile producers experienced a severe depression during the Civil War, producers of fabrics using these other inputs did not face input shortages. In fact, producers of woollen (and worsted) textiles, the second largest textile sector in Britain during this period, actually benefited from the war because of the need for wool goods for military use as well as a reduction in competition from cotton goods. However, these other textile types were not easily substituted for cotton goods, particularly in warm climates. As

---

[4] John Habakkuk (1962), *American and British Technology in the Nineteenth Century: Search for Labor Saving Inventions*, Cambridge.

[5] See, for example, Daron Acemoglu, 'Why Do New Technologies Complement Skills? Directed Technical Change and Wage Inequality', *The Quarterly Journal of Economics*, 113 (4) (1998): 1055–1089, and Daron Acemoglu (2002), 'Directed Technical Change', *Review of Economic Studies*, 69 (4): 781–809.

[6] Another example is provided by work looking at a rise in the price of energy, which is difficult to substitute with other inputs, as in R. G. Newell, A. B. Jaffe and R. N. Stavins (1999), 'The Induced Innovation Hypothesis and Energy-Saving Technological Change', *The Quarterly Journal of Economics*, 114 (3): 941–957, and David Popp (2002), 'Induced Innovation and Energy Prices', *American Economic Review*, 92 (1): 160–180. These papers show that high energy prices induce innovation in energy-saving technologies, consistent with the predictions of the theory.

a result, directed technical change theories make different predictions about how we expect innovation in other textile technologies to respond relative to cotton textile technologies, which are discussed in detail later.

The second question explored in this chapter has do to with path dependence in innovation, that is, whether a temporary change in the direction of technological progress can have a persistent effect on the future path of invention. Whether technological progress exhibits path dependents is an important question in economics. One reason to care about path dependence is that if the direction of technological progress today can affect the direction of innovation in the future, then temporary interventions that change the direction of innovation today can have long-run effects.

As an example, this idea has recently been applied to think about the impact of innovation policies in clean (low-carbon) versus dirty (carbon-intensive) energy technologies. Recent work suggests that path dependence represents an important reason why much of the research effort in the energy sector continues to focus on relatively dirty technologies such as internal combustion engines; they argue that firms may continue to innovate in dirty technologies because they are good at that type of research, having gained experience through innovating in dirty technologies in the past.[7] One important implication of this idea is that a temporary government policy that provides incentives for firms to develop clean energy technologies can lead to a long-run change in the direction of innovation. Not only could the policy cause firms to produce clean energy technologies today, it may also make them better at innovating in clean energy technologies in the future, causing them to focus more effort on those technologies even after the policy was removed. If true, it means that temporary innovation incentives today could provide a long-run solution to rising carbon emissions at a relatively low cost. This example shows that path dependence in innovation is a potentially important idea. However, at present this hypothesis remains largely untested.[8]

One way to think about the idea of path dependence is to divide the relationship between research undertaken in previous periods and the incentives for innovation in the future into two possible effects. One of these, which I will call the 'standing on the shoulders of giants' effect, suggests that previous research in an area lays the groundwork for future work. If this is true, then there will be greater incentives for firms to innovate in areas where they have already done research. More practically, we can think of workers gaining experience in particular forms of research over time or firms making capital investments needed for research in a particular area. Opposing that, we have what I will call the 'low-hanging fruit' effect. This is the idea that research within an area focuses on the easiest problems first (the low-hanging fruit) and further innovation in the same direction becomes increasingly difficult and costly, that is,

---

[7]   See D. Acemoglu, P. Aghion, L. Bursztyn and D. Hemous (2012), 'The Environment and Directed Technical Change', *American Economic Review*, 102 (1): 131–166.

[8]   One of the few recent papers to make progress in this area is P. Aghion, A. Dechezlepretre, D. Hemous, R. Martin and J. Van Reenen (February 2016), 'Carbon Taxes, Path Dependency, and Directed Technical Change: Evidence from the Auto Industry', *Journal of Political Economy*, 124 (1): 1–51, which studies the automotive industry.

innovation in a particular direction exhibits decreasing returns. If the low-hanging fruit effect dominates, then we should not expect a temporary increase in innovation in one type of technology to have a long-term positive effect on research effort in that area.

The impact of the Civil War on the British textile industry provides us with an opportunity to look for evidence of path dependence in innovation. As we will see, the cotton shortage caused by the Civil War generated substantial short-run changes in the types of inventions developed in Britain during this period. After the war, cotton supplies rapidly returned to pre-war levels. Thus, we can study path dependence in innovation by looking at whether innovation patterns also returned to those observed prior to the war, or if, on the other hand, the experience gained in working on new types of inventions during the war had a long-run impact on the types of technologies developed in the post-war years.

## Context

When the Industrial Revolution took place in Britain in the late eighteenth century, it started in the cotton textile industry. From that point through the early twentieth century, this industry would form one of the largest and most important sectors of the British economy. During the 1860s, cotton textile production was Britain's largest manufacturing sector. The Census of 1861 shows that in that year cotton textile manufacturing employed over 450,000 workers in England and Wales, while tens of thousands of other workers were employed in related sectors such as textile dying and printing. Cotton textile products were also Britain's largest single export during this period. The textile industry was also one of the most innovative sectors of the British economy; textile technologies, most of them related to cotton, made up over 10 per cent of British patents over the 1852–1883 period.[9] This rapid rate of innovation kept British textile firms at the forefront of world technology and made Britain's machinery firms the world's main supplier of textile machinery.

The cotton textile industry in Britain was entirely reliant on imported supplies of raw cotton, a necessary input into the production process. In fact, raw cotton was Britain's largest single import; in 1860, Britain imported £35 million worth of raw cotton, almost twice the value of wheat imports, the next largest at £16.5 million.[10] By far the most important supplier of cotton was the Southern United States, which provided 77 per cent of British imports, by value, in 1860.[11] India was the second largest supplier, accounting for 16 per cent of the market. The next largest suppliers, Egypt and Brazil, were much smaller, with each accounting for about 3 per cent of the market.

However, there were important quality differences between cotton from the United States and India. These differences arose from the fact that, for climatic reasons, the

---

[9] Author's calculations from data given in the section 'Tracking innovation'.
[10] Trade values from the *Annual Statement of Trade and Navigation of the United Kingdom in the Year 1860*.
[11] Data from Thomas Ellison (1886), *The Cotton Trade of Great Britain*, London.

cotton grown in the United States was biologically different from the cotton grown in India, as well as differences in the structure of the market in these two locations. The majority of U.S. cotton had a medium staple length.[12] By contrast, Indian cotton was a short-stable variety that was more difficult to spin and produced weaker fabrics. Another important difference was in the level of adulteration. While U.S. cotton came to the market in a clean state, cotton supplied from India before the war often came to market in a dirty state. In many cases, substances such as dirt and saltwater were intentionally added to cotton bales by middlemen in order to increase weight and therefore the selling price. While the Government of India took steps to combat this adulteration, particularly during the Civil War, these proved to be largely unsuccessful. As a result, Indian cotton required more processing before it could be used. This cleaning process was done by a variety of machines, such as scutchers and carding machines, at the beginning of the production process. The Indian cotton was also tightly compressed for shipment, to save on transport costs during the longer voyage from India to England. As a result, once the cotton arrived it needed additional processing to decompress the fibres. This was done using machines called openers. These machines will play an important role in our analysis, as they will allow us to track changes in innovation patterns in technologies that were particularly important when using Indian cotton.

Another important difference between the U.S. and Indian cotton varieties was the ease with which the seeds could be removed. Seed removal was a major issue in cotton production, which is why Eli Whitney's cotton gin – which successfully removed the seeds from the main variety of American cotton – had such an impact. However, Whitney's gin design, called a 'saw gin', was much less successful in removing the seeds of Indian cotton, which more strongly adhered to the fibres. As a result, for most of the cotton grown in India prior to the war, the seeds were removed using simple hand- or foot-powered Churkas, a contraption that typically resembled a pair of rolling pins that squeezed out the cotton seeds as the cotton fibres were passed between them. This was an extremely slow and labour-intensive process. Thus, gins provide another technology, in addition to the openers, scutchers and carding machines described above, which was potentially important for improving the ability of manufacturers to use Indian cotton.

An increase in the use of Indian cotton thus raised demand for technologies that cleaned the cotton, those that opened the tightly packed cotton bales and gins that could remove the seeds from the main Indian cotton varieties. Prior to the war, these sorts of technologies had been largely neglected, as innovators focused on machinery that was more suited for the needs of U.S. cotton. Thus, I look for changes in the direction of innovation by studying whether the Civil War led to an increase in innovation in the types of machinery needed for the use of Indian cotton.

While the main focus of the analysis is on the cotton textile industry, it is also useful to compare this sector to the other important textile industries present in Britain

---

[12]  Staple length refers to the length of the individual cotton fibres. Longer fibres were easier to spin and produced stronger fabrics.

during this period: wool (woollen and worsted), linen and silk. Of these, the wool textile industry was by far the largest, employing around 240,000 people by the 1861 Census. The 1861 Census shows silk employment of 122,000 workers. The number of linen and flax workers is more difficult to ascertain because some of these workers were mixed into industries such as fustian, which combined linen with other materials. Furthermore, the centre of the linen industry at this time was in Northern Ireland, outside the area studied here.

## The impact of the U.S. Civil War

The onset of the U.S. Civil War (1861–1865), which was due in part to Southerner's belief that European nations would intervene in order to maintain their cotton supplies, ultimately resulted in a sharp disruption of this trade. Cotton flows from the United States to Britain, which stood at over 2.5 million bales in 1860, fell to around 100,000 bales by 1862, as shown in the left-hand panel of Figure 10.1. This shortage drove prices up from a pre-war level of around 7 pence per lb. to over 25 pence per lb., as shown in the right-hand panel. In response to these high prices, other countries, led by India, sharply increased their supplies. But their efforts were not enough to completely offset the shortage of U.S. cotton. As a result, evidence suggests that industry output fell by as much as 50 per cent during the Civil War years, while hundreds of thousands of mill operatives found themselves out of work or working short time.

These graphs highlight a couple of important features of this historical case. First, the relative input shares changed dramatically, with cotton from India becoming much more abundant relative to U.S. cotton. Second, the shock was largely unanticipated and temporary; we see no evidence of a substantial price increase before 1861, and prices fall fairly rapidly after the end of the war in 1865.

An important feature, for our purposes, of the shock caused by the U.S. Civil War is that it had little direct impact on the British economy outside of the cotton textile industry. As discussed in Hanlon (2017), there is no evidence that it impacted major

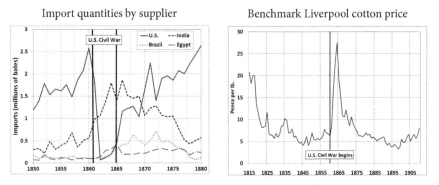

**Figure 10.1** Cotton import quantities and prices during the Civil War.

British imports other than raw cotton.[13] In addition, there does not appear to have been any substantial impact on exports other than textile goods. Within textiles, the direct effect of the war was largely confined to the cotton sector, though the lack of competition from cotton textiles meant that 1861–65 were generally good years for producers of other textile fabrics.

## Tracking innovation

Tracking the development of new technologies is always a difficult task. While there are many potential ways to track technological progress, perhaps the leading approach used by economists is to use patent data. While patent data are not perfect, they are widely used because they provide a systematic and quantifiable measure of technological progress, and virtually the only measure available over long periods across many technology types. Moreover, in the absence of changes to patent laws, patent data benefit from the fact the filing of patents is a response to a consistent and transparent set of incentives.

The patent data used in this chapter were gathered by digitizing around 1,500 pages of printed patent office reports obtained from the British Library and combining these with additional information from the previously available *Cradle of Inventions Database*.[14] The data cover all patents from 1852 to 1883, though some of the information, such as patent titles, is available only for a limited time period. The reason for choosing this particular time period is that it avoids major patent law changes. Patent laws changed in 1852 and 1883 but were stable between these dates.

The entries for each patent contain several useful pieces of information. For each patent, we have a unique patent identifier, the name of the inventor(s) who applied for the patent and a patent title. Also, each patent is classified into one or more of 146 technology categories by the British Patent Office (BPO). Furthermore, within each of these technology categories, the Patent Office divided patents into multiple technology subcategories.

The patent data provide two ways of identifying patents of interest for this study. One useful tool is the patent classifications provided by the BPO. The two BPO categories of interest here are *Spinning* and *Weaving*. Within these categories, I have also collected more detailed subcategory data, which allows me to identify different types of textile machinery. In particular, within the Spinning technology category, I can identify the types of early-stage machines – gins, openers, scutchers and carding machines – that were most needed by producers who wanted to take advantage of the lower-quality Indian cotton. The drawback of the BPO categorizations is that they do not indicate the type of fibre (cotton, wool, silk, etc.) that the machine was intended for or whether the machine could be used with a variety of different fibres. To obtain these

---

[13]  See W. W. Hanlon (2017), 'Temporary Shocks and Persistent Effects in the Urban System: Evidence from British Cities after the U.S. Civil War', *Review of Economics and Statistics*, 99 (1): 67–79.

[14]  These data were originally compiled for W. W. Hanlon (2015), 'Necessity Is the Mother of Invention: Input Supplies and Directed Technical Change', *Econometrica*, 83 (1): 67–100.

details, I conduct a text search of the patent names, looking for mentions of 'cotton', 'wool' and so on.

In today's patent system, once a patent application is filed it will be reviewed by experts in the patent office, a process that can take some time, and only a subset of patent applications will ultimately be approved. However, once a patent is approved, it is assumed to be valid, which makes challenging patents in the court system more difficult. The system worked somewhat differently in nineteenth-century Britain. At this time patents were not reviewed by experts, so nearly all of the patent applications filed were approved as long as the applicant took the necessary steps. However, invalid patents were often challenged and defeated in court after being granted. This provided the necessary check on the filing of invalid patents.

These features have some implications for the patent data that I use. In particular, while the data I use cover patent applications, almost all of these applications ultimately became patents. Also, by focusing on applications I avoid having to worry about delays between the time at which the application was filed and when the patent was actually granted. This is an important fact to keep in mind as we look at how patenting patterns respond to the sharp change in incentives generated by the Civil War.

It is worth pausing to discuss two important drawbacks of using patent data to track innovation. One concern, pointed out by Petra Moser, is that many useful technologies may not be patented.[15] For example, instead of patenting their innovations, companies may decide to protect their intellectual property through secrecy. However, secrecy is likely to be less of a concern for the textile technologies considered here, because new innovations were relatively easy to copy in this industry. A second important concern when looking at patent data is that simple counts of patents may not do a very good job of capturing the true value of the underlying technologies. For example, a few technologies may be quite valuable, while many others are nearly worthless. Even more troubling, for our topic of interest, is that changes in the number of patents filed may be driven primarily by marginal low-value patents. One way to help deal with this concern is to look at other indicators of patent quality. In the case of this analysis, I will consider evidence based on patent renewal payments, which were paid for by a subset of more valuable patents in order to extend the length of patent protection.

## Scarcity and innovation

In this section, I analyse the impact of the cotton shortage on British innovation in two steps. I begin by looking at innovations within the cotton textile industry, comparing technologies that were particularly important for the use of Indian cotton to innovation rates in other types of technologies. Then, I broaden the scope of the enquiry to look at innovation rates across different textile sectors, comparing what we see in cotton textile technologies to patterns observed for technologies related to wool, linen and silk.

---

[15] Petra Moser (2012), 'Innovation without Patents: Evidence from World's Fairs', *Journal of Law and Economics*, 55 (1): 43–74.

As a first step in the analysis, it is useful to look at how patenting patterns evolved across the two textile technology categories identified in the BPO data, spinning and weaving. The *Spinning* category covers all of the technologies used in the early stages of the production process, including those used to clean and prepare raw cotton. The *Weaving* category includes technologies used in the later stages of textile production, where spun yarn was converted into fabric. Figure 10.2 shows how the number of patents in each of these categories evolved across the period from 1855 to 1883, when the BPO categorizations are available. The striking feature here is the substantial increase in spinning patents during the U.S. Civil War. Spinning patents jumped upwards in 1862 and remained high until 1864, before returning to more normal levels in 1865. This contrasts with weaving technologies, where we see no evidence of an increase in patents during the 1861–1865 period. Finally, note that both types of technologies show substantial reductions in patenting in 1865, a year in which the strain of the cotton shortage precipitated a broader financial crisis that led to widespread bankruptcies.

At first glance, it is somewhat surprising to see in Figure 10.2 that during the Civil War years, a period in which the textile industry underwent a massive depression, the number of new textile technologies being patented actually increased. This provides a first look into the surprising ways that input scarcity and innovation interact. Another fact to take away from Figure 10.2 is that the major changes in textile technology innovation patterns occurred in the early (spinning) stage of the production process.

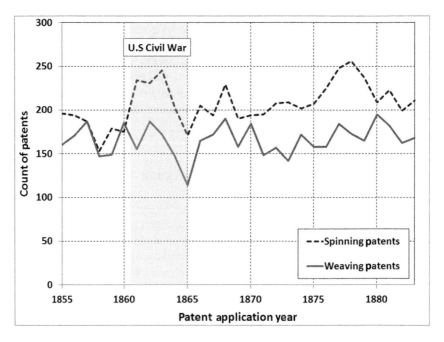

**Figure 10.2** Innovation in spinning and weaving technologies.

To unpack the patterns in Figure 10.2, we can take the more detailed BPO subcategories to look at patenting patterns for specific types of machinery. Figure 10.3 does this for a selection of six of the most important subcategories of the BPO spinning technology. In the top row, I describe patenting patterns for three technologies that were particularly important for cleaning and preparing raw cotton: gins, openers and scutchers, and carding machines. All of these technologies would have been particularly important for the use of Indian cotton, which was more difficult to gin, required additional cleaning and was more tightly packed for shipment. The notable feature in all three of these graphs is the high levels of patenting that took place during the Civil War years.

The bottom row in Figure 10.3 shows patenting in three technologies used at a slightly later stage of the spinning process. The first of these, mules, was the most important single piece of machinery used in spinning. Rollers, the next technology, was a component used in a variety of machines, while finishing technologies were used at the end of the spinning process. Unlike the technologies in the top row, we do not see any increase in patenting in these technology categories.

Figure 10.3 shows that there was a sharp increase in patenting in technologies related to the use of Indian cotton during the period in which U.S. cotton was in short supply, while we see no change in patenting patterns in technologies, in the bottom row of figures, that were less important for the use of Indian cotton. This suggests that the shortage of U.S. cotton affected the direction of invention and in a very particular way: it biased innovation towards technologies that used Indian cotton, the relatively more abundant input during the Civil War years. Though there were important differences between U.S. and Indian cotton, we expect that overall these inputs were fairly substitutable in the production process (more so than, say, cotton and labour). Given this, the patterns shown in Figure 10.3 are consistent with the predictions of the directed technical change theories discussed earlier.

Despite the clear patterns shown in Figure 10.3, one may worry that these results will not hold if we look across a broader set of different spinning technology subcategories or if a more sophisticated econometric approach is applied. However, after these concerns are addressed the basic conclusions are unchanged;[16] the shortage of high-quality U.S. cotton pushed innovation towards improving technologies that were used with alternative, lower-quality cotton varieties.

There is a second important feature visible in Figure 10.3; while we see substantial increases in patenting in the gins, openers and scutchers, and carding machine categories during the Civil War, there is no clear evidence that this continued in the years after 1865. While patenting in these categories was volatile and may have remained high for a couple of years after 1865, by 1870 patenting levels had returned close to their pre-war averages in all three categories. This feature speaks directly to questions about path dependence in innovation. In particular, there is little evidence here that the increase in innovation in these categories during the 1861–65 period led to a persistent change in the incentives for innovation in later years. Looking back at

---

[16] See Hanlon, 'Necessity Is the Mother of Invention', pp. 67–100.

**Technologies used to clean and prepare cotton**

**Technologies used mainly later in the spinning process**

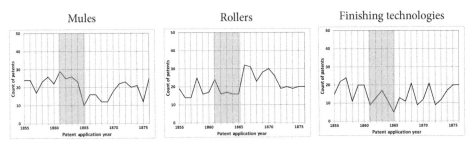

**Figure 10.3** Patents of specific spinning technologies.

Figure 10.2, we can see that roughly the same pattern is observable for spinning patents overall. Thus, it does not appear that path dependence in innovation is a strong feature of the innovation process in textile technologies during this period.

Next, I shift my focus to a comparison of patenting patterns in cotton textile technologies compared to those that use wool, linen or silk. The BPO technology categories do not separate technologies related to these different sectors. Instead, I turn to data from the *Cradle of Inventions Database*, which includes patent titles and identify the sector depending on whether a patent mentions 'cotton', 'wool', 'linen' or 'silk' (or related terms like 'worsted') in the title. It is worth noting that this analysis ignores a fairly large number of textile technology patents that did not specifically mention the material the machinery is used with. This will not affect the validity of the analysis as long as we are willing to assume that the set of patent titles mentioning a specific input did not change in a systematic way during the Civil War, which seems reasonable.

Figure 10.4 describes patenting patterns for the four largest textile industries, cotton, wool, linen and silk, over the study period. One notable feature of these graphs is that the shortage of cotton during the U.S. Civil War led to a substantial increase in the number of cotton-related patents. Similar patterns do not appear in any of the other textile industries. The fact that cotton textile patents increase relative to patents in other textile sectors during the U.S. Civil War suggests that the shortage of cotton also influenced the distribution of innovative effort across sectors. However, unlike the pattern observed within the cotton textile industry, here we see evidence of innovation

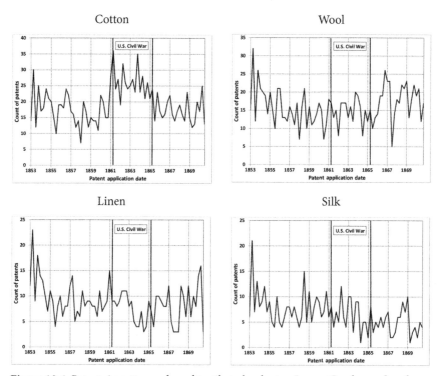

**Figure 10.4** Patents in cotton and wool textile technologies. *Source*: Graphs produced using data from the Cradle of Inventions database.

directed towards the sector that uses the input – raw cotton – that had become relatively more scarce. This pattern is consistent with directed technical change theories under the assumption that there is relatively low substitutability between cotton textiles and wool, linen or silk textiles. There is reason to believe that this assumption is reasonable; for example, providing relatively inexpensive clothing to workers in tropical climates was a major source of demand for cotton textiles. Wool textiles were unlikely to be a reasonable substitute under these conditions, because wool is less comfortable to wear in warm weather, while linen and silk were generally too expensive to compete with cotton in this market.

How can we reconcile the fact that at the industry level it appears that innovation was directed towards the sector in which inputs had become relatively scarce, but that once we look within cotton textile technologies innovation was directed towards using the input that had become relatively more abundant? The answer points back to substitutability. If many people were unwilling to substitute alternative fabrics for cotton goods, then it makes sense to focus innovation on making the most of the available cotton inputs. However, within the set of cotton inputs, whether goods were made out of American or Indian cotton made relatively little difference, so at this level innovation focused on taking advantage of supplies from India, which became relatively more important due to the shortage of U.S. cotton. These patterns demonstrate the complex relationship between scarcity and innovation, but they also suggest that relatively simple economic models can be helpful for understanding these interactions.

The results in Figure 10.4 also tell us something about path dependence in innovation. As in previous results, the graphs in Figure 10.4 provide no evidence that the temporary increase in patenting in cotton textile technologies, relative to other textile sectors, had any long-term impact on innovation patterns. Instead, after 1865 the overall number of cotton patents rapidly returned to roughly the levels observed in the pre-war period. It is interesting to note that despite the fact that we observe different patterns in terms of how the cotton shortage affected the direction of innovation, for path dependence the evidence consistently shows no effect.

One interesting feature in Figure 10.4 is the very rapid increase in cotton patents right at the beginning of the Civil War. This is a surprising pattern given that we expect there to be a delay between when the incentives for new innovation change and when the technologies are actually ready to be patented. The likely explanation here is that there were a set of technologies developed before the onset of the Civil War that were not immediately patented because they were not sufficiently valuable given the dominance of U.S. cotton. However, the start of the war, and the looming shortage of U.S. cotton, increased the value of these technologies, resulting in their inventors rapidly filing patents.

As mentioned above, one potential concern in using patent data to track innovation is that raw patent counts may not be a good measure of the value of the technologies being generated. To help address this potential concern, Figure 10.5 focuses on patents

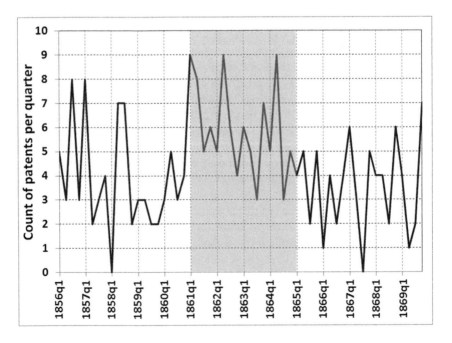

**Figure 10.5** Cotton textile patents renewed after three years, by date of filing.

for which a renewal fee was paid to keep the patent in force for longer than three years. Because the renewal fee of £50 represented a substantial sum in the 1860s, it only made sense for inventors to pay the renewal fee on the most valuable patents. Figure 10.5 shows that these more valuable cotton textile patents also experienced a substantial increase during the Civil War period, mirroring the increase in the total number of patents shown in Figure 10.4. This demonstrates that the effect of the cotton scarcity was not just to generate a bunch of low-value cotton patents.

## Discussion

The cotton shortage caused by the U.S. Civil War had a devastating effect on British workers, leading historians to label this period the 'Cotton Famine'. However, despite causing mass unemployment, the cotton shortage also triggered a wave of new innovation. Faced with a shortage of U.S. cotton, manufacturers invested in new technologies that allowed them to take advantage of alternative suppliers, particularly cotton from India.

What lessons can we draw from this experience to inform our understanding of scarcity more broadly? Perhaps the key message is that when thinking about the impacts of scarcity in one particular resource – be it cotton, land, water, etc. – it is important to account for how technology will respond. This also has implications for how we conceptualize and measure scarcity. Had British cotton spinners been better at using Indian cotton before 1861 or had better substitutes for cotton been available, the reduction in cotton caused by the U.S. Civil War might have had little effect. Scarcity, in this case, depended on the necessity of using U.S. cotton, a necessity that diminished over time as technology adjusted.

This experience provides one illustration of how innovation responds to shortage. Of course, given that we have considered a very specific example, it is natural to wonder whether we might expect to see similar patterns in other contexts. It is clearly not possible to answer that question decisively. However, the link between the results described here and existing economic theory suggests that the connections between scarcity and innovation may be systematic. In particular, under very reasonable assumptions, the relationship between the cotton shortage and innovation that I have described matches the predictions of existing directed technical change theories. Because these theories were developed with a very different context in mind – the modern United States – the fact that the theory offers predictions that perform well in the context that I study suggests that the theory is capturing a salient feature of the world.

While there does appear to be a clear connection between the cotton shortage and concurrent innovation patterns, there is no evidence that innovation exhibited path dependence. This is a potentially interesting result which, notably, looks quite different than the findings of existing work on this topic.[17] It appears that whether or

---

[17] See Aghion et al., 'Carbon Taxes, Path Dependency, and Directed Technical Change', pp. 1–51.

not innovation 'stands on the shoulders of giants' or suffers from the 'low-hanging fruit effect' is likely to be context-specific. However, while there is little evidence that the temporary shortage of cotton had a persistent effect on the direction of innovation, it is important to keep in mind that the new technologies developed during the Civil War remained available in the post-war period.

In the end, the extent to which technology can adapt to scarcity is likely to play a key role in determining how scarcity affects people. If innovators quickly adjust, as was the case with nineteenth-century British inventors faced with a severe cotton shortage, then innovation may play an important role in cushioning the impact of scarcity. However, my setting also makes it clear that even when innovators do react quickly, technological change is often not enough to compensate for the direct effects of shortage.

# 11

# China's Great Leap Famine: Malthus, Marx, Mao and Material Scarcity

## Sigrid Schmalzer

*Do not worry about scarcity; worry about uneven distribution.*

*– The Analects, c. 285 BC*

*To distribute resources evenly will only ruin the Great Leap Forward.*

–Mao Zedong, 1959

In 1958, Mao Zedong announced that the People's Republic of China (PRC) was ready to take a 'Great Leap Forward' into full-fledged communism. By mobilizing the revolutionary energy of the masses, China would produce steel surpassing that of Britain, increase agricultural yields to support not only the domestic population but also China's international allies and achieve the utopian communist society envisioned by Marx and Mao, in which the divisions between city and countryside, worker and peasant, intellectual and manual labour would be overcome.[1] State organs around the country soon began producing visions of the bounty that awaited those willing to endure 'three years of struggle' in order to achieve 'ten thousand years of happiness'.[2] The propaganda poster from 1959 depicted in Figure 11.1 is one such example: the caption reads, 'The vegetables are green, the cucumbers plump, and the yield is abundant.'

But during those same years, China experienced the worst famine in human history. Tens of millions of people died. Even as propagandists painted the portrait

---

[1] Felix Wemheuer (2012), 'Dining in Utopia: An Intellectual History of the Origins of the Public Dining', in Matthias Middell and Felix Wemheuer (eds.), *Hunger and Scarcity under State-Socialism*, 277–301, Leipzig: Leipzig University, 287; Felix Wemheuer, '"The Grain Problem Is an Ideological Problem": Discourses of Hunger in the 1957 Socialist Education Campaign', in Kimberly Ens Manning and Felix Wemheuer (eds.) (2011), *Eating Bitterness: New Perspectives on China's Great Leap Forward and Famine*, 107–129, Vancouver: University of British Columbia Press, 124.

[2] Maurice Meisner (1982), *Marxism, Maoism, and Utopianism: Eight Essays*, Madison: University of Wisconsin Press; 'Zou San Xian, fang Xincun' [Going to Three Counties, Visiting the New Countryside] (1959), *People's Daily*, 27 April 1959: 11. See also Matthew D. Johnson (2014), 'Cinema and Propaganda in the Great Leap Forward', in James A. Cook et al. (eds.), *Visualizing Modern China: Image, History, and Memory, 1750-Present*, 219–239, Lanham, MD: Lexington Books.

**Figure 11.1** Jin Meisheng, *Cailü guafei chanliang duo* [The vegetables are green, the cucumbers are plump, the harvest is abundant] (Shanghai: Shanghai renmin meishu chubanshe, 1959), archived on http://chineseposters.net/gallery/e11-992.php.

of imminent paradise, local cadres began filing reports on the mounting devastation. By 1961, a report from Sichuan documented, 'Villagers have resorted to living on wild herbs and tree bark. Every day in [Chongqing's] Beifu district more than 100 people have been seen going out in groups to search for food. All the banana trees in the People's Park, the old people's home in the district, and the local state farm have been ripped up and the roots consumed by hungry villagers.'[3] The most chilling reports told of people resorting to cannibalism, including parents eating their children and people murdered for human consumption.[4]

For historians of modern China, and especially of rural China, questions of abundance and scarcity are inescapable. They fill both the rhetoric and the reality of our field of study. In recent years, one period in particular has captured the attention of scholars: the Great Leap Forward (1958–1960) and the devastating famine (1959–1961) that accompanied it. Explaining what brought the utopian vision of the Great Leap to its knees, how many people were lost and above all what caused them to die has increasingly occupied scholars – and of course the Great Leap's survivors and their descendants have their own understandings of what happened and who was to blame.[5] This chapter will not seek to add any new answers to such questions. Rather, it will focus on the differing ways material scarcity and the distribution of limited resources have been understood over time, and the role these concepts played both in the lead-up to the Great Leap famine itself and in ensuing debates over its historical significance. In particular, the famine offers a valuable, if very painful, opportunity to consider Marxist interpretations of scarcity and the interesting historical twists that have occurred when those Marxist interpretations have confronted famine in a state-socialist context – a context in which, the PRC state promised, 'no one would starve to death'.[6]

Two puzzles lie at the centre of this discussion. First, Marxism teaches that food scarcity is primarily a political, rather than a natural, phenomenon. Yet, in the wake of the Great Leap, the socialist Chinese state determined the cause of the shortages to be largely weather-related and refused to use the term 'famine' at all, referring only to 'three years of natural disasters'. Among scholars, critics hostile to socialism have been among the most likely to reject the notion that weather played a significant role in the famine, while those more sympathetic to socialism have been more inclined to grant some role to natural causes or at least to insist on the need to test the data before dismissing weather as an influence.

---

[3] Zhou Xun (ed.), *The Great Famine in China, 1958-1962: A Documentary History*, New Haven, CT: Yale University Press, 132. In fact, facing desperate scarcity, the state had itself developed a programme to promote such 'food substitutes'. See Gao Hua, 'Food Augmentation Methods and Food Substitutes during the Great Famine', *Eating Bitterness*, 171–196.

[4] For a review of the literature documenting cannibalism, see Cormac Ó Gráda (2011), 'Great Leap into Famine: A Review Essay', *Population and Development Review*, 37 (1): 191–202, on 197–198.

[5] Scholarly interpretations will be discussed in detail below. On popular memories and assigning of responsibility, see especially Ralph Thaxton (2008), *Calamity and Contention in Rural China: Mao's Great Leap Forward Famine and the Origins of Righteous Resistance in Da Fo Village*, Cambridge: Cambridge University Press; Felix Wemheuer, 'Dealing with Responsibility for the Great Leap Famine in the People's Republic of China', *The China Quarterly*, 201 (2010): 176–194.

[6] Felix Wemheuer, (2014), *Famine Politics in Maoist China and the Soviet Union*, 7, New Haven, CT: Yale University Press. See also Matthias Middell, 'Famine: A Global Perspective', *Hunger and Scarcity in State-Socialism*, 9–27.

Second, we might think that as Marxists and socialists, Mao and his followers would have specifically recognized uneven distribution of resources as a political problem underlying poverty and starvation; indeed, the vision of the Great Leap was coloured with a radical egalitarianism that promised to dissolve society's most fundamental inequities. And yet, at key moments, Mao and other leaders vehemently defended the practice of uneven distribution as necessary to socialist development. On the other side, critics of the socialist state have leaped to criticize the inequities of Maoist policies and have invoked Amartya Sen's concept of food entitlement to highlight the Chinese state's failure to distribute food where it was needed.

This chapter begins with a discussion of the concept of scarcity in Marx's writings and how a Marxist analysis allowed Mao in 1949 to conceptualize famine in political, rather than natural, terms. The second section shows how Mao's distinctively voluntarist brand of Marxism shifted the balance from political to ideological factors in analysing food shortages. The third section explores a central paradox of Great Leap policy as communist utopianism bumped up against the practical needs of distributing scarce resources for socialist economic construction. The final section surveys diverse interpretations of the Great Leap famine, demonstrating the unexpected ways in which Malthusianism, Marxism and Maoism have provided intellectual resources for the analysis of natural, political and ideological causes of scarcity and famine in the Great Leap Forward.

## Dialectical materialism: Food problems as political problems

Among the most important intellectual legacies of Karl Marx and Friedrich Engels is the critique of theories that interpret social and political phenomena as facts of nature. Marx identified this problem even in the work of Charles Darwin, whose contributions to materialism were greatly appreciated by Marx. In a letter to Engels in 1862, Marx wrote, 'It is remarkable how Darwin has discerned anew among beasts and plants his English society with its division of labor, competition, elucidation of new markets, "discoveries" and the Malthusian "struggle for existence."'[7] With his critical awareness of the influence of capitalist ideology, Marx saw in Darwin an unconscious tendency to interpret nature through the lens of specific social experience, and then to bring the natural 'laws' thus identified back into the interpretation of society, with all the supposedly objective force of science.

But far more than Darwinism, it was specifically Malthusianism that troubled Marx, though he rarely tackled Malthus as directly as one might expect.[8] In volume 1 of *Capital* (1867), Marx zeroed in on what superficially appeared as a recent confirmation of Malthusian principles: the Irish Great Famine and the apparent solving of the problem through mass exodus from Ireland to the United States. As Marx wrote with

---

[7]   Marx to Engels (1979), 18 June 1862, in *The Letters of Karl Marx*, 156–157, ed. and trans. Saul K. Padover, Englewood Cliffs: Prentice-Hall, Inc.

[8]   Michael Perelman (1987), *Marx's Crises Theory: Scarcity, Labor, and Finance*, 27–55, New York: Praeger.

dripping sarcasm, 'Here, then, under our own eyes and on a large scale, a process is revealed, than which nothing more excellent could be wished for by orthodox economy for the support of its dogma: that misery springs from absolute surplus population, and that equilibrium is re-established by depopulation.' However, as Marx went on to explain, Ireland had not suffered an 'absolute surplus' of population (i.e. a surplus defined according to some law governing how many people can be supported by natural resources), but rather a 'relative surplus' (i.e. a surplus created by the demands of capitalist production). Marx asked, 'What were the consequences for the Irish laborers left behind and freed from the surplus population?' He answered, 'That the relative surplus population is today as great as before 1846; that wages are just as low, that the oppression of the laborers has increased, that misery is forcing the country towards a new crisis.' Why? Because capitalist agriculture had 'crushed' small farmers and forced them to become labourers desperate to work even for pitifully low wages.[9] Thus, for Marx, poverty and famine in Ireland were the result not of any natural law of population dynamics but rather of historical processes accompanying capitalism.

By no means was Marx's critique of Malthusianism a denial of the natural world: Marxism is first and foremost a materialist philosophy. However, for Marx and his followers, a materialist analysis must include not only the means of production (the land, its mineral resources, etc.) but also the social and political structures that govern who controls those means. For Marxists, scarcity can never signify merely a lack of sufficient land, water and fertilizer to produce grain. It must also take into account the organization of labour and resources. It is this dialectical relationship between nature and society that lies at the heart of Marxist understandings of scarcity and allows for a critical understanding of the way Malthusian claims to represent natural processes have shored up the 'dogma' of the 'orthodox economy' of capitalism.

Writing in 1949, on the eve of communist victory in the Chinese civil war, Mao Zedong invoked Marx's dismissal of Malthusianism in his own triumphant dismissal of U.S. imperialism as propounded by Secretary of State Dean Acheson, whom Mao dubbed the 'spokesman of the bourgeoisie'. Reacting to Acheson's recent analysis in a white paper on China, Mao especially took issue with Acheson's characterization of China as wracked by two centuries of mounting overpopulation that had resulted in 'unbearable pressure upon the land', which 'so far none has succeeded' in overcoming. Mao further suggested that behind Acheson's history lesson lay his 'hope' that the Chinese communists would similarly fail, such that 'China will remain in perpetual chaos and that her only way out is to live on U.S. flour, in other words, to become a U.S. colony.' Rebutting Acheson's analysis and challenging his alleged 'hope', Mao wrote, 'It is a very good thing that China has a big population. Even if China's population multiplies many times, she is fully capable of finding a solution; the solution is production. The absurd argument of Western bourgeois economists like Malthus that increases in food cannot keep pace with increases in population was not only thoroughly refuted in theory by Marxists long ago, but has also been completely exploded by the realities in

[9]   Karl Marx (2001 [1867]), *Capital*, Vol. 1, trans. Samuel Moore and Edward Aveling, 1006, London: Elecbook.

the Soviet Union and the Liberated Areas of China after their revolutions.' For Mao, it came down to a Marxist 'truth': 'revolution plus production can solve the problem of feeding the population'.[10]

## Voluntarism: Food problems as ideological problems

Thus for Mao in 1949, as for Marxists more generally, food problems were fundamentally questions of political economy and not the products of insurmountable natural laws governing the relationship between population and resources. What distinguished Maoism from many other forms of Marxism was an extraordinary faith in the ability of the masses to overcome material obstacles, given only their revolutionary spirit and the wise guidance of the party. This Maoist emphasis on 'voluntarism' intensified the degree to which social and political explanations of phenomena were preferred over natural ones, added a strong ideological component to the analysis and raised the bar for utopian visions of communist paradise rapidly achieved.[11] In the same 1949 essay cited above, Mao declared, 'Of all things in the world, people are the most precious. Under the leadership of the Communist Party, as long as there are people, every kind of miracle can be performed. We are refuters of Acheson's counter-revolutionary theory. We believe that revolution can change everything, and that before long there will arise a new China with a big population and a great wealth of products, where life will be abundant and culture will flourish. All pessimistic views are utterly groundless.'[12]

In this oft-quoted speech were some of the seeds of the PRC state's early reluctance to interpret its swelling population numbers in Malthusian terms – it was only after Deng Xiaoping came to power in 1978 that the infamous 'one-child policy' came into being, and even then Chinese leaders studiously avoided appearing to endorse Malthusianism.[13] And here too were seeds of the Great Leap Forward – Mao's boldest, and ultimately deadliest, endeavour. Dissatisfied with the slow pace of development China had pursued under the guidance of Soviet advisors, in 1958 Mao sought to propel China directly into full-fledged communism. In just a few years, Chinese communes (ranging from about 10,000 to about 100,000 members) were expected to become self-reliant entities capable of providing a high living standard to all. Long-standing social distinctions would vanish, as peasants acquired the products of industry and people across social classes learned to participate both in material production and in the arts and sciences. Meanwhile, dining halls would facilitate gender equality, freeing

---

[10]  Mao Tse-Tung (1969), 'The Bankruptcy of the Idealist Conception of History', *Selected Works of Mao Tse-tung*, Vol. IV, 451–453, Beijing: Foreign Languages Press. For Dean Acheson's white paper, see U.S. Department of State (1967), *The China White Paper, August 1949*, Stanford, CA: Stanford University Press.

[11]  Frederic E. Wakeman (1973), *History and Will: Philosophical Perspectives of Mao Tse-tung's Thought*, Berkeley: University of California Press; Meisner, *Marxism*.

[12]  Mao, 'The Bankruptcy', p. 454.

[13]  Susan Greenhalgh (2008), *Just One Child: Science and Policy in Deng's China*, Berkeley: University of California Press.

women for participation in collective labour, and would establish that, in Mao's words, 'communism is eating for free'.[14]

What would make this metamorphosis possible? Nowhere was Mao's voluntarism more apparent than in his expectations that the Chinese people could achieve 'every kind of miracle', including 'leaping' over stages of economic development to arrive at communism before any other nation in the world. And as further foreshadowed in Mao's 1949 speech, during the Great Leap Forward, doubts as to the people's ability to achieve such feats would be considered 'pessimistic' and 'utterly groundless'. Worse yet, those who expressed such doubts risked being labelled 'rightist' or 'counter-revolutionary', which came with dire, and not infrequently deadly, political consequences.

Especially relevant here is the shift in attention from the political to the ideological realm. Although politics and ideology are obviously related, they are importantly distinct. Political problems are rooted in power imbalances and may be addressed through collective struggle to gain control over resources and decision-making. Ideological problems are rooted in the mind and are typically addressed by using education and propaganda to mould consciousness. Consistent with a voluntarist analysis, the Mao-era state emphasized ideological transformation as fundamental to socialist economic construction.[15] *People's Daily* articles frequently addressed the relationship between problems of labour power, method, technology or other practical concerns and problems of 'thought' – often concluding that ideological shortfalls constituted the most important stumbling blocks on the road to economic development.[16]

In the summer of 1957, the state determined that it had paid insufficient attention to 'thought work' in the countryside and launched a 'socialist education campaign' to rectify the situation.[17] In August, *People's Daily* published an article, 'Grain Problems and Thought Problems', that cast recent complaints about food shortages in ideological terms. It reported the example of one county in Shanxi Province, where 90 per cent of commune members had been complaining that they were experiencing a grain shortage, but after undergoing education and discussion, only 10 per cent concluded they actually

---

[14] Wemheuer, 'Dining in Utopia', 287. See also Xin Yi, 'On the Distribution System of Large-Scale People's Communes', *Eating Bitterness*, 132. On the abuses that accompanied calls for gender 'equality', see Kimberley Ens Manning, 'The Gendered Politics of Woman-Work: Rethinking Radicalism in the Great Leap Forward', *Eating Bitterness*, 72–106.

[15] Franz Schurmann (1966), *Ideology and Organization in Communist China*, Berkeley: University of California Press; Aminda M. Smith (2013), *Thought Reform and China's Dangerous Classes: Reeducation, Resistance, and the People*, Lanham, MD: Rowman & Littlefield. Note that the post-Mao state has also often sought to promote adherence to new models of economic development through ideological moulding.

[16] 'Shi jishu wenti, ye shi sixiang wenti' [It's a technology problem, but also a thought problem], *Renmin ribao* [People's Daily], 28 March 1958, 2; 'Laoli wenti he sixiang wenti' [Problems of labour power and problems of thought], *Renmin ribao* [People's Daily], 6 October 1958, 2; 'Shi sixiang wenti, haishi shiji wenti' [Is it a thought problem or a practical problem?], *Renmin ribao* [People's Daily], 4 August 1963, 2; 'It's a methodological problem, but also a thought problem' *Renmin ribao* [People's Daily], 18 August 1963, 2.

[17] Ralph Thaxton and Felix Wemheuer have described this campaign as an extension into the countryside of the far better remembered Anti-Rightist Campaign, which targeted intellectuals and political cadres in the urban areas. Thaxton, *Calamity and Contention*; Wemheuer, '"The Grain Problem"'.

lacked sufficient grain. Selfish individualism was reportedly to blame for the peasants' unreasonable expectations, and if it were not overcome, socialist construction in China would 'suffer serious harm'. Incorrect thought was said to run through the ranks of cadres as well. At the local level, cadres suffered from 'departmentalism' that led them to focus only on securing 'immediate small advantages' for the peasants in their own commune or village, while overlooking 'the peasants' long-term interests and the state's fundamental interests'. Meanwhile, even cadres at the county level and above possessed too 'narrow' an understanding of collectivism, seeing it as 'simply a way right now of distributing to everyone a bit more, letting them eat a bit better', instead of 'thinking about the entire country's socialist enterprise and the problem of the peasants' future trajectory'.[18] At every level, the problem reportedly lay in an ideological failure to grasp the principles of socialist development and commit to the sacrifices required for its achievement.

## Socialist construction: Defending uneven distribution

In the *People's Daily* article just cited, the specific ideological problem of concern to state leaders was the desire on the part of peasants and cadres to spread existing resources more evenly to boost local or individual consumption, rather than concentrating it at the national level to achieve rapid industrial development. Felix Wemheuer characterizes this as a specific manifestation of a 'permanent struggle between the state and the peasants over the agricultural surplus', which 'resulted in a politicization of hunger in which the definition of an adequate ration became part of the conflict itself'.[19] This was where the rubber met the road: it was all well and good to critique Malthusianism and capitalism, but once in power the PRC state had to make hard decisions about how to invest scarce resources in socialist economic construction while still supplying the people's basic needs.

The tension between local and national needs represented one of the fundamental paradoxes of the Great Leap Forward. The promise of the Great Leap was society's imminent arrival at the stage of communism itself: an egalitarian society in which all Chinese people, urban and rural, could achieve their full human potential while satisfying their needs freely from the pool of collectively produced wealth.[20] In 1958, Mao had even spoken of communism as the 'three no' (no government, no state, no nationalities), suggesting that he envisioned (at least momentarily) the withering away of the state that Marx had predicted would occur naturally when communism was achieved.[21] Replacing the nation state would be myriad self-reliant communes; indeed,

---

[18] 'Liangshi wenti he sixiang wenti' [Grain problems and thought problems], *Renmin ribao* [People's Daily], 5 August 1957, 1. See also Wemheuer, '"The Grain Problem"', p. 115.

[19] Wemheuer, *Famine Politics*, p. 258.

[20] On the difficulties of the 'free-distribution system' and its quick abandonment, see Xin Yi, 'On the Distribution System'.

[21] Wemheuer, 'Dining in Utopia', p. 287.

the discourse of self-reliance achieved a salience during the Great Leap Forward not found since the days of the revolutionary base areas when Chinese Communists faced economic blockades.[22] Given the strength of this vision, we can understand why the Great Leap would have encouraged a strongly localist mentality. However, the chariot engineered to carry China to this paradise operated according to strikingly different economic principles. Before China could arrive at communism, it needed to accomplish economic development based on rapid industrialization at the national level. And this intermediate goal apparently required drastic measures to extract massive quantities of grain from the countryside. Ten thousand years of happiness was said to lie on the horizon for China's peasants, but *first* they would need to sacrifice, withstanding profoundly unequal treatment to subsidize the immediate needs of China's industrial development.

This economic pattern was in fact already established in the early 1950s. The irony is well captured in Mao's 1953 attack on rural reformer and latter-day Confucian Liang Shuming. During the 1930s, Liang had been among the most influential Chinese figures grappling with the rural economic crisis in efforts to 'reconstruct' Chinese villages from the bottom up. He was highly attuned to the threats Western economic imperialism posed to rural China, and he was committed above all to the welfare of Chinese peasants. In the early 1950s, he decried the income gap between peasants and workers produced by the Soviet model of economic development, and he cited the guidance found in the Confucian classics – 'Do not worry about scarcity; worry about uneven distribution'[23] – when he called upon the state to allocate some of the workers' income to peasants. Indeed, the notion that the government bore responsibility for the redistribution of resources to guarantee the welfare of the empire's subjects had long been a fundamental principle of Chinese statecraft.[24]

Perhaps Liang imagined that he would be successful in his appeal to a leader known for his commitment to abolishing the 'great divide' between peasants and workers.[25] Instead, Mao harshly criticized Liang at a 1953 conference: 'Your idea is not to have the peasants increase their income through their own efforts in production but to equalize the earnings of the workers and peasants by taking away part of the former's earnings to distribute among the latter. If your idea were adopted, wouldn't that spell the destruction of China's industry? Such a diversion of the workers' earnings would mean the ruin of our country.'[26] Mao thus argued that the solution to Chinese rural poverty

[22] Sigrid Schmalzer (2014), 'Self-Reliant Science: The Impact of the Cold War on Science in Socialist China', in Naomi Oreskes and John Krige (eds.), *Science and Technology in the Global Cold War*, 75–106, Cambridge, MA: MIT Press.

[23] *Lunyu* [The Analects] 16:1. For the full passage, and a somewhat different translation, see E. Bruce Brooks and A. Taeko Brooks (1998), *The Original Analects: Sayings of Confucius and His Successors*, 153, New York: Columbia University Press.

[24] Pierre-Etienne Will and Roy Bin Wong (1991), *Nourish the People: The State Civilian Granary System in China, 1650–1850*, Ann Arbor: Center for Chinese Studies, University of Michigan.

[25] Guy Alitto (1979), *The Last Confucian: Liang Shu-ming and the Chinese Dilemma of Modernity*, 324–328, Berkeley: University of California Press.

[26] Mao Tse-Tung (1977), *Selected Works of Mao Tse-tung*, Vol. V, Peking: Foreign Languages Press, 127.

lay not in redistribution but rather in the increases that a collectivist economy would bring to agricultural production – a position not entirely unlike that of conservative U.S. politicians who are sceptical of redistribution and instead seek to address poverty through economic growth.[27]

During the Great Leap Forward, a *People's Daily* article criticized the same Confucian adage that Liang had quoted to make a more specific point related to economic planning:

> To construct a steel rolling mill requires steel, and steel is just what is most lacking at present and just the thing that everyone most needs. So how do we use the limited steel we have? Should it be according to the principle 'Do not worry about scarcity; worry about uneven distribution', whereby we divide it all up so that each person has the same amount? Or do we first concentrate it in order to construct a steel rolling mill? Without doubt, we should choose the latter. It's much like eating eggs. When there are few eggs and many people, the eggs can be divided up to make one meal. Although that would solve a few immediate needs, the next step would be difficult to take. But if everyone temporarily exercises restraint, and allows the eggs to hatch into chickens, the chickens will produce more eggs. In this way, not only will people eat more eggs, but they will regularly have eggs to eat.[28]

On its surface, this explanation appears very logical – even obvious. But understood within its historical context it takes on a different significance. Here, in very plain language, is a justification of policies that required enormous sacrifice on the part of local communities and individual peasants, and that appeared to fly in the face of the egalitarian vision of communism the state had promised in return for peasant labour. In what must be the most widely cited example of Great Leap policy at the grassroots level, peasants were asked to surrender their cooking pots (which the communal dining halls promised to make redundant) to help the state produce steel for its industrialization drive. This form of resource management was neither as innocent and logical as the *People's Daily* analysis would suggest, nor as brutal and irrational as the cooking pot example is typically taken to imply. Rather, the extraction of resources from the countryside was a central element of China's economic plan for socialist development through rapid industrialization fuelled by agricultural collectivism.

I would further argue that this is the context in which we should understand Mao's alleged suggestion, which Mao's critics have seized as evidence of his barbarism, that

---

27  Writing on both the Soviet Union and China, Wemheuer notes, 'The Communist parties made it clear that a distribution of wealth and resources alone could not solve the problems of the country but that huge sacrifices had to be made to build up a modern industrial nation.' Wemheuer, *Famine Politics*, 242.

28  'Bian gang chengcai' [Turning steel into raw material], *Renmin ribao* [People's Daily], 17 November 1958, 1.

the state should allow half the people to starve in order to feed the other half.[29] He made the comment at a conference in Shanghai in March 1959 during a discussion of economic planning. While the final, most disturbing line is often taken in isolation, a fuller account of his argument reads:

> In the next three months we need to put our efforts into developing our industry. We must be forceful, relentless, and precise. Our leadership in charge of industry should act like the First Emperor of Qin.[30] To distribute resources evenly will only ruin the Great Leap Forward. When there is not enough to eat, people starve to death. It is better to let half the people die so that the other half can eat their fill.[31]

Placed in this larger context, Mao's comment remains characteristically unfeeling and undiplomatic, but it also becomes more obviously a statement about the necessity of uneven distribution of resources in the effort to industrialize, rather than a literal proposal to solve existing food shortages by starving half the population. As Anthony Garnaut puts it, 'The "people" whom Mao was willing to let die of starvation turn out to be not people at all, but large-scale industrial projects.'[32]

My intention here is neither to defend nor to vilify, but rather to emphasize the importance of the principle of uneven distribution in Maoist economic planning, including in the Great Leap era. The kind of radical, egalitarian redistribution that offends right-wing critics of socialism did appear vividly in the propagandists' portraits of the promised utopia that awaited, and a 'taste' of this future might perhaps have been found in the communal dining halls.[33] However, even the dining halls represented part of a larger plan to concentrate scarce resources for investment: they facilitated

---

[29] Zhou, *The Great Famine*, 25; Frank Dikötter (2010), *Mao's Great Famine: The History of China's Most Devastating Catastrophe, 1958–1962*, New York: Walker, 88; Alexander V. Pantsov with Steven I. Levine (2012), *Mao: The Real Story*, 466, New York: Simon & Schuster. Note that Yang Jisheng has disputed that Mao ever said this (http://insideoutchina.blogspot.ie/2011/12/yang-rebuts-Dikötter-on-famine-research.html); see also Cormac Ó Gráda (2013), 'Great Leap, Great Famine: A Review Essay', *Population and Development Review*, 39 (2): 333–346. For a related Mao quotation about letting half the people die, see Jung Chang and Jon Halliday (2005), *Mao: The Unknown Story*, 458, London: Jonathan Cape; for a critique of Chang and Halliday's interpretation of the quotation, see Thomas P. Bernstein (2006), 'Mao Zedong and the Famine of 1959–1960: A Study in Wilfulness', *The China Quarterly*, 186: 421–45, 443–44.

[30] The first emperor of Qin (Qin shi huangdi) was a famously autocratic leader despised especially by the Confucians for his inhumane policies but credited for standardizing the written language, currency and units of measurement, and for developing transportation and other economic infrastructure.

[31] Zhou, *The Great Famine*, 25.

[32] Anthony Garnaut, 'Hard Facts and Half-Truths: The New Archival History of China's Great Famine', *China Information*, 27 (2): 223–246, on 235–238; see also Wemheuer, *Famine Politics*, pp. 56–57. Garnaut further supplies an important phrase left out of Zhou's version of the document, which makes still clearer the context of the quotation as it relates to industrialization.

[33] David Zweig argues that it also was reflected in the practice of transferring resources from wealthier to poorer which he says was 'widespread during the Great Leap' despite being criticized by Mao in 1959. He also shows, however, that such transfers occurred not just among units at the same bureaucratic level but also from the local level up the chain to concentrate resources at higher levels. David Zweig (1989), *Agrarian Radicalism in China, 1968–1981*, Cambridge: Harvard University Press, Chapter 7.

increased state control over grain and so increased procurement to feed Chinese cities and international allies aiding China's industrialization, and they further allowed the state to extract resources from peasants in the form of their cooking pots. This is one face of what Engels, Lenin and other Marxists have referred to as 'state capitalism': the state replaced the bourgeoisie as the owner of the means of production, but it behaved in a somewhat parallel manner, extracting resources from the people for investment in state industrialization projects.

## Interpreting the Great Leap famine

Very few people today deny the Great Leap famine outright. Those who continue to express scepticism must do so in the face of overwhelming evidence. However, the extreme sensitivity of the issue for the PRC state, its salience for much larger questions and perhaps most importantly the ontological flexibility of the concept of scarcity all make for great variability in the explanations people have produced as to what happened and why. The scholarly literature on the Great Leap famine has mushroomed over the past decade, and I cannot hope to do justice to it all here. Instead, I will focus on how Malthusian, Marxist and Maoist perspectives have continued to inform interpretations of the famine's causes and broader significance.

Widely remembered in present-day scholarship is the story of Liu Shaoqi, then China's president and Mao's heir-apparent, who visited his home village in Hunan Province in 1961 and not only personally witnessed the devastation but also heard from a peasant what was reportedly a common understanding among locals at the time: that only three-tenths of the calamity was attributable to natural causes, while man-made factors were to blame for the remaining seven-tenths.[34] This acknowledgement of the political reasons underlying the famine would not survive the resurgence of radicalism in the mid-1960s, when Mao sought to re-establish party authority and popular commitment to the revolution through an expanded Socialist Education Campaign (1964–66) followed by the Cultural Revolution (1966–76). Skirting both the severity of the crisis and its causes, the leadership studiously avoided mention of the famine at all, instead adopting the term 'three years of natural disasters'.[35] While natural disasters are a different form of 'nature' than Malthus's supposedly 'natural' law of population dynamics, it is nonetheless striking that when confronted with famine in a state-socialist context, these particular Marxists avoided analysing the famine from the perspective of political economy and instead resorted to blaming nature.

---

[34] This episode appears in many places. Among the most useful is Wemheuer, 'Dealing with Responsibility', 180.

[35] This phrase first appears in *People's Daily* already in 1961. See, for example, a report on a speech by Zhou Enlai: 'Zhou Enlai zongli juxing shengda guoqing zhaodaihui' [Premier Zhou Enlai Holds a Reception for National Day], 1 Oct. 1961, 1.

After the Cultural Revolution, party leaders took stock of recent history under the new paradigm established by Deng Xiaoping. The official verdict on the Great Leap Forward was that 'Mao Zedong and many leading comrades … were impatient for quick results and overestimated the role of man's subjective will and efforts'; moreover, Great Leap policy 'overlooked objective economic laws', and the political campaign against so-called Rightists 'gravely undermined inner-party democracy from the central level down to the grassroots'. The document did not acknowledge the famine per se, but recognized the 'serious losses to our country and people' from 1959 to 1961, which it attributed 'mainly … to the errors of the Great Leap Forward and of the struggle against "Right opportunism" together with a succession of natural calamities and the perfidious scrapping of contracts by the Soviet Government'.[36] Preserved in this assessment is a prominent role for natural forces outside of state control, alongside a familiar scapegoating of the Soviets for the effects of the Sino-Soviet split, but in first place an attribution of 'errors' to Mao and other leaders. While hardly an analysis worthy of Marx's treatment of the Great Famine of Ireland, this assessment contains some of the germs of what has become a burgeoning field of scholarly research into the causes of the Great Leap famine.

The role of the weather has declined steadily in scholarship, but a number of works have continued to insist that it at least be formally confronted and not summarily dismissed. Y. Y. Kueh provides the most systematic analysis of the effects of weather on agricultural yields in China during a sixty-year span including the Great Leap era. He concludes that poor weather conditions did negatively impact yields during the Great Leap, but further argues that policy errors, especially the reduction of cultivated land and excessive state procurement, were an 'equally and potentially more important factor' leading to the famine: 'even without bad weather, the peasants could not possibly have survived'.[37] Building on Kueh's analysis, along with meteorological research by Chinese scholars, Cormac Ó Gráda concludes that patterns of drought mapped convincingly onto patterns of harvest shortfalls.[38] It is perhaps not surprising that Chris Bramall, one of the Western economists most sympathetic to Mao-era collectivism, has also insisted on serious treatment of the weather hypothesis, though his analysis resulted in the conclusion that weather did not play a significant role.[39] For Li Minqi, a far more committed Leftist, the weather continues to be an important factor under-acknowledged by mainstream scholarship – and while he recognizes political causes, he assigns these not to Mao but to Liu Shaoqi and other revisionists.[40]

---

[36] Chinese Communist Party (1981), 'Resolution on Certain Questions in the History of Our Party since the Founding of the People's Republic of China', in *Resolution on CPC History*, Beijing: Foreign Languages Press, 28–29.

[37] Y. Y. Kueh (1995), *Agricultural Instability in China, 1931–1991: Weather, Technology, and Institutions*, 207, Oxford: Clarendon Press.

[38] Cormac Ó Gráda (2008), 'The Ripple that Drowns? Twentieth Century Famines in China and India as Economic History', *Economic History Review*, 61 (S1): 5–37.

[39] Chris Bramall (2011), 'Agency and Famine in China's Sichuan Province, 1958–1962', *The China Quarterly*, 208: 990–1008, esp. 994.

[40] Li Minqi (2008), *The Rise of China and the Demise of the Capitalist World-Economy*, New York: Monthly Review Press, 42–44.

Interestingly, it is from one of the most passionately anti-communist scholars that we hear an argument on the weather most inspired by Marxist dialectics: Frank Dikötter asks us to remember that human and natural factors are 'intertwined', and so the effects of weather on agriculture are greatly dependent on how humans have altered the landscape. In the case of 1950s China, Dikötter argues, grandiose state projects undertaken with the kind of shoddy workmanship one expects from forced labour produced dams ready to collapse under inclement weather. Ironically, however, Dikötter's argument ultimately rests more on ideological than political causes – more on a Maoist than a strictly Marxist explanation. He follows Judith Shapiro's analysis in suggesting that it was the belief that humans were separate from, and in Shapiro's terms were at 'war' with, nature that 'lay at the root of environmental degradation in China at the time'.[41] Felix Wemheuer, meanwhile, makes a similar point about the dialectical relationship between politics and weather, but does so in the broader context of famine in nineteenth- and twentieth-century China, and moreover cites Mike Davis's important environmental history of 'late Victorian' famines as they related to political economy, in particular to the ramifications of imperialism and capitalism.[42]

Scholars have increasingly eschewed weather-based analyses and have placed far greater emphasis on political and social factors. The question of who bears the most personal responsibility has been of consistent concern to scholars. Consensus seems to be growing that top leaders knew about the unfolding crisis and made conscious decisions to continue the Great Leap policies in the face of disaster; meanwhile, some scholars have further suggested that the degree to which localities suffered was closely related to the behaviour of local leaders.[43] While Mao himself has come in for his share of criticism, people have been eager to avoid being seen as simplistically pinning the blame on a single person – a 'great man of history' interpretation whose widespread and longlasting unpopularity among scholars is another of Marx's important academic legacies.[44]

Instead of assigning personal blame, many scholars have highlighted problems said to be intrinsic to the political economy of state socialism itself. If Marx used the Irish potato famine to explain the problems inherent in capitalism, these scholars have sought in the Great Leap famine evidence as to problems allegedly inherent in state socialism. Some political scientists and economists have specifically identified

---

[41] Dikötter, *Mao's Great Famine*, Chapter 21, especially 178. Here it is worth remembering the material limitations facing Mao-era China and the magnitude of the task of modernizing the economy. This, more than any anti-nature ideology, should help us understand the drive to plunder natural resources.

[42] Wemheuer, *Famine Politics*, 27; see also 193. Mike Davis (2001), *Late Victorian Holocausts: El Niño Famines and the Making of the Third World*, New York: Verso.

[43] For this argument, see especially Bramall, 'Agency and Famine'.

[44] In his review of Yang Jisheng's *Mubei* (Tombstone), Frank Dikötter criticizes Yang for pinning the blame on Mao personally, rather than offering a structural or systemic explanation, a charge Yang adamantly refuted (see http://insideoutchina.blogspot.ie/2011/12/yang-rebuts-Dikötter-on-famine-research.html). Interestingly, Ó Gráda's assessment is precisely the opposite: 'While Dikötter and Zhou blame the famine on Mao Zedong personally, for Yang – who is no apologist for Mao – it proves that "a system without a corrective mechanism is the most dangerous of all systems"'. Ó Gráda, 'Great Leap, Great Famine', p. 333.

incentive problems and a kind of 'tragedy of the commons' as root causes of the famine. The tragedy of the commons, a theory popularized in 1968 by ecologist Garrett Hardin, emerges from a Malthusian concern about the realities facing communities with limited resources; it suggests that given a system of collective ownership, people will ruin resources held in common as they seek to satisfy their individual needs at the expense of the larger social good.[45] For political scientist Dali Yang, the communal dining halls represented just such 'a tragedy of the commons in a world of scarcity'; he argues that when offered unlimited access to food, peasants ate more than the system could accommodate, leading to shortages in the following seasons.[46] Justin Yifu Lin has disputed the role of the dining commons but similarly adopts an explanation rooted in the behaviour of individuals. Using game theory (which has taken the tragedy of the commons as a central example), he suggests that when Great Leap policy eliminated the right of peasants to withdraw from agricultural collectives, what had been a 'repeated game' became a 'one-time game', eroding the 'self-enforcing contract' and thus causing agricultural productivity to collapse.[47] For Wei Li and Dennis Tao Yang, the fault lies even more explicitly in 'central planning' itself, as the 'impatient central planner, believing in the magic power of collectivization', diverted too many resources from agriculture (including nutritional resources for agricultural labourers) and so precipitated a decline in agricultural production.[48] And for Xin Yi, the very egalitarianism of the Great Leap's promise represented 'contempt for basic human values' and so 'destroyed the driving force behind society and undermined the social order'.[49] Implicit in all of these interpretations is a belief in the necessity of market economics. If Karl Marx were alive to offer a critique, he would likely see in these theories a reflection of the 'orthodox economy' in which they were generated, just as he saw the ideology of capitalism to have informed the theories of Malthus and Darwin. And indeed, the influence of both these figures is very much at play in the analyses just discussed.

In the work of Frank Dikötter, the Great Leap famine serves still more explicitly as evidence of the inviolability of markets and, moreover, the essential brutality of collectivism. Godfather of neoliberalism Friedrich Hayek provides the critical piece of wisdom: as Dikötter paraphrases Hayek, '[O]nce you start stripping away every kind of freedom – the freedom of association, freedom of speech, freedom of movement, *freedom to trade* – once you replace it by a one-party dictate, there can only be one road, and that is the road to serfdom.' And for Dikötter, 'the Great Leap Forward illustrates

---

[45] Garrett Hardin (1968), 'The Tragedy of the Commons', *Science*, 162 (3859): 1243–1248. For a Marxist critique, see John Vandermeer (1977), 'Ecological Determinism', in Ann Arbor Science for the People Editorial Collective (ed.), *Biology as a Social Weapon*, 108–122, Minneapolis: Burgess Pub. Co.

[46] Dali Yang (1996), *Calamity and Reform: State, Rural Society, and Institutional Change since the Great Leap Famine*, 55, Stanford, CA: Stanford University Press.

[47] Justin Yifu Lin (1990), 'Collectivization and China's Agricultural Crisis in 1959–1961', *Journal of Political Economy*, 98 (6): 1228–1252.

[48] Wei Li and Dennis Tao Yang (2005), 'The Great Leap Forward: Anatomy of a Central Planning Disaster', *Journal of Political Economy*, 113 (4): 840–877. On 842–843.

[49] Xin Yi, 'On the Distribution System', 142.

that better than anything else in twentieth-century history'.[50] Perhaps the boldest argument in Dikötter's widely read book *Mao's Great Famine* is that collectivism could not work without the imposition of state terrorism of the most brutal kind: peasants died not just because the socialist economy produced food shortages but because their leaders beat them to death in a futile attempt to circumvent the inevitable incentive problems associated with collectivization.[51]

However, it is not just proponents of capitalism and devotees of Hayek who have emphasized the significance of markets in the Great Leap famine. The authors of several village studies (Friedman, Pickowicz and Selden's *Chinese Village, Socialist State* and Ralph Thaxton's *Catastrophe and Contention* stand as premier examples) have drawn inspiration from James C. Scott in highlighting the disruptions caused to rural society by state socialism. Markets play an important role in these studies, but in a more abstract sense than that in Dikötter's work. For these scholars, what was at stake was less 'the free market' and more the actual rural markets that served as both social spaces and economic networks for peasant households. The disruption of these markets not only represented an assault on rural society but also eroded the family and community survival strategies that had protected rural people against the worst consequences of food shortages in the past. Excessive grain procurement thus came on top of a ruined rural landscape, where the most important traditional safeguards had been broken. In these accounts, the dining commons play an important role, but in a different way than in Dali Yang's analysis: the problem was not overconsumption leading to a 'tragedy of the commons', but rather the wrecking of an existing robust system founded on the kind of 'moral economy' that Scott has argued underlies most peasant societies.[52] Although the language employed is sometimes quite similar to that used by Dikötter, from a political perspective these works do not naturalize capitalism so much as 'traditional' society.

The authors of these village studies tend to share Dikötter's perspective that the economic process of collectivization was inextricable from the political violence that accompanied it. However, it should also be possible to argue that the political violence of the 1950s is reason *not* to equate the famine with collectivization per se; such an argument would depend on the notion that collectivization can occur without systemic state violence and persecution. Felix Wemheuer, for one, has been cautious not to use the Great Leap famine as evidence against all collectivist efforts: 'Collectivization did not necessarily produce famine, but it contributed to the starvation of millions when it was implemented in a very radical way.'[53] Here, what is important is the specific implementation of Great Leap collectivization – the speed with which it was attempted and, more importantly, the political persecution that not only resulted in many deaths but also prevented local leaders from making sound decisions about

[50] Frank Dikötter as interviewed on *The Alex Jones Show*, 23 Sept. 2010, archived at https://www.youtube.com/watch?v=Y9zASJEIusk (emphasis added). See also http://www.frankDikötter.com/interviews/interviews-5.html.

[51] Dikötter, *Mao's Great Famine*.

[52] James C. Scott, *The Moral Economy of the Peasant: Rebellion and Subsistence in Southeast Asia*, New Haven, CT: Yale University Press, 1976.

[53] Wemheuer, *Famine Politics*, 248.

grain procurements and distribution. The famine thus would not provide evidence against agricultural collectivism as a form of economic organization, but only against authoritarian forms of governance. A related argument is put forward by economist Zhun Xu, who holds that 'stratification' (political and economic inequalities), rather than egalitarianism, was responsible for any failures of Mao-era collectivization.[54] Jeremy Brown's work also helps shift the focus away from discrediting socialism per se. In highlighting the urban bias of Mao-era economic policy – showing how leaders systematically shifted resources to shelter urban people while villagers died – Brown avoids attacking socialist collectivism and instead condemns the PRC state for failing to live up to its own promises of an equitable society.[55]

Whether or not it is understood as part and parcel of a collectivist economy, totalitarianism represents the chief culprit in an increasing number of scholarly treatments of the famine. The work of Amartya Sen, who argued so influentially that democracy is the most important factor in preventing famines, has been clearly influential in this respect. Sen combines Marx's central insight as to the political character of famine with a special focus on the contrasts between democratic and totalitarian forms of government, an angle that today enjoys broad appeal across the political spectrum.[56] Much current scholarship on the Great Leap famine, representing a wide range of political positions, seems to follow Sen, as baldly summarized in Ralph Thaxton conclusion that 'Mao's anti-democratic politics' constituted the 'primary cause' of the famine.[57]

On the other hand, Felix Wemheuer has noted that one-party dictatorships have been able to pull themselves out of famine, and he credits the PRC state for its ability, after 1962, to 'prevent deadly famines'.[58] Moreover, and perhaps more importantly, both Wemheuer and Ó Gráda have called for a broader view of the famine, placing it in a longer historical context. Without discounting the distinctive features and unprecedented scale of the Great Leap famine, they insist on recognizing the ways in which it was in fact consistent with earlier patterns of famine, especially since the nineteenth century. They take Dikötter in particular to task for ignoring earlier famines and failing to recognize the material constraints Mao's regime faced; Wemheuer goes as far as to flag these gaps as evidence of Dikötter's political bias against the socialist state.[59] While neither scholar lets Mao or his authoritarian regime off the

---

[54] Zhun Xu (2012), 'The Political Economy of Agrarian Change in the People's Republic of China', Ph.D. Diss. University of Massachusetts, Amherst.

[55] Jeremy Brown (2012), *City versus Countryside in Mao's China: Negotiating the Divide*, Cambridge: Cambridge University Press.Others have highlighted this urban bias, but none so fully and compellingly as Brown.

[56] Amartya Sen (1981), *Poverty and Famines: An Essay on Entitlement and Deprivation*, Oxford: Clarendon Press;; Amartya Sen (1999), *Development as Freedom*, New York: Knopf.

[57] Thaxton, *Catastrophe and Contention*, p. 334. Thaxton directly engages with Sen on 27n8 and 155. For other examples of engagement with Sen, see Bramall, 'Agency and Famine', 992n4; Justin Yifu Lin and Dennis Tao Yang (2000), 'Food Availability, Entitlements and the Chinese Famine of 1959–61', *The Economic Journal*, 110: 136–158. Felix Wemheuer engages critically with Sen in his *Famine Politics* (150–153), concluding that 'Sen's theses are accurate but [too] general' to provide sufficient insight into the Chinese case.

[58] Wemheuer, *Famine Politics*, pp. 22, 252.

[59] Ibid., p. 28; Ó Gráda, 'Great Leap into Famine', pp. 192–193.

hook, in their accounts the famine is not simply an indictment of state socialism. For Wemheuer, the Great Leap famine, along with the Soviet famine of the early 1930s, 'should be understood as deadly escalations of the general conflict between the state and the peasantry over agricultural surpluses'.[60] For his part, Ó Gráda emphasizes the 'backwardness' of the Chinese economy in the 1950s. This isn't necessarily in Mao's favour, since as he points out, 'to engage in radical economic experimentation in such an extremely backward economy was to risk disaster'.[61] However, over all, Ó Gráda seeks to provide 'more room ... for the supply side factors stressed by Malthus', by offering 'more historical context ... drawing attention to China's relative poverty and the overlap between high excess mortality regions and those previously vulnerable to famine'. With such an analysis, he argues, 'The famine remains an outlier, but to an extent fits a pattern established by the mid-nineteenth century'.[62]

The growing abundance of scholarship on the Great Leap famine reflects the twists, and the ironies, of history in the production of knowledge about scarcity. Marx's analysis of the Irish potato famine as a problem of capitalism, rather than a Malthusian population crisis, represents an important historical predecessor for the work of scholars across the political spectrum today, many of whom have taken a similar position in refuting claims about the 'natural' causes of the Great Leap famine and instead pinning the blame firmly on the political economy of state socialism. But Malthusian understandings of scarcity and population dynamics are also alive here – in the work of game theorists interested in determining how people make choices in resource-constrained situations and in the work of historians and social scientists seeking a larger historical perspective than merely the specific travesties of any one form of political economy. And the kind of ideological analysis that Mao favoured, in which incorrect ideas (rather than material scarcity or unjust economic structures) lay at the root of development problems, also crops up here and there – not just in the official interpretations of the PRC state but also in the writings of critics of Maoism, who see Mao's ideology of the separation of humans and nature as the root cause of environmental degradation in Mao-era China.

Politics and ideology can act in vulgar ways to bias perception. Political and ideological commitments certainly prevented Mao-era officials from acknowledging the man-made causes of the Great Leap famine, even though Marxist materialism should have pushed them to do so. Meanwhile, political and ideological commitments have arguably limited the subtlety with which some scholars, on both the right and the left, interpret the significance of the Great Leap famine and advance understandings of the meaning of scarcity.

But politics and ideology will always play a role in our discussions, because scarcity is a conceptual, rather than a natural, category. The quantity of grain can be measured, but whether or not that quantity constitutes scarcity requires theorizing, which necessarily involves a set of understandings about political relationships and the role of ideas in shaping human action. Awareness of the contexts in which we are doing that

---

[60]  Wemheuer, *Famine Politics*, p. 243.
[61]  Ó Gráda, 'The Ripple', p. 10.
[62]  Ibid., p. 32.

theorizing, and of the influence of our intellectual forebears, should help us approach the task more critically and therefore more subtly and more robustly.

## Acknowledgements

I thank Jeremy Brown, Fredrik Albritton Jonsson, Felix Wemheuer and Zhun Xu for their helpful recommendations, but these fine scholars are not responsible for any errors or analytical weakness in this chapter.

# 12

# Encounters with Scarcity at a Micro-Scale: Householders' Responses to Drought as a Continuum of Normal Practice

Heather Chappells

## Introduction

Recollections of the 1976 drought in England suggest it was patriotic to have a dirty car, normal to flush washing-up water down the toilet and that everyone knew the golden rule about bath time: use five inches of water at most and then pour it onto the garden.[1]

Evoking such encounters with extreme drought conditions is more than an exercise in nostalgia. A micro-scale vantage point can reveal deep layers of understanding about variable social experiences of normality and disruption, and how this shapes the relative flexibility of practices. Understanding how people have coped with a lack of resources in the past can elucidate social and material interactions that can influence the effectiveness of responses to the normalized scarcity conditions that are anticipated for the future.

Drought is usually considered a temporary decrease of average water availability, while scarcity occurs where there is insufficient water to meet long-term average requirements.[2] While drought is episodic and exceptional in relation to normal conditions, scarcity reflects a long-term imbalance between supply and demand that can come to be seen as a normal state of affairs.[3] In this chapter, both episodic drought and long-term water scarcity are seen as simultaneously natural and social phenomena. Although water scarcity relates to resource problems of different

---

[1]   I. Herbert (2006), 'Drought of 1976 Brought Standpipes and Shared Baths', *The Independent*, 17 May. Available from: http://www.independent.co.uk/environment/drought-of-1976-brought-standpipes-and-shared-baths-478513.html (accessed 23 September 2017).

[2]   European Commission (2007), 'Water Scarcity and Droughts', Second Interim Report, DG Environment, June.

[3]   A. F. Van Loon and H. A. J. Van Lanen (2013), 'Making the Distinction between Water Scarcity and Drought Using an Observation-Modeling Framework', *Water Resources Research*, 49 (3): 1483–1502.

intensity and duration to drought, analysing experiences of relatively short-lived disruptions can be a multifaceted revelatory tool for informing future adaptations to scarcity. Memories of coping with drought in the past can help to uncover how people understand and experience shortages today and whether they are perceived to be intensifying.[4] Times of temporary disruption can offer a useful moment to uncover the importance of routinized practices in the lives of different people and their relative flexibility.[5] Investigating how consumers have coped with disruption in the past, and through recurrent drought experiences, can shed light on shifting meanings of essential uses, normal consumption and consequently what it means to get back to normal.[6] How consumers engage with or resist specific measures introduced to manage disruption provide further insights into variable sociopolitical notions of scarcity and resilience that frame individual, collective and institutional responses. Moments of disruption can offer a means for tapping into the roles that incumbent socio-technical infrastructures, involved in the delivery of resources, play in defining the scope for consumer adaptation. Reflecting on variable approaches to coping with drought can be used to expose how different consumers interpret, experience and manage shortages in relation to local environments. These multiple layers of insight that temporary disruptions can expose makes them integral to informing future approaches for sustainable adaptation to living with scarcity in relation to water and other critical resource sectors.

Water resource scarcity has been examined within the social sciences at both macro- and micro-scales. Studies in the former realm have focused on the role of hydraulic paradigms in constructing the social and political contexts of shortage and on the reinforcing role of infrastructures in defining how disruption manifests in different geographical settings.[7] Implicit in such accounts is the notion that scarcity is not just a natural or physical phenomenon but is produced within specific socio-technical regimes that are the products of a certain politics, place and time.[8] Though consumers feature in macro-scale investigations of scarcity and drought, the fine-grained details of how disruptions intersect with routine aspects of daily life are often sidelined in such accounts. Cultural geographers, sociologists and anthropologists have addressed this imbalance through detailing how social structures and cultural dynamics of everyday

---

[4]  F. Furedi (2007), 'From the Narrative of the Blitz to the Rhetoric of Vulnerability', *Cultural Sociology*, 1 (2): 235–254. J. Garde-Hansen, L. McEwen, A. Holmes and O. Jones (2016), 'Sustainable Flood Memory: Remembering as Resilience', *Memory Studies*, 1–22. Available from: http://journals.sagepub.com/doi/pdf/10.1177/1750698016667453 (accessed 23 September 2017).

[5]  H. Chappells, W. Medd and E. Shove (2011), 'Disruption and Change: Drought and the Inconspicuous Dynamics of Garden Lives', *Social and Cultural Geography*, 12 (7): 701–705.

[6]  F. Trentmann (2009), 'Disruption Is Normal: Blackouts, Breakdowns and the Elasticity of Everyday Life', in E. Shove, F. Trentmann and R. Wilk (eds.), *Time, Consumption, and Everyday Life*, 67–84, Oxford: Berg.

[7]  L. Del Moral Ituarte and C. Giansante (2000), 'Constraints to Drought Contingency Planning in Spain: The Hydraulic Paradigm and the Case of Seville', *Journal of Contingencies and Crisis Management*, 8 (2): 93–102. M. Kaika (2003), 'Constructing Scarcity and Sensationalizing Water Politics: 170 Days That Shook Athens', *Antipode*, 35 (5): 919–954.

[8]  E. Swyngedouw (2004), *Social Power and the Urbanization of Water: Flows of Power*, Oxford: Oxford University Press.

life frame consumer understandings of, and responses to, water shortages.[9] Questions addressed in this context include how different notions of normal consumption evolve, how habits become ingrained, how routines are performed, and as a consequence, how resource-intensive social practices might be adapted during drought.

Informed by these macro- and micro-scale perspectives on the social, technological and cultural construction of droughts, this chapter offers a distinctive interpretation of what it may mean to cope with longer-term scarcity. Utilizing disruption as a *micro-scale* methodological lens, the chapter explores the meanings embedded in routine consumer practices and their dynamics under drought conditions. Key questions addressed are how pre-existing structures of normal life materialize and change in relation to periods of water stress, both temporary and long-lived, and how this influences variable methods of coping employed over time. Focusing on the negotiability of household practice is instructive to uncover how consumer responses to drought-related disruptions are related to deep-seated memories, cultural orientations and material arrangements that support certain water-consuming practices. The chapter takes a long-term view of disruption, situating a recent experience in historical context in order to highlight shifting ideas about the flexibility of household practices and socio-technical resilience. Moving across time reveals different scales of drought management and connects these to varied incumbent institutional and grid arrangements, which ultimately structure consumer responsiveness and resilience to scarcity. Comparing disruption experiences is used to explore the cultural specificity of consumer response and resilience, as well as to consider the wider applicability of drought as a lens on the flexibility of micro-practice and infrastructure under intensifying conditions of scarcity.

The chapter begins with an evaluation of householders' interpretations of the worsening resource situation as they lived through a specific period of drought in South East England in 2006. Ostensibly, the drought appeared as an exceptional, isolated and relatively short-lived disruption intruding within otherwise normal conditions. Through a sociologically informed lens, however, householders' varied interpretations suggest that the drought, and responses to it, acted within a series of continuums that connected the past to the present and normality to disruption. These connections are explored through four key strands of investigation.

The first strand focuses on the role of memory in connecting current incidents of water shortage to past disruptions; how did people living through the current drought talk about past experiences of living without, and how did they invoke such memories to explain their responses to more recent events? A second strand relates to the remarkable diversity of what counts as normal practice. Talk of coping, maintaining, suffering or adapting during times of drought speaks to a plurality of normal states and expectations, driven by diverse social orientations. These multiple states stand in contrast to the often unitary visions of governing authorities and their subsequent infusion in the formulation of standardized responses, such as a universal hosepipe

---

[9] E. Shove (2003), *Comfort, Cleanliness and Convenience: The Social Organization of Normality*, Oxford: Berg. Z. Sofoulis (2005), 'Big Water, Everyday Water: A Sociotechnical Perspective', *Continuum: Journal of Media & Cultural Studies*, 19 (4): 445–463. V. Strang (2004), *The Meaning of Water*, Oxford: Berg.

ban. A third investigative strand relates to embedded infrastructures and their ongoing role in reproducing ideas about normal access, use and response. This connects to macro-structuring ideas about the socio-technical ordering of societal response, but with a distinctly micro-scale focus on everyday technologies like the hosepipe. A fourth line of exploration considers drought as a means to uncover changing ideas about householders' roles as active participants in alleviating water shortages. This engages with different ideas about the meaning of socio-technical resilience at a micro to macro organizing scale.

Exploring what it means to live through a drought proves to be a powerful revelatory tool that has further relevance in thinking about sustainable adaptation to longer-term scarcity in the future. The conclusion revisits the themes of memory in shaping experience, the plurality of normal practice, infrastructural roles in shaping responses and contrasting interpretations of resilience from a micro-household and macro-provider perspective. It briefly draws on experiences of coping with prolonged droughts in California to consider the wider value of such investigations in dealing with anticipated situations of scarcity as the norm in future.

## Drought as a lens on changing household practices

'Across the south east of England, rainfall has been much lower than for the same period in 1974–76, and in some places it is the lowest since the drought of 1920–22. Continued dry weather through the spring and into the summer would give us one of the most serious droughts of the last hundred years.'[10]

This was the stark warning to residents issued at the beginning of 2006, when parts of Britain faced diminishing water supplies. This drought is taken here as a methodological lens through which to examine the hidden dynamics of everyday life under conditions of scarcity.

Drought is increasingly understood as a product of the interplay between natural, social and material conditions. Human influences on both drought and water scarcity include regionally variable pressures of overpopulation or overconsumption and the influence of incumbent sociopolitical regimes that define resource access rights. Evaluations of the severity of drought conditions are further contingent upon local indicators and experiences of shortage. How drought recurs and is remembered in relation to other periods of shortage thus has a bearing on the orientation and scale of response.

The drought culminating in 2006 resulted from two successive winters of below average rainfall. Deemed to be one of the region's most serious droughts of the last century, groundwater and river levels in many areas were exceptionally low. A key mechanism used to manage the drought was a hosepipe ban, which targeted outdoor demand, deemed to be more discretionary and therefore more flexible. Eight water companies introduced such bans with 15.6 million customers affected. For 3.4 million people this was the second consecutive summer of water restrictions.[11] Householders

---

[10]  Environment Agency (2006), 'Drought Prospects 2006', Bristol: Environment Agency, February: 2.
[11]  Environment Agency (2007), 'Early Drought Prospects', Bristol: Environment Agency, November.

did not face the disruption of standpipes or rota cuts as they had in some previous droughts. Even without these measures regional estimates reported that demand was between 5 and 15 per cent lower than expected.[12] In some water resource zones, however, peak demand did reach near-record levels in July and there was a genuine concern among water managers here that a third dry winter would bring significant disruption to daily life. In the end this scenario did not materialize and it was in fact flooding that wreaked havoc the following year.

The conceptualization of drought and the coping strategies employed to alleviate it have been variable over the course of the twentieth century in Britain. Situating the 2006 drought within the context of these shifting approaches is important in both charting the variable experience of droughts in Britain and tracing the evolution of these experiences over time.[13] Householders' understandings of water scarcity, and of the need to adapt, form over time with relation to historical experiences of drought.[14] Connecting disruptions past to those of the present is a means to track the shifting legitimacy of consumption practices and methods to regulate them.[15] Though historical comparisons are made throughout this chapter, the first strand of inquiry directly asks how householders assessed the drought with relation to their own personal memories and experiences of disruption in the past.

## Memories connecting the past to the present

'I certainly feel as though it's probably drier [than usual] and the only time I can really relate it to was 1976 when it was particularly dry then.'

Ostensibly, the drought appeared as an unusual event amid long-term average conditions but disruptions rarely exist in isolation in the minds of those who live through them. People define droughts relative to past moments of living without water that they have experienced. In turn, drought memories shape how people view the severity of shortages and opinions of what needs to be done to alleviate them. Situating talk of the current drought within reflections about past disruptions has another key purpose; it reveals the temporal variability of social practices, and memories of disruption can provide a platform for developing lay knowledge, social learning and resilience.[16] Drought memories in this sense can be seen as an opportunity to consider how householders repurposed their knowledge of past droughts to interpret the current event and how this subsequently fed into their responses.[17]

---

[12] J. Duggin, G. Jeal and B. Piper (2007), 'UKWIR Drought and Demand: Modelling the Impact of Restrictions on Demand during the Drought', UKWIR Report No. 07/WR/02/3, London: UKWIR.

[13] V. Taylor, H. Chappells, W. Medd and F. Trentmann (2008), 'Drought Is Normal, the Socio-technical Evolution of Drought and Water Demand in the UK, 1893–2006', *Historical Geography*, 35 (3): 568–591.

[14] Ibid.

[15] F. Trentmann and V. Taylor (2006), 'From Users to Consumers: Water Politics in Nineteenth-Century London', in F. Trentmann (ed.), *The Making of the Consumer: Knowledge, Power and Identity in the Modern World*, 53–79. Oxford and New York: Berg.

[16] Garde-Hansen et al., 'Sustainable Flood Memory'.

[17] Furedi, 'From the Narrative of the Blitz'. Garde-Hansen et al., 'Sustainable Flood Memory'.

In terms of the physical drought conditions many people talked in general terms about how they had experienced other situations of comparable 'dryness' prior to the current event. Evidence for this referenced media reporting about the relative seriousness of the situation along with various gauges in the local environment, including dry riverbeds, falling stream levels or parched lawns. Observations varied depending on the fluctuating local water situation. A serious drought to many people was equated with images of dry reservoirs. This situation was to be found in some water supply areas but this sign of major drought was absent elsewhere, both on the ground and in the media. To some extent this was an invisible drought affecting mainly groundwater reserves hidden away underground. Drought was also a situation equated with long, hot summers, and though July 2006 saw record temperatures, August and September were relatively wet.[18] The lack of visible signs of drought, along with media speculation about mismanagement, meant that some householders questioned if it was a real drought at all. At least one water company responded by filming water levels in boreholes to prove to their customers that the situation was indeed real and more serious than usual. Other companies relayed messages that aimed to challenge perceptions of England as a wet country and to instill instead a sense of how the south-east of the country in particular was drier on average than some desert states. These efforts were intended to fundamentally challenge peoples' long-held understandings of average regional climatic and environmental conditions and to educate people on the reality of the local water situation.

Water consumers shared their own ideas about whether the drought was real or not. One householder who had lived in East Anglia all his life explained how he understood that this was a particularly dry summer but questioned whether this was indicative of wider climatic change or the consequence of heightened awareness through the media.[19] Media reports and company representations of the severity of the water shortage failed, in some cases, to equate with the dynamic and variable local situations in which people found themselves. Reports about the hosepipe ban extending into the winter were hard to equate with heavy rainfall being experienced in some areas: 'I hear stories now, they say it's going to be a struggle like this winter and I find it quite amazing because of all the rain we've had.'[20]

Another popular gauge for the relative severity of the 2006 drought was the long, hot summer of 1976 – an iconic event etched into the collective memories of those generations old enough to recall the standpipes, shallow baths or bricks in the cistern. As one middle-aged householder recalled of the earlier drought measures: 'I didn't hear any of that stuff this year, so rightly or wrongly, I feel as though the water problems were greater in '76 than they are now.' For this householder the current hosepipe ban seemed a measured and logical response as it targeted the most wasteful or unnecessary practices, such as cleaning the car or watering the grass. He and others who had lived through 1976 expressed relief that more serious restrictions, like standpipes or rota cuts, had not been introduced. At the same time, what people were asked to do, or not

---

[18] Met Office (2006), 'Weather records tumble', News release, 1 August.
[19] Interview household (#5), Drought and Demand project.
[20] Interview household (#22), Drought and Demand project.

to do, had framed their perception of the severity of the present-day water problem they were facing.

Technology-wise, the 'brick in the cistern' campaign seemed to be emblematic of the drought in 1976 but its absence in 2006 again served for some householders as evidence that things were not quite so bad. Targeting toilet flushing seemed to have become almost a taboo topic in the later drought and when the Mayor of London compelled Londoners to restrict the frequency of flushing,[21] this was not advice welcomed by many water companies. Reduced flushing belonged, along with other 'draconian' measures such as standpipes and rota cuts, in the past not in the privatized customer service–driven water industry of the modern day. There were, however, some inconsistencies in this message, as in early 2006 when national environmental regulators urged consumers to be cautious in the use of water in order to avoid standpipes.[22] This was much to the chagrin of most water managers, who saw standpipes as a very last resort and as indicative of perceived deficiencies in their ability to manage their supply systems. Responses to drought appear here as symptomatic of changing social and institutional conventions.

The long, hot summer of 1976 was remembered for its series of interruptions to everyday life. Householders recalled how the absence of water had halted both indoor and outdoor practices; sharing bathwater became the norm, while local authorities stopped filling community pools denying citizens their usual summer pleasures. People had to find other ways to get clean or cool off. In thinking about how they had coped in the past, householders caught up in both the 1976 and 2006 droughts provided comparative evidence of shifting everyday resilience. One householder recalled how in the past when water supply had been restricted at certain times, they had initiated strategies for collecting and storing water in saucepans, kettles and any other containers they could find. The legitimacy of implementing more extreme drought strategies was questioned in light of social controversies arising in the past. An elderly woman recounted how timed supply cut-offs in London in 1976 had caused outrage due to the impact on new mothers and the very elderly and pondered how authorities in the current drought would possibly be able to navigate the complexities of which users or supply zones to serve or restrict should the situation worsen.[23] Drought-management measures like water cut-offs and standpipes were incomprehensible for some consumers in 2006, and from a company perspective unsuited to the contemporary political climate, but previous experiences of these harsher restrictions continued to have a bearing on how people perceived drought and the sorts of adaptations they anticipated. The expectancy of standpipes, should the situation worsen, was a concern

---

[21] Muir, H. (2005), 'Think before you flush – Mayor's latest message to Londoners', *The Guardian*, 29 June. Available online: http://www.guardian.co.uk/environment/2005/jun/29/water.greaterlondonauthority (accessed 23 September 2017).

[22] DEFRA (2006), 'Drought in the south east – Minister urges 'use water sensibly now', DEFRA News Release, 2 February Available from: http://web.archive.org/web/20060216164257/www.defra.gov.uk/news/2006/060202e.htm (accessed 23 September 2017). Environment Agency (2006), 'Drought Prospects 2006', Spring update, Bristol: Environment Agency, May.

[23] Interview household (#20), Drought and Demand project.

articulated by those who had lived through the long, hot summer of 1976 and when the weather broke in the late summer of 2006 there was collective sigh of relief.

Droughts, such as those that culminated in water restrictions in 1976 and 2006, may be relatively short-lived but they live on in peoples' memories and are a reference point that are likely to frame future understandings of whether scarcity is real and how it should be handled. Peoples' experiences of each drought are also remarkably diverse and understanding why this is the case is important because it has a bearing on the longer-term resilience of water resources and demand.

### Drought and the micro-variability of household practices

Drought is used here to unpack the meaning and dynamics of normal consumption. Changing sensibilities about what is a wasteful or acceptable use of water are reflected in which water consuming technologies and practices have been the foci of restraint policies and media debates. During the interwar years and again in the 1970s and 1990s, water providers called for voluntary economy in the use of water used for gardening, toilet flushing and bathing, suggesting that these have been persistently perceived as more wasteful or more adaptable demand components. As early as the 1890s, the wasteful lawn watering routines of affluent suburban consumers were highlighted in media accounts as an uncivil form of behaviour during shortages.[24] Suburban gardening practices have remained at the forefront of debates about profligate and unnecessary consumption ever since. Yet when the hosepipe ban was introduced in 2006 it was not unanimously commended as a common-sense approach to beating the drought. A concern articulated by certain water managers was that the emergency restriction of water use sent out the wrong message to their customers. They saw the need for a continued and sustained message to develop a sense of care and caution in water use as the norm rather than responding only in exceptional circumstances.[25] As the impacts of the drought were not spread evenly over the south-east region, managers in areas where resources were at relatively healthy levels were also prompted to question the relevance of restrictions for their customers.

The hosepipe ban that was introduced in 2006 provides one means to interrogate variability, flexibility and resilience in relation to household practices. The ban proved effective in terms of significant reductions in water demand regionally, but more interesting from a sociological perspective was the question of how consumer adaptations made to 'beat the ban' challenged or reinforced different conventions of normal practice. When considering water from a sociological perspective, the usual starting point is to acknowledge that resources are of value, not directly, but for facilitating an array of social and cultural practices, such as bathing, relaxing or cooling off.[26] Every one of these micro-consumption practices involves a distinctive

---

[24] Taylor et al., 'Drought Is Normal'.
[25] W. Medd and H. Chappells (2011), 'Resilience in Practice: The 2006 Drought in Southeast England', *Society and Natural Resources*, 25 (3): 302–316.
[26] Shove, *Comfort, Cleanliness and Convenience*.

coordination of bodies, minds, resources and technologies.[27] The practice of showering, for example, became normal in the context of particular ideas about health and hygiene as well as through developments in plumbing, heating and power.[28] Understanding the dynamics of micro-consumption practices, at times of both normal and exceptional conditions, thus requires an appreciation of the integration of such elements and of their simultaneous coordination by individuals and by attachments to wider social, economic and political systems.[29]

This way of thinking about normal practice can be applied to experiences of coping with drought in 2006, which centred primarily on outdoor water use. Interviews with households living with the hosepipe ban clearly showed that habits and routines of garden life both before and during the ban related to different social obligations, material arrangements and life stages.[30] Those who valued gardens as a site of productive horticulture, for example, made extra efforts to keep lawns and flower beds well watered despite the hosepipe ban, allocating more time to these tasks and using an impressive array of water storage and distribution systems (e.g. multiple watering cans, rainwater collection tanks and grey water reuse systems). Others stated that they did not worry about the lawn going brown and just accepted this as an inevitable fact of life given Britain's notoriously unpredictable weather. Some actually welcomed the chance to do less in the garden. Others saw it as a chance to plan for the future – as in the case of a young couple who had recently moved into a new home and were planning a lower maintenance garden to cope with predicted longer-term changes in climate they anticipated to produce scarcity conditions.[31]

Other responses to the ban varied depending on diverse social obligations that defined the need for water use, for example, filling paddling pools to keep children cool on hot days or washing down patios and garden furniture to prepare for summer barbeques. In other situations, where work or other family obligations took precedence garden watering constraints were often welcomed as it meant one less task to perform. The timing of the drought and its coincidence with a particular phase in people's life cycle or familial situation further reinforced drought responses, as witnessed through phases of active maintenance or abandonment of gardens. In other words, how change to normal practice materialized reflected the amplification of existing social orientations that placed different values on sustaining garden life.[32]

How householders talked about living through the 2006 drought – in terms of coping, adapting, suffering or giving up – speaks volumes about the plurality of normal situations and expectations that exist. These plural existences are underpinned by diverse social orientations and conventions, and they relate to specific practice

[27] A. Reckwitz (2002), Toward a Theory of Social Practices, *European Journal of Social Theory*, 5 (2): 243–263.

[28] M. Hand, E. Shove and D. Southerton (2005), 'Explaining Showering: A Discussion of the Material, Conventional and Temporal Dimensions of Practice', *Sociological Research Online*, 10 (2). Available online: http://www.socresonline.org.uk/10/2/hand.html (accessed 23 September 2017).

[29] Shove, *Comfort, Cleanliness and Convenience*. W. Medd and E. Shove (2007), *The Sociology of Water Use*, UKWIR Report No. 07/CU/02/2. London: UKWIR.

[30] Chappells et al., 'Disruption and Change'.

[31] Interview household (#20), Drought and Demand project.

[32] Chappells et al., 'Disruption and Change'.

constellations framed by different configurations of family life. Some parents might willingly give up the lawn as one less job in chaotic lives, but would struggle to live without the paddling pool to cool down their suffering children in the midst of a heatwave. Other elderly gardening enthusiasts would find despair in the deadened landscape of the brown lawn and wilted flower beds.

Normal life is by no means uniform or one-dimensional. It is an experience enriched with all kinds of diverse comforts and small pleasures. Giving these up can be easy or difficult depending on the perceived social or emotional cost. This diversity stands in contrast to the often unitary visions of normal life represented by governing authorities and their subsequent infusion in the formulation of standardized responses such as the hosepipe ban that see giving up the pleasures of outdoor life as a small price to pay for future water security. However, habits and routines associated with water-consuming practices were decided not only by individual preferences or by social obligations and conventions; they were reinforced by infrastructures in place and consequently by the macro socio-technical regimes underpinning such micro-infrastructural arrangements.

### Embedded infrastructures and the (in)flexibilities of household adaptations

Water infrastructures are integral to everyday life, but the value of these systems and the services they provide in the lives of different consumers have varied over time. Means of coping without water need to be considered in light of these developments as technologies have evidently framed both interpretations of normal use and the strategies that households can employ to manage drought over time.

At a macro–scale, infrastructure networks that connect households to an endless supply of drinking water have a role in creating expectations and defining what becomes normal and thereby legitimate consumption.[33] Arrays of smaller devices embedded in homes also play an ongoing role in reproducing ideas about normal access, levels of use and acceptable response. Technologies can effectively promote their own use; once people have invested in appliances these can offer unlimited access to cleanliness and convenience with very little effort.[34] Hosing down the car is generally easier and more effective than hauling buckets of water to do the same job. Indoor labour-saving devices, such as the washing machine or the dishwasher, allow people to use and dispose of water invisibly and without much thought. Though, as happened in 2006, these appliances may be repurposed, at least one householder described collecting water from the washing machine to use on the garden.

Most homes in Britain have been routinely equipped with hot and cold running water since the 1950s. New plumbing infrastructures facilitated an array of new water consuming appliances from the 1960s, including automated washing machines, dishwashers and power showers. Such arrangements have supported new household

---

[33] Z. Sofoulis (2006), 'Changing Water Cultures', in E. Probyn, S. Muecke and A. Shoemaker (eds.), *Creating Value: The Humanities and Their Publics*, 105–115, Canberra: The Australian Academy of the Humanities.

[34] Strang, *The Meaning of Water*.

routines, such as the trend for daily showering rather than weekly bathing, but these have not been uniformly or unanimously practised across households. It is within a varied landscape of evolving consumer dependencies on different water infrastructures and devices that droughts have emerged. Domestic plumbing and appliances had clearly changed radically in the lifetimes of households living through the 2006 drought. Seniors vividly recalled the first time indoor bathrooms were plumbed in, or the arrival of the washing machine in place of the washtub and mangle. Stark contrasts were made with household standards and living arrangements today, including questioning of why the younger generations needed two or three bathrooms when one would suffice. When pressed on such matters, those living in multi-bathroom homes emphasized issues of convenience and changing convention such as the emerging norm for en suite bathrooms and expanding home or family size. Besides acknowledging the broad sweep of changes in household technologies, standards of living and associated domestic practices, householders' adjustments to drought showed the micro-variability of cultural and material arrangements within households and how these structured capacities for water saving.

Cultural perceptions of different water uses, and their associated technologies, as a root cause of scarcity have ebbed and waned in popular consciousness, in line with views about their necessity or optionality. For example, languishing in a deep bath is now considered more wasteful than the available alternative of a quick shower, but many water-saving experts now view power showers as worse than baths in terms of volume of an average use.[35] Though restrictions on the depth of bathwater was not an official drought policy in 2006, shifting ideas about wasteful washing practices played into water-saving advice such as fitting flow restrictors or using a timer to monitor shower time. In terms of the drought-affected families interviewed, however, very few made bathing decisions based solely on wastefulness. Instead elements of relaxation, sensation and hygiene intersected with family organization and differently paced lives. Responses revealed that habits and technologies had changed significantly – from experiences of shared, and often tepid, baths of childhood recounted by older generations to present-day preferences for private bathroom space and the fierce jets of power showering favoured by younger generations today.

Materially, the incredible canvas of domestic devices and plumbing fittings framed water-saving contexts. Talking of a hosepipe or a shower in generic terms overlooks a multitude of attachments and configurations that influence how people undertake activities and what constrains them. For example, an elderly couple living in a rented apartment reflected on how their landlord had replaced the old hot water tank with a smaller one. It was this rather than water restrictions that had hindered their ability to take the deep and hot bath they desired or to do multiple tasks such as washing-up dishes and bathing at the same time. In homes where water pressure was generally poor, showers were often not even a feasible option for truly getting clean. What emerges

---

[35] C. Cooper (2011), 'Now Baths Are Green Option as Eco-groups Go Cold on Showers, *The Independent*, 22 November. Available online: http://www.independent.co.uk/environment/green-living/now-baths-are-green-option-as-eco-groups-go-cold-on-showers-6265904.html (accessed 23 September 2017).

from these examples is a sense of how coping with scarcity can be constrained by the configuration of household technologies, water distribution infrastructures as well as by diverse social needs or routines. To talk in general terms of restricting showering or regulating bath size fails to account for the multiple constellations of bathing practices and devices that already exist as part of the entrenched pre-drought landscape.

Droughts have persistently opened discussions about how much water is actually needed to perform a given activity – questions that inevitably interface with infrastructure. In 1921 and again in the 1970s, voluntary restrictions, such as 5" baths, were urged upon citizens. In the 1970s, placing a brick in the toilet cistern became the common practice to reduce the volume of water used in each flush. From the 1990s onwards, the 'Hippo' and other forms of water-saver cistern device have been enrolled to do the same job. In the drought people talked of such devices as a simple option for conserving water without expending too much effort, but whether they were accepted as part of household water-saving strategies was related to water pressure and the capacity to produce a 'proper' flush to eliminate waste. Again, this was related to plumbing infrastructure alongside differing conventions of hygiene. Water-saving experts further acknowledged that such devices could have the consequence of double flushing, ironically negating their benefit in alleviating pressure on water resources. Interactions with water-saving devices represent one example of consumer adaptation to drought conditions but evidence indicates that householders' roles in dealing with disruption go far beyond such simple acts.

## Moving between micro- and macro-scale resilience in coping with scarcity

Shifting perceptions about the passive or active role of consumers in overcoming water stress can be discerned across time. During many of the major droughts to hit England and Wales since the 1950s, the need for consumer responsiveness was strongly mediated by the level of political and institutional support for supply-side measures. The 1959 drought saw localized water shortages alleviated by laying of emergency pipelines to overcome supply shortages while in 1976 reservoirs and rivers were utilized to their limits to overcome drought.[36] Both these examples indicate the dominant emphasis on meeting consumer demand through macro management of supply capacity. This did not mean that consumer activities were left untouched but it suggests that, historically, there has been limited interest in engaging households directly in water management at a micro-scale.

Possibilities of reusing or recycling water have been a common topic highlighted during droughts, from the shared baths of 1976 to debates about the value and safety of rainwater or grey water use in 2006. During the latter drought a tension emerged between the perceived need for managing resilience through reinforcing big supply infrastructure and promoting flexibility through adaptive management of water demand at a household level. This became evident in discussions about the value of alternative, non-mains household water collection systems during the drought.

---

[36] Taylor et al., 'Drought Is Normal'.

Rainwater collection for outdoor water use was already an established practice for many at the time of the drought, and many homeowners reported plans to upgrade existing systems in light of continued uncertainty over water resource availability in future and in the context of likely recurrent restrictions.[37] Relatively simple forms of rainwater collection had taken on new momentum in the years preceding the drought, as water companies had responded to concerns over climate change and peak demand associated with garden watering with promotions for water butts.[38] During the 2006 drought, householders who aimed to maintain garden practices had attempted to purchase more though in some cases had been thwarted, and frustrated, by lack of availability at retail outlets. Other householders aimed even higher, developing more sophisticated techniques for grey water reuse on the garden. One elderly man explained how he had diverted used water from the washing machine and was collecting it in storage boxes outside the house to use on his flower beds. He explained how he had been inspired to recycle water by a neighbour who had constructed an even more sophisticated system that involved laying pipes from his bath down across the lawn to water his shrubbery and vegetable plot.[39]

In light of the perceived scope for rainwater collection or water recycling as a means of coping with short-lived drought or long-term scarcity, some householders questioned why water regulators and managers were not doing more to promote such micro-scale, in-house systems as a resilient solution. Though the answer to this question is politically complex, and beyond the scope of this chapter, it was clear from talking to representatives of water companies in South East England that their idea of a resilient solution diverged considerably from some consumer visions. On the one hand, household-scale systems were seen as a marginal and temporary solution, and on the other, they were presented as a long-term solution that saw the regular utilization of a virtually free source of water as part of domestic infrastructure.

The example of rainwater collection and recycling further reinforces the points made previously that different conjunctions of social orientations and technologies influence the interest in and capacity for adaptation in outdoor living. Collecting rainwater in the garden was supported by the majority of our householders in theory, but not all had translated this into practice. For those households with an avid interest in gardening, rainwater butts were a long-standing feature and natural response to drought. For other households, such as those with young children, or those lacking green fingers, they were a source of danger or an unnecessary hassle.

## Conclusion

Reviewing household experiences of a specific drought in South East England has shown the value of a micro-scale focus on disruption as a lens to reveal the plurality

---

[37] Medd and Chappells, 'Resilience in Practice'.
[38] R. Bisgrove and P. Hadley (2002), *Gardening in the Global Greenhouse: The Impacts of Climate Change on Gardens in the UK*, Technical Report, November, Oxford: UK Climate Impacts Programme.
[39] Interview household (#12), Drought and Demand project.

of normal ways of life that underpin peoples' capacities to comprehend and to cope with scarcity. Situating this drought in the context of earlier ones, and in relation to the evolution of water-related practices and infrastructures, has illuminated further the cognitive, cultural and material connections across time that feed into the experience of disruption and the shaping of resilience.

Focusing on a specific disruption has produced key revelatory moments through which social dynamics and resiliencies of consumer practice are exposed. This singular case of drought is by no means unique and exploring others can undoubtedly expand understandings of what it means to cope with scarcity. California, for example, has recently emerged from a decade-long drought that featured some of the most extreme water-resource shortages facing a developed society.[40] Drought is a recurrent feature of this region making it possible to trace the historical development of crisis discourses and responses. Uncovering the social and material dimensions of past Californian droughts may therefore prove invaluable in informing discussions about coping with persistent scarcity in the future. Although this is beyond the scope of this chapter, some connections are made below in relation to the British case discussed.

In both regions the domination of a supply-oriented logic is evident until at least the 1970s, when large schemes to store and transfer water over long distances were a key component of maintaining supply during disruption, though geographical scales varied. A shift to conservation management is often associated with the severe droughts of the 1970s in both Britain and California and to a rising environmental consciousness. In Britain the drought of 1976 is commonly credited with raising consciousness of conservation needs, while the dry Californian weather of 1977 brought widespread water rationing and a serious interest in conservation through efficiency devices. However, in both these drought regions engaging consumers in efforts to save water was not a new approach; it had been a recurrent feature of past droughts alongside supply measures.

Just as droughts have been a normal feature of everyday life, so to have consumer adaptations been a normal practice. Faced with shortages consumers have continually sought out creative and innovative solutions to manage water use, often on their own initiative. In South East England this manifested in the form of water recycling, while Californian cases have shown how people have built backyard wells to access groundwater.[41] These forms of consumer adaptation have not, however, always been recognized as a legitimate form of resilience from a provider perspective. Water regulators and managers have also played a key role in shaping the meaning of excess consumption and the types of adaptation that consumers are encouraged to make. Mandatory or voluntary measures to overcome drought (e.g. rationing, policing, penalties, publicity) are influenced by the severity of physical drought conditions, but

---

[40]  'The California drought is officially over but the next could be around the corner', *The Guardian*, 7 April 2017. Available online: https://www.theguardian.com/us-news/2017/apr/07/california-drought-over-jerry-brown-future-climate-change (accessed 23 September 2017).

[41]  P. Hartlaub (2014), 'Remembering the California droughts of 1977 and 1991', *San Francisco Chronicle*, 24 October. Available from: http://blog.sfgate.com/thebigevent/2014/01/16/remembering-the-california-droughts-of-1977-and-1991-photos/ (accessed 23 September 2017).

also institutionalized interpretations of normal or rational consumer practice that are in turn the product of particular hydraulic regimes. This in a sense brings us full circle, closing the gap between the micro- and macro-organization of water scarcity as options for resilience and adaptation are sidelined within the bigger regime.[42]

It is also debatable whether evidence of more recent shifts to engaging consumers in conservation measures indicates a meaningful appreciation of the differentiated cultural meanings assigned to water-consumption practices in everyday life. The meaning of non-essential usage that underpins water restrictions varies by region and jurisdiction, but outdoor use has been the universally common target. Gardeners' concerns about plants and lawns have been deprioritized during severe shortages as other essential uses have taken precedence. A question that emerges in focusing at the micro-scale of practices is how the deep-seated values that people attach to a myriad of indoor and outdoor practices might be incorporated in the formulation of more flexible coping methods for addressing future scarcity. Another question to contemplate is the role of drought and conservation measures in facilitating new forms of resilience. During droughts Californian and British gardeners have been regularly cast in the role of wasteful water guzzlers and have been subject to intense public and media scrutiny. At the same time, gardens have become an important site of innovation as residents have worked out a way to beat the drought and maintain their existing ways of life. Some of these methods may prove crucial in dealing with situations of scarcity going forward.

Droughts have been recognized as a revelatory crisis – one that can disrupt routines sufficiently to allow people to innovate and perhaps even bring about accelerated rates of social and technological change.[43] In viewing droughts not so much as a revelatory crisis but as a revealing encounter with normal and continuing disturbances of everyday life, pathways for innovation or change appear quite differently. One might ask, for example, how people might become more engaged in routine responsiveness and flexible adaptation to the inevitable, and very probably more frequent, disruptions to be encountered in the future? What is clear is that the potential for change will be defined by pre-existing ways of life and social and cultural values in conjunction with macro-structuring regimes. This challenges the legitimacy of unitary calls for restraint. Scarcity and the means to cope with it is fundamentally part of a continuum. What it means to live without water is sustained by memory and by infrastructure and by routinized practice. Capacities to adapt to times of shortage thus depend on how these pre-existing elements interact within the more time sensitive and household-specific micro-organizational contexts of specific droughts. Disruptions are not a short-lived deviation from normal life; they are part of its past, present and future.

Scarcity is predicted to be the usual state of affairs in many regions over the coming decades. Conceptually, this means we need to move away from episodic thinking where disruptions upset the equilibrium of normal life to thinking in terms of a continuum where imbalances between supply and demand are normal even if they vary in intensity or frequency. In turn this signals a different way of thinking about what it

---

[42] Sofoulis, 'Big Water, Everyday Water'.
[43] J. S. Solway (1994), 'Drought as a "Revelatory Crisis": An Exploration of Shifting Entitlements and Hierarchies in the Kalahari, Botswana', *Development and Change*, 25 (3): 471–495.

means to cope with scarcity. Rather than coping as something people are expected to do to alleviate temporary disruptions, it needs to be integrated into routines of daily life. When summer arrives switching to recycled water for the garden might become as normal as fitting winter tyres to deal with icy roads. Scheduling for scarcity in this way may offset more serious imbalances in resource availability. Scarcity, in the future, may not be something that policymakers strive to avoid at all. It may be something that societies learn to accept as more effort is put into instilling a sense of care and caution for the future by dealing with scarcity as part of everyday life.

Beyond the household there is an important role for institutions in reshaping perceptions of scarcity and embedding long-term resilience in domestic infrastructures. Addressing material imbalances is not restricted to sorting out the supply problem; it requires intensified attention to imbalances in demand. There is scope for this to go far beyond the implementation of standardized measures such as a hosepipe ban but this will require the in-depth evaluation of demand and its micro-dynamics. Demand represents the outcome of many practices that are valued very differently by consumers. This diversity of practice means that scarcity will not be experienced consistently. Understanding how scarcity affects different social groups is one priority but sociological evaluation shows the relevance of opening up the micro-details of practice to unpack multiple options for resilience. 'Measuring' scarcity in this sense means evaluating its propensity to produce pleasure, comfort and security – as well as discomfort, despair or even pain. These emotions, senses and feelings will affect how scarcity is experienced. How policymakers will navigate this complex landscape of consumer orientations upon which experiences of scarcity are predicated – or indeed whether they will see this as a priority at all – remains to be seen, but it may open up an array of options to cope with scarcity that people find more palatable than standardized responses that can have a disproportionate cultural impact.

## Acknowledgements

The case study of UK drought explored in this chapter draws on research undertaken by the author in conjunction with Dr Will Medd for the Drought and Demand 2006 project. The Drought and Demand project was funded by the Economic and Social Research Council (RES-177–25-0001) in collaboration with UKWIR, Defra, OFWAT, the Environment Agency, Anglian Water, Essex and Suffolk Water, Folkestone and Dover Water, Three Valleys Water and South East Water. Interviews with twenty-two householders in South East England, managers from four water-resource teams and representatives from the four main national regulatory bodies and regional teams were undertaken by the author during the drought in the summer of 2006.

Part Four

# Dynamics of Distribution

# 13

# A Climate of Scarcity:
# Electricity in India, 1899–2016

Elizabeth Chatterjee

## Introduction

In August 2016 a working group of the International Commission on Stratigraphy provisionally recommended that the current time interval be renamed to recognize the new geological 'age of mankind': the Anthropocene. Interpretations of the new epoch are hotly contested. Nonetheless, at the heart of many popular and historical understandings of the new era lies a dilemma of abundance.

The mainstream historical narrative locates the key moment of the Anthropocene's emergence in the West around 1800 with the invention and spread of steam engines. In this account, the modern economy was founded on the shattering of the old Malthusian constraints imposed by the natural world. Britain tore past its previously successful counterparts in Asia, thanks in large part to its access to abundant land and especially coal.[1] This fossil fuel revolution, and its second waves based on electricity and oil, brought with it the promise of apparently endless economic growth. Such a narrative has been echoed both by climate scientists and by perhaps the most influential critique of the Anthropocene to come out of the humanities thus far: the claim that the new era's hallmark was the emergence of the steam-driven capitalist socioeconomic system – 'fossil capitalism' – and that it might therefore be more accurately labelled the 'Capitalocene'.[2] While the Anthropocene Working Group has shifted instead towards

---

[1]  Kenneth Pomeranz (2000), *The Great Divergence: Europe, China, and the Making of the Modern World Economy*, Princeton, NJ: Princeton University Press; E. A. Wrigley (2010), *Energy and the English Industrial Revolution*, Cambridge: Cambridge University Press. At least until the Anthropocene Working Group announced that it provisionally favoured an official start-date around 1950, the emphasis on Europe around 1800 was the 'dominant scholarly consensus' on the Anthropocene; see Alan Mikhail (2016), 'Enlightenment Anthropocene', *Eighteenth-Century Studies*, 49 (2): 211–231, 222.

[2]  Andreas Malm and Alf Hornborg (2014), 'The Geology of Mankind? A Critique of the Anthropocene Narrative', *Anthropocene Review*, 1 (1): 62–69; Andreas Malm (2016), *Fossil Capital: The Rise of Steam Power and the Roots of Global Warming*, London; New York: Verso. The most vociferous exponent of the 'Capitalocene' label, Jason W. Moore, emphasizes the opening of the New World colonies over coal, but abundance in the Euro-Atlantic world still lies at the heart of his account; see *Capitalism in the Web of Life: Ecology and the Accumulation of Capital* (2015), London; New York: Verso.

a date around 1950, economic historians have continued to argue that 'the decisive process was that which launched what became the incomplete but worldwide spread of industrialization'.[3]

All this came at the cost of environmental and social degradation. The apparent material abundance enjoyed by Western elites in particular was revealed to be running headlong into systemic planetary limits, limits which do not neatly coincide with 'peak' coal, oil or natural gas. This is the popular tragedy of the Anthropocene, and the root of fundamental debates about the future of economy and society, at least in the Global North: '[W]e cannot agree on whether the world we relate to is one fundamentally defined by scarcity (and thus limits) or by abundance (and thus unlimited potential).'[4]

But what of the world beyond the north-western corner of Europe and its North Atlantic offshoot? Imitating standard, Enlightenment-tinged accounts of 'the birth of the modern world', the influential 'Capitalocene' thesis that dominates the still-emergent economic history literature on the Anthropocene locates virtually all the key actors – inventors, colonialists and capitalists – in Europe and the United States. The fossil economy's beneficiaries are depicted as an industrial and commercial elite minority, in contradistinction to the mass of the population. Beyond this heartland, the rest of the world features largely as a passive resource pool[5] or imitators of a peculiarly Euro-American development model. Such literature often assumes a neat process whereby fossil capitalism was transmitted from north-west Europe to its colonial peripheries, either through a process of mechanistic diffusion – the "westernisation" of the world'[6] – or via coercion by 'a clique of white British men'.[7] This is perhaps unsurprising, given that its authors are typically specialists on early modern or Victorian Europe, but it neglects a rich body of revisionist history on the economy, the environment and technological development in the Global South.

This chapter suggests that in its focus on abundance, the Capitalocene thesis misdiagnoses both the dynamics of fossil capitalism's spread beyond its original heartlands and the degree of hegemony and coherence it displayed thereafter. Late development is a condition characterized by new forms of, and a new consciousness

---

[3]  Gareth Austin (2017), 'Introduction', in Gareth Austin (ed.), *Economic Development and Environmental History in the Anthropocene: Perspectives on Asia and Africa*, London: Bloomsbury Academic, 6. The impact of the Capitalocene thesis likely owes much to lack of competition, given the persistent gulf between economic and environmental history.

[4]  Joshua J. Yates (2012), 'Abundance on Trial: The Cultural Significance of Sustainability', *Hedgehog Review*, 14 (2): 8–25, 22–23.

[5]  This is true even of one recent attempt to grant colonialism a central place in the Capitalocene narrative, the idea of the 'Plantationocene', in which world history is read off the unusual colonial experience of the Americas. See Donna Haraway (2015), 'Anthropocene, Capitalocene, Plantationocene, Chthulucene: Making Kin', *Environmental Humanities*, 6 (1): 159–165, 162.

[6]  Elmar Altvater (2007), 'The Social and Natural Environment of Fossil Capitalism', in Colin Leys and Leo Panitch (eds.), *Coming to Terms with Nature: Socialist Register 2007*, 37, London; New York; Halifax: Merlin Press. See similarly Christophe Bonneuil and Jean-Baptiste Fressoz (2016), *The Shock of the Anthropocene*, London; New York: Verso. As Julia Adeney Thomas argues in her forthcoming review of the latter for *Social History*: 'The old diffusionist model of "human technology" arising exclusively in the West until the 1850s when it "reached a global scale" is recuperated without acknowledging the research dislodging this Eurocentric modernization narrative.'

[7]  Malm and Hornborg, 'Geology of Mankind?', 3; Malm, *Fossil Capital*, 267.

of, scarcity – of remaining behind in the waiting room of Malthusian subsistence while the elites of the developed world revel in the new material surfeit. Indeed, the starting point for one recent collection was the speculation that scarcity acts as a totalizing discourse of modernity in the Global South in the way that risk does in the North, naturalizing a turn to scientific and technological fixes.[8] If abundance was the precondition of the Euro-American fossil economy, how did fossil capitalism spread and develop in settings where scarcity was the norm? Were the beneficiaries of the fossil economy always fossil capitalists, and to what degree did they succeed in ensuring that electricity was governed along recognizably capitalist lines? More fundamentally, can Northern living standards be universalized for the South's huge populations without asphyxiating humankind or must the latter be expected to embrace comparative scarcity voluntarily?

To answer these questions, this chapter focuses on India, now a key case as the world's third-largest national carbon emitter, and takes as its lens the spread of electrification. On-grid, utility-scale electricity was *the* great macro-technology of the twentieth-century fossil economy (and a critical enabler of the twenty-first-century knowledge economy), a crucial input that reshaped capitalism from factory technologies to the rise of finance. It also lies at the intersection of fossil capitalism and distributive politics, touching virtually every dimension of everyday life, at least in electrified areas. Finally, power generation is now the single largest source of anthropogenic carbon emissions worldwide, placing it at the centre of the contemporary environmental crisis. The history of electricity in India therefore provides a rich case through which to view one trajectory of fossil capitalism beyond its Atlantic origins and into the postcolonial era.

The following analysis first examines how this crucial macro-technology of fossil capitalism arrived in India. Against the assumption of a seamless dissemination of the fossil economy, the elements of colonialism, fossil capitalism and rising energy consumption did not neatly align before 1947, the year of Indian independence. Outside favoured elite pockets the imperial regime was largely indifferent to electrification, which instead often relied on local initiative and capital. In this way colonialism helped to produce a new consciousness of scarcity, as power became a crucial industrial input and, for nationalists, a defining characteristic of the modernity that the colonial regime denied its peripheries.

Yet, against the emphasis on corporate, export-driven manufacturing that so preoccupies Capitalocene theorists,[9] it was not only industrial capitalism that relied on fossil fuels. Agriculture, infrastructure, lighting, welfare provision, urban life, household labour, public communication and even democracy have also become increasingly dependent on energy abundance. We might thus more accurately analyse the spread of a broader *fossil developmentalism* than fossil capitalism.

The chapter therefore turns to explore how the persistent scarcity of electricity came to intersect with fossil developmentalism in the formally democratic context

---

[8]  Lyla Mehta (ed.), *The Limits to Scarcity: Contesting the Politics of Allocation*, London; Washington, DC: Earthscan, 2010, xxi.
[9]  See especially Malm, *Fossil Capital*.

of postcolonial India, examining this question from first a society-centric and then a state-centric perspective. Against the Capitalocene emphasis on the hegemony of industrial and commercial capitalists and the seemingly inexorable process of the commodification of natural resources, political pressures to obtain scarce power came to be exercised both within and without the democratic process in ways that often undermined fossil capitalists' access to electricity in favour of agricultural and residential consumers, and subverted attempts to impose conventional economic rationality on bureaucratic power governance. As this suggests, it is important to separate out a 'hard', absolute scarcity of electricity (the quantity of power *generated*) from the 'soft' scarcity created through the unequal politics of its frontline *distribution*, which creates asymmetric shortages for different categories of consumer; both types of scarcity are socially produced – though they are also inseparable from natural resource constraints and electricity's physical characteristics – but their policy implications are quite different. Neither the political economy nor the governing logic of the Indian electricity supply industry is well captured by Capitalocene historiography derived from Euro-American experiences. Defined by endemic scarcities, the history of electrification in India thus illustrates the complexity of the much-debated relationships between energy abundance and colonialism, fossil capitalism and democracy outside the Global North.

## Generating scarcity: Electricity in the colonial era

Mainstream Anthropocene–Capitalocene literature condemns colonialism for spreading carbon-intensive technologies such as '[t]rans-continental canals, railways, steamships, docks, grain silos and telegraph lines', as noted above.[10] But did European colonialism really lead to such a neat diffusion of fossil capitalism? A substantial body of revisionist economic and environmental history scholarship suggests this is too simplistic: even if it did not actively encourage *de*industrialization, colonialism did not simply gift capital- and energy-intensive development to its peripheries.[11]

This is especially true if we move beyond the 'canonical' technologies of empire such as railways and telegraphs to examine *absences* in the archival record and on the ground alike. No absence is more notable than electricity. Electrification, as the political scientist Sunila Kale recently noted, was largely 'incidental' to imperialism into the early twentieth century – and therefore to subsequent historical scholarship on the British Empire.[12]

Colonial India illuminates the limits of imperial interest. In the capital, the Calcutta Electric Supply Corporation (CESC) began operations in 1899, only seventeen years

---

[10] Bonneuil and Fressoz, *Shock*, 238.

[11] In India the deindustrialization debate dates back to the early nationalist movement. It remains much contested, especially around textiles. Even if colonialism did not crush local production, as sceptics suggest, technological transfer was clearly limited; see Tirthankar Roy, *The Economic History of India, 1857–1947*, New Delhi; Oxford: Oxford University Press, 2000, 114–153.

[12] Sunila S. Kale (2014), 'Structures of Power: Electrification in Colonial India', *Comparative Studies of South Asia, Africa and the Middle East*, 34 (3): 454–475, 455.

after London and New York's first generating stations. But outside colonial residential zones, military complexes and industrial belts around the major cities, electrification was rare. Before 1920 the limited capacity additions that did materialize were generally used more to regulate the population – lighting prisons, government offices, arms factories and lighthouses – rather than directly prioritizing economic development in the fossil-capitalist mode.[13] There was a slow, regionally differentiated take-off of hydroelectric projects from the 1920s. Nonetheless, senior officials often remained indifferent, despite growing calls from local elites – both Indian and occasionally colonial – to install grids and support new provincial generation capacity.

The situation was somewhat better in some princely states, such as Mysore under the celebrated administration of M. Visvesvaraya, or in Bombay, where a hydroelectric plant owned by the local entrepreneurial Tata dynasty contributed half of all India's installed capacity as late as 1917.[14] As this suggests, indigenous rulers, officials, entrepreneurs and investors were crucial in electricity's early spread. The share of foreign ownership in installed generation capacity correspondingly fell from around 80 per cent in 1913–14 to only 31 per cent in 1928–32.[15] This was no passive process of technological 'diffusion', but a collaborative process in which local capital and initiative played a key role.

Cultural diffusion and skill transfers did not seamlessly accompany the geographical relocation of technologies, however. Torn between a dearth of imported personnel and scepticism about Indians' technical abilities, the colonial regime was slow to encourage engineering education.[16] Senior engineers, even in Indian utilities, were often British, German or American, and even after independence India continued to rely on imported technology and foreign or multinational technical expertise for some years. British engineers and managing agencies stayed on in some utilities well into the 1950s.

As a result, in 1947 the entire generation capacity of the Indian electricity sector stood at a mere 1,362 MW, less than 0.5 per cent of installed capacity in 2016. One historian concludes: 'At the time of its Independence, India had an electrical industry which reached the level of European nations just before 1914'; the reason it did not opt for full nationalization was 'that there was actually nothing much to nationalize.'[17] This underdevelopment was castigated by nationalists, who argued in 1938 that electricity was 'the very life blood of the industrial nation which must flow abundantly and without interruption if the nation's strength and well-being are to be preserved'.[18] Even

---

[13] Srinivasa Rao and John Lourdusamy (2010), 'Colonialism and the Development of Electricity: The Case of Madras Presidency, 1900–47', *Science, Technology & Society*, 15 (1): 27–54.

[14] Ibid.; Kale, 'Structures of Power'.

[15] William J. Hausman, Peter Hertner and Mira Wilkins (2008), *Global Electrification: Multinational Enterprise and International Finance in the History of Light and Power, 1878–2007*, Cambridge; New York: Cambridge University Press, 32.

[16] See Daniel R. Headrick (1988), *The Tentacles of Progress: Technology Transfer in the Age of Imperialism, 1850–1940*, New York; Oxford: Oxford University Press.

[17] Pierre Lanthier (2014), 'From the Raj to Independence: British Investment in the Indian Electricity Sector', *Utilities Policy*, 29: 44–53, 46, 49.

[18] K. T. Shah (1949), *Power and Fuel: Report of the Sub-Committee*, Indian National Congress Planning Committee, Bombay: Vora, 71.

Gandhians, often parodied as hostile to every trapping of industrial modernization, recognized the practical benefits of large-scale power generation.[19]

India's fate strikingly contrasted with that of Japan. The latter quickly developed a prodigious local electricity industry and by 1935 had electrified 89 per cent of households, significantly outstripping Britain and the United States.[20] This was in spite of a lack of natural resources in some ways even more striking than that of India. Asian societies were evidently more than able to assimilate electrical technologies outside colonial control. The continent's divergent histories of electrification again suggest the significance of imperial ambivalence about technological transfer to the colonies, as well as the heterogeneity of non-Western energy histories.

Instead of a simplistic and linear process of diffusion, then, the electric avatar of Euro-American-style fossil capitalism arrived in India haphazardly, reluctantly and belatedly; and it was translated into new contexts with the collaboration of indigenous players. As the novelist Amitav Ghosh recently argued, in relation to climate change 'it is demonstrably the case that the imperatives of capital and empire have often pushed in different directions, sometimes producing counter-intuitive results'.[21] The history of electricity in India thus provides a much more ambivalent account of colonialism and its relationship to industrial capitalism and climate change than that admitted by historians of the 'Capitalocene'.

More than this, there were already signs that electricity's role in postcolonial India was to be expanded well beyond private industry. B.R. Ambedkar – famous as the leading advocate for India's Dalits (formerly 'untouchables') and later the principal drafter of India's constitution, but who also chaired the committee on public utilities and electricity under the colonial regime – declared in a 1943 speech that 'without cheap and abundant electricity no effort for the industrialization of India can succeed'. This was not for the sake of capitalist enterprise, Ambedkar emphasized: '[W]e want industrialization in India as the surest means to rescue the people from the eternal cycle of poverty in which they are caught.'[22] The stage was set for the shift from narrow fossil capitalism towards a far more ambitious vision of fossil developmentalism that would draw quite different constituencies into its ambit.

## Democratizing scarcity: The politics of allocation

At independence, then, India inherited a new, hitherto unimagined scarcity in electricity. This was exacerbated by a series of related and overlapping scarcities in

---

[19] Michael Adas (2006), *Dominance by Design: Technological Imperatives and America's Civilizing Mission*, Cambridge, MA: Belknap Press of Harvard University Press, 273.

[20] Brett L. Walker (2015), *A Concise History of Japan*, Cambridge: Cambridge University Press, 174.

[21] Amitav Ghosh (2016), *The Great Derangement: Climate Change and the Unthinkable*, Gurgaon, India: Allen Lane, 117.

[22] Quoted in Sunila S. Kale (2014), *Electrifying India: Regional Political Economies of Development*, Stanford, CA: Stanford University Press, 32.

technology, skilled personnel, capital and wealthy consumers willing and able to pay for service. Yet if the Japanese counterexample appears to suggest a link between national sovereignty and the uptake of electricity, the shift from colonial autocracy to democratic independence in India would not neatly provision fossil capitalists with electricity. The new government's developmental vision and democratic politics instead intersected with these multiple scarcities in complex ways, undermining the consolidation of fossil capitalism even while fostering the broader spread of fossil developmentalism beyond private industry.

If the relationship between colonialism and fossil capitalism is an ambivalent one, the connection between fossil capitalism and democracy is even more fraught. Several scholars have suggested it is no coincidence that the expansion of formal rights and the advent of fossil capitalism broadly coincided in western Europe. Dipesh Chakrabarty has argued that '[t]he mansion of modern freedoms stands on an ever-expanding base of fossil-fuel use'.[23] It does seem that some minimum level of individual wealth and consumption is generally necessary for democracy's consolidation: political science orthodoxy predicts that democracy is much more likely to survive in wealthier countries – where, almost universally, energy consumption is higher.[24] The mainstays of *substantive* democratic engagement – basic health, education, public safety, political communication, mass media, even voting itself – are all facilitated by electrification. Turning from energy consumption to production, Timothy Mitchell has (controversially) argued for a more direct link, contending that democracy's development owed much to the physical characteristics of the coal industry and its empowerment of the labour movement, even as the shift to oil has undermined democracy in turn: 'Fossil fuels helped create both the possibility of modern democracy and its limits.'[25] To complicate matters, this is a two-way relationship: drawing on satellite light data, Brian Min finds that democracies are in general more likely to provide electricity than authoritarian states.[26] Energy consumption thus facilitated both the development and the consolidation of democracy, while democracy in turn encouraged a broadening of electricity consumption.

In such terms, India is an outlier. There universal voting rights preceded a dramatic take-off of economic development, widespread literacy or per capita energy consumption, and yet formal democracy was successfully consolidated.[27] The very

[23] Dipesh Chakrabarty (2009), 'The Climate of History: Four Theses', *Critical Inquiry*, 35 (2): 197–222, 208.

[24] Seymour Martin Lipset (1959), 'Some Social Requisites of Democracy: Economic Development and Political Legitimacy', *American Political Science Review*, 53 (1): 69–105. The democratic deconsolidation occurring in some advanced economies today might call this into question, of course.

[25] Timothy Mitchell (2011), *Carbon Democracy: Political Power in the Age of Oil*, London: Verso, 1, 12–27. By attributing mass mobilization to the structure of the coal industry, Mitchell's materialism ignores the long pre-mining history of labour activism with its many alternative sources of radicalism. I am grateful to Fredrik Albritton Jonsson for this point.

[26] Brian Min (2015), *Power and the Vote: Elections and Electricity in the Developing World*, New York: Cambridge University Press.

[27] The exception is the 21-month Emergency of 1975–77, Indira Gandhi's brief suspension of formal democracy. During this time electricity featured as a weapon of both state coercion and populism: one of Mrs Gandhi's first moves was to cut power supplies to major newspapers, while her 20-point programme promised rapid electrification.

fact of democracy's survival in India thereby defies conventional wisdom, let alone the Capitalocene thesis. How, then, did fossil capitalism and democracy intersect in a situation where multiple scarcities persisted?

Examining the contrast between the famines of colonial India and independent India's relative freedom from dramatic starvation, Amartya Sen famously argued that food scarcity is often socially produced.[28] He thereby usefully shifted attention from supply to questions of access and distribution – though subsequent scholars have noted that while sensational famines ceased, democratic India has failed to solve the problem of chronic malnutrition.[29] The Indian power sector, too, has witnessed a slow-burning crisis virtually from independence. Yet, as in the case of food, this has not been solely a question of increasing overall supplies. As one commentator noted, from 1947 India consistently invested substantial sums in electricity; the sector is not at the global technological frontier and so catch-up should not have been difficult; and the country boasted a number of energy experts, often producing official reports that astutely diagnosed the sector's difficulties.[30] As in the case of food, then, the interaction of democracy and scarcity in India means that the sector's difficulties have more often revolved around distribution than simple supply – literally in this case, around the 'last mile' of low-voltage electricity distribution to different categories of consumers. The fundamental drivers of this power crisis lay not (only) in an absolute scarcity of power generated, but in the politics of allocation that developed around access to the limited electricity supply, which in turn helped to drive the sector further into crisis.

Worldwide, the post-war years witnessed rapid expansion of physical electricity assets within broadly state-owned frameworks. A commitment to fossil capitalism was no prerequisite: the Soviet Union's first-ever strategy for state-led development and the prototype for later Five-Year Plans, the GOELRO plan, focused on a distinctively centralized mode of electrification as the pillar of economic modernization, although not until after 1926 did it accelerate (from a very low, foreign-dominated base under tsarist rule).[31] Lenin's famous formula for communism, 'soviet power plus the electrification of the whole country', would later be frequently invoked in India's Constituent Assembly debates around independence. India's installed capacity grew eightfold and actual generation tenfold during the first two decades of its own Five-Year Plan system. During these early years, electrification continued to follow the patterns of privilege established in the colonial period. As in the Global North, industrial consumers' bulk tariffs were lower than those of residential consumers, in

---

[28] *Poverty and Famines: An Essay on Entitlement and Deprivation* (1981), Oxford: Clarendon Press. See also Mehta, this volume.

[29] Dan Banik (2007), *Starvation and India's Democracy*, London: Routledge.

[30] Thomas B. Smith (1993), 'India's Electric Power Crisis: Why Do the Lights Go Out?', *Asian Survey*, 33 (4): 376–377.

[31] Jonathan Coopersmith (1992), *The Electrification of Russia, 1880–1926*, 151–191, Ithaca; London: Cornell University Press. Nonetheless, the broad relationship between democracy and electrification holds true in the longer term: a large *n*-study found that while poor countries experienced legacy infrastructure benefits from central planning, across formerly planned economies this came at the cost of long-term 'quality handicaps'; see Wendy Carlin, Mark Schaffer and Paul Seabright (2013), 'Soviet Power plus Electrification: What Is the Long-Run Legacy of Communism?', *Explorations in Economic History*, 50 (1): 116–147, 134.

accordance with Nehruvian India's vision of economic development driven by heavy industry, the public sector and technological progress.[32] The icon of this development in the early phase was non-fossil, however: mega-scale hydroelectric dams, Nehru's famous 'temples of modern India'.

Yet, as in the wider economy and society, the need to accommodate non-industrial elites began to undermine the Nehruvian project of socio-economic transformation.[33] A distinctly different tariff pattern began to emerge from the mid-1960s, as non industrial users instead received increasingly large subsidies. Much of the inter- and post-war world had granted power policy an increased emphasis on social objectives and distribution goals rather than narrow profitability. In India power had already been bracketed in the same ministry as irrigation, and the rise of concerns about food security after the droughts of the 1960s only solidified this linkage. The ensuing Green Revolution policies helped to spread irrigated agriculture via electric tubewells and pumpsets; their numbers leapt from 192,000 in 1960–61 to over 1 million in 1968–69, solidifying an 'energy-irrigation nexus'. Agricultural power consumption grew at an annual average compound rate of over 14 per cent in the decade after 1960–61. India thereby became the largest groundwater user in the world, dwarfing even the United States and China and creating a burgeoning environmental crisis.

If cross-subsidization in, for example, the United States had sought to accelerate the electrification of the most marginal rural households, in India the subsidies 'leaked' to wealthier recipients. This was not accidental. India had inherited from the British a federal division of powers over electricity, confirmed in the much-debated Electricity (Supply) Act of 1948.[34] This left the crucial distribution segment in the hands of state-level governments. The key institutions were state electricity boards (SEBs), vertically integrated monopolies usually lacking insulation from political administrations. As Min suggests, policymakers who must rely on re-election are more likely to provide public goods than their insulated, unelected counterparts – and where possible they will seek to leverage this provision for electoral gain.[35]

Accordingly, the rural shift in tariffs was regionally variegated. It was especially striking in states where farmer lobbies were powerful, such as Punjab, Haryana, Tamil Nadu, Gujarat, western Maharashtra and western Uttar Pradesh. In the 1960s, these groups formed the bedrock of the earliest resistance to the ruling Congress's one-party dominance at the national level. If farmers mobilized to protect their interests, state-level politicians – often drawn from wealthy agrarian classes themselves – in turn benefited electorally from catering to this powerful voting bloc. In the context of increasing party-political competition, agricultural power subsidies became a recognized political

---

[32] While the 1956 Industrial Policy Resolution confirmed public-sector dominance of electricity, pre-existing private generation firms such as CESC continued to be tolerated. On the 'fetishistic' reliance of the Nehruvian regime on massive monuments to modernity and scientific progress such as mega-dams and atomic reactors, see Itty Abraham (1998), *The Making of the Indian Atomic Bomb: Science, Secrecy and the Postcolonial State*, London; New York: Zed Books.

[33] The classic exposition of this argument is Francine R. Frankel (1978), *India's Political Economy, 1947–1977: The Gradual Revolution*, Princeton, NJ; Guildford: Princeton University Press.

[34] For an excellent analysis of this federal settlement and the regionally variegated political economies it fostered, see Kale, *Electrifying India*.

[35] Min, *Power and the Vote*.

idiom. Their origins appear to lie in Punjab, where the Congress lost its majority for the first time in 1967; the administration introduced flat-rate (unmetered) consumption the following year, a practice that quickly spread to other politically competitive states.[36] Less dramatically, too, middle-class residential consumers underpaid for their power, though their growing size made this subsidy a substantial financial burden upon state governments.[37] Once introduced, power subsidies only reinforced the strength of farmer and middle-class groups, and politicians' incentives to continue delivering the subsidies as a symbol of their commitment to such interests. Farmers were swift to mobilize around any threat to reduce subsidies through protest marches and other extra-electoral action, while politicians competing for votes drove tariffs ever lower – virtually to zero, as in Tamil Nadu. At the same time, the Nehruvian preference for mega-dams increasingly ran into opposition from landholders and environmentalists alike, accelerating the country's turn towards coal (nationalized in 1971–73 in the name of improved productivity and working conditions).

This pattern of consumer subsidies looked quite different to that which predominated in the Global North, where industrial and commercial consumers – fossil capitalists – continued to be favoured with cheap bulk tariffs. Instead, the older urban bias of Indian power policy was increasingly replaced by rural bias. Industrialists came to cross-subsidize this system through some of the world's highest power tariffs. Accordingly, one of the most celebrated analyses of India's political economy in the 1980s treated power subsidies as an archetypical symptom of the strength of wealthy farmers as they competed for state favours against India's two other 'dominant proprietary classes', industrial capitalists and the professional bureaucracy, the three classes together driving the state towards financial profligacy.[38] As this suggested, the dominance of fossil capitalists was strongly challenged by other groups in ways which decommodified electricity, treating it as an entitlement rather than a paid service. Nonetheless, these rival groups were also elite. Even where they sought to use democratic channels to secure their influence, then, electric scarcity was far from democratic.

---

[36] For example, by the early 1970s Tamil Nadu saw fierce competition between two regional parties, each offering ever lower agricultural tariffs; Andhra Pradesh followed later that decade with its own brand of competitive 'electric populism'; see Kale, *Electrifying India*, 170, 142. Conversely, one-party communist dominance in West Bengal between 1977 and 2011 helped to facilitate higher agricultural tariffs there than elsewhere; see Elizabeth Chatterjee (2018), 'The Politics of Electricity Reform', *World Development*, 104: 128–139.

[37] Although farmer subsidies have received most scholarly attention, domestic subsidies remain sizeable. In 2010, 87 per cent of all residential electricity consumption was subsidized, accounting for almost a quarter of all consumption and 0.4 per cent of GDP. In 2011–12, the all-India average tariff for domestic consumers was 314 paise/kWh, compared to 144 for agricultural, 514 for industrial and 690 for commercial consumers. Domestic subsidies were estimated to cost Rs. 37,047 crore nationwide, compared to Rs. 57,901 crore for agricultural subsidies. Data from Kristy Mayer, Sudeshna Ghosh Banerjee and Chris Trimble (2015), *Elite Capture: Residential Tariff Subsidies in India*, Washington, DC: World Bank, 32, ix; Planning Commission, *Annual Report (2013–14) on the Working of State Electricity Boards & Electricity Departments* (New Delhi: Government of India, 2014), 195, 208–11.

[38] Pranab Bardhan (1998), *The Political Economy of Development in India*, expanded edition, 129–130, Delhi: Oxford University Press. On the resilience of this political economy of subsidies into the twenty-first century, see Elizabeth Chatterjee, 'The Limits of Liberalization: The Power Sector', in R. Nagaraj and Sripad Motiram (eds.), *India's Political Economy*, New Delhi: Cambridge University Press.

Alongside skewed tariffs, this politics of scarcity also had more informal forms. First, electricity theft became virtually ubiquitous: almost 60 per cent of Delhi's power was going missing before the city privatized its electricity sector in 2002. The sheer quantity of stolen power suggested that poor users were less culpable than wealthy urban dwellers and even some industrialists. While illegal connections ('hooking') and amateur fraud (meter tampering) were contributors to this theft, frontline professionals also often received pay-offs to reduce long waits for new connections or to cut electricity bills.[39] Rising levels of losses around elections confirm that this theft was institutionally tolerated and politicized.[40]

Second, in the context of scarce supply power officials made strategic choices about managing demand through 'load shedding', or deliberate power cuts. While in some cases this targeted areas with high levels of power theft, it often spared politically influential constituencies or areas where politicians lived. At times this took the form of a 'zero-sum game' between industrial and more numerous users, with government-mandated power cuts targeting industrial rather than agricultural consumers.[41] The economic impact on industry was substantial. Many larger firms resorted to their own captive generation to reduce dependence on the irregular and expensive public system.

By 1991, the year of India's 'big-bang' economic reforms, the result was a politically stable but economically and environmentally dysfunctional system. There developed a self-perpetuating cycle of scarcity: cost under-recoveries from theft and subsidized consumption led to mounting financial losses and thus to dramatic shortages of cash for reinvestment; the ensuing poor performance further reduced consumers' willingness to pay. The gap between demand and supply widened, while more than a half-century after independence the 2001 census found that only 55.8 per cent of households used electricity as their primary lighting source. If power policy favoured certain elites – albeit within a low-level equilibrium that in the longer term was suboptimal for all users – it was not the industrial capitalists of the Capitalocene thesis who were the prime beneficiaries. Instead, the scarcity of electricity combined with the corrosive political economy of power subsidies to prevent the consolidation of fossil capitalism.

## Governing scarcity

If societal contests over scarce power threatened fossil capitalists' access to this key energy input, the distortionary effects of scarcity also reached deep into the

---

[39] Thomas B. Smith, 'Electricity Theft: A Comparative Analysis', *Energy Policy*, 32 (18) (2004): 2067–2076. Robert Wade's classic analyses of irrigation suggest that this was merely the street level of an elaborate system of corruption and patronage. Many of these fees were likely funnelled upwards to superiors in a quid pro quo for access to public-sector employment. See 'The System of Administrative and Political Corruption: Canal Irrigation in South India' (1982), *Journal of Development Studies*, 18 (3): 287–328.

[40] Brian Min and Miriam Golden (2014), 'Electoral Cycles in Electricity Losses in India', *Energy Policy*, 65: 619–625.

[41] Kale, *Electrifying India*, 149.

state itself, in ways that would perpetuate and exacerbate shortages. Administering scarcity is in some sense the organizing principle of all mainstream economics and public policy planning, as noted elsewhere in this book. Yet neoclassical economic rationality – the archetypical capitalist mode of public governance – developed in parallel with the high noon of fossil capitalism and the prospect of limitless growth that abundant energy promised. Mitchell goes as far as to argue that there was no such concept as 'the economy' before the development of grid electricity or cheap oil.[42] Capitalocene literature similarly argues that one of the hallmarks of fossil capitalism was its commodification of the natural world: the gradual extension of prices and 'the cash nexus' to everything, dating this moment to colonial expansion in particular.[43] Again, then, how did this capitalistic ideology of public governance fare where the expansionary dynamic that underlay it in the Global North was missing?

In the Indian power sector, the endemic and highly politicized character of scarcity helped to undermine the consistent application of a recognizably capitalistic mindset in electricity governance, either at the state apex or within the implementing bureaucracy. Inside the public electricity utilities, the logic governing power was 'administrative' rather than economically rational – the organizational corollary of fossil developmentalism rather than fossil capitalism. As the French economist Joël Ruet found after years of ethnographic research, 'what is decided on paper counts more than what actually happens'; SEB officials typically operated in a system driven by procedures and paperwork, in which cost–benefit analysis and profitability was an 'alien notion'.[44] They consequently failed to take simple profitable measures like timely repairs, preventive servicing or anticipated investments. Meanwhile, under pressure from political administrations data were massaged. Figures on electricity theft were systematically depressed. Losses were instead attributed to subsidies on wealthy farmers, costs which SEBs could at least in theory claim back from state governments, although many of the latter did not reimburse them in full.[45] State politicians exploited soft budget constraints, the classic moral hazard of the socialist 'economy of shortages', knowing that they would rarely be penalized for their short-termist financial management.[46]

As in the Soviet Union,[47] the apex planning apparatus began to give way under such persistent difficulties with implementation and faulty data. Under pressure to display

---

[42]  Mitchell (2008), 'Rethinking Economy', *Geoforum* 39 (3): 1116–1121; *Carbon Democracy*. While Fredrik Albritton Jonsson disputes Mitchell's belated dating, he agrees that mainstream post-war economics rests on a promise of cornucopianism; see 'The Origins of Cornucopianism: A Preliminary Genealogy', *Critical Historical Studies*, 1 (1): 151–168.

[43]  See especially Jason W. Moore, 'The Rise of Cheap Nature', in Jason W. Moore (ed.), *Anthropocene or Capitalocene? Nature, History, and the Crisis of Capitalism*, Oakland, CA: PM Press, 2016.

[44]  Joël Ruet (2005), *Privatising Power Cuts? Ownership and Reform of State Electricity Boards in India*, 46, 43, New Delhi: Academic Foundation; Centre de Sciences Humaines.

[45]  This was evidenced by the sudden upward spike in transmission and distribution loss figures across states as the World Bank applied pressure for accurate estimates in return for loans in the late 1990s.

[46]  János Kornai (1980), *Economics of Shortage*, 2 vols., Amsterdam; London: North-Holland. State-level power utilities have enjoyed three central bailouts over the past fifteen years, for example.

[47]  See, for example, Alec Nove (1958), 'The Problem of "Success Indicators" in Soviet Industry', *Economica*, 25 (97): 1–13.

results in accordance with the apex vision of fossil developmentalism, power planning increasingly became a utopian ritual detached from these realities, explaining away failure while setting unrealistically ambitious targets to correct for past shortfalls. In 1983, the Planning Commission's own journal, *Yojana*, lamented the 'total chaos' in power planning: 'If one were to cite an example where the government says one thing and acts quite differently while implementing, the energy sector may take the cake.'[48] Glorious futures were projected on paper, while in reality targets were missed with glaring consistency (Table 13.1). Not only did the contested politics of distribution shift to the detriment of fossil capitalists, then, but managing resource allocations in the context of electrical, financial and human capital shortages also placed intolerable demands on the state administration, in which the conventional economic rationality of profit maximization was subordinated to alternative logics.

By the economic opening of 1991, the power sector's problems were obvious and widely acknowledged. Power generation was the first major sector opened to private investment that year, ushering in a quarter-century of attempted reforms. Yet the multiple and overlapping character of scarcities in the power system complicated any solution. Policymakers often misdiagnosed or misprioritized the core scarcities, so that reforms either failed to tackle scarcity or even produced simultaneous overabundance and scarcity in different segments of this complex industry. In this way the politicized allocation of electricity between competing elites and the failures of apex power planning interacted to perpetuate the sector's persistent low-grade crisis.

The initial phase of reforms after 1991 – the introduction of independent power producers (IPPs) – targeted the generation segment. This measure, attempted in many Asian countries, nominally echoed the early stages of a model developed in the Global North which fit the pattern of abundance and commodification highlighted above. Developed in England and Wales (alongside New Zealand) in the 1980s, pre-existing cheap infrastructure and cheap North Sea gas permitted the introduction of competitive markets that treated electricity as a commodity rather than a core service.

**Table 13.1** Repeatedly missed targets in the power sector

| Five-Year Plan | 1st | 2nd | 3rd | 4th | 5th | 6th | 7th | 8th | 9th | 10th | 11th |
|---|---|---|---|---|---|---|---|---|---|---|---|
| % generation capacity addition target achieved | 84.6 | 64.3 | 64.2 | 49.5 | 81.6 | 72.3 | 96.2 | 53.8 | 47.5 | 51.76 | 69.84 |

*Source*: Figures from the Planning Commission's Five-Year Plans (New Delhi: Government of India, various years).

---

[48] Quoted in Smith, 'India's Power Crisis', 381. See also Elizabeth Chatterjee (2012), 'Dissipated Energy: Indian Electric Power and the Politics of Blame', *Contemporary South Asia*, 20 (1): 91–103.

Under the aegis of the World Bank, this post-Keynesian energy regime would become consolidated into a blueprint for global power reform.[49]

In India, however, the rationale for reform was quite different to the solidifying commodification framework. By 1991, the country was facing a serious balance-of-payments crisis and turned to the International Monetary Fund for an emergency loan. The balance-of-payments crisis became the lens through which the dilemmas of the power sector were reframed. Not the mismanagement and politicization of distribution but scarce finance was the overriding concern, as became evident when the reform amendment was introduced in Parliament.[50] The IPP policy ill fit the sector's more fundamental problems, neglecting entirely the distribution segment. Its appeal lay in the perceived need to access capital, especially foreign finance, and to increase generation at virtually any cost.

This concern with increasing generation capacity – 'pouring more water in the leaky bucket', in one commentator's memorable phrase[51] – has been a hallmark of Indian power reforms. Renewable energy sources have been persistently plagued by underinvestment in transmission infrastructure, which has left assets underutilized or exacerbated grid instability problems, for example in Tamil Nadu's prodigiously wind-heavy power system. The ultra mega power projects of the 2000s or the recent surge in private thermal capacity have also continually run up against the old problems of subsidy politics in many states.[52]

Later phases of power reform did belatedly attempt to tackle the politics of distribution, first through restructuring SEBs and the import of independent regulatory agencies and later through ambitious legislation. Since the Electricity Act of 2003, the Government of India has hoped that competition – primarily through 'open access' to the retail market for large consumers – would force power governance reform. Distribution remains the purview of the state governments, however, which are typically loath to alienate the sizeable and wealthy constituencies who currently benefit from subsidized tariffs and theft, yet equally loath to lose lucrative industrial and commercial consumers; they have all but blocked open access in practice. More than this, competition may be structurally difficult to legislate: it requires good data, a serious private-sector presence, improved governance and pricing reforms – all of which remain in scarce supply.

The persistent crisis of power distribution has led to the coexistence of abundance in some sectors with continued scarcity at the street level. Recently, the crisis of coal supply for thermal power plants that characterized the first half of this decade has abruptly shifted in the face of swifter mining by the state-owned behemoth Coal India Limited. Today India instead faces a major glut of thermal power, with up to one-third

---

[49] See World Bank (1993), *The World Bank's Role in the Electric Power Sector*, Washington, DC: World Bank.

[50] Kale, *Electrifying India*, 54.

[51] Deepak Parekh, then chairman of the Infrastructure Development Finance Corporation, quoted in N. Ramakrishnan, 'Decade of Power Reforms – Hardly Electrifying', *Hindu Business Line*, 4 September 2001.

[52] See Navroz Dubash, Sunila Kale and Ranjit Bharvirkar (eds.) (2018), *Mapping Power: The Political Economy of Electricity in India's States*, Delhi: Oxford University Press.

of plants lying idle and power sold on exchanges at rates that barely cover the cost of fuel.[53] State governments proudly announce that they now enjoy a 'power surplus'. This privately sponsored crisis of overinvestment, mirroring China's state-driven glut, will only be exacerbated by the current push for a vast expansion of renewable energy.

This counterintuitive situation bespeaks the absence of the cost-benefit rationale that is argued to have historically accompanied the Northern avatars of fossil capitalism.[54] On the one hand, private firms did not always behave with long-term engagement in the sector in mind. Rather, 'every Tom, Dick, and Harry' poured into the thermal power sector, including many steel and cotton companies with no commercial power experience, hoping to exploit or speculate on cheap loans and preferential access to state-administered coal blocks.[55] The result of this irrational exuberance was a rising proportion of stranded assets and non-performing loans, especially in public-sector banks.

More fundamentally, the politicized problems of the distribution segment remain an overriding constraint in many states and overlap with the alternative rationalities of power governance that emerged to manage scarcity. Faced with political unwillingness to reduce the subsidy burden and haemorrhaging cash, the huge, impoverished state of Uttar Pradesh has at times all but given up on power procurement planning and instead resorted to the type of unscheduled over-drawing from the inter-state grid that helped cause the world-record blackouts of July 2012. Meanwhile, utility officials in the poor (but coal-rich) eastern state of Jharkhand appear to operate with a fixed maximum amount of spending in mind: today they are opting to ration power even while cheap sources are available via short-term markets. Elsewhere demand remains constrained by absent connections and high costs. One official thus complained that state-level boasts about power surplus were 'like saying India is a beef-surplus country when it is mostly vegetarian'[56]: on-paper abundance masks persistent inequalities of access to and underinvestment in electricity. India's fragmented federal polity thus continues to stymie the development of a fossil-capitalist power system in many areas.

India's economic trajectory has itself been reshaped by these features. The absolute scarcity of electricity combined with mismanagement and the corrosive political economy of power subsidies to prevent the consolidation of fossil capitalism in its traditional form. Businesses consistently report that India's unreliable power supply is *the* biggest obstacle to their sustained economic growth, more so than taxation or corruption.[57] They have compensated in ways that distinctively shifted Indian industrialization away from the exemplary 'Capitalocene' cases of Britain and the United States. Infrastructure bottlenecks, electricity prime among them, helped

---

[53] Around one-tenth of Indian power is now traded on short-term power exchanges. The remainder continues to be sold largely through long-term power purchase agreements.

[54] Cases such as the collapse of Enron might warn us against exaggerating the longer-term cost-benefit rationality of Euro-American energy firms, however.

[55] Power Trading Corporation official, quoted in M. Rajshekhar, 'Chhattisgarh Power Boom That Never Was', *Economic Times*, 25 October 2012.

[56] Interview, former central power official, Kolkata, 28 July 2016.

[57] Sadiq Ahmed and Ejaz Ghani (2007), *South Asia: Growth and Regional Integration*, Washington, DC: World Bank, 11.

to undermine the development of a large manufacturing sector like that in China. Instead, the Indian economy today has been characterized by 'jobless growth' and a reliance on services, including dense clusters of IT firms with their own private power supplies. In place of traditional factories where industrialists bore the costs of power cuts, large firms sought to shift the risk onto small subcontractors who could compensate through power theft or by exploiting unwaged family labour. The result was an expansion of India's vast and growing informal economy, estimated to account for up to 90 per cent of livelihoods today. Most recently, ambitious projections for demand growth made a decade ago have failed to materialize. Although on paper India is now the world's fastest-growing major economy, in practice power demand – especially from industrialists – is not rising in line with these figures as historical precedent would lead us to expect. In such ways the shape of India's fossil capitalism was fundamentally altered by electric scarcities: not solely or even primarily the 'hard' scarcity of limited fuel supplies or power generation capacity, but by the competitive political economy of scarce electricity allocation and the troubled planning apparatus for managing shortages.

## Conclusion

While the dilemma of abundance forms the backdrop to climate change in the Global North, electricity in India has throughout its history been characterized by multiple and overlapping scarcities of capital, technology, personnel, lucrative consumers and natural resources. Looking at this critical case, the dynamics and hegemony of fossil capitalism look quite different to the assumptions of the Capitalocene narrative. The foregoing analysis has troubled three elements of this narrative: the spread of electricity as a key macro-technology of fossil capitalism; the degree of dominance enjoyed by fossil capitalists over this crucial industrial input; and the expansion of a capitalistic economic rationality that seeks to commodify energy, and indeed all of 'nature', within a profit-making framework.

Against the Capitalocene assumption that the European mode of production was disseminated in a seamless and mechanistic manner, the British imperial government in the subcontinent was surprisingly indifferent to electrification. Grid electricity was installed only haphazardly across a few favoured areas, often relying on local entrepreneurship. This unsettles the notion of any simple relationship between colonialism, fossil capitalism and climate change. Instead colonialism produced a new scarcity in electricity both through the visible successes of electrified, industrial modernity in the metropole and the relative neglect of electrification in the peripheries, as nationalists argued. The relative scarcities produced by lack of technology transfer became a defining feature of the construction of a 'developing world'.

Even after independence in 1947, fossil capitalists did not enjoy a consistent acceleration of electricity provision. Questions of distribution became politicized and institutionally conditioned by the democratic context and federal structure. A distinctive politics of elite democratic mobilization and power rationing emerged across many Indian states, in which subsidized overuse coincided with deliberate cuts, penalizing industry alongside the hundreds of millions of Indians left without access to the grid. The public management of such endemic scarcity looked very different to the economic rationality that emerged to govern the abundant resources of the Global North. Against the equation of the Anthropocene with capitalist commodification, electrification did not coincide with the installation of a commercial, cost-benefit logic across the country. In many utilities, scarcity was not conceptualized in purely economic terms. Instead, the public management of scarcity was guided by a non-economic rationality shaped around administrative protocols and political exigencies. Simultaneously, scarcity contracted political time horizons. Power planning became increasingly divorced from the realities of short-term, zero-sum calculations around regional political economies of resource allocation and soft budget constraints. Fierce competition for scarce resources thus undermined long-term 'developmental' state planning and market-based policies alike.

Alongside the 'hard' absolute scarcity of electricity generated, the underperformance of India's electricity sector shows the importance of 'soft', politically mediated scarcity created by inequalities of access and the institutional complex that evolved to govern them. This distinction has been neglected by Indian policymakers, who have often favoured the easier solution of increasing generation capacity over the riskier work of subsidy rollbacks or organizational reform. As this suggests, scarcity's multiple forms (physical, financial, human capital and more) have led to misdiagnoses of the sector's problems, so that overabundance and scarcity have come paradoxically to coincide. Nonetheless, the line between hard and soft scarcities is blurred. Both are man-made. Both are inseparable from the external world, whether through natural resource constraints, electricity's physical characteristics (such as the inevitability of technical losses during low-voltage distribution) and their environmental implications. And both are mutually conditioning, as conditions of persistent hard scarcity shape demand politics and governance, and subsidies and mismanagement in turn discourage investments upstream.

India's variant of fossil developmentalism was itself reshaped by the pressures of the politically mediated scarcity of electricity. This and other infrastructural bottlenecks helped to discourage the conventional growth of factory-based manufacturing in favour of services and a vast informal economy in which own-account workers shouldered the risk of breakdowns. None of these features – electricity's dissemination around the subcontinent, the political economy of the Indian power sector, the non-commercial logic of power governance and India's unusual industrial trajectory – are well captured by Anthropocene–Capitalocene literature derived from Euro-American experiences founded on energy abundance.

Meanwhile, the threat of climate change itself has prompted a move to revalue scarcity. India's dysfunctional power system had one beneficial side effect from a long-term, global perspective: energy production and consumption was constrained. Such energy-scarce late development has been reconfigured as a moment of opportunity to move beyond fossil capitalism and its environmental consequences, either to alternative fuels or, more radically, towards more parsimonious modes of living. In this vein India's power cuts are occasionally reinterpreted with only a little irony as a prodigiously well-developed system of 'demand-side management'. Nonetheless, the domestic allure of this revaluation is limited. The right to overcome the persistent scarcity of power – to 'develop' – has long remained the pillar of India's international climate negotiating stance.[58] Abundant electricity is at present a non-negotiable component of modernity. The history of electrification in India thus illustrates the complexity of the much-debated relationships between voracious energy consumption and industrial capitalism, colonialism and democracy outside the Global North – relationships which look unlikely to become less fraught in the near future. As revealed here, the postcolonial Anthropocene is defined as much by the perception of relative scarcity as by the dilemma of abundance.

## Acknowledgements

I am grateful to conference participants at the University of Chicago, the Australian National University and Boston College, and especially to Tyler Williams, Faridah Zaman and Fredrik Albritton Jonsson, for their thoughtful responses to earlier versions of this draft.

---

[58] Navroz K. Dubash (2013), 'The Politics of Climate Change in India: Narratives of Equity and Cobenefits', *WIREs Climate Change*, 4 (3): 191–201.

14

# Lagos 'Scarce-City': Investigating the Roots of Urban Modernity in a Colonial Capital, 1900–1928

David Lamoureux

Originally established in the fifteenth century, Lagos Island developed by the early decades of the nineteenth century into a trading post for the transatlantic slave trade. It was because of this role that the British decided to invade it in 1851 as part of their anti-slavery campaign. The period that followed was revolutionary for more than just political reasons. Missionaries started building churches and schools. Administrators and merchants, eager to trade with the hinterland where palm oil replaced slaves as the region's principal export, began to arrive. Steamers from Britain brought new technologies and products.[1] There was no better illustration of the changes introduced than alterations brought in the physical landscape of Lagos. Of course, the city that the British had conquered was not a blank slate. Lagos presented a complex urban structure before the arrival of the British. Yet, existing houses were built in what Europeans conceived as being primitive materials such as mud, palm leaves, bamboo and clay. A thick forest encircled its shores, swamps covered most of its landmass and the settlement did not occupy more than a third of the island.[2]

Fifty years after the invasion, more than half of Lagos Island was urbanized. Twenty years later, it was the entire island. Lagos now had an extensive commercial, religious and public infrastructure. In 1898, a train station was opened at Iddo, on the mainland, linking it with the hinterland. By the turn of the twentieth century, the city emerged as an international commercial gateway. A British journalist who visited the city in 1900 was so optimistic about its prospects that he felt it was 'the most enlightened spot in West Africa'.[3]

[1] A. B. Aderibigde (1975), 'Early History of Lagos to about 1850', in A. B. Aderibigde (ed.), *Lagos: The Development of an African City*, 1–27, Lagos; K. Mann (2007), *Slavery and the Birth of an African City: Lagos, 1790–1900*, 23–51, Bloomington.

[2] L. Bigon (2005), 'Sanitation and Street Layout in Early Colonial Lagos: British and Indigenous Conceptions 1851–1900', *Planning Perspectives*, 20: 247–269 (pp. 253–256).

[3] A. F. Mockler-Ferryman (1900), *British West Africa: Its Rise and Progress*, 112, London.

Yet, this situation was not only a cause to rejoice. Thousands of hinterland traders and rural migrants came every year attracted by the booming colonial economy, increasing the pressure on the resources of this island-city constrained by its natural geography. Strikingly, its population had increased from approximately 20,000 inhabitants in 1861 to 41,847 in 1900.[4] Furthermore, these estimates were often incomplete, excluding informal settlements, unmarried women and people who did not pay tax. In 1946, when anticolonial mobilization reached a peak, British intelligence officers estimated the *real* population as around 350,000 inhabitants.[5]

The social effects of these demographic and geographic forces were disastrous. As Ayodeji Olukoju has noted, Lagos grew without sufficient access to key sources for modern industrial, commercial and domestic activity.[6] At the beginning of the century, the scarcity of freshwater and land threatened the very survival of the city. Density and poor sanitation, as a local newspaper editor wrote in 1924, had turned poor Lagosians into 'beasts' and opened the door to repetitive outbreaks of yellow fever, cholera, tuberculosis and even plague.[7] Yet, despite this catastrophic situation, Lagos continued to develop. By the end of the 1920s, its British administrators even felt confident enough about its prospect to promise their African subjects a modern urban future that would grant them more municipal rights than anywhere else in their African empire, especially within Nigeria, and a greater living comfort than many urbanites enjoyed in Europe.

The story of Lagos between 1900 and 1928 poses an interesting challenge to the standard view of British imperial history where the introduction of socially progressive and politically inclusive colonial policies is usually attributed to the period after the Second World War, with its rhetoric of freedom and self-determination.[8] The seminal works of Frederick Cooper, particularly, have presented this 'second' or 'late' form of colonial occupation in Africa as an attempt by the colonial state to reduce the mobilizing 'opportunity' that the war provided to African nationalists. A model of state that provided 'modern' services 'with general appeal and rewarding followers with state resources' has been seen as part of this strategy after 1945.[9] The history of the extension of modern municipal services, such as running water, electricity, social housing and participative, in Lagos in the first three decades of the twentieth century modifies this classic interpretation.

The coexistence of rapid demographic development and scarcity of resources fundamental to urban life – freshwater and constructible space in this case – raises fundamental questions. How was the growth of Lagos sustainable or even possible?

---

[4]  P. O. Sada and A. A. Adefolalu (1975), 'Urbanisation and Problems of Urban Development', in A. B. Aderibigde (ed.), *Lagos: The Development of an African City*, 79–107, Lagos (p. 79).

[5]  Nigerian National Archives, Ibadan, COMCOL 1/307/187/Vol. 10, 'Blue Book 1944/1945', From Ag. Commissioner of the Colony E.A. Care, 19 May 1945; Divisional Office Ikeja to Commissioner of the Colony, 'Blue Book 1944/1945'.

[6]  A. Olukoju (2004), '"Never Expect Power Always", Electricity Consumers' Response to Monopoly, Corruption and Inefficient Services in Nigeria', *African Affairs*, 103: 51–71.

[7]  'The Health of the People', *African Messenger* (7 August 1924).

[8]  D. Birmingham (2009), *The Decolonization of Africa*, 4, London:.

[9]  F. Cooper (2011), *Africa since 1945: The Past of the Present* (2002), 34–88, Cambridge.

And how could it happen in a system as unequal as colonization? This chapter provides an answer by highlighting the effect that 'scarcity politics' had as a motor for the political development and physical improvement of Lagos. It does so through the prism of ongoing debates about the meaning of urban modernity at the time. This chapter begins with these debates before looking at how they translated in practice in Lagos in a context of extreme scarcity.

## Modernity, sanitation and the colonial city

Early twentieth-century Lagos was not the first imperial city to experience rapid demographic growth. Between 1850 and 1900, Calcutta and Bombay doubled to almost a million people. Likewise, the population of Nairobi tripled at the start of the twentieth century. The same was true for the populations of Liverpool and Manchester, which spectacularly increased from less than 100,000 to almost a million between 1801 and 1931. The sanitary reality known to Lagosians was by no means novel to British administrators.[10]

Density even lay at the roots of what could be described as Britain's first wave of 'modern' urban reforms. In the second half of the nineteenth century, the widely noted squalid conditions of life that predominated among British industrial workers, their growing number and the spectre of popular revolutions in mainland Europe led to an extension of the vote. In turn, electoral reforms brought marginalized grievances concerning the need for sanitary and housing reforms to the forefront of the political agenda.[11] The Metropolis Management Act (1855) appointed 'health officers' in major British cities. The Local Government Act (1894) allowed city councils to be fully elected. In 1909, the Town Planning Act enabled councils to enforce population density maximums and set up boards of improvement to extend access to lighting, sewages and waterworks.[12]

For an early twentieth-century British audience, urban modernity was, in that sense, a largely 'imagined' idea that summarized a patchwork of new or relatively new urban experiences.[13] In economic terms, it envisaged a city that fuelled its growth through industrial production and international commerce. In political terms, it meant new forms of municipal politics that created spaces for its various communities to express their grievances, guaranteeing the stability necessary for a shared prosperity. More generally, it was essentially used to describe the possible application of new technologies to the problems associated with urban density.[14] Instead of a coherent

---

[10] O. Goerg and X. Huetz De Lemps, *La Ville Coloniale XVe-XXe Siècle. Histoire de l'Europe Urbaine*, 205–237, Vol. 5, Paris; G. M. Howe (1976), *Man, Environment and Disease in Britain*, London.

[11] R. J. Evans (1988), 'Epidemics and Revolutions: Cholera in Nineteenth-Century Europe', *Past & Present*, 120: 123–146.

[12] P. J. Waller (1984), *Town, City, and Nation: England in 1850–1914*, Oxford.

[13] See Charles Taylor's work (2004), *Modern Social Imaginaries*, London, for a definition of modern social imaginaries.

[14] R. Denis (2008), *Cities in Modernity: Representations and Productions of Metropolitan Space, 1840–1930*, Cambridge.

vision of the 'modern city', pioneering science fiction writings in the years around
1900 tellingly envisioned it symbolically, through the absence of dirt and diseases,
mass vertical housing, rapid public transportation systems and through the centralized
'bureaucratic' management of the city's water, electrical and food supplies, for the
comfort of all urban dwellers.[15]

The reality and inclusiveness of these new urban reforms, however, varied greatly
between British cities. As Martin Daunton has noted, their scale and social priorities
did not conform to a single model. Industrial cities in the North, with their organized
factory workers, did not reform alongside the same lines as commercial cities in the
South, with their powerful tax-paying middle class.[16] New urban reforms heavily
depended on the personal agendas of individuals who made up local pressure groups,
councils and governments.[17] Revealingly, private companies and philanthropists,
rather than town councils, were often responsible for the development of Britain's first
social housing estates.[18]

New housing and water systems also captured the imagination of inhabitants in
major colonial cities that developed alongside similar patterns. But, as Robert Home
has pointed out, while in Britain 'new forms of municipal government' ultimately
emerged to help share the cost of these reforms, in the colonial world urban populations
lacked these institutions precisely because of their colonized status.[19] The vast majority
of their inhabitants were de facto excluded from new 'modern' urban reforms. A plan
for sewage works in Calcutta, for instance, had been made as early as 1857 based on
similar works in Britain. The city would have to wait sixty years to see some of its
aspects implemented.[20]

This lack of consideration for the modernization of the colonial city was
especially pronounced in British West Africa: a region that lacked significant
European settlements. In 1901, less than 300 of Lagos's 41,847 official inhabitants
were Europeans.[21] Minimal intervention was even embraced as a model of colonial
governance that can be traced back to the idea of 'indirect rule' of Frederick Lugard,
the commissioner and governor of Northern Nigeria (1899–1906), Southern Nigeria
(1913–14) and Nigeria (1914–18).[22] Africans, in his own words, needed to be led 'by
their own efforts … to raise themselves to a higher plane of social organization'.[23]

---

[15] For examples, see J. Vernes (1879), *The Begum's Fortune*, London; H. G. Wells (1905), *A Modern Utopia*, London; H. G. Gernsback (1925), *Ralph 124C 41+*, New York.

[16] M. Daunton (2001), 'Introduction', in M. Daunton (ed.), *The Cambridge Urban History of Britain*, 1–56, Vol. 3, Cambridge.

[17] B. Doyle (2001), 'The Changing Functions of Urban Government: Councillors, Officials and Pressure Groups', in M. Daunton (ed.), *The Cambridge Urban History of Britain*, 287–314, Vol. 3, Cambridge.

[18] Vickerstown (1901), New Earswick (1904), Whiteley Village (1907), the Garden Village (1908) and the Woodlands (1908).

[19] R. K. Home (1997), *Of Planting and Planning. The Making of British Colonial Cities*, 68, London.

[20] Goerg and Huetz de Lemps, *La Ville Coloniale XVe-XXe Siècle*, 227–233.

[21] MacGregor to Chamberlain, 4 February 1901, 'Correspondence between Governor, Lagos and Foreign/Colonial Office 1880–1905'.

[22] M. Perham (1956–60), *Lugard*, London.

[23] Quoted in 'Indirect rule in West Africa' (1948), *The Round Table*, 39: 125–130 (p. 125).

Where urban modernity was concerned, this policy posed a profound dilemma. To link sanitary reforms to an 'enfranchised colonised constituency' – in essence a contradiction – made little sense in the face of epidemics that threatened the colonial project in a region long nicknamed the 'white man's grave'.[24] This contradiction did not escape colonial administrators. At the turn of the twentieth century, they were more divided than ever about the best response to adopt, between partisan of segregated European health stations, on one side, and advocates of sanitary campaigns directed towards all potential carriers of tropical diseases, on the other.[25]

If the colonial establishment remained divided, its members nonetheless agreed that urban problems in African cities were of a medical rather than political nature. In colonial Africa, this inevitably led to an increased identification of disease victims and agents defined on the basis of medical conditions that matched ethnic conditions and living spaces. Progressive voices now justified this development. In 1904, the *OED*'s definition of segregation was a quote by Patrick Manson, the 1902 Nobel Prize laureate in Medicine, praising it as 'the first law of hygiene for Europeans'.[26] In 1916, another leading British physician described African children as pathological agents.[27] As sanitation became the focus of debates concerning the modernization of African cities, this Conradian conception would profoundly affect the European imaginary. In 1932, one of the earliest official textbooks about architectural development in tropical Africa still referred to 'the darkness of the tropical village'.[28]

By the beginning of the twentieth century, a new model of centralized modern urban reforms started to appear in British Africa. Yet, the political developments that characterized urban modernization in Britain were absent here. Instead, it promoted a vision of the modern African city that excluded Africans. In Cape Town, for instance, Europeans used an epidemic of bubonic plague in 1900 to seize control of an urban space occupied by Africans. They had their houses characterized as insalubrious by medical experts, whose judgement they could not contest, and were forced to relocate to the urban margins where the absence of developed housing solutions only furthered negative stereotypes about their hygiene. Modern sanitary works were being implemented for minority settlers.[29] Such developments did not escape West Africa either. In 1904, thirty-two years after it was first refused on the grounds of its prohibitive cost, Whitehall authorized the construction of an expensive segregated station in Freetown, on the grounds of a modern medical experiment, for the comfort of less than 400 Europeans.[30]

---

[24] Curtin (1990), 'The End of the "White Man's Grave"? Nineteenth-Century Mortality in West Africa', *The Journal of Interdisciplinary History*, 21 (1): 63–88.

[25] J. W. Cell (1986), 'Anglo-Indian Medical Theory and the Origins of Segregation in West Africa', *The American Historical Review*, 91 (2): 307–335 (pp. 328–334).

[26] Quoted in ibid., p. 308.

[27] W. J. R. Simpson (1916), *The Maintenance of Health in the Tropics*, 2nd edition, London.

[28] B. Blacklock (1932), *An Empire Problem: The House and Village in the Tropics*, 363, Liverpool.

[29] M. W. Swanson (1977), 'The Sanitation Syndrome: Bubonic Plague and Urban Native Policy in the Cape Colony, 1900–1909', *The Journal of African History*, 18 (3): 387–410.

[30] S. Frenkel and J. Western, 'Pretext or Prophylaxis? Racial Segregation and Malarial Mosquitos in a British Tropical Colony: Sierra Leone', *Annals of the Association of American Geographers*, 78 (2): 221–228.

## The changing dynamics of urban works in Lagos, 1900–1904

In 1897, the first of many public hygiene experts to visit Lagos observed that the need of a radical sanitary reform was 'so fully established that further discussion [was] unnecessary'. Everything, he noted, was missing in Lagos. The most worrying problem was how scarce access to freshwater and dry land for construction were.[31] The next inspector to visit the island shared his pessimism. He simply suggested relocating Europeans outside of Lagos.[32] His proposal came at the same time when Whitehall authorized the establishment of Freetown's segregated station. Yet, despite an aggravated sanitary situation, and an overcrowding of 20,000 inhabitants per square mile in 1900, no similar project was being discussed for Lagos Island.[33]

Notwithstanding its restricted geography and even poorer sanitation, the British felt more reluctant to exclude Africans in Lagos than anywhere else. This highlighted an important aspect of the city, namely: the social complexity on which its development historically relied. By the early 1900s, alongside indigenous landowning *Aworis* and European settlers, Lagos counted a diverse African population, which played a full part in its transformation from a slave-port to an imperial hub. West African merchants, for instance, were key intermediaries between imperial firms and the hinterland.[34] The same was true for indigenous market women who organized most of the food trade around the lagoon.[35] The city also counted a large European-educated African population, trained in law, medicine or classics that helped sustain the colonial administration.[36]

The physical development of the island reflected these sociological foundations. First and covering much of the north-west, there was Isale Eko, the predominantly indigenous district organized around the *Oba*'s (King's) palace and the main markets. This was the historical heart of Lagos, its chief trading-point for food and the most overcrowded neighbourhood. It was characterized by traditional compounds that had changed little since the pre-colonial era.[37] Second, east of Isale Eko lived the Brazilian and West Indian returnees in Oke Popo. Their architecture was impressive. They transposed Portuguese colonial architecture to idiosyncratic West African needs. The services of their craftsmen were sought throughout West Africa.[38] Third, south of Lagos Island and bordering the lagoon was Marina: the European district with most

[31]  O. Chadwick (1897), *Memorandum on the Sanitation of Lagos*, 1, London.
[32]  S. H. Brown (1994), 'Public Health in US and West African Cities, 1870–1900', *The Historian*, 56: 685–698.
[33]  P. H. Baker (1996), *Urbanization and Political Change: The Politics of Lagos 1917–1967*, Berkeley: 21–45.
[34]  A. Olukoju (2004), *The 'Liverpool' of West Africa. The Dynamics and Impacts of Maritime Trade in Lagos*, 10, Trenton.
[35]  C. Johnson (1982), 'Grass Roots Organizing: Women in Anticolonial Activity in Southwestern Nigeria', *African Studies Review*, 25 (2/3): 137–157 (pp. 138–139).
[36]  F. O. Ogunlade (1974), 'Education and Politics in Colonial Nigeria: The Case of King's College, Lagos (1906–1911)', *Journal of the Historical Society of Nigeria*, 7 (2): 325–345.
[37]  J. Hetherton (1936), *A Travel Guide to West Africa*, 22–27, London.
[38]  M. M. Dolapo Alonge (1994), *Afro-Brazilian Architecture in Lagos State: A Case for Conservation* (unpublished) PhD thesis, University of Newcastle.

public and commercial offices, which had some running water, drainage and electrical facilities. Finally, west of Marina stood Olowogbowo. Similar to Oke Popo, the district was populated by *Saros*, immigrants from Sierra Leone, who constituted most of the European-educated African elite.

If the quality of public infrastructure varied between districts and communities, the spatial ordering of Lagos remained largely opportunistic.[39] Under the tenets of Indirect Rule, government intervention was limited. If Isale Eko was deprived of proper drainage, leaving its compounds at the mercy of floods, it was because British administrators were reluctant to intervene in its inhabitants' affairs.[40] Yet, limited colonial interventions did not prevent the city to develop commercially. Rather, those who made up its transformation as an imperial bridgehead shared the cost of development. Many African inhabitants perceived themselves as loyal imperial subjects in an imperial project rather than indigenous colonial subjects.[41]

At the beginning of the twentieth century, there was a high degree of cooperation between Saros and Europeans. Both benefited from Lagos's expanding influence over the hinterland, at the expense of the indigenous elite. The motto of one Saro newspaper was 'For God, the King and the People' and suggests why the British were reluctant to alienate them and do in Lagos what they had done in Freetown.[42] The cost of segregation outweighed its gains. The only planning law in existence at the beginning of the twentieth century was a Town Improvement Ordinance (1863) that mainly authorized limited water works and official buildings.[43]

The arrival of Governor MacGregor (1899–1904) was a turning point. A physician by training, MacGregor not only refused to accept calls to relocate the government outside of Lagos but inaugurated a new culture of government intervention. A self-defined modernizer, he completed in 1901 the city's first continental bridge, the Carter Bridge, linking Lagos Island to Iddo, where the train station was situated. In 1902, he established a steam tramway line that ran from the southern wharves of Lagos Island, over the Carter Bridge, to Iddo, in an attempt to reduce the burden of overcrowding. The tramway was not only the first modern means of urban transportation in West Africa: it was also open to Africans and Europeans alike.[44] In 1904, in an attempt to increase available building land, he ordered an impressive reclamation of the largest swamps of the island, redirecting its rivers into a 25-foot-wide (later called) MacGregor canal.[45]

---

[39] A. Vaughan-Richards and K. Akinsemoyin (2009), *Building Lagos (1976)*, 6–53, Lagos.

[40] Nigerian National Archives (1911), Ibadan, CSO 26/13001/Vol. 3, 'Outbreak of Plague in Lagos 1924', Recent Outbreak of Yellow Fever in West Africa, March.

[41] J. S. Coleman (1958), *Nigeria: Background to Nationalism*, 182, Berkeley; R. L. Sklar (2004), *Nigerian Political Parties: Power in an Emergent African Nation* (1963), 41–45, Princeton, NJ.

[42] The *Lagos Standard*. J. E. Flint, 1969, 'Nigeria: The colonial experience from 1880–1914', in L. H. Gann and P. Duignan (eds.), *The History and Politics of Colonialism 1870-1914, Colonialism in Africa*, Vol. 1, Cambridge pp. 220–226.

[43] M. Echeruo, *Victorian Lagos: Aspects of the Nineteenth Century Lagos Life*, London, 1977.

[44] Miller, *Lagos Steam Tramway*, pp. 1–18.

[45] Public Record Office, National Archives of the UK, Kew, CO 147/164, 'Lecture on Malaria by Sir William MacGregor, 1901', pp. 5–10.

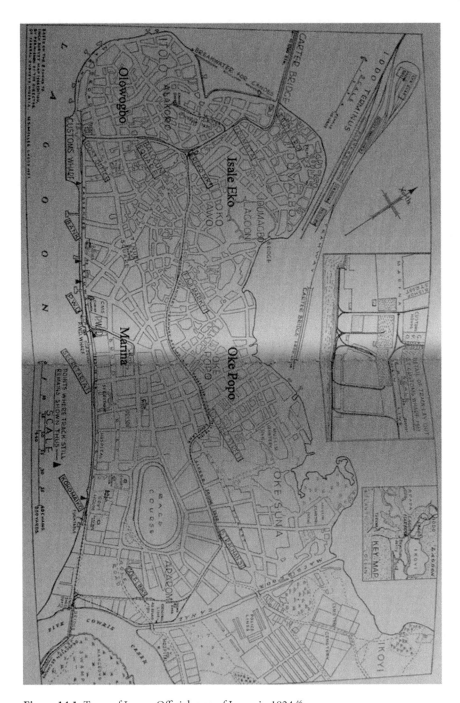

**Figure 14.1** Town of Lagos: Official map of Lagos in 1924.[46]

46  N. S. Miller (1958), *Lagos Steam Tramway, 1902–1933*, London.

This culture of greater government intervention reflected the growing status of the city in the region. Its designation as the new capital of Southern Nigeria in 1905 unlocked unprecedented projects, with revenues exceeding £1 million in 1905, compared to £200,000 just a few years earlier. In the following two decades, the Lagos Government Railway and the Baro-Kano Railway would be amalgamated and Lagos, Ibadan and Oyo connected by road.[47] The administration also started to invest directly in a new port at Apapa, opposite Lagos Island, to welcome more international maritime traffic.[48]

Its designation of Lagos as a colonial capital meant that British authorities grew increasingly active in controlling its unregulated but limited urban landscape. Its new standing justified improvement works to attract major businesses and civil servants.[49] In this context, however, MacGregor's policies were the exceptions rather than the rule. Almost immediately after assuming power, Governor Egerton (1904–1912), MacGregor's successor, passed a Cantonment Proclamation that authorized, for the first time, the establishment of separate services for Europeans on the grounds of sanitation.

In the first decades of the twentieth century, all these developments would start to marginalize the African elite on which the city's development had historically relied. European companies could now access the interior directly and Egerton felt so convinced in his ability to bypass European-educated Africans that he even banned them from serving in several governmental functions, such as army doctors. By 1910, the city counted segregated hospitals, clubs, churches and cemeteries, all funded by rising taxes from European expatriates.[50]

## Water scarcity and the advent of modern municipal politics, 1905–1919

The increasing arrival of Europeans, however, was not only a cause to rejoice for the colonial administration. Newcomers only added more pressure on Lagos's already scarce resources and nowhere more so than for freshwater. Since the British invasion, the absence of sustainable water sources on the island had repeatedly posed an obstacle for development. The 'water system' of Lagos consisted of rainwater tanks and wells essentially dug in the mid-nineteenth century. In the early twentieth century, the island had more than 1,400 of those wells. Not only was water scarce, but the medical department also lacked the human resources to monitor its quality. Cases of bacterial contamination were common.[51] The idea of a scheme to collect an increased volume of freshwater from streams situated on the mainland had been an ambition for some time

[47] Olukoju, *The 'Liverpool' of West Africa*, 16–18.
[48] A. Olukoju (1996), 'Transportation in Colonial West Africa', in G. O. Ogunremi and E. K. Faluyi (eds.), *Economic History of West Africa since 1750*, 149, Ibadan.
[49] Nigerian National Archives, Ibadan, CSO 1/65/43/Vol. 2, 'Correspondence between Governor, Lagos and Secretary of State for the Colonies, 1903–1966', Lugard to Bonard Law, n.a.
[50] G. O. Olusanya (1975), 'The Evolution of the Nigerian Civil Service, 1861–1960: The Problems of Nigerianization', 22–23, in *Humanities Monograph Series 2*, Lagos.
[51] A. Olukoju (2003), *Infrastructure Development and Urban Facilities in Lagos, 1861–2000*, 48–67, Ibadan.

but was repeatedly thwarted by its prohibitive cost.[52] In 1899, proposals had been made to fund it through taxation but the colonial administration feared that this would raise 'violent objection' among its precious African allies.[53]

Faced with rising European demands, however, the question of the water scheme returned to the forefront of debate. This time, with the African elite marginalized, the administration felt it could be implemented. In 1905, Egerton ordered the acquisition of 151 acres of land around the Iju River, north of Lagos on the mainland. Three enormous steam-infused pumps were commissioned from Britain, as well as a considerable number of pipes to transport the water. The scheme, it was hoped, would draw two million gallons a day, sufficient to fill the daily needs of 115,000 people. The £300,000 needed for its construction were to be funded through direct taxation on all Lagosian households, irrespective of their actual ability to connect to water pipes. More importantly, in an effort to achieve a complete modernization of the water system of Lagos, the government declared its intention to close all wells and formalize water sales through communal rate payments for Africans.[54]

Here was the greatest paradox of the era: by the end of the first decade of the twentieth century, Lagos had become a bastion of British imperialism because of its formidably cosmopolitan and qualified African community. They were responsible for turning the city into something that was not a mere trading post but a colonial capital perceived as a worthy recipient of modern urban amenities associated with Europe. Yet, in the process, Africans were deprived of a say in discussions concerning the city's most fundamental problems and the management of an existing resources as scarce and vital as water. To say that the scheme was perceived as being intended for Europeans alone would be an understatement. It was justified precisely on the ground that the current freshwater scarcity represented a threat to their health. Little provisions were made for African inhabitants of Lagos Island.

Not surprisingly, they did not take long to denounce the scheme. In 1908, John Randle, an Edinburgh-educated Saro physician, established the first political party in the history of Nigeria, the Lagos People's Union (LPU), to protest against it. Yet, the most innovative change his LPU induced was that it brought together a European-educated elite –who had largely cooperated with the British –with indigenous landowning Lagosians, which they had traditionally opposed. In that sense, it introduced a new form of political activism in Lagos: one that demanded better representation for all taxpayers, irrespective of their racial or cultural background. The British attempt to seize control of scarce water supplies by characterizing all Africans as non-European homeowners, without distinctions of social standing or ancestry, had paradoxically enabled the emergence of the kind of constituency that had been crucial in the advancement of new 'modern' urban projects in nineteenth-century Europe.[55]

---

[52] Nigerian National Archives, Ibadan, CSO 187, 'Lagos Water Supply', Osbert Chadwick to the Crown Agents for the Colonies, 15 March 1900.
[53] Olukoju, *Infrastructure Development*, p. 48.
[54] D. Lamoureux, *Developing Lagos as a Modern Capital City, 1900–1976* (unpublished PhD thesis, University of Cambridge, 2016), pp. 56–58.
[55] *Idem.*

In February 1909, after Egerton decided to disregard the LPU's critique, and inspectors were authorized to access private properties to determine their water tax, Saros and indigenous Lagosians declared all markets and businesses closed in protest. Led by Oba Eleko, an impressive crowd of 15,000 people marched on to Government House.[56] The British decision to send Eleko into exile revealed the level of their anxiety.[57] In reaction, on 2 April 1909, all markets were closed again and 3,000 market women gathered to discuss a boycott of food sales to Europeans. This put the very stability of the colonial enterprise at risk. Their firm stand can directly be linked to the British attempt to formalize the sale of freshwater, one of their main sources of income.[58] Despite the *Oba's* exile, 1909 ultimately proved a victorious year as the scheme was dropped.[59]

Yet, this victory did not usher in material improvements for African Lagosians. If the colonial authorities recognized that modernizing Lagos would be difficult without including constituents upon which the city still largely depended, they also grew increasingly wary of this dependence. In 1909, Egerton introduced a Sedition Act destined to limit the freedom of expression of African-owned newspapers.[60] The next year, in a landmark case, the Supreme Court of Southern Nigeria authorized the colonial administration to seize indigenous lands for their urban projects, such as a new water scheme. This decision caused uproar with traditional chiefs who argued that it amounted to a profound misunderstanding of customary law.[61] Furthermore, the problem of water scarcity per se remained unsolved and prospects for a constructive dialogue limited.

This blockage illustrates the kind of political atmosphere that had developed in Lagos. Two figures came to personify this era. On the African side, Herbert Macaulay, a Saro of Yoruba origin, the grandson of Bishop Crowther – the first African Anglican bishop – and a former PWD and Land Department surveyor, who had studied engineering in England and owned anticolonial newspapers, represented the new 'modern' kind of African politics that emerged from British attempts to control the city's scarce resources for the benefit of a Eurocentric vision of a future 'modern Lagos'.[62] Macaulay's importance was enhanced by the return in Nigeria of a second figure: Lord Lugard, the Governor General (1914–19) of the newly amalgamated colony of (Northern and Southern) Nigeria.

Lugard was even less eager than Egerton to demonstrate flexibility in front of individuals whom he described as 'plotting … ceaselessly'.[63] Immediately after his arrival, and ignoring the ongoing legal dispute concerning the ownership of Lagosian

[56] 'The Lagos Water Mail', *African Mail* (26 February 1909).
[57] T. Folami (1981), *History of Lagos, Nigeria: The Shaping of an African City*, Smithtown.
[58] P. Cole (1975), *Modern and Traditional Elites in the Politics of Lagos*, 236, Cambridge.
[59] Legislative Council of Nigeria (1922), *Opening Speech Explaining the Details of the Proposed New Constitution for Nigeria Made by His Excellency the Governor Sir Hugh Clifford*, 3–13, Lagos.
[60] 'Editorial: Political Status of the Native', *Lagos Standard* (22 September 1909).
[61] 'Taslim Olawale Elias: Makers of Nigerian Law', *West Africa* (31 December 1955).
[62] Coleman, *Nigeria*, pp. 181–182; T. Falola (2001), *Culture and Customs of Nigeria*, 55–76, Westport,.
[63] F. D. Lugard (1968), 'Amalgamation Report', in K. Greene (ed.), *Lugar and the Amalgamation of Nigeria*, 78, London.

lands, he passed an ordinance that effectively authorized the government to acquire land compulsorily for public use. Then, he introduced the water scheme without any public consultation, warning Lagosians about inevitable future land-seizures. He agreed that Africans owning 'fine houses' that conformed to 'modern European standards' should be able to be connected to the system, but only at their own expense. Furthermore, he confirmed the implementation of direct taxation and water rates.[64]

Unsurprisingly, as in 1908, these events caused uproar among the African elite and the government ignored them, igniting a new wave of protests. This time, however, it was Macaulay, rather than Randle and Eleko, who became its figurehead. Macaulay argued that the scheme was meant for the benefit of European expatriates whose houses were already connected to water pipes. He observed that it would only reduce ordinary Lagosians' access to already-limited but relatively cheap well and rainwater, for the benefit of a system that they would pay for twice over: first through taxation and second through rate payments. Through his newspapers and many public meetings, he encouraged Lagosians to question whether the aim of the scheme was indeed modern sanitation or to make the city unliveable for them. Macaulay's charisma, his intellectual and professional credentials, troubled Lugard. The man he faced was an opponent contesting his policies through scientific reasoning and political rhetoric, not an agitator who could be easily silenced by police action.[65]

In September 1916, the situation escalated rapidly. Following the government's refusal to abandon its plans, the Oba and market women declared a boycott of all food sales to Europeans. A few days later, when two Lagosians were arrested for non-payment of the water tax, a crowd of around 18,000 marched onto Government House. This was the largest and most important protest the city had ever seen. Macaulay warned his supporters that this show of strength would not be well received in the context of the First World War. Unfortunately for them, they did not listen. The events gave Lugard a free hand. Two hundred policemen and soldiers repressed the protest, beating protesters, arresting their leaders and imposing restrictions on the press. By the end of September, no Lagosians were to be found protesting the scheme on the streets of Lagos anymore.[66]

Nonetheless, not all was lost for Africans in Lagos. Lugard recognized the difficulty of bypassing them. In 1917, he introduced a new Lagos Town Council (LTC), modelled on British town councils, in an attempt to ease tensions. Of course, there were limits to the inclusiveness of these schemes. The governor still nominated its African members. New African-managed 'Native Areas' and European-managed 'European Reservation Areas' (ERAs) also meant that if Africans were now able to access services previously limited to Europeans, they could only do so if they were willing to pay for them.[67] Still, the reforms signalled an important shift: the earlier 'medical' understanding of urban

---

[64] Lagos State Government (1987), *Lagos State Handbook 1987*, Ikeja-Lagos, p. 210; 'Iju Waterworks', Department of Public Works to CSG, 28 May 1928.

[65] H. O. Danmole (1987), 'The Crisis of the Lagos Muslim Community, 1915–1947', in A. A. Babatunde (ed.), *The History of the Peoples of Lagos State*, pp. 290–305, Ikeja-Lagos.

[66] Lamoureux, *Developing Lagos*, pp. 59–62.

[67] F. D. Lugard (1919), *Revision of Instructions to Political Officers on Subjects Chiefly Political and Administrative 1913–1918*, 417, London.

modernization had been replaced with a 'political' understanding of urban modernity. The African elite was not fooled by Lugard's concessions. An editor of the *Lagos Weekly Record* even accused the governor of establishing an 'infernal system'.[68]

Once Lugard had left in 1919, African elites found the British administration more willing to make concessions to avoid further protests. In 1919, the Crown's Privy Council judged that the 1910 decision of the Supreme Court of Southern Nigeria concerning the question of land ownership in Lagos was indeed based on a misunderstanding of customary law. The solution to Lagos Island's infamous lack of freshwater supplies would therefore not be achieved without consensus.[69] Governor Hugh Clifford (1919–25), Lugard's successor, even agreed to bear the high cost of the water scheme and scrap rates for public fountains as a peace-seeking measure. In 1922, he also introduced a new constitution that opened voting and elective rights to the Legislative Council of the colony and the LTC for Africans. This measure only concerned men with a minimal income of £100 (approximately 3,000 individuals). Still, it meant that leading Africans had regained their position as participators in the modernization of Lagos.[70] The political crisis induced by water scarcity had proved a turning point.

## 'Like herrings in a barrel': The scarcity of space and the advent of modern Lagos, 1919–1928[71]

In the midst of these constitutional changes a new Lagos started to emerge. With the water scheme, funded largely at government's expense, demands for the democratization of other markers of a desired European urban modernity also grew. This was notably the case for electrical street lighting. Since the 1880s, African Lagosians, who perceived it as a necessary measure to deter burglaries, had offered to pay for it. In 1891, the colonial authorities had even started to assess potential hydroelectric and coal-based generating projects. Such ambitious plans, however, were thwarted by more pressing problems, such as the water scheme. In 1919, only a modest coal-powered steam station existed on the island, powering street lighting around key administrative buildings until 11 pm.[72]

With the new constitution, ordinary Lagosians, even if they themselves did not have the vote, could now hold 'their' representatives accountable for such services. Almost immediately after taking power, representatives of Macaulay's new Nigerian National Democratic Party (NNDP) thus started calling for the introduction of a new electrical system. This time, their demands and their willingness to participate financially matched that of the Europeans. Accordingly, in 1920, the government commissioned a new power station. Opened in 1923 across the lagoon, Ijora Power Station was the

---

[68] 'The Retirement of Frederick Lugard', *The Lagos Weekly Record* (23 February 1919).
[69] Coleman, *Nigeria*, pp. 181–182.
[70] Legislative Council of Nigeria, *Opening Speech, 1922*, pp. 3–13.
[71] 'Deputy Director of Sanitary Services to Editor', *Nigerian Pioneer* (5 December 1924).
[72] Olukoju, *Infrastructure Development*, pp. 21–25.

tallest industrial structure in West Africa at the time, with a chimney 152 feet high and a steam turbine capable of generating up to 7 megawatts.[73] Electrical street lighting progressively became a reality on Lagos Island; the LTC's electrical spending grew from approximately £1,000 to £6,000 per annum.[74]

The democratization of new modern urban services hid a bigger problem, however. Demands for services and resources previously limited to Europeans skyrocketed alongside the population of Lagos Island, which had risen from approximately 41,000 in 1900 to 98,000 in 1921.[75] Inevitably, this tested the supplies of a city already renowned for multiple scarcities. Two years after its opening, the PWD already had to raise electrical rates to discourage demand.[76] Political enfranchisement simply did not create the necessary financial mechanism to fund the modernization of Lagos Island for all its inhabitants. Despite the modernization of its water and electrical infrastructure, Lagos was only becoming more insalubrious. The port city, a local journalist wrote, had become a 'time bomb' for epidemics, ravaged by outbursts of Spanish influenza, tuberculosis and cholera that only benefited from the ever-growing demographic density of the city.[77]

It did not take long before major European firms started to criticize the new status quo that had emerged after the water rate protests. Political peace, they argued, had been bought at the expense of an effective modernization of Lagos, one that, in their mind, would have guaranteed the health of their employees. They started to lobby the government and wanted to take the matter into their own hands, demanding an area where they could freely build housing, medical and recreational facilities, in a 'modern European style' for the safety of Europeans. Yet, they, too, quickly faced the seemingly insurmountable challenge of another scarce resource in Lagos: constructible dry land. The shortage of land was partly the result of overcrowding but was exacerbated by the difficulty of seizing African-owned land under the new constitutional agreements. In fact, the government's first reaction was to suggest land on the mainland but European firms judged it to be too far away.

As in 1905, British authorities in 1922 came up with a radical solution to this seemingly impossible problem of natural scarcity. They authorized imperial companies to conduct the reclamation of Ikoyi, unoccupied swamps situated east of the Macgregor Canal, almost half of the physical space in Lagos Island. By the end of the year, works had started to prepare Ikoyi for its new purpose.[78] The government's decision to spend £100,351 on the construction of government bungalows for its European civil servants in Ikoyi left little doubts about its intentions. As a PWD surveyor remarked, in terms that could be have been taken directly from Lugard's own writings, 'the native', not the

---

[73] Legislative Council of Nigeria (1923), *Address by the Governor Sir Hugh Clifford*, 100, Lagos.

[74] Nigerian National Archives, Ibadan, COMCOL 1/1532, 'Street Lighting in Lagos', Commissioner for Lands to CSG, 23 September 1932.

[75] P. O. Sada (1969), 'Differential Population Distribution and Growth in Metropolitan Lagos', *Journal of Business and Social Studies*, 1 (2): 117–132.

[76] Quoted in Olukoju, *Infrastructure Development*, p. 26.

[77] 'Overcrowding in Lagos and the Spread of Pulmonary Tuberculosis', *Nigerian Pioneer* (29 August 1919).

[78] Legislative Council of Nigeria, *Address by the Governor, 1923*, pp. 98–99.

colonial government, ought to 'assume responsibility' for his own 'development'.[79] The outcome of the political modernization that followed the water rate protests, then, was deeply paradoxical: ultimately, it enabled the authorities to impose the sort of two-speed vision for modern Lagos that Africans had successfully challenged in the past.

Africans in Lagos were unsurprisingly consternated by the development of Ikoyi. They realized how marginalized they remained within a colonial system, despite constitutional reforms. In 1922, their leaders presented the governor with a 'monster petition' of 17,000 signatures warning him that segregating Ikoyi, instead of making it available to the whole of the population, was putting at risk the majority of Lagos with the spectre of a bubonic plague already hitting Ghana and Sierra Leone.[80] The development of an exclusively European district 'compelled' the 'native community' to 'huddle themselves together under the insanitary conditions'.[81] Ikoyi effectively ended the possibilities for 'natural' African 'expansion', forcing them to live 'like herrings in a barrel'.[82]

Yet, Governor Clifford was unconvinced. '17,000 signatures', he wrote, represented 'a poor show of "unanimity" on the part of a community numbering more than 99,000 souls'.[83] The historical reversal that had occurred since the water rate protests could not be clearer. Africans were excluded on the grounds that they were unable to participate equally in financial terms in the modernization of their districts alongside European lines and thus presented a sanitary threat to the health of Europeans. It was even the 'medical' officer of the colony who was put in charge of Ikoyi now justified their exclusion.[84] In less than half a decade, most Europeans had relocated to the new district and Clifford declared that it was the proudest achievement of his career in Nigeria.[85]

Paradoxically, it was the confirmation of the African community's worst fears that would prove to be of the greatest help to them. In 1924, bubonic plague broke out in Lagos. By the time the presence of the disease was confirmed, the density of Lagos Island had ensured it spread quickly, all the way to Ikoyi. Although less devastating than other epidemics – 509 deaths in 1925 – the psychological impact of the plague on European colonial administrators was very significant, triggering fears of the Black Death of fourteenth-century Europe.[86] Indeed, the Colonial Office in London itself became so worried about the handling of affairs in Lagos that it decided in 1924 to appoint an expert with executive powers to solve the matter. The source of the problem, as the expert discovered, was simple: the uneven distribution and development of constructible dry land had generated a land scarcity that effectively put Lagos Island in

[79] F. V. Meyer (1947), '*Nigeria*'. *Public Works in the British Colonies*, 15, London.
[80] Legislative Council of Nigeria, *Address by the Governor, 1923*, p. 32.
[81] *Nigerian Pioneer* (24 March 1922).
[82] 'Deputy Director of Sanitary Services to Editor', *Nigerian Pioneer* (5 December 1924).
[83] Legislative Council of Nigeria, *Address by the Governor, 1923*, p. 33.
[84] Nigerian National Archives, Ibadan, LAG PWD 3.1/96/C.181/Vol. 2, C series, 'Town Planning in Lagos, 1929–30'.
[85] Legislative Council of Nigeria, *Address by the Governor, 1923*, p. 33.
[86] Lamoureux, *Developing Lagos*, pp. 68–69.

a state of sanitary siege. It was 'more overcrowded', he wrote, 'than any other town' that he had visited 'in the last twenty-five years'.[87]

Yet, despite good intentions, the solution he suggested did not solve the political tensions that had built up. In the mind of Africans, his decision to authorize unexpected sanitary visits in private Lagosian homes to deal with disinfection or the imposition of heavy restrictions on street sellers (accused of dropping waste in the drains) contrasted sharply with the development of Ikoyi for Europeans.[88] The measures were not enough. At a colonial conference in London, the head of the powerful Association of West African Merchants now also urged the governor to realize that Lagos was 'perhaps the most insanitary town in West Africa' and it was time 'that some real and consistent thought' was given by the government to 'modernize' and expand its 'sanitary system'.[89] Ultimately, the failure of past policies that attempted to reduce the pressure of scarcity on the European minority by making access to key scarce resources even scarcer for the African majority ended up forcing Clifford, as he prepared to leave Nigeria, to initiate consultation for a large-scale modernization of all of Lagos Island – one that would paradoxically enfranchise most of its inhabitants, in the collective interest, as recipients of urban modernity.

In 1925, H. Howard Humphreys and Sons, a leading British civil engineering company, was commissioned by the Lagos government to write a report on the sanitary situation of Lagos and identify priorities for a future improvement scheme. This was the first time that an attempt was made to audit independently the state of the city. The report was damning for the British authorities. What was called the '"sanitary system" of the City', J. D. Wall – the expert – wrote, was 'scarcely worthy of the name'.[90] Concerning the issue of constructible land scarcity, the establishment of Ikoyi, he observed, had led to the concentration of 'four-fifths' of the population of Lagos into 'less than two-thirds of Lagos Island'.[91] The modernization of Lagos existed only in name. There were just thirty available latrines connected to drains in Lagos Island for 'more than 80,000' inhabitants. Perhaps the fact that since 1913 the authorities had judged that it was more profitable to use the tramway for waste collection than passenger transportation illustrated how bad overcrowding really was.[92] Faced with these appalling conclusions, the colonial administration agreed to invest resources in a large-scale programme that expanded the benefits already enjoyed by Europeans in Ikoyi to African inhabitants.[93]

The proposed programme of 'physical' modernization of Lagos was unique by British African colonial standards. The British government promised to spend £200,000 for the voluntary relocation of 10,000 people from the Island to the mainland

---

[87]  Public Record Office, National Archives of the UK, Kew, CO 583/144/9, 'Plague Report in Nigeria, 1925'.
[88]  'Deputy Director of Sanitary Services to Editor', *Nigerian Pioneer* (5 December 1924).
[89]  Nigerian National Archives, Ibadan, CSO 26/1/09947/Vol. 2, 'Merchants and H.M. Ships', Association of West African Merchants, 27 October 1925.
[90]  Nigerian National Archives, Ibadan, RG/H3 (1926), *Howard Humphrey: Report upon the Main Drainage of Lagos*, 4, Lagos.
[91]  Ibid., p. 3.
[92]  Olukoju, *Infrastructure Development*, p. 85.
[93]  Legislative Council of Nigeria, *Address by the Governor, 1923*, pp. 31–54; p. 120.

north of Iddo, across the Carter Bridge, in a district built in a quality equivalent to that of Ikoyi and connected to Lagos Island by modern means of transportation, as well as running water, electricity and a state-of-the-art sewage system. Furthermore, it was agreed that the colony would establish a central planning agency, the Lagos Executive Development Board, and hire, for the first time in its history, a full-time professional town planner to coordinate the completion of the works fairly and independently from the chaos of scarcity politics.[94]

## Conclusion: Scarcity at the roots of urban modernity?

The extension of running water, limited political representation and state-sponsored housing as early as the 1920s in Lagos forces us to revise a dominant narrative that locates such developments in the context of the Second World War. In Lagos, it was earlier attempts to control the distribution and ownership of scarce but vital resources that triggered new forms of indigenous political mobilization that would forever alter the British administration's approach to the modernization of the city and the modernity of its inhabitants. In 1928, the modernity of Lagos was already intrinsically linked to debates concerning the modernity of municipal rights. Crucially, group-specific responses, by colonial administrators, to a state of scarcity best comprehended as a generalized existential threat to the whole of Lagos led to the unprecedented mobilization of previously scattered African masses in the defence of a modern definition of the general interest never truly articulated before by European colonists in Lagos. In that sense, Cooper was certainly right to observe that urban 'density' and 'its consequences' were 'crucibles of social, cultural and political change'. The explosive politics of water and land scarcity in Lagos were indeed accentuated by an ever-denser demographic urban reality. Yet, that in 1928, already, the urban modernity imagined for Africans in Lagos to reduce the pressure of scarcity corresponded to the same infrastructural and visual terms as those that had defined urban modernity in Britain was revolutionary.

Certainly, these visions had clear geographic limits, extending not much further than Lagos Island itself and its most immediate continental shores. There were limitations to how 'African' or even 'urban' these modern responses to freshwater and constructible space scarcity indeed were. The colonial government's insistence that Wall's foundational survey should only concern Lagos Island and Ikoyi ignored in practice the problems of the thousands of rural migrants who had come to amalgamate around the island. The lack of freshwater and their claims to urban modernity were simply ignored.[95] In that sense, indigenous struggles in the rest of Nigeria remained disconnected from debates that concerned Africans in the colonial capital. This would, indeed, only change after the Second World War.

The urban modernity promoted by the British neither amounted to a full infrastructural reform of Lagos seeking to eliminate completely scarcities nor did

---

[94] Legislative Council of Nigeria (1925), *Address by the Governor*, 230–232; Meyer, *'Nigeria'. Public Works in the British Colonies*, p. 15.
[95] Nigerian National Archives, *Howard Humphrey*, p. 1.

it include all of its inhabitants. Rather, it aimed to deliver limited modern urban services, in specific districts, for an extended but still limited enfranchised community. The promised modern Lagos was a hybrid that still reflected the economic essence and cynicism of scarcity politics. If the proposed reforms marked a revolutionary precedent in the context of British Africa, where racial segregation constituted the norm, their direct beneficiaries remained a very small group of European-educated and landowning Africans who dominated municipal politics and commerce and who the British treated as the legitimate 'voices' of the greater Lagosian masses.[96]

Scarcity politics in early twentieth-century Lagos led to a new imperial social contract between the colonial administration and this African elite rather than a full democratization of the numerous new services it introduced. Macaulay's NNDP, for instance, remained anchored in a struggle for equal participation rather than a call for self-determination that increasingly characterized political movements elsewhere in West Africa.[97] Indeed, its leaders seemed greatly satisfied with the proposed scheme, even if it made no real provision for the qualitative upgrade of Lagos Island. As one of them remarked, it was simply too 'difficult' to rebuild the entire town on 'proper sanitary lines'.[98] Their inclusion in a prospective urban modernity defined alongside European lines, in that sense, symbolized Lagos's entry into the only sphere that really mattered: one that comforted their elitist position and granted them dominance, alongside Europeans, over the vast market and resources of 'their' new Nigerian colony. In the following decades, the extreme concentration of investments and development funds in Lagos, as opposed to the rest of Nigeria, would prove to be no less of a mobilizing factor for these 'new' Nigerian masses. Scarcity, albeit conceptualized in a different but no less vital, financial way, would continue to be a political motor for change.

---

[96] K. Oke (2013), 'The Colonial Public Sphere in Nigeria, 1920–1943', *Stichproben. Wiener Zeitschrift für Kritische Afrikastudien*, 25 (13): 29–56.

[97] G. I. C. Eluwa (1971), 'Background to the Emergence of the National Congress of British West Africa', *African Studies Review*, 14 (2): 205–218.

[98] 'Editorial', *Nigerian Pioneer* (2 July 1926).

15

# Energy Shortages and the Politics of Time: Resilience, Redistribution and 'Normality' in Japan and East Germany, 1940s–1970s

Hiroki Shin and Frank Trentmann

In contemporary memory, the 1973 oil crisis appears as the watershed between a post-war era of affluence and a new period of pessimism worried about the limits of growth and resources shortages.[1] Yet energy shortages were a recurrent feature of the twentieth century, as well as in earlier periods. Today, shortages are associated with underdeveloped or developing countries, with sometimes serious consequences to public health. Zanzibar in Tanzania, for example, was without power for a month in the early summer of 2008 and for three months in 2010. The 2008 blackout was accompanied by a reduction in the birth weights of babies with in utero exposure to the blackout.[2] Nor does economic growth on its own eliminate the severity of cuts; the biggest blackout in history occurred in an emerging economy, India, in late July 2012 and affected 620 million people.[3]

It is easy to forget that the most advanced industrial societies also went through periods where they battled with shortages. Some of these were the result of military conflict, most notably the coal shortages and rationing of the two world wars. But peacetime was equally disrupted by intermittent shortages, the result of strikes (e.g. Germany in 1919–20), austerity (1932), technical failures and natural disasters, and sometimes a combination of these. Europe's cold winter of 1963 and the New York blackout of 1965 were only the most dramatic instances of disruption.[4] Britain faced severe electricity shortages in 1947–48 and 1963, Japan in 1946–49, 1951–53 and

---

[1] For example, see Dominic Sandbrook's (2010), *State of Emergency: The Way We Were: Britain 1970–1974*, London and his (2012) *Seasons in the Sun: The Battle for Britain, 1974–1979*, London. For other perspectives, see Frank Bösch and Rüdiger Graf (eds.), *Historical Social Research: Special Issue 'The Energy Crisis of the 1970s'*, 39 (4) (2014).

[2] Alfredo Burlando (2010), 'The Impact of Electricity on Work and Health: Evidence from a Blackout in Zanzibar'. Available at https://www.aeaweb.org/conference/2011/retrieve.php?pdfid=523.

[3] Sunila Kale (2014), *Electrifying India: Regional Political Economies of Development*, pp. 176–178, Stanford, CA; International Energy Agency (2005), *Saving Electricity in a Hurry: Dealing with Temporary Shortfalls in Electricity Supplies*, Paris. See also the chapters on Lagos, India and China in this volume.

[4] David Nye (2010), *When the Lights Went Out*, Cambridge, MA.

1956–57, in addition to gas shortages in 1961, 1965 and 1969. Industrial growth and the rapid expansion of private electricity use made developed societies worry about energy security well before OPEC announced its oil embargo in October 1973.

In this chapter, we revisit real and feared energy shortages between the end of the Second World War and the first oil crisis in 1973, focusing on the experience of two societies: Japan and East Germany (GDR). Our aim is, partly, to overcome amnesia and to suggest that shortages were an integral feature of affluence and growth – and not only of recession. But we are equally interested in shortages for what they can reveal about the coping mechanisms of advanced modern societies. Attention to the two oil crises of the 1970s tends to highlight external factors and causes. But most shortages were also shaped by internal social and political dynamics. Instead of focusing on immediate causes, we use shortages to illuminate how societies cope under stress by comparing the priorities and mechanisms at play in a capitalist regime with those in a planned socialist economy.

At the centre of this discussion is the distributional politics of who gets what and when. It also concerns distribution across times of day and seasons. Shortages have distinct temporal features, depending on both the seasons and the daily evening peak of electricity use. Disruption in the flow of resources sets in motion a politics of time that favours some users at the expense of others and some practices (such as night work) at the expense of others (like daytime housework). How this is worked out in reality can tell us not only something about priorities and interests in different societies but also about the relative flexibility or rigidity of 'normality' in everyday life.

## Not all consumers are equal

The German Democratic Republic (GDR) was born into a particularly precarious energy situation in 1949. In addition to the destruction of plant and transport networks at the end of the Second World War and by Soviet dismantling thereafter, the new socialist country lost ready access to the hard coal (*Steinkohle*) deposits in the Ruhr which now lay in the capitalist West. Life and labour now hinged almost exclusively on *lignite* (*Braunkohle*), a fuel which in addition to being of low energetic value and highly polluting had the additional drawback of containing 30–60 per cent water, which spelled disaster in a cold winter because the coal froze to the ground or in transport. On top, there were constant problems with old plant, the flight and shortage of skilled workers and engineers, poorly repaired boilers and lagging production of transformers and other core parts for the generation and distribution of electric power.

On their own, coal and electricity have fundamentally different qualities: one can be stored, the other cannot. Electricity users are linked by a shared network, resulting in collective peaks and troughs very different from the coal used by separate users. However, since lignite was the main source of electricity as well as for heating homes, the fortunes of coal and electricity were intimately tied. Energy shortages vary considerably by type of fuel, duration and geographic scale. In addition, countries vary in their energy mix, relative autonomy and stage of economic development. Japan depended on hydropower for nearly 60 per cent of its electricity until 1960. Ten years later, 41 per cent of the country's electricity generation came from oil. Socialist East Germany, by contrast, depended on lignite for 83 per cent of its electricity in 1970. By the time the Wall came down in 1989, the East German population still relied on solid fuels for 56 per cent of all its energy needs, notwithstanding the expansion of the gas network in the 1970s–1980s.[5]

Shortages were a way of life in the GDR but their site shifted decisively in the course of the 1950s. Rolling blackouts had been common in both the Western allied and Soviet zones of Berlin in 1947–48. Unlike in West Germany, however, electricity cuts and rationing continued in the GDR after 1949 – West Germany did face severe gas shortages in the early 1950s, but here shortages of electricity were an anxiety rather than a reality.[6] In East Germany, small rather than big users were initially expected to reduce the energy deficit. The priority was on rapid industrial recovery and growth. Industries were urged to be economical with their coal, but the main burden fell on the shoulders of household consumers. Posters, radio and the ruling Communist Party (SED) in 1951 called on the population to save for industry. As the SED central committee explained in support of its campaign for strict economy in February 1953, 'to awaken the initiative and enthusiasm among the masses for practising an energy saving regime will be an important lever to erect the foundations of socialism'. Energy saving was not a temporary emergency measure but the 'constantly intelligent principle of socialist economic policy', preventing the waste of collective resources.[7] Cuts during peak hours were the norm. In March 1953, the GDR decided on a 30 per cent cut. In East Berlin, the situation was especially problematic. Not only were households here responsible for 40 per cent of all electricity used, but from 1952 East Berlin had to export energy to the rest of the GDR to help alleviate shortages there.

Electricity cuts and discontent over coal deliveries earlier that year hardly helped the public mood in the first half of 1953. In January, there had been long queues for coal. In Nordhausen, a public official was confronted by heavy engineering workers who had waited since 4 o' clock in the morning: 'If one is lucky, one receives 50 kg of briquettes after having waited four hours.'[8] Deliveries met targets in Berlin and Cottbus, but there were serious problems in Dresden, Potsdam, Leipzig and Karl-Marx Stadt, where inhabitants were either left short or refused to take low-grade unsieved lignite altogether.[9] Lack (or uncertainty) of coal drove more and more people to switch on electric heaters instead, thus intensifying the peak problem. Overcrowding and damaged housing increased the popularity of electric hot plates; these gave lodgers the chance to cook in their own room in the evening and avoid tension with the main tenant over the use of the kitchen, one energy inspector noted.[10]

---

[5]  Bundesarchiv (BArch) Berlin-Lichterfelde, DF 4/32283, Institut für Energetik, 'Abrechnung der Komplexbilanz Energie der DDR 1987'.

[6]  "Am Ende der Gasversorgung?" in *Energiewirtschaftliche Tagesfragen*, III/24, 18 Feb. 1954, pp. 213–214.

[7]  BEWAG Archive, Berlin, A 14: Bewag Ost, 7, director Quade 'Stellungnahme', 18 Feb. 1953.

[8]  BArch Berlin-Lichterfelde, DC/16/23, Kopietz to Koordinierungs- und Kontrollstelle für Industrie und Verkehr, 19 Jan. 1953.

[9]  BArch Berlin-Lichterfelde, DC/16/23, Abt. Grundstoffindustrie to Politbüro and ZK, 24 July 1953.

[10]  Landesarchiv Berlin (LAB), C Rep. 149–06 nr 28, Protokoll, Tagung der bezirklichen Energiekommission, 11 Dec. 1953.

**Figure 15.1** 'Helft Stromsperren vermeiden' 1950 ['Help prevent power cuts', Berlin 1950]. *Source*: Berlin, Landesarchiv.

**Figure 15.2** 'Mehr Strom für den Aufbau des Sozialismus' 1952 ['More electricity for building socialism', East Germany 1952]. *Source*: Berlin, Landesarchiv.

The uprising of 17 June 1953 tipped the balance between industry and households. The main demands of the protesters had been free elections, more humane work quotas and better living conditions. The regime would not give them the first two. But it now made it a priority to give them energy. A week after Soviet tanks had quelled the uprising, the council of ministers ordered the end of electricity cuts (*Stromsperren*) for households, with effect from 1 July. The population was already spared any cuts in the following week. Then levels of consumption started to rise and made it necessary to roll out cuts again in July and early August. The state secretary for energy blamed industries that 'refused' to switch to night shifts but also the more liberal use of energy in households; total energy use jumped from 2,698 MW to 2,912 MW in the course of July, requiring cuts of between 100 MW and 300 MW in these weeks.[11] The campaign for greater energy awareness never entirely disappeared. In 1954, at 7 am in the morning, lorries would drive through the streets of East Berlin, with loudspeakers appealing to residents to 'Remember that we are now in peak time: save energy.'[12] Energy saving was promoted in film and leaflets. In 1957–58, the party's youth movement (FDJ) initiated a campaign against the 'Wattfrass' (watt glutton) that carried echoes of the Hitler Youth's earlier pursuit of the 'Kohlenklau' (coal thief). Members pledged to switch off electricity-hungry appliances in their homes and schools and save at least 100 W each;[13] that citizens were reckless 'energy sinners' would remain a complaint among local energy deputies in the 1950s and 1960s. But the political will for more stringent measures had disappeared. The political masters had no desire to confront the people and enforce energy discipline within their private four walls.

This left industry as the main site of intervention. The main lever was electricity quotas for peak hours for consumers using more than 500 KW. Energy deputies (*Energiebeauftragte*) worked on behalf of local government districts (*Räte*). In addition, there were energy inspectors within enterprises. Some firms excelled. The VEB Berliner Glühlampenwerk, the publicly owned light-bulb producer, was praised as 'exemplary' by the district inspector in February 1962. The firm had appointed its own full-time energy inspector who checked that quotas were not exceeded, with the help of hourly meter readings and half-hourly studies of electric curves. A specially designed clock sounded a signal when quotas were being reached. Excessively large engines were replaced. In 1961, the plant spent 30,000 marks on the cleaning of existing lights. It whitewashed rooms to reflect light better. For every shining example, however, there was a failure not very far away. The VEB Fahrzeugausrüstung – a vehicle equipment plant – did not even have a schedule for the operation of its machines. It repeatedly breached both electric and gas quotas. The energy delegate was unqualified and 'seen as a brake on the production process'. For many foremen, energy delegates were 'deceitful' and a pain in the neck, pointing out pipes that were not insulated, criticizing fellow workers for opening windows and interfering with work routines.[14]

[11]  BArch Berlin-Lichterfelde, DC/16/23, Stellungnahme, Büchner, 3 Aug. 1953.
[12]  *Energiewirtschaftliche Tagesfragen*, III/24 (1953–4), p. 235.
[13]  LAB, C Rep. 135–01, no. 253, Protokoll über die Kohle- und Energiekonferenz, 6 Feb. 1958.
[14]  LAB, C Rep. 135–01, no. 253, Schmiga, Informationsbericht über die Versorgung mit Elektroenergie', 14 Feb. 1962; see also ibid.: Andrae to mayor and ZK, 24 Nov. 1961.

The mixed career of the local energy deputies illustrates the problems of making energy a greater priority in a planned economy. Energy deputies were first appointed in 1952. A year later, an official investigation found few were living up to the job. Deputies were used for all sorts of other tasks where there was a shortage of officials and resources. The one in Fürstenwalde registered the sale of livestock. In Magdeburg, many were also in charge of collecting scrap metal. Those in Stendal and Calau had qualifications but as a barber and brewer. Most industries either did not have any energy plans or lacked the meters and instruments to monitor them. In the newly christened Karl-Marx-Stadt (today's Chemnitz), the chair of the city council was not even aware of the energy delegates' existence. In Neubrandenburg, shops and retailers did not know that it was prohibited to light shop windows during peak hours. Most firms simply refused to take part in 'socialist competitions' (*sozialistischer Wettbewerb*) for energy saving.[15]

In November 1953, the Ministry for Heavy Industry tried to give the status of the lowly energy delegates a lift with new ranks and uniforms – a grey blue jacket and trousers, with beige for special festivities, and piping rising from bronze to gold for officials in ministries. The new clothes failed to impress. In June 1954, the frustrated energy delegate in Berlin Weissensee was still waiting for forty-eight enterprises to provide their energy consumption cards, documenting their electricity consumption.[16] By the late 1960s, the government found few signs of improvement. In Karl-Marx-Stadt, for example, 1,095 enterprises had pledged energy-saving measures. In Leipzig, on the other hand, 39 per cent of enterprises did not have any energy plan, and 20 per cent did not use any energy norms for their own production plans. In Berlin, only every third firm entered the energy strand of socialist competitions.[17]

The frustrations of the energy delegates were endless and point to the systematic difficulties of managing scarcity, let alone overcoming it. On 1 October 1954, for example, Berlin's mayoral office explained to the local districts that the present shortage could not just be blamed on yet another technical failure at the Klingenberg power station but resulted from industries feverishly trying to overcome their planning backlog.[18] Energy delegates called for fines, only to see these softened or thrown out by local government. As the lawyer for the VEB Grossdrehmaschinenbau stressed in his appeal to the council in February 1955, the mechanical engineering enterprise produced vital exports for the USSR. Yes, it had repeatedly exceeded its electricity quotas in October of the previous year, but it had no option, given the delays and fluctuations with raw materials. To slow down production when materials finally arrived and fail to meet export orders purely to stay within energy norms was unreasonable. The fine for the director was transmuted into a 'stern warning'.[19] Other firms burnt through their monthly electric peak-use quota well before the end of the month with the simple

---

[15] BArch Berlin-Lichterfelde, DC 16/21: Staatssekretariat für Energie, HV Energie, Zentrale Kommission, report 13 May 1953.

[16] LAB, C Rep. 148–06, nr 43, Wehlmann, Tätigkeitsbericht 17 June 1954.

[17] BArch Berlin-Lichterfelde, DC 20/11885, Opitz to Rauchfuss, 14 Nov. 1969.

[18] LAB, C Rep. 148–06, nr 43, Harry Krebs to council of district Berlin-Weissensee, 1 Oct. 1954.

[19] LAB, C Rep. 148–06, nr 43, Gaulke to VEB 16 Dec. 1955.

realization that energy, once used, could not be clawed back.[20] In general, it did not matter how many new power stations the GDR built and how much it increased the supply of coal – the amount of lignite doubled in the 1960s – energy continued to be outpaced by industrial production. Energy was too cheap to encourage saving – only in 1968 did the GDR government introduce a higher price for peak-time electricity for heavy users, coupled with a feed-in tariff to reward those who fed energy back into the grid during peak time.[21] Energy scarcity was a normal feature of an economy marked by general material scarcity.

Local authorities were in an ambivalent position. Officials were consumers of energy as well as arms of the government. In December 1952, police reported that the lights were always on in 8,000 buildings managed by the state-owned housing administration.[22] A year later, the government prohibited the public and private use of electric space heaters between the hours of 6 am and 10 pm, but could not even enforce it among its own officials. In October 1954, the ruling party made the Berlin electricity provider BEWAG sent out a '50-Mann Brigade' to do spot checks on 155 government offices and eighty-nine enterprises: it discovered 377 electric radiators, of which 205 were running (in early October!), and thirty-one cookplates, of which two were used as heaters. Many offices had a well-oiled early warning system for such inspections and managed to hide away their appliances in time.[23]

******

Japan faced an even more frightening challenge in the post-war period. Defeat isolated Japan from international energy supplies. Domestic coal production collapsed at the end of the war, yielding only 23 million tonnes in 1946, compared to 49 million tonnes in 1938.[24] Traditional fuel resources had also been depleted, as deforestation during the war had eaten into already limited domestic resources of firewood and charcoal; Japan lost 15 per cent of its forest in the course of the war.[25] Desperate to overcome fuel shortages, domestic consumers turned to electricity. There were few alternatives; charcoal rations had been curtailed and gas supply was unreliable because of reduced coal production and damaged gas mains. In 1946, electricity consumption for lighting and domestic purposes jumped to 63 TWh, nearly twice the figure during the war. There was an additional 20 TWh of illicit use, ranging from electricity theft to the installation of unauthorized appliances and higher wattage light bulbs.[26] Since 90 per cent of Japan's electricity at the time came from hydropower, shortages were inevitable

[20]  LAB, C Rep. 148–06, nr 43, Hohmann, Tatigkeitsbericht, nd (Sept. 1956).
[21]  BArch Berlin-Lichterfelde, DY/30/J IV 2/2J, Ministerrat, Beschluss 10 Sept. 1968.
[22]  LAB, C Rep. 106–02, nr 616, Protokoll, Energiekommission 2 Dec. 1952.
[23]  LAB, C Rep. 752, nr 38, Energiekommission, Kurzbericht, Oct. 1954.
[24]  *Shōwa Kokusei Sōran*, Vol. 1 (Tokyo, 1991), p. 460.
[25]  William Tsutsui (2003), 'Landscapes in the Dark Valley: Toward an Environmental History of Wartime Japan', *Environmental History*, VIII: 294–311.
[26]  S. Kotake (1980), *Denryoku Hyakunen Shi Zen hen*, p. 620, Tokyo; M. Tanahasi (1948), *Denki Senyō Bōshihou Yōtei*, p. 5, Funabashi.

in unusually dry seasons. A series of winter droughts between 1946 and 1952 made electricity crises a regular event. In 1946, electricity was added to the list of controlled resources that already included charcoal and firewood. For the Japanese government under the American Occupation, the overwhelming priority was economic recovery. Under the 'priority production policy', available energy was thus directed to industries – particularly coal and steel – at the expense of domestic consumers.[27]

The control of electricity supply was ad hoc and arbitrary. Because electricity supply largely depended on rainfall, the extent of necessary saving tended to be difficult to predict. In August 1948, Kanto Electric Supply announced that the month's electricity supply would be reduced by 10 per cent, 25 per cent or more from the previous year's level.[28] Voltage reduction and power cuts were executed without warning, especially in residential areas.[29] Both the occupying American authorities and Japanese civil servants believed that turning off electricity in households to deliver fuel to factories was justified to make the country stand on its own feet. This was a top-down – even authoritarian – approach. U.S. officials opposed the formation of voluntary energy-saving groups for fear of reviving wartime patriotic associations or spreading socialism.[30] Instead, savings in household consumption were achieved through compulsory measures, such as disconnection or setting ceilings for consumption, that were monitored by meter readers and supply companies' patrols.[31] Industries, by contrast, had their electricity allocated and maximized their use through efficiency, such as thermal management in the steel industry.[32] Osaka city sent electricity rationalization instructors to factories.[33]

The main site of intervention for Japanese policymakers, however, was the residential sector. Households were told to use only 'one lamp, [and] one radio' during peak hours.[34] Between 1949 and 1953, the Resource Investigation Council widened its ambitions well beyond electricity cuts. The Council, for example, recommended shifting demand from electricity and charcoal to town gas in urban areas and replacing in rural areas traditional cook stoves (*kamados*) altogether.[35] The number of town gas consumers increased from 1.2 million in 1948 to 2.2 million in 1954.[36] The rural cooking reform was introduced in 43,000 villages.

Although the sites of intervention were different in Japan and the GDR, energy disruption dramatically affected everyday life. In Japan, intervention hit domestic

---

[27] For example, the 'Electric Power Five Year Plan' referred to in H. Inaba (ed.) (1948), *Nihon Keizai no Shōrai*, pp. 166, 287, Tokyo.

[28] *Denki Shimbun*, 9 Aug. 1948.

[29] Ministry of Commerce and Industry, 'Kinkyū Denryoku Chōsetsu Jissi Youryō', 10 Nov. 1947, National Archives of Japan.

[30] Tōkyō Denryoku (1983), *Tōkyō Denryoku Sanjyūnen Shi*, p. 159, Tokyo.

[31] Tōkyō Shōkō Kyoku (1948), *Juden no Tebiki*, Tokyo.

[32] S. Kobori (2010), *Nihon no Enerugī Kakumei*, pp. 135–144, Nagoya.

[33] *Denki Shimbun*, 9 Aug. 1948.

[34] Taro Ishikawa (1999), *Chūbu no Denki Bunka no Ayumi Tenbyō*, p. 198, Nagoya.

[35] Traditional cooking stoves had 17–18 per cent thermal efficiency, while improved cooking stoves had 24–25 per cent efficiency. Shigen Chōsa Kai (1953), *Katei Nenryō Gōrika ni kansuru Kankoku*, pp. 5, 39, Tokyo,.

[36] Ministry of Internal Affairs and Communications (2006), *Historical Statistics of Japan*, new edn., Vol. 2, p. 570, Tokyo.

consumers directly.[37] In the GDR, by contrast, the primary focus after the 1953 uprising was on the industrial workplace. Of course, this did not mean that daily life and domestic use were untouched. Additional night shifts upset daily rhythms of cooking, washing and childcare, affecting women and mothers especially. We now turn to the temporal manifestations of energy disruptions.

## The politics of time

Energy shortages are interesting cases of scarcity because they illuminate transfers of limited resources not only between groups but also across time. In this section, we focus on two types of such temporal transfers: efforts to move energy use out of peak times (a characteristic of grid systems) and responses to severe seasonal shortages affecting bundles of fuel, such as coal, water and electricity.

Japan's post-war energy policy rested on assumptions about the 'normal' time for work and domestic life. Policymakers and energy providers believed that daytime was for productive work, while the evening belonged to family life. These were powerful social and cultural conventions rather than official regulations.[38] Temporal management of industrial demand was rarely attempted unless electricity supply became extremely tight.[39] Electricity quotas for industry consumers were not intended to alleviate peak load. It was only after 1953 that large factories were offered off-peak pricing to incentivize operation outside peak hours. There was little official control over the temporal pattern of electricity consumption in factories and business offices.

In real life, it proved impossible to expect cultural conventions to split electricity use neatly into day- and night-time activities. To prepare dinner in time for the return of workers, cooking in the home had to start before the evening; a typical load curve in this period had a pronounced peak between 5 pm and 8 pm.[40] Restaurants, bars and entertainment districts also opened for business around 5 pm, boosting electricity load. Some factories kept operating into the evening. In the Kanto region, for example, 25 per cent of industrial consumers exceeded their allocation between September 1951 and January 1952.[41] Factories also offered their workers baths, cooking facilities and even permanent hair wave machines, which drew additional electricity outside work hours.[42]

---

[37] Takuji Okamoto (2001), 'The Reorganization of the Electric Power Industry', in Shigeru Nakayama, Kunio Goto and Hitoshi Yoshioka (eds.), *A Social History of Science and Technology in Contemporary Japan*, Vol. 1, pp. 323–324, Melbourne.

[38] Barbara Molony (1993), 'Equality versus Difference: The Japanese Debate over "Motherhood Protection", 1915–50', in Janet Hunter (ed.), *Japanese Women Working*, p. 141, London.

[39] An exception was an official order in November 1947 that prohibited industry electricity use between 4 pm and 10 pm. Ministry of Commerce and Industry, 'Kinkyū Denryoku Chōsetsu Jissi Youryō', 10 Nov. 1947, National Archives of Japan.

[40] Nihon Hassō Den, 'Kinkyū Seigen no Jitsuyō Chōsa', 10 Oct. 1948, Central Research Institute of Electric Power Industry, Nippatsu Library, Tokyo; Chugoku Denryoku (1996), *Kaisō* p. 239, Hiroshima.

[41] Kantō Denki Kyōkai (1952), *Denki Gasu Jigyō Nenpō*, p. 77, Tokyo.

[42] *Denki Shimbun*, 27 Aug. 1948.

The competing demand for energy caused frequent evening blackouts. Instead of being privileged users in the evenings, it was often households that had to carry the burden of disruption. Reports in the Housewives' Association's (Shufu-ren) newsletter highlighted how blackouts ruptured the normal rhythm of everyday life. Housewives complained that blackouts slowed down meal preparation, leaving them with disgruntled husbands and crying children who were afraid of the dark.[43] Household fuel was one of the association's crusading issues. In November 1950, it secured over 6,600 tonnes of charcoal for its members.[44] In early 1952, blackouts drove the association to take political action, and its delegates were sent to government offices and utilities companies, demanding better management of electricity supply. Negotiations between the association and the Public Utilities Commission resulted in a 2 per cent cut of the electricity tariff, pro rata for days when a power cut of more than two hours occurred.[45]

Small discounts on utility bills, however, did not appease the association. When blackouts continued later in 1952, it organized a mass boycott against electricity bills. The movement attracted one million supporters, ranging from domestic consumers to small businessmen running cinemas, beauty salons, laundry shops and medical clinics. The utility companies initially threatened disconnection and penalties for late payment, but the association held its ground. After three months, the companies yielded and agreed to reduce customers' utility bills in proportion to the number of power cuts.[46]

The housewives' protest illustrates the gendered response to energy disruption in post-war Japan. Following the wartime emphasis on women's role on the home front (*Jugo no Mamori*), the post-war shortages of food and fuel highlighted the role of housewives in procuring necessities. In a contemporary photograph, a drawing of an electricity bulb was overlaid on the association's rice-paddle-shaped placards, showing that, for the association's members, electricity was as essential as food (Figure 15.3). Being tasked with ensuring a bright and warm home in the evening, Japanese housewives saw evening power cuts as a threat to family life.

The Japanese story brings into view deep-seated assumptions about 'normal' customs and habits and about what were considered acceptable forms of intervention in the organization of work time versus domestic time. East Germany picked a radically different course. Here the focus was on enterprises and on getting industrial users to save energy at peak time by introducing additional shifts in evenings and night-time. In January 1954, VEB Siemens-Plania, for example, won the first prize in the competitive 'battle against electricity cuts in the GDR' for managing to use 55 per cent of its entire electrical energy in night-time. But there were clear limits, not least since many enterprises in the steel and chemical industries were already running three shifts. Encouraging firms to make use of their night-time quotas also had bizarre counter-effects that will be familiar to students of planned economies. In spring 1953, for example, the Magdeburg Konsumkleiderfabrik (clothing factory) was found to

---

[43] *Shufu-ren Tayori*, 15 Jan. 1952 and 15 Nov. 1952.
[44] *Shufu-ren Tayori*, 1 Nov. 1950.
[45] *Shufu-ren Tayori*, 15 Mar. 1952.
[46] *Shufu-ren Tayori*, 15 Feb. 1953.

be fully lit at night to reach its night-time electricity target, even though only four employees were at work.[47]

**Figure 15.3** Housewives' Association protest against electricity tariff increase (1954). *Source*: Japan Archives, Hygo.

---

[47] BArch Berlin-Lichterfelde, DC 16/21: Staatssekretariat für Energie, HV Energie, Zentrale Kommission, report 13 May 1953. In general, see: André Steiner (2004), *Von Plan zu Plan: eine Wirtschaftsgeschichte der DDR*, München.

In 1961, after years of pressure and intervention, the night-time share of electrical consumption in Berlin stood at 23 per cent (up from 20 per cent in 1960),[48] a considerable but hardly impressive figure and certainly not sufficient to eliminate the peak problem. Many enterprises routinely exceeded their energy quotas in the evening peak by 30 per cent, like the VEB Werk für Fernmeldewesen (telecommunications) in 1962.[49] A spot check of 120 enterprises in October 1963 revealed that only forty-five had moved their work hours, affecting 8,500 workers, including 2,800 women. The National Economic Council concluded that 'this was in no way satisfactory, given all the effort'.[50] One third of the enterprises said they had not even received the energy-saving guidelines.

Peak-time restrictions also seriously affected agricultural work rhythms. In November 1953, for example, the use of electric energy was prohibited during the hours of 6 am and 1 pm and, again, from half an hour before sunset until 10 pm. Electrical fodder steamers were only to be switched on between 10 pm and 6 am.

These temporary introductions of additional shifts and night-time work had major repercussions for the coordination of all sorts of other daily routines and rhythms as workers suddenly had their work, leisure and sleep patterns disrupted. Women workers with children were especially affected – the official protection of mothers and teenagers from the consequences of night-shifts was simply being ignored. Additional shifts required nurseries to stay open longer. In administrative offices, peak-hour restrictions limited the flexible use of overtime. On 15 December 1953, for example, the energy delegate in Berlin Pankow reminded officials that it was strictly forbidden to keep working after 5 pm in order to catch up on planned targets: employees were told to use Saturday afternoons.[51] There appears to have been surprisingly little conscious reflection on the spillover of interventions at work for domestic life and leisure.

The response of the population to appeals to change their habits in peak times was muted. Few were responsive to radio alerts and newspapers publicizing peak hours; indeed, many professed (or preferred) not even to be aware of their existence. An energy delegate in Berlin Pankow in December 1954 found that most workers were reasonably economical; he blamed the high energy use on a minority of the bourgeois intelligentsia, who lacked the will to 'sacrifice their personal comforts'.[52] Pointing the finger at the class enemy was probably too simple. At a SED conference on the energy programme in Berlin in October 1957, Else Kuss, a deputy of the Democratic Women's League (Demokratischer Frauenbund), reported that none of her neighbours had followed the exhortation to reduce the use of appliances during peak hours.[53] The spread of electric heating and electrical appliances put an additional strain on an already fractured energy system and proved difficult to deal with for a socialist regime

---

[48] LAB, C Rep. 135–01, nr 253, Schmiga, 'Informationsbericht über die Versorgung mit Elektroenergie', 14 Feb. 1962.
[49] LAB, C Rep. 135–01, nr 253, Andrae to SED, mayor and ZK, 24 Nov. 1961.
[50] LAB, C Rep. 135–01, nr 253, Aktenvermerk, 14 Oct. 1963.
[51] LAB, C Rep. 149–06, nr 28, Sielaff to chair of Pankow council, 15 Dec. 1953.
[52] LAB, C Rep. 149–06, nr 28, Sielaff to Magistrat, 8 Dec. 1954.
[53] LAB, C Rep. 902, nr 139, Kuss at SED conference, 3 Oct. 1957.

which saw energy (like water) as a basic need. Further restrictions followed in the late 1950s.

The range of infractions and disregard might be read as 'ruses' in the tradition of Michel de Certeau, little everyday acts of resistance.[54] This probably would be an overinterpretation. Habits were resilient, shaped in part by infrastructure and equipment or by their absence.[55] Even if people had wanted to heed the appeals of the 70 W and 100 W campaigns in the 1950s, there were simply not enough of the lauded 15 W or 25 W light bulbs for sale to dim their living rooms. In poorly heated blocks of flats, the electric heater was a welcome friend. With single-pipe heating systems and in the absence of thermostats, it was natural for most residents to open their windows to regulate the temperature – even after insulation and central heating programmes from the 1970s, there were 1 million homes without any thermostat in 1983.[56] In the early 1980s, a directive required users to hand over all electrical heaters and night-storage heaters unless they held a licensed exemption. Between 1982 and 1984, this succeeded in lowering the connected wattage of direct electric space heaters by 46 per cent or 268 MW and that of night-storage heaters by 13 per cent or 66 MW. Still, only one-third of electric heaters were handed back in. Energy combines received tens of thousands of applications for exemptions and only a quarter of these were rejected.[57]

Prolonged seasonal disruptions produced distinctive predicaments and reactions in East Germany. The situation was particularly tense in the autumn and winter of 1958, in the winters of 1963 and 1970/71 and in the autumn of 1971. In September 1958, grid problems led to many districts and rural populations in particular being cut off. Heavy snow in January 1963 saw coal wagons stuck in snow and Berlin and other cities without supplies. On 14 January 1963, Berlin ordered hot water to be limited to the period from 12:00 on Saturday to 12:00 on Sunday, including on the prestigious Karl-Marx-Allee; to restrict hot water to a few hours every day was rejected as wasteful because it would have required repeatedly heating up boilers. Some schools were closed, others ran shifts in one room, heated to a minimum. Firms and institutions were ordered to move staff into the same office; nurseries and medical buildings were exempted. Industrial and commercial use of gas was lowered to 50 per cent of the volume normal for that time of year.[58] In 1971, the 'week of winter preparation' began as early as 18 October.

Seasonal shortages led to the general mobilization of the population, with students and soldiers sent to mines and helping to defrost tracks and coal wagons. The National Front (NF), assisted by the FDJ youth organization, was the regime's voice at street level. In January 1963 in Erfurt, it mobilized 1,160 activists to get scarce coal to

[54] Michel de Certeau (1984), *The Practice of Everyday Life*, Berkeley, CA; cf. Vanessa Taylor and Frank Trentmann (2011), 'Liquid Politics: Water and the Politics of Everyday Life in the Modern City', *Past and Present*, 211: 199–241.

[55] See Frank Trentmann and Anna Carlsson-Hyslop (2018), 'The Evolution of Energy Demand: Politics, Daily Life and Public Housing, Britain 1920s–70s', *Historical Journal*, 61 (3): 807–839.

[56] BArch Berlin-Lichterfelde, DC20/27420, AG Rationelle Energieanwendung, Vorlage, 27 June 1984.

[57] BArch Berlin-Lichterfelde, DC20/27420, AG Rationelle Energieanwendung, Vorlage, 10 Feb. 1984.

[58] LAB, C Rep. 135–01, nr 253, Hornig to Hoeding, 'Massnahmen in der Kohleversorgung', 14 Jan. 1963.

suffering households and drum up support for energy saving. Unsurprisingly, the reports by the NF showcase the enthusiasm of their volunteers but they also give some insight into the reactions of the public. In Erfurt, inhabitants of the flats on Triftstrasse 48, 49a and 50 pledged to save energy – presumably, those living in numbers 1 to 47 were less heroic. The NF set up 13 Wärmestuben (warm chambers) for Erfurt pensioners, who were entertained by Young Pioneers and actors whose theatres had closed. How attractive these were is doubtful: in Rostock in 1963 often no more than two to four pensioners found their way to them.[59] Internal reports by the NF registered considerable popular frustration. People saw the latest shortage as evidence that 'the GDR was near collapse', others wondered 'why do our newspapers report about the poor conditions in capitalist countries but so little about ours?'[60] In January 1971, in Suhl, some Hausgemeinschaften (block communities) offered suggestions about how to save energy, from unscrewing light bulbs in chandeliers to lowering the light in staircases. The same meetings, however, also revealed scepticism about such individual responses to systemic problems. 'Why is the energy situation getting worse and worse every year', asked one. Many voices asked 'why have not more power stations been built' and 'why has there not been more investment in energy'. A 'Brigade' of the PGH 'Figaro' (hairdressers) complained: '21 years GDR and still not enough electricity.'[61] A collective farmer put it bluntly: 'now again, the GDR has run out of coal: it is all the fault of socialism.'[62] In Rostock, shops kept selling hot water boilers – against orders. In most cases, officially sponsored local efforts at energy saving were short-lived. Erfurt and the surrounding area measured the response to the FDJ's campaign on 29 January 1963 to dim lighting and to turn off electrical appliances. There was an immediate saving of 8 per cent of electricity in Erfurt and 5 per cent in Gotha compared to 25 January, but the following day consumption jumped back up by 3 per cent and 7 per cent, respectively.[63]

In contrast to the GDR, Japan in the 1950s wholeheartedly embraced affluent lifestyles. Already before regaining independence in 1952, Japan's electricity industry was restructured into nine regional monopolies. The nine electric power companies soon started to fend off official restrictions as interfering with private business. As commercial operations, they also began to take a more conciliatory stance towards domestic consumers. A rapid series of tariff increases could only be justified by raising customer satisfaction. Between 1951 and 1956, national electricity consumption grew from 37 TWh to 61 TWh. The diffusion of the so-called three sacred treasures – black-and-white television, the washing machine and the refrigerator – was now locking Japanese households into the electricity grid. Industrial electricity consumption saw an even larger jump, with a boom in the chemical, steel and metal industries, and added to the pressure on energy providers. Northern parts of Japan were especially hit by electricity shortages, because the relatively low price of electricity there had attracted

---

[59] BArch Berlin-Lichterfelde, DY 6/4678, Nationale Front, report, Rostock, end of Jan. 1963.
[60] BArch Berlin-Lichterfelde, DY 6/4903, Nationale Front, report, Erfurt, 31 Jan. 1963.
[61] BArch Berlin-Lichterfelde, DY 6/4990, Nationale Front, report, Suhl, 11 Jan. 1971.
[62] BArch Berlin-Lichterfelde, DY 6/4678, Nationale Front, report, Rostock, end of Jan. 1963.
[63] BArch Berlin-Lichterfelde, DY 6/4903, Nationale Front, report, Erfurt, 31 Jan. 1963.

new electrolysis plants and electric furnaces. In January 1957, rainfall was 20 per cent lower than average, leading to a nationwide electricity shortage. Disconnecting domestic consumers was no longer the utilities' preferred method for managing scarcity. Instead, many large industrial customers were now obliged to reduce their consumption in exchange for off-peak pricing. Large factories were the first to lose electricity, followed by voluntary reductions in smaller firms. The priority of industrial over domestic consumers had been reversed.

The change in Japan's approach to disruption coincided with a major energy transition. Japan's entry into the international oil market in 1951 stimulated investment in thermal power plants. The opening up to oil imports from the Middle East in 1964 meant that electricity supply was now stabilized by oil-fired power plants.[64] Kerosene and liquid petroleum gas (LPG) further eased the pressure on household energy supply, especially for heating and cooking. By the end of the 1960s, kerosene and LPG met about half of all household energy requirements.

But the conversion to oil came at a price. In 1971, when 92 per cent of its primary energy came from abroad, policymakers realized that any disturbance in the international oil market would jeopardize the country's entire energy supply.

On the surface, Japan's domestic energy consumers in the 1960s enjoyed an energy-intensive lifestyle enabled by cheap imported oil and expanded electricity supply. Most energy users believed disruption was a thing of the past. In reality, they were living in the shadow of energy disruption. A new type of vulnerability was emerging as a result of two factors. The first was Japan's excessive dependence on imported oil. The second was that electricity demand growth exacerbated the peak load problem. By 1970, around 90 per cent of Japanese households had a washing machine, electric refrigerator and television set, and about 70 per cent owned an electric vacuum cleaner. Between 1961 and 1971, domestic electricity consumption almost quadrupled, from 15 TWh to 56 TWh per annum. And the diffusion of colour televisions and air conditioners in the late 1960s shifted the country's annual peak demand from winter to summer. In early August 1971, the country was on the verge of new electricity restrictions. The utilities tried to prevent government intervention by controlling industrial demand. Almost 1,400 firms responded to the Kansai Electric Power Co's demand reduction campaign, which eased pressure from the supply network. The narrow escape was repeated in the following year.

In the 1960s, domestic electricity users temporarily disappeared from the Japanese story of energy disruption. No longer were they targeted first at moments of energy shortage. For them, blackouts now belonged to the realms of exceptional circumstances such as typhoons, floods and earthquakes. The electricity supply was far more reliable than in previous decades.[65] That new 'normality' made domestic consumers complacent about the risk of disruption. In 1971, with the prospect of large-scale blackouts looming over Japan, the journalist Tokuro Irie observed that 'Japanese people are inclined to believe that they have a limitless supply of water, liberty and electricity.'[66]

---

[64] Japan's electricity supply industry, in 1968, consumed more than 30 million kilolitres of heavy and crude oil for generating power.

[65] Ministry of International Trade and Industry (1970), *Electricity White Paper*, p. 243, Tokyo.

[66] *Tōden Graph*, Aug. 1971.

# Outlook

Disruptions offer an unusual lens for the study of developed societies, which are normally treated as functional and productive, societies that 'work' and follow a script from which societies suffering from famine, internal strife and underdevelopment deviate. However, developed societies have also faced disruptions, and studying these can shed light on the inner workings of societies that tend to take basic services for granted. Rather than treating shortages as aberrations, we can view them as facilitating the production of a new normal.[67] It was shortages of coal and charcoal, for example, that pushed many people to electric heaters and cookers, moving these societies one step closer to an electrified world of consumption, with its inherent vulnerability and dependency.

Reflecting on energy disruptions in the past is an opportunity to reconceptualize energy scarcity in the present. Conventionally, research on energy disturbance has been preoccupied with supply-side problems, chiefly those resulting from technological failures and human errors.[68] However, as the sociologists Hugh Byrd and Steve Matthewman have recently argued, energy disruptions in modern societies largely stem from a failure of 'exergy' – the amount of energy available for use.[69] Energy becomes scarce when supply and demand fail to synchronize. Put differently, energy disruption is a loss of energy *flow* when demanded by users. The level of disturbance thus correlates with the mismatch between available supply and the demand involved in users' pursuit of what they perceive to be a 'normal' life. Since the nature of this 'normality' changes over time, and especially so in modern consumer societies – think of heating, cooling and mobility – the demand of daily practices and expectations needs to be recognized as a critical factor in the creation of energy shortages. This chapter has revealed how consumer expectations of energy use hinged upon energy users' daily routines, assigned to specific times of the day by social and cultural norms and conventions. Consumers, we have shown, were particularly sensitive to disruptions in their core routines, such as sleeping, eating, working and leisure. Modern energy systems have not eliminated disturbances. In fact, they have often made them more frequent and left users more vulnerable than in the past.[70] It is therefore just as crucial to build user-side resilience as it is to improve the technical reliability of supply. A first step towards mitigating the impact of future disruptions will be a better understanding of how time-anchored daily routines spread the impact of disruption to diverse social activities. This question is only becoming more urgent as societies are expanding their use of renewable energy, such as solar, wind and tidal power – resources that are susceptible to supply fluctuations caused by natural temporal cycles and deviations.

---

[67] See also Hendrik Vollmer (2013), *Sociology of Disruption, Disaster and Social Change: Punctuated Cooperation*, Cambridge.

[68] For example, U. G. Knight (2001), *Power Systems in Emergencies: From Contingency Planning to Crisis Management*, p. 7, Colchester.

[69] Hugh Byrd and Steve Matthewman (2014), 'Exergy and the City: The Technology and Sociology of Power (Failure)', *Journal of Urban Technology*, 21 (3): 85–102.

[70] Byrd and Matthewman, 'Exergy and the City', pp. 97–98; Charles Perrow (1984), *Normal Accidents: Living with High-Risk Technologies*, updated edn., Princeton, NJ.

Responses to energy disruption are historically and politically contingent. What emerges are forms of material politics that develop in conjunction with a constantly changing energy mix. Their development is dynamic and interdependent. At the same time as they eliminate some bottlenecks, new fuels and new technologies create new kinds of vulnerability. Resilience to disruption is conditioned by political regimes and their citizens' coping mechanisms as well as by the availabilities of different fuels.

One striking thing about the history of energy disruption in the GDR and Japan is the way political regimes and consumers helped shape supply and supply shortages. Political ideas determined the official distribution of energy in the first place, by prioritizing certain types of consumers over others. However, consumers were not necessarily the obedient servants of their political masters. Consumer resilience and outright political mobilization sometimes forced policymakers and energy providers to revise their priorities. Shifting the site of intervention could have long-term consequences. When Japan's utilities abandoned household power cuts as the quick way to deal with supply shortages, they simultaneously paved the way for the new summer peak in consumption that would call for additional supply capacity to avoid disruption in the future. Consumption, in other words, was not just the result of supply: to an extent, it also shaped supply and supply shortages.

The GDR and Japan had their own distinct political regimes but they were by no means exceptional in having distinct national approaches to energy crisis. As Robert Lieber has stressed, Western Europe's response to the 1973 oil crisis was characterized by the absence of international coordination. Each country followed its own national self-interest and strategy.[71] Indeed, Britain and Norway initially opposed joining the International Energy Agency, on the grounds that such an international body would threaten national sovereignty and limit their ability to deal with specific domestic issues. The energy shortages after the Second World War cast a long shadow. In the case of Britain, its fuel emergency policy was a direct child of the fuel shortages between 1946 and 1951. Like the GDR after 1953, post-war British governments tried not to interfere with domestic energy users directly. Unlike the GDR, the presence of strong trade unions also made it difficult to force night work on factory workers. Instead, the British government relied on electricity quotas for industry and moral appeals to domestic consumers. By leaving both working patterns and domestic consumption largely untouched, Britain's electricity system carried its two vulnerabilities into the 1960s and 1970s. In the winter of 1973–74, during the first oil crisis, it was trade union activity and domestic heating demand which caused the electricity crisis. Given how intertwined domestic policy and energy shortages have been in the twentieth century, it is not surprising that during the oil crisis in 1973, countries looked for solutions in national strategies rather than international coordination.

Discussions of moral economy have been dominated by food and food riots.[72] Energy, like food, is a basic good on which human life and survival depend. There are

[71] Robert Lieber (1976), *Oil and the Middle East War: Europe in the Energy Crisis*, Cambridge, MA; Vessela Chakarova (2013), *Oil Supply Crisis: Cooperation and Discord in the West*, Lanham.

[72] E. P. Thompson (1971), 'The Moral Economy of the English Crowd in the Eighteenth Century', *Past and Present*, 50: 76–136. Cf. Didier Fassin (2009), 'Les économies morales revisitées', *Annales*, 64 (6): 1237–1266; Frank Trentmann (2007), 'Before "Fair Trade": Empire, Free Trade, and the Moral Economies of Food in the Modern World', *Environment and Planning D*, 25 (6): 1079–1102.

major differences, however, between what happens when the lights go out and what happens when the price of flour or bread goes through the roof. Energy shortages have rarely sparked the kind of riots and popular mobilizations that struggles over food have done. Only recently have there been sporadic protests against power cuts, such as the ones in Myanmar in 2007 and 2012.[73] One reason for the relative absence of such protests is the potential for substituting one fuel for another – an ability that changes during the course of energy transitions. A second is displacement in political discourse and institutions. Energy shortages are usually framed in a different political register from famine. They are treated in terms of a welfare policy such as 'fuel poverty' or as a question of monopoly power and pricing. In this chapter, we have attempted to widen the terms of the debate regarding distributional fairness and power. Discussion of moral economy has favoured a view of society as a conflict between citizens/consumers on the one hand and state/merchants on the other over the 'fair' price of food. But this is only one of several constellations. By integrating different users into the same system, modern energy networks made themselves vulnerable, at times of shortage, to additional conflicts: between different groups of consumers, between work and home, different energy-hungry activities, night and day and between different seasons. At a time when societies are debating the future of the grid, the history of energy shortages is a reminder that energy transitions involve moral and political as much as technological challenges.

## Acknowledgements

We would like to thank the AHRC research grant (AH/K006088/1) and our colleagues of the 'Material Cultures of Energy' research project.

---

[73] http://www.aljazeera.com/news/asia-pacific/2012/05/20125235117172891.html (accessed 1 September 2017).

# 16

# Food Shortages: The Role and Limitations of Markets in Resolving Food Crises during the 2012 Famine in the Sahel

Emma C. Stephens

## Scarcity, markets and redistribution

The concept of scarcity, where unlimited wants are met with limited means, inherently contains a spatial dimension, in that the underlying issue of a mismatch between demand and supply applies to a given population in a particular time and place. The degree of scarcity experienced is greatly influenced by the ability of those impacted to arbitrage between pockets of scarcity and reservoirs of abundance. This could mean contemporaneous redistribution of supply, through transport mechanisms, from a source region to a scarce destination. Or, it could mean inter-temporal arbitrage, via storage technology, from a time when supplies are available into a future when they are no longer sufficient to meet demand. Or, we may be able to innovate our way out of scarcity,[1] which again is a costly redistribution of our current collective resources across time and space into a better future formulation to resolve scarcity.

In examining important past and present episodes of scarcity, the redistribution mechanisms in play have significantly shaped the outcomes and eventual solutions. And in some cases, existing mechanisms have been found inadequate, leading to huge costs in terms of human health, welfare or the environment and subsequent changes in our redistribution networks and capabilities. Public sector or political processes have often been employed to redistribute resources, for example, in subsidizing technological innovation out of resource scarcity or supporting a social safety net via tax and transfer schemes from rich to poor in society. However, private markets remain key mechanisms in play around the world for resolving many forms of scarcity. For fundamental concerns, like ensuring adequate food availability for a given population, market mechanisms often pre-date the introduction of public-sector redistribution programmes, coexist alongside them and are often more ubiquitous than political

[1] U. Neren (2011), 'The number one way to innovation: Scarcity', Harvard Business Review, 14 January 2011. Available from: https://hbr.org/2011/01/the-number-one-key-to-innovati

institutions dedicated to resolving scarcity of this type. Thus, understanding how a network of private markets performs when large-scale scarcity appears is critical to our understanding of the distribution issues associated with mismatched demand and supply of important goods and services and the persistence of scarcity overall. This chapter examines the functioning of such network market mechanisms during a recent food shortage in the African Sahel and analyses the distribution networks to highlight some of the shortfalls that exacerbated the food crisis.

## The 2012 food crisis in the Sahel

The Sahelian region in Africa traverses the north of the continent and is made up of the semi-arid agro-ecological zone between the Sahara Desert and the Sudanian Savanna. The West African states within the Sahel of Burkina Faso, Cape Verde, Chad, Gambia, Guinea Bissau, Mali, Mauritania, Niger and Senegal are currently home to 100 million people, with population expected to approach 200 million by 2050.[2]

There is one agricultural season in the region, with harvests coming every fall, after the summer rains in July and August. There is a lot of seasonal variation every year in food availability due to the high prevalence of subsistence farming, where farmers rely primarily on their own food production for consumption needs. Food stocks are generally plentiful from harvest in October until early spring the following year. Late spring and summer are known as the 'hungry season', where farmers' own food supplies are lowest, regional food supplies are dwindling and food prices begin to rise. During this time, many rural households seek work off-farm to earn income to purchase food and then return for harvest season.[3]

Since the turn of the twenty-first century, the region has experienced several significant food crises in 2005, 2010 and 2012. In 2017, an estimated 135,000 people in Niger were assessed at a food insecurity scale of 3 or higher. Almost 7 million people in the Lake Chad region in the eastern Sahel were classified as food insecure in the 2017 lean season. Final accounts for 2018 are expected to be similar FSIN (2018).[4] There is some variation in the causes of these crises, but all relate to some combination of drought or natural disaster in the region during the summer production season that significantly lowers production, in conjunction with large increase in food prices. For example, locusts impacted grain production across the region in summer 2004, leading to the 2005 crisis. Political instability was a factor in the 2012 crisis, which coincided with an armed rebellion in northern Mali. This displaced families from their farms as they fled the violence, causing food insecurity by abandoning their own production, as well as harming local production by leaving crops in the fields and

---

[2] IRIN (2008). 'Backgrounder on the Sahel, West Africa's poorest region', IRIN News Network. Available from: http://www.irinnews.org/feature/2008/06/02.

[3] See, for example, a typical seasonal calendar for Mali (http://www.fews.net/west-africa/mali/seasonal-calendar/december-2013).

[4] FEWS NET (Famine Early Warning System Net). USAID. Retrieved from https://www.fews.net (http://www.fsincop.net/fileadmin/user_upload/fsin/docs/global_report/2018/GRFC_2018_Full_report_EN_Low_resolution.pdf).

putting resource pressure on towns that received refugees.[5] Political instability with Boko Haram in the Lake Chad region is one of the causes behind the 2017 crisis. In 2000, food production also fell below regional averages, but a food crisis did not occur that year as food markets were able to continually supply the region and keep prices relatively low.[6]

The seasonal hunger cycle and times of food crisis usually end with the next harvest. Aid organizations have been criticized for their slow response to the 2005 and 2010 crises, but have increased efforts to more proactively send food aid to affected regions earlier and to develop better early warning systems, such as USAID's Famine Early Warning System (www.fews.net). International aid agencies thus also contribute to resolving a food crisis when it occurs.

As in previous episodes, the 2012 crisis has been attributed to lower-than-average harvests brought on by low rainfall, as well as political instability in Mali, causing several hundred thousand refugees to flee to neighbouring countries.[7] The 2012 crisis was unique in that it was more widespread than earlier crises (the 2005 crisis mainly impacted Niger, for example). This meant that redistribution of food from traditional source areas within the Sahel was more difficult, which exacerbated the crisis. In the final analysis, 18.7 million people in the Sahel faced extreme food insecurity in 2012, including 1 million children, with steep increases in malnutrition rates. As well, 1 million people fled their homes due to a combination of political violence and food insecurity.[8] Analysts have also determined that the 2012 crisis made families more susceptible to subsequent food crisis episodes. In summary, a combination of local supply shocks and high food prices has contributed to the most recent food crises in the Sahel. The relationship between scarcity in food supply and problems with food redistribution through markets, leading to unsustainable price increases, has been an important subject for academic research on food crises and how to prevent them.

## Food security, markets and entitlements: Concepts and definitions

In 1996, the Food and Agriculture Organization established what is now the most widely used definition of food security: 'Food security exists when all people, at all times, have physical, social and economic access to sufficient, safe and nutritious food

---

[5] Emergency Capacity Building Project (ECB) (2012), 'Northern Mali conflict and food insecurity Disaster Needs Analysis'. Available from: http://www.ecbproject.org/resource/18328.

[6] J. Aker (2008), 'Rainfall Shocks, Markets and Food Crises: Evidence from the Sahel', Center for Global Development Working Paper 157. Available from: https://www.cgdev.org/publication/rainfall-shocks-markets-and-food-crises-evidence-sahel-working-paper-157.

[7] OXFAM (2012), 'Food crisis in the Sahel: Five steps to break the hunger cycle in 2012'. Available from: file:///C:/Users/estephen/Google%20Drive/summer%202017%20research/ib-food-crisis-sahel-31052012-en.pdf.

[8] OXFAM (2013), 'Learning the lessons? Assessing the response to the 2012 food crisis in the Sahel to build resilience for the future', Oxfam briefing paper 168. Available from: https://www.oxfam.org/sites/www.oxfam.org/files/bp168-learning-the-lessons-sahel-food-crisis-160413-en_1.pdf.

which meets their dietary needs and food preferences for an active and healthy life.'[9] Within this, stakeholders in the food security community have identified that food security is comprised of four main features:[10,11]

1 *Food availability*, which includes domestic production, stocks, imports and food aid receipts.
2 *Food access*, which differs from the availability dimension in that local food stocks may be sufficient in terms of quantity, but there may be physical, economic or sociocultural barriers to obtaining food.
3 *Food utilization*, which brings into consideration food quality and safety issues, which again might differ from overall assessments of supply.
4 *Stability* of dimensions 1, 2 and 3 over time as an additional critical aspect of food security.

In the context of the most extreme form of food insecurity, when a food crisis occurs, the proximate causes can be found in the collapse of one or more of the above dimensions.

The common perception of food crises usually centres on the first dimension, where a crisis is the result of a collapse in *food availability*, via a large negative shock to a region's food supply, either due to a drought or a flood or other natural disaster. However, in his seminal work *Poverty and Famines*, Amartya Sen created a paradigmatic shift in our understanding of food crises as being primarily food supply driven to seeing them more broadly as a reflection of what he called entitlement failure.[12] In Sen's entitlements framework, individuals can acquire food by converting their endowments and resources into food in a variety of ways: by growing their own food; by buying food in the market; by working for food; and by obtaining food from transfers from other individuals or institutional entities. Thus food crises, like the one experienced in 2012 in the Sahel, can be caused by the collapse of any of these mechanisms or a collapse of the individual's right (or 'entitlement') to employ any of these channels to get access to food. Entitlement failure in this context for areas and populations that experience food crises can then be the result of a 'direct entitlement decline', which is a decline in the ability to produce your own food for a variety of reasons (e.g. natural disaster) but could also be the result of a decline in the 'exchange entitlement' of an individual to purchase food and/or exchange labour or other resources for food. Sen's insights in particular about the second scenario, where in practice a food crisis might still occur even when aggregate food supplies appear to be sufficient to support the local population, have led to the explicit analysis of the functioning of food markets and food market participants in understanding food crises and famines and predicting when new crises might occur.

[9] FAO (1996), World Food Summit: Rome Declaration on World Food Security and World Food Summit Plan of Action, Rome.
[10] WFP (2009), 'Hunger and Markets', World Hunger Series, WFP, Rome and Earthscan, London.
[11] G.-A. Simon (2012). 'Food security: Definition, four dimensions, history'. Available from: www.fao.org/fileadmin/templates/ERP/uni/F4D.pdf.
[12] A. Sen (1981), *Poverty and Famines: An Essay on Entitlement and Deprivation*, New York: Oxford University Press.

Although there are many critiques of the entitlements approach[13] for ignoring other forces that are also critical in causing food crises, such as war, agricultural sector disruption via internal displacement to escape food shortages, concurrent health crises during famine episodes and complex intra-household decision-making processes about food resources, the entitlements framework has persisted and provides key insights into how famines occur and what role markets might play in explaining these phenomena. It also provides some theoretical boundaries that can help assess how markets might remain limited in addressing food crises.

## Market response to the 2012 food crisis

Analysts had already observed higher-than-average food prices in key markets leading into the start of the 2011 harvest season across the Sahel region.[14] Drought in the region had reduced harvests, and carry-over food stocks were already depleted by November 2011. The drastic increase in food prices continued into the summer of 2012, with key food grains like millet doubling in price between September 2011 and September 2012. The figures below show the spot prices for 100 kilo bags of millet, a main staple food in the region. Spot prices represent prices local farmers and traders would expect to pay for a bag of grain in their local market. Each series represents a key regional market centre spread across the country.[15] The severity of the food price increases for millet in Burkina Faso and Mali in 2012 is evident. For reference, average annual per capita income in each nation is around $700 USD, or about 380,000 CFA in local currency units. A poor, rural small farm family produces and consumes a few hundred kilos of millet per year. [16, 17]

### Spatial market integration during the 2012 food crisis

A key feature of interest in understanding and anticipating the severity of food crises is the level of spatial market integration between key regional food markets. Particularly in the case of food crises brought on by exchange entitlement failures, analysts looking at past events would like to observe the level of responsiveness of local markets to food price spikes and also get a sense of when extremes in food prices might be expected to dissipate. Further, in attempting to prevent future food crises associated with poorly functioning food markets, it is imperative to be able to characterize areas in the market network that are particularly slow in responding to food price shocks. Spatial market integration speeds up when trading costs fall, due to improved transportation

---

[13] S. Devereaux (2001), 'Sen's Entitlement Approach: Critiques and Counter-critiques', *Oxford Development Studies*, 29 (3): 245–263.

[14] ODI (2012), Special Feature: The Crisis in the Sahel. Humanitarian Exchange, Volume 55.

[15] Figures 16.3 and 16.4 provide maps of the locations of each market.

[16] FAO (2012), Statistical Year Book Africa. Retrieved from http://www.fao.org/docrep/018/i3137e/i3137e03.pdf.

[17] All prices are deflated and account for inflation pressures, and represent real spot prices for grains in these regions (FAO-GIEWS http://www.fao.org/giews/food-prices/tool/public/#/home).

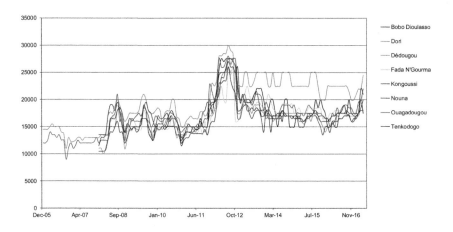

**Figure 16.1** Burkina Faso millet prices (CFA/100 kg) (FAO-GIEWS Food Price Monitoring Tool).

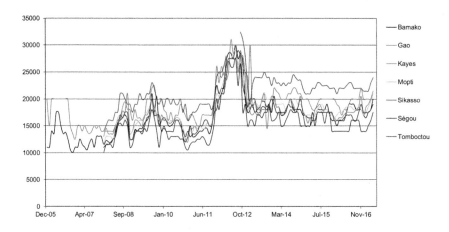

**Figure 16.2** Mali millet prices (CFA/100 kg) (FAO-GIEWS Food Price Monitoring Tool).

infrastructure, or when traders and market participants have better information about prices across the network.[18]

One useful way to do this has been through application of time series econometric models of food price differences between two distinct markets.[19] One such model is

[18] See, for example, R. Jensen (2007), 'The digital provide: Information (technology), market performance, and welfare in the South Indian fisheries sector', *Quarterly Journal of Economics*, 122 (3): 879–924.

[19] S. Johansen (1988), 'Statistical Analysis of Cointegration Vectors', *Journal of Economic Dynamics and Control* 12: 231–254.

the vector error correction model, or VECM. Time series models like the VECM take observations of price data for grains over time and identify statistically significant patterns in the data that tell us something about how prices respond to shocks and how prices in spatially distinct markets can influence each other. These models account for autocorrelation (essentially the time dependency) in food prices and isolate out the *speed of adjustment* of food prices between market pairs and can identify particularly sluggish adjustments within the network. Markets that respond slowly to large positive food price spikes are thought to be more likely to be associated with exchange entitlement failures for households that participate in those markets. Food price crises are thus more likely in those areas, and further, aid organizations can attempt to combat these types of crises by directly targeting food aid to households in those areas to make up for their access shortfall through markets.[20]

The VECM in this instance is built around the notion that in the long run, food market pairs are expected to be in *spatial equilibrium* with one another, as food markets, particularly in this region, tend to be mostly competitive, with numerous traders participating and little marketing margins observed for either farmers or traders.[21]

Spatial market equilibrium conditions for markets $i$ and $j$ that trade staple grains, $Q_{ji}$, with one another were first outlined by Takayama and Judge[22] as follows:[23]

$$P_{it} - P_{jt} = TC_{jit}, \quad Q_{jit} > 0 \ (16.1)$$

$$P_{it} - P_{jt} \leq TC_{jit}, \quad Q_{jit} = 0 \ (16.2)$$

With two markets in spatial equilibrium at any given time $t$, the condition in equation (16.1) thus indicates that market prices for a staple grain in a destination market $i$ should be separated from prices in the source market $j$ only by the transaction cost of transporting the grains between the two ($TC_{jit}$) if trade is positive ($Q_{jit} > 0$). Equation (16.2) assumes that if no trade occurs ($Q_{ji} = 0$), it is because the spatial arbitrage potential between the two markets is not large enough to cover the transaction costs (i.e. $P_{it} - P_{jt} \leq TC_{jit}$).

Subsequent analysis has tested the validity of these assumptions in the basic spatial market equilibrium model and has found exceptions. These include when trade might occur even in the case where price differentials might fall below transaction costs or

[20] The World Food Programme, for example, defines a useful summary statistic called the 'alpha value', which is the ratio of the price of a unit of food in the market over the cost per unit to deliver it as food aid. Alpha values greater than one indicate potential exchange entitlement failure, where direct food aid might be more effective. See the WFP's 'Market Analysis Framework' for further reference (https://documents.wfp.org/stellent/groups/public/documents/manual_guide_proced/wfp243856.pdf).

[21] Aker, 'Rainfall Shocks, Markets and Food Crises'.

[22] T. Takayama, T. & G. G. Judge (1964), 'Equilibrium among Spatially Separated Markets: A Reformulation', *Econometrica*, 32 (4): 510–524.

[23] Note that the subscripts on the trade volume variable, $Q_{ji}$, indicate the direction of trade from market $j$ to market $i$, with a similar convention on the transactions cost variable, $TC_{ji}$.

when trade does not occur even when spatial arbitrage seems profitable.[24] There is also a literature on asymmetric or non-linear adjustment to price shocks, where the process returning prices to long-run equilibrium might differ depending on whether shocks are positive or negative (see von Cramon-Taubadel[25] for a very recent summary). However, most vector error correction models of spatial market equilibrium patterns follow the basic model outlined above. In the interests of parsimony, this model is also followed here.

The vector error correction model makes use of the presence of the long-run equilibrium condition in equation (16.1) to define an *error correction term* defined as the deviation, $e_{jit-1}$, away from the long-run linear relationship between the previous month's prices (indicated by the '$t$-1' subscript) for the two markets $i$ and $j$ as follows:

$$P_{it-1} = \beta_0 + \beta_1 P_{it-1} + e_{jit-1} \quad (16.3)$$

The error correction term, $e_{jit-1}$, is assumed to be a stationary, random shock away from the long-run equilibrium that should exist between the markets, while the coefficients $\beta_0$ and $\beta_1$ represent various fundamental aspects of the market network structure, including level trade costs associated with transporting grains between the markets ($\beta_0$), as well as the degree of price transmission between the markets ($\beta_1$).[26] Full data on level trade costs, $TC_{jit}$, are rarely available so these are usually estimated with the price data at hand via parameter $\beta_0$. The coefficient on the price in the destination market is also normalized to 1.

In summary, observed food prices in month '$t$' ($P_{it}$ and $P_{jt}$), if they are not exactly following the estimated long-run relationship (see equation (16.1)), are said to be observed with an 'error' that is an unexpected deviation in either the source or destination price (or both) away from the long-run relationship. However, if the long-run relationship accurately describes the underlying fundamentals of food trade between the two markets, then these 'errors' are likely to be short-lived, with traders, food producers and food consumers participating in food markets and responding to price shocks in such a way as to bring the markets back into long-run equilibrium. For example, if the food price in a destination market, $P_{it}$, suddenly exceeds, $\beta_0 + \beta_1 P_{jt}$, due to a negative supply shock there, this should encourage traders from market $j$ to ship more food from market $j$ to market $i$. The impact of this should be to lower the price in destination market $i$ as more food arrives, and also to potentially raise the price in source market $j$ if a lot of supply leaves, bringing the two market prices back into long-run equilibrium with one another.

Taking into account the potential autocorrelation between market prices over time, where today's prices at time $t$ are often well predicted by yesterday's prices at time

[24] C. B. Barrett & J. R. Li (2002), 'Distinguishing between Equilibrium and Integration in Spatial Price Analysis', *American Journal of Agricultural Economics*, 84 (2): 292–307.

[25] S. Von Cramon-Taubadel (2017), 'The Analysis of Market Integration and Price Transmission – Results and Implications in an African Context', *Agrekon*, 56 (2): 83–96.

[26] For example, imports of grain from market $j$ to market $i$ might not lead to one-for-one price transmission between $P_{it}$ and $P_{jt}$, thus $\beta_1$ may not necessarily be equal to 1.

*t-1*, as well as other dynamic exogenous shocks ($X_t$) that might independently impact prices beyond the spatial market pattern, like oil price shocks or a known disruptive event like a trade policy change, the full vector error correction model specification used here can be written as:

$$\begin{bmatrix} \Delta P_{it} \\ \Delta P_{jt} \end{bmatrix} = (\alpha_i, \alpha_j)(1, \beta_1, \beta_0)' \begin{bmatrix} P_{it-1} \\ P_{jt-1} \\ 1 \end{bmatrix} + \sum \Gamma_k \begin{bmatrix} \Delta P_{it-k} \\ \Delta P_{jt-k} \end{bmatrix} + \gamma X_t + error_t \qquad (16.4)$$

**Adjustment speeds**

Within the VECM framework in equation 16.4, the $\alpha_i$ and $\alpha_j$ parameters represent the 'speed of adjustment' to shocks in each market price. For example, a large, negative, estimated $\alpha_i$ would mean that the price of the staple grain in destination market $i$ quickly falls and returns to long-run equilibrium in response to a positive price shock, while a small parameter indicates slow adjustment speed.

A useful transformation of the adjustment parameter is into a 'half-life' indicating the amount of time necessary to reduce any temporary deviation from long-run equilibrium to half its value, with short 'half-lives' indicating relatively quick adjustment to price shocks:

$$T_{half} = \frac{\ln(0.5)}{\ln(1-|\hat{\alpha}|)} \qquad (16.5)$$

## VECM analysis of Burkina Faso grain markets

Burkina Faso markets for millet were deeply impacted by the food price crisis in 2012. Average price increases for millet were up 57–83 per cent between September 2011 and September 2012. The government at the time estimated that 2.8 million people in Burkina Faso were negatively impacted by the food price crisis, including 100,000 children at risk for severe malnutrition.[27]

To characterize the impact these price increases had on the market network, we conducted a VECM analysis of four market pairs between Ouagadougou, which is the national capital and largest city in the country (and largest market, well integrated into not just local but regional and international grain trade networks), and four other important grain markets in the country: Bobo-Dioulasso, Dori, Fada N'gourma and

---

[27] A. Hirsch (12 July 2012), 'Mali refugees struggle to settle in Burkina Faso as food crisis deepens', *The Guardian*. Available from: https://www.theguardian.com/global-development/2012/jul/12/mali-refugees-burkina-faso-food-crisis.

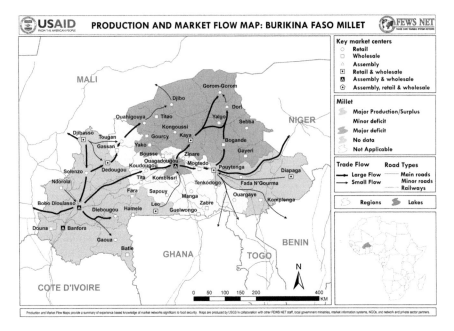

**Figure 16.3** Production and trade flow for millet (Burkina Faso) (FEWS NET).

Kongoussi. Analysis was conducted using the JMulTi package.[28] Figure 16.3 shows the main production and grain trade flows across these markets in a typical production year, indicating the direction of trade to contextualize the VECM results. As can be seen, Dori, Fada N'gourma and Kongoussi are major deficit regions for staple grain production and were some of the hardest hit by the food price crisis. By contrast, we also compare their dynamics to the patterns between Bobo-Dioulasso and Ouagadougou, noting that Bobo-Dioulasso is the second largest city in Burkina Faso and is located in a surplus production region.

A sample VECM analysis for the Ouagadougou–Dori market pair for millet is shown in Table 16.1. Additional exogenous factors included in the analysis are the price of Brent crude oil as an important component of transportation costs (converted to current West African franc CFA[29]), as well as a dummy variable accounting for the lean season months of March–August, when prices typically rise, due to consistent patterns of seasonal price variation, and finally a time trend variable to capture longer-term dynamics. Akaike information criteria were used to assess autocorrelation, but the optimal model did not contain any lags of the endogenous variables.

---

[28] H. Lütkepohl and M. Krätzig (2005), VECM Analysis in JMulTi. Available from: http://www.jmulti.de.

[29] U.S. Energy Information Administration. Petroleum and other liquids data summary. Available from: https://www.eia.gov/petroleum/.

**Table 16.1** VECM for millet prices between Ouagadougou and Dori, January 2006–May 2017

|  | $\alpha$ | $\beta$ | | Oil | Lean dummy | Trend |
|---|---|---|---|---|---|---|
| Dori | −0.300 *** | 1 | | −1.279 | 637.600 *** | 9.782 *** |
| Ouagadougou | 0.250 *** | − | 0.896 *** | 0.189 | 352.162 | −11.062 *** |
| Constant ($\beta_0$) | | | −1517.488 | | | |

Notes: *, **, *** = 10%, 5% and 1% statistical significance (*t*-tests).

The half-lives for Dori millet and Ouagadougou millet prices are calculated as (using equation 16.5):

$$T_{half,\,Dori} = 1.94 \text{ months}, \; T_{half,Ouagadougou} = 2.41 \text{ months}$$

As can be seen, the Dori millet market price responds a bit more quickly to disequilibrium shocks than Ouagadougou. In general, as a large market integrated into multiple trading networks, it is not unexpected that the Ouagadougou market responds relatively slowly and can better absorb price shocks from smaller regional markets. This pattern is consistent across most of the different market pairs studied. Ideally, however, the price responsiveness should be mostly on the destination market, and the source market should be able to absorb increased demand with little price movement, so the apparent responsiveness in the capital is not necessarily a positive observation. Ouagadougou serves as the source market for many regions in the country. Price shocks in Dori that are the result of a food crisis there are less damaging if they do not spread throughout the network, but as will be seen below, even Ouagadougou was impacted by the severity of the 2012 crisis. If the spread of food crises across markets is severe enough, the price transmission process can completely breakdown, as happened in the more remote markets of Mali during this time period (see Figure 16.2). In addition, the fact that the adjustment time frame can be multiple months is in general a sign of weakness in the market network, as this time frame is very long when thinking about the food security needs of subsistence net grain buyers in a smaller remote market area like Dori.

Other indicators of market integration quality are the size and volatility of the error term from equation 16.3. Not only should prices in destination markets that are well integrated start to fall quickly from positive spikes, but in general, with well-functioning trade networks and constant movement of grains throughout the year, the error term should not be very volatile overall, indicating only small shocks, quickly resolved, away from long-run equilibrium. The graph in Figure 16.4 shows the error term for the long-run relationship between millet prices in Dori and Ouagadougou, but as can be seen, it is highly volatile, with large deviations observed before being eventually corrected, particularly during the 2012 crisis. Also of concern is the very large negative error at the height of the food price crisis. In general, the error term should be mostly positive between a large surplus source market and a smaller deficit destination, with food shortages in the destination temporarily driving up prices, followed by increased trade from the source market that resolves the shortage and brings the price back

*Scarcity in the Modern World*

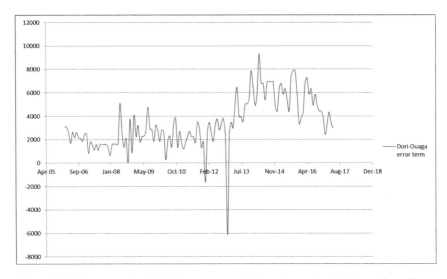

**Figure 16.4** Error term $(e_{jit})$ in the long-run equilibrium (equation 16.3) state for millet prices between Dori and Ouagadougou (x $10^4$).

down. However, the large, negative error during the crisis indicates a sudden increase in millet prices in Ouagadougou, which then got transmitted to Dori, indicating shortages in *both* markets, rather than a market network that can consistently help resolve food crises in deficit areas.

By way of comparison, the half-lives for Ouagadougou and other representative markets are given in Table 16.2.

Out of these comparisons, the market pair that shows up as the most robust is Ouagadougou and Bobo-Dioulasso. This can be ascertained through a few observations. First, the speed of adjustment to shocks to the long-run equilibrium is the fastest for Bobo-Dioulasso, at only a few weeks. As a source market, this means positive price signals in Ouagadougou will spur a quick increase in trade from Bobo-Dioulasso to the capital to resolve any shortages. Also, Ouagadougou appears to be relatively immune to price shocks from Bobo-Dioulasso, as the adjustment parameter is not statistically significant, indicating price stability. Finally, Figure 16.5 shows the error term graph for this pair overlaid with the Dori–Ouagadougou error term. It is more balanced than for the Dori–Ouagadougou pair and shocks are more easily resolved.

**Table 16.2** Average adjustment speeds for millet, Burkina Faso

|  | Ouaga to → | Kongoussi | Ouaga to → | Fada N'gourma | Bobo-Dioulasso to → | Ouaga |
|---|---|---|---|---|---|---|
| $\alpha$ | 0.484*** | −0.273*** | 0.060 | −0.549*** | 0.598*** | −0.112 |
| $T_{half}$ (months) | 1.05 | 2.17 | 11.20 | 0.87 | 0.76 | 5.83 |

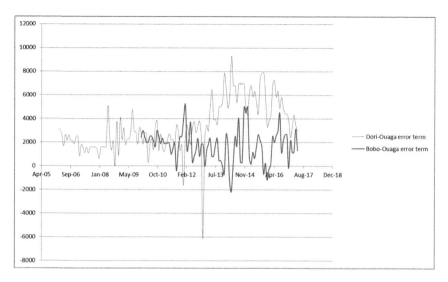

**Figure 16.5** Error term $(e_{jit})$ in the long-run equilibrium (equation 16.3) state for millet prices between Bobo-Dioulasso and Ouagadougou.

## VECM analysis of Mali grain markets

Market stress was even more pronounced in Mali during the 2012 food price crisis due to both food market failures and the start of the violent takeover of northern Mali by Tuareg rebels and other armed groups. The World Food Programme estimated very large deviations in grain prices all over Mali during this time period due to both crises playing out simultaneously in the region. In the final analysis, the 2012 crisis in Mali led to approximately 400,000 refugees from northern Mali (half of whom fled to other neighbouring countries) and an estimated 1.76 million of those who remained suffering extreme food insecurity.[30] Given the level of overall insecurity in the region, it is difficult to isolate the impact of the drought and food production from the severe disruptions to trade brought on by the large numbers of people displaced and insecurity in the transportation networks from the presence of armed groups. Nonetheless, all of these shocks eventually translate down to food markets and their ability or inability to resolve shortages and food insecurity, being priced into commodity trade in a variety of ways.

Some key market pairs for millet trade in Mali are assessed below, using the same VECM methodology as for Burkina Faso. One pair included is Bamako and Kayes, in the southwest of the country. This is trade from Bamako, which is the capital and serves a similar role in the Mali market network as Ouagadougou does in Burkina Faso, as a large, well-integrated grain source, to a deficit region for millet (and one which was not directly impacted by the political situation in northern Mali).

[30] ECB, 'Northern Mali conflict and food insecurity Disaster Needs Analysis'.

Sourcing the north of Mali, the main supply comes from the city of Ségou. The longest price data time series in this region comes from the northern gateway city of Mopti, which also gets grain from another key source region, Sikasso. Finally, the largest, most stable markets in the country, with the most traders, are Bamako and Ségou, and an analysis is offered for this pair as well. Given the gaps in the price series during the height of the crisis in Gao and Tombouctou in the northern part of the country, the VECM cannot be estimated for these series, but the estimates for the Ségou–Mopti relationship can serve as a proxy and a best-case scenario for trade from Ségou, Mopti or Sikasso to Gao and Tombouctou. The level of disruption during this time period was severe enough that traders sought new sources, including from typically more remote markets in Algeria.[31]

**Table 16.3** Bamako–Kayes spatial market integration

|  | $\alpha$ | $\beta$ | Oil | Lean dummy | Trend |
|---|---|---|---|---|---|
| Kayes | −0.548 *** | 1 | −0.005 | −92.881 | 0.529 |
| Bamako | 0.201 ** | −0.858 *** | −0.001 | 922.173*** | −3.910 |
| Constant $(\beta_0)$ |  | −4871.490 *** |  |  |  |

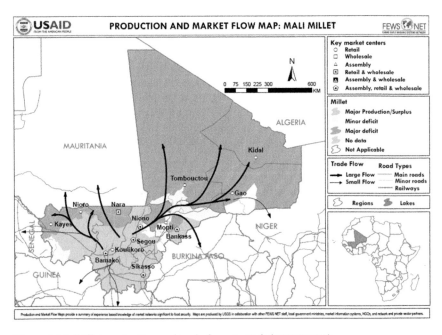

**Figure 16.6** Millet production and trade flows in Mali (FEWS NET).

---

[31] Ibid.

The estimated half-life for Kayes is 0.87 months and for Bamako it is 3.09 months. Thus, price spikes in Kayes can be resolved relatively quickly with trade from Bamako, and the long-run relationship between the two market prices is quick to return to the equilibrium state. Other components of the estimates to take note of are the relatively large estimated trade costs along this route (4871.490 CFA/100 kg). The average price of a 100 kg bag of millet ranges between 10,000 CFA and 30,000 CFA, thus these trade costs are a significant proportion of spot market prices. In terms of entitlement failure, even in a year without significant price shocks, high trade costs limit exchange entitlements for the poor in Mali who purchase up to 50 per cent of their food needs and are an important driver of endemic food insecurity.[32]

By way of comparison, the estimated half-lives between other important market pairs are shown below.

The adjustment parameters for these representative markets closer to the regions most impacted by both the drought and the conflict zones tell a different, and much more troubling, story. Both Ségou and Sikasso serve as source markets for deficit zone Mopti. As such, the best-case scenario for markets successfully resolving price spikes associated with food shortages would be to observe a relatively stable price in the source and a quickly responding price in the destination (or stable prices in both areas). However, for both of these pairs, the opposite is observed. The source markets are extremely sensitive to price volatility in Mopti, while the prices in Mopti take a very long time to adjust. As prices on average in Mopti are 1000–2000 CFA higher than the source regions, this means that high prices in the destination are not coming down much in response to trade from the source areas, severely limiting food access in the region. Despite the uncertainty that comes from an incomplete time series, prices in the most remote region for which there is consistent data (Tombouctou) were up to 6000 CFA higher than Ségou and have not yet returned, as of this writing, to more typical lows last observed in the 2008–2009 season.

A comparison of the error correction terms for all market pairs in Mali is shown below. To reiterate, a market network that on average successfully resolves food shortages should display relatively small errors away from a stable long run set of equilibrium prices and there should be few negative errors indicating volatility in source markets, which might limit their ability to insure against food shortages consistently by being susceptible to food price spikes rather than stable food reservoirs that can ship out grains and satisfy excess demand in distant deficit areas.

**Table 16.4** Adjustment parameters and 'half-lives', Mali millet markets

|  | Ségou to → | Mopti | Sikasso to → | Mopti | Bamako to → | Ségou |
|---|---|---|---|---|---|---|
| $\alpha$ | 0.624*** | −0.151* | 0.677*** | 0.122 | 0.431*** | −0.441*** |
| $T_{half}$ (months) | 0.71 | 4.23 | 0.61 | 5.33 | 1.23 | 1.19 |

[32] Ibid.

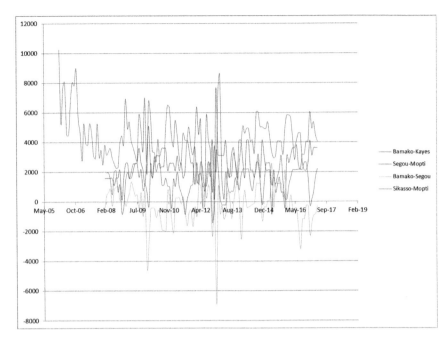

**Figure 16.7** Error correction terms for Mali markets.

In the case of staple grain trade in Mali, none of the examined trading relationships demonstrate all of these characteristics. Between the two arguably 'deepest' grain markets, Bamako and Ségou, the errors are the smallest, indicating relatively quick responsiveness. However, the source market Bamako was not immune to the 2012 price spikes, as evidenced by the large negative errors in the spring of 2012. The Sikasso–Mopti market pair is more characteristic of a successful market process for resolving food price spikes, with no apparent negative errors and quick adjustment in the destination. However, the mostly positive errors, which indicate positive price spikes in the destination, are still large, showing that market participants in these regions suffer routinely from high price shocks. The Ségou–Mopti and Bamako–Kayes pairs are the most volatile of all, and with persistent large, positive errors indicate a large degree of food price instability in these destinations, which has a devastating impact on food security in regions where people rely heavily on markets to obtain subsistence consumption.

## Conclusion

The level of spatial market integration and price adjustment for key grain markets in Burkina Faso and Mali varies greatly, with more remote markets sending weaker signals to the market network in times of food insecurity, leading to broad exchange entitlement failure in the 2012 crisis. In addition to tackling supply conditions to prevent crop failure and insure against production risks associated with natural disasters and climate change, attention needs to be paid to the trading network and its ability to move staple grains from surplus to deficit areas quickly and efficiently (FEWS NET). Currently, across the market networks in Burkina Faso and Mali studied here, there is insufficient capacity to minimize exchange entitlement failure when future food price crises arise. In looking at some simple estimated parameters that can characterize the properties of these market networks, this is due to either slow adjustment speeds in remote markets or instability even within large markets and susceptibility to food price spikes.

It will take several initiatives to begin to make these markets more effective in preventing future food crises: trade costs need to be lowered; information about food price spikes needs to be communicated across the network earlier; more trader participation; more integration of the large source markets into regional and international trade networks that can reliably call upon imports more consistently in times of need. Several domestic and international initiatives are under way to improve market networks with the goal of boosting food security, including through NEPAD (New Partnership for Africa's Development), the African Development Bank, the World Bank and other development and food security partners.[33] It is anticipated that the Sahel region will face repeated cycles of food insecurity in the coming years, and significant investment in both supply productivity and market network strengthening needs to be made to break this cycle. Markets can be powerful tools to resolve food shortages and crises, but they need to be greatly strengthened in this region to cope with future shocks.

## Market networks and scarcity

Making use of private market networks to resolve different types of scarcity is typically a first-order response by participants to an unexpected mismatch between supply and demand in a given time and place for a tradable commodity. If market networks respond quickly to shocks, local scarcity is minimized for many. If the market network is both responsive and large, then scarcity on a regional, national or even international scale can be constrained as well. More detailed analysis of the capabilities and properties of these market networks can help us better understand both how they contribute to the existence of scarcity and their ability to resolve it, especially as concerns critical commodities for human welfare, like staple foods.

---

[33] http://www.nepad.org/content/about-nepad.

# Acknowledgements

This book has its origins in a meeting in Pasadena in November 2014 at the California Institute of Technology that brought together a number of scholars to look at scarcity from a range of perspectives. Interdisciplinary conferences have, of course, become a regular feature of academic life, but we knew that our topic called for an unusually large mix. Scarcity is of interest to historians and social scientists, but engineers and natural scientists wrestle with it, too. The workshop proved as stimulating as the mix of approaches and questions raised by the contributors. Subsequently, we identified additional experts to come on board. We would like to thank all speakers, chairs and commentators who contributed to this project. In particular, we would like to thank the Division of the Humanities and Social Sciences and the Resnick Sustainability Institute at Caltech for their warm and generous support. Caltech offered an ideal platform for bringing experts and disciplines together. The practical success of the gathering owed a good deal to Sabrina Hameister and her administrative expertise and assistance. We are also grateful to the "Material Cultures of Energy" project funded by the Arts and Humanities Research Council (UK), and Laura Bevir for the index. For their generous support from start to finish, we would like to thank everyone at Bloomsbury and especially Emma Goode, Dan Hutchins and Shamli Priya Vijayan.

November 2018

# Index

Note: page numbers in *italics* refer to illustrations and page references with letter 'n' followed by locators denote note numbers.